THE PRIME TIME CLOSET

THE PRIME TIME CLOSET

A HISTORY OF GAYS AND LESBIANS ON TV

BY STEPHEN TROPIANO

APPLAUSE
THEATRE & CINEMA BOOKS

The Prime Time Closet
By Stephen Tropiano
Copyright © 2002 by Stephen Tropiano
All rights reserved

Photo Credits

Unless noted, all photos courtesy of Photofest.

Library of Congress Cataloging-in-Publication Data

Tropiano, Stephen.
  The prime time closet / by Stephen Tropiano.
    p. cm.
  ISBN 1-55783-557-8
  1. Homosexuality on television. I. Title.
  PN1992.8.H64 T76 2002
  791.45'653--dc21

                                                                    2002003220

British Library Cataloguing-in-Publication Data

A catalogue record for this book is available from the British Library

ISBN: 1-55783-557-8

APPLAUSE THEATRE & CINEMA
151 West 46th Street
New York, NY 10036
Phone: 212-575-9265
Fax: 646-562-5852
Email: info@applausepub.com
Internet: www.applausepub.com

SALES AND DISTRIBUTION:

NORTH AMERICA:

HAL LEONARD CORP.
7777 West Bluemound Road
P.O. Box 13819
Milwaukee, WI 53213
Phone: 414-774-3630
Fax: 414-774-3259
email: halinfo@halleonard.com
internet: www.halleonard.com

UNITED KINGDOM

COMBINED BOOK SERVICES LTD.
Units I/K, Paddock Wood Distribution Centre
Paddock Wood, Tonbridge, Kent TN12 6UU
Phone: (44) 01892 837171
Fax: (44) 01892 837272

TABLE OF CONTENTS

This book was written with the financial assistance of a James B. Pendleton Grant from the Roy H. Park School of Communications, Ithaca College. I would like to extend my appreciation to Dean Thomas Bohn, Elizabeth Nonas, and Patricia Zimmermann for their encouragement. In addition, thanks to all of my students and colleagues at the Ithaca College Los Angeles Program, especially Robert Meunier, Grant Rickard, and David Kelley for their support and patience.

I am also grateful to the staffs of the One Institute Gay and Lesbian Archives (www.oneinstitute.org), now located in its new home near the University of Southern California campus, and the Human Sexuality Collection at Cornell University (rmc.library.cornell.edu/HSC) in Ithaca, New York. Rosemary Rotondi conducted valuable research for me in the Manuscripts and Archives Division of the New York Public Library (www.nypl.org/research/chss/spe/rbk/mss.html). Thanks for doing such a thorough job!

I was able to track down copies of several hundred gay-themed episodes with the help of my friends and fellow collectors around the country. My thanks to Matthew Beck & Michael Santori, Ron Becker, Lance Clement, Paul D'Ambrosio, Greg Daskalogrigorakis, David Garland, Jeff Greenberg, Joe Griffin, Ted Johnson, Allen Lane, Marla Leech, Chris Nickerson, David Pendleton, Greg Richman, Ilka Rivard, Jamie Schmidt, John Shaffner & Joe Stewart, Lloyd Scott, Mike Werb, and Bonnie Zane. Special thanks to Steven Capsuto, author of the informative *Alternative Channels: The Uncensored Stories of Gay and Lesbian Images and Television*, for exchanging information and tapes with me on an ongoing basis. I also appreciate the support I have received from James Robert Parish, author of *Gays and Lesbians in Mainstream Cinema*, which is also an invaluable resource.

This book would not have been possible without the groundbreaking scholarship of film historian and author Vito Russo. I had the privilege of hearing Mr. Russo speak when I was in college. His dedication to the study of homosexuality in film and television, which culminated with the publication of *The Celluloid Closet*, continues to be an inspiration to me.

On a personal note, thanks to my family, Faith Ginsberg, Linda Bobel, Barry Sandler, Neil Spisak, Christine Tucci & Vincent Angell, Peter Kaufman at TV Books, Arnold Stiefel, Mart Crowley, Matthew Beck, Ted Johnson, Shannon Kelley & my friends at OUTFEST, Tom Teves, and all my friends at SEFAL. Thanks also to Mark Glubke and Matthew Callan at Applause Theatre & Cinema Books.

This book is dedicated in loving memory to Gary Petrillo, Brian Lasser, David Fox, Bill Strouse, and Brad Wojcoski; to the writers, directors, producers, and actors in the television industry, past and present, who approached the subject of homosexuality with honesty and integrity; and to my lover and best friend, Steven Ginsberg.

Stephen Tropiano
West Hollywood, California

primetimecloset@aol.com

INTRODUCTION

OPENING THE PRIME TIME CLOSET DOOR

When I was a junior in high school, I saw an episode of the television series *The White Shadow* entitled "One of the Boys." The story focuses on a teenager named Raymond Collins (played by *thirtysomething*'s Peter Horton), who transfers to Carver High School and is recruited to play on the school's basketball team. His teammates soon discover Collins left his other school to escape a rumor that he's gay. When the rumor follows him to Carver, Collins feels he has no choice but to drop out of school. However, in the final scene, he has a heart-to-heart talk with Vice Principal Buchanan (Joan Pringle), who tells him he must not let hatred and bigotry control his life. As a result of their talk, Collins changes his mind and decides to return to his old school.

The episode had a profound effect on me because as a gay teenager, I identified with Collins's confusion, pain, and loneliness. I too felt different from everyone else. And I was also in need of a heart-to-heart talk with someone as sympathetic, understanding, and wise as V.P. Buchanan — someone to assure me everything was going to be all right.

Nine years later, I am sitting with my lover Steven in a Los Angeles movie theatre, waiting for the film to start. When I look over at the guy who just sat down next to me, I realize it's Peter Horton. For a brief moment, I consider striking up a conversation and maybe even mentioning the impact the *White Shadow* episode had on me. But I'm not the type of person to initiate a conversation with a total stranger, let alone a recognizable actor. And he probably would have thought I was crazy.

My Peter Horton "sighting" made me think more about the integral role television has played in the formation of my identity as a gay man. Many of my older gay male friends have described how the negative stereotypes of gays and lesbians in Hollywood films of the 1940s, 1950s, and 1960s served as their first introduction to the subject of homosexuality. As a member of the post-Kennedy generation, I consider myself fortunate to have grown up (and come out) in an era when some television programs (like *The White Shadow*) and made-for-TV movies were beginning to tackle the subject of homosexuality in a sensitive, intelligent manner.

In 1992, I started to research, catalogue, and view hundreds of hours of television programming. My goal was to gain some insight into the evolution of the images of gay men, lesbians, bisexuals, and transgender people on television as well as the medium's treatment of homosexuality and gay-related issues. As I began to research TV programs from the 1960s and 1970s, the number of current television series with regular and recurring gay and lesbian characters was increasing at such a rapid rate, it became difficult to keep up.

Then, in April of 1997, history was made when Ellen DeGeneres, along with her television alter-ego, Ellen Morgan, declared on the cover of *Time* magazine those three little words: "Yep, I'm gay." By opening the prime time closet door, Ms. DeGeneres told all of America — gay and straight — that we can and will no longer remain invisible. For the gay and lesbian youth who were among the 36 million viewers who watched that evening, Ms. DeGeneres delivered the most important message of all: *It's O.K. to be gay. Be who you are.* For Ms. DeGeneres's act of courage, this gay man is truly grateful.

The title of this book is *The Prime Time Closet: A History of Gays and Lesbians on TV*. The reason it's *A* History and not *The* History is because this isn't a traditional historical account of homosexuality on television. Instead, it examines, in a historical context, the representation of gay men, lesbians, bisexuals, and transgender characters, and the treatment of gay subject matter and themes in relation to the major television genres.

The book is divided into four sections, each of which focuses on a major television genre: 1) medical dramas; 2) "law and order" dramas, which includes police and detective shows and courtroom dramas; 3) dramatic series, including prime time soap operas, teen dramas, made-for-TV movies, and mini-series; and 4) situation comedies. I am by no means a purist when it comes to categorizing TV series in terms of genres. Some programs are grouped on the basis of their content (i.e. *Popular*, a comedy-drama hybrid, is discussed in the section on teen dramas rather than in the comedy section).

While this study concentrates on television programming dating back as early as 1954 through the present day, some programs will be discussed in greater detail than others. I have included an appendix, which contains a fairly comprehensive listing of program and episode titles as well as of regular and recurring characters. If you don't see your favorite series, episode, made-for-TV movie, mini-series, or character on the list, please feel free to drop me a line.

A word about language: when referring to gay, lesbian, bisexual, and transgender characters, instead of using an acronym like GLBT (which always reminds me of a BLT), I use the word *gay*. The term *gay* will also be used in reference to male homosexuals when it precedes the word *male* or *males*, as in the sentence, "My, there are so many gay males on prime time television!"

PRIME TIME CLOSET CHRONOLOGY

April 25, 1954	*Confidential File*, a Los Angeles based tabloid talk show, examines "Homosexuals and the Problems They Present."
September 11, 1961	*The Rejected*, the first documentary about homosexuality produced for television, premieres on San Francisco public TV station, KQED-TV.
November 13, 1963	*The Eleventh Hour*, an NBC drama about psychiatry, is the first TV drama to address the subject of homosexuality. In "What Did She Mean By Good Luck?" a paranoid, neurotic stage actress with lesbian tendencies seeks treatment.
March 7, 1967	Mike Wallace hosts *CBS Reports: The Homosexual*, the first major network news special about homosexuality.
September 5, 1967	*N.Y.P.D.* premieres with "Shakedown," in which a team of New York detectives enlist the help of a closeted gay man to help crack a homosexual blackmail ring.
February 9, 1971	In "Judging Books by Covers," *All in the Family*'s Archie Bunker discovers his drinking buddy, an ex-pro football player, is gay. It's the first sitcom episode to tackle the subject of homosexuality.
June 21, 1972	*The Corner Bar*, an ABC comedy set in a New York saloon, debuts. The sitcom is the first show to feature a gay series regular, designer Peter Panama.
November 1, 1972	*That Certain Summer*, the first made-for-TV movie about homosexuality, premieres. The story revolves around a teenager who discovers his dad is gay.
February 20, 1973	*Marcus Welby, M.D.* features an episode entitled "The Other Martin Loring" about an alcoholic diabetic with homosexual tendencies whose marriage is falling apart. Gay activists object to Dr. Welby treating his patient's homosexuality as an illness.
October 8, 1974	In "The Outrage," *Marcus Welby, M.D.* treats a teenager molested by his teacher. Gay activists fear that, although the script states that the teacher is not a homosexual, the public will think otherwise. Several advertisers agree and pull their commercials, while two affiliates choose not to air the episode.
November 8, 1974	An episode of *Police Woman* entitled "Flowers of Evil" focuses on three lesbians who slay the residents of a retirement home. Although some changes were made prior to airing, it's still clear the killers are lesbians.
January 24, 1975	Debut of *Hot l Baltimore*, a sitcom about a group of "social outcasts" who live in a low-rent hotel. The residents include a gay couple in their 50s, George and Gordon, who have been together for many years. The controversial series lasts only 13 episodes.

PRIME TIME CLOSET CHRONOLOGY

September 13, 1977	The premiere of *Soap*, which features Billy Crystal as a gay man who plans to have a sex change so he can be with his lover, a closeted pro football player. Before the first episode airs, ABC receives 30,000 letters demanding the show be canceled.
December 21, 1983	*St. Elsewhere* is the first network dramatic series to devote an episode to the subject of AIDS. In "AIDS and Comfort," a married, closeted gay city councilman is diagnosed with the disease.
July 13, 1984	On the premiere episode of Showtime's *Brothers*, the first original situation comedy produced for cable, the youngest of three siblings comes out on his wedding day.
November 11, 1985	*An Early Frost*, the first made-for-TV movie about AIDS, focuses on a young gay lawyer who is diagnosed with the disease.
March 23, 1988	Premiere of *Heartbeat*, a short lived medical series that features the first lesbian regular character in a prime time drama. Gail Strickland plays Nurse Marilyn McGrath, who lives with her lover, Patti (Gina Hecht).
December 13, 1988	San Francisco AIDS activists are outraged when NBC airs "After It Happened," an episode of *Midnight Caller* in which a bisexual man knowingly infects his male and female sexual partners.
November 7, 1989	ABC reports a loss of $1.5 million in advertising revenue when it airs an episode of *thirtysomething* ("Strangers") that depicts two men in bed together having a post-coital conversation.
February 7, 1991	On *L.A. Law* ("He's a Crowd"), history is made when C.J., a bisexual lawyer, kisses her heterosexual female colleague on the lips.
July 16, 1991	PBS airs Marlon Riggs's *Tongues Untied*, which examines the black gay experience in America. Half of PBS's affiliates choose not to air the program. The FCC receives numerous complaints about those that did.
April 29, 1993	CBS demands producer David E. Kelly reshoot a kiss between two teenage girls with the lights out for a controversial episode of *Picket Fences* ("Sugar and Spice") that takes an honest look at adolescence and homophobia.
1994	A commercial for the Swedish-based furniture store IKEA features a gay couple, Mitch and Steve, picking out a dining room table. The ad runs after 9:30 pm in New York and Washington, D.C.

PRIME TIME CLOSET CHRONOLOGY

May 2, 1994	On *Northern Exposure* ("I Feel the Earth Move"), the residents of Cicely, Alaska gather to celebrate the spring wedding of innkeepers Erik & Ron.
January 10-12, 1994	Over the course of three nights, PBS presents *Tales of the City*, based on the first of Armistead Maupin's series of novels about life in San Francisco. The mini-series receives the highest rating in PBS history.
March 1, 1994	In "Don't Ask, Don't Tell," Mariel Hemingway plants a kiss on an unsuspecting *Roseanne*. The episode is the highest rated show of the week.
June 23, 1994	The San Francisco cast of *The Real World* includes Pedro Zamora, a gay man who is HIV positive. Over the course of the season, Pedro exchanges rings with his lover, Sean Sasser. Pedro dies of complications from AIDS on November 11, 1994.
January 18, 1996	In "The One With the Lesbian Wedding," the *Friends* gang attends the wedding of Ross's ex-wife Carol to her lover Susan.
April 30, 1997	On "The Puppy Episode," Ellen DeGeneres's TV alter ego Ellen Morgan comes out of the closet. DeGeneres did the same on the April 14 cover of *Time* magazine.
September 21, 1998	*Will & Grace* debuts on NBC.
December 3, 2000	*Queer as Folk*, an American series based on a British mini-series, debuts on Showtime.
March 14, 2002	In a report on gay parenting, *Prime Time Live* host Diane Sawyer interviews talk show host/actor Rosie O'Donnell, who reveals she is a lesbian.

CHAPTER ONE

DIAGNOSIS: HOMOSEXUAL
HOMOSEXUALITY AND THE
TELEVISION MEDICAL DRAMA

After World War II, homosexuals had become a more visible minority in American society. Upon completing their military service, many gay men and lesbians headed straight to New York and San Francisco instead of returning to small town life. Gay bars and hangouts, open for business in many major cities and some smaller urban areas, offered their patrons a place to socialize and be part of a community.

Consequently, increased visibility fueled society's intolerance toward homo-sexuals or, as they were more commonly referred to, *fags, dykes, queers, deviants*, and *sex perverts*. As the American public became more vocal in expressing their hatred, fear and ignorance, the oppression of homosexuals became more wide-spread and extreme. Homosexual bars were subject to constant raids. Gay men and lesbians were continually harassed and interrogated by the police, and unjustly imprisoned by the judicial system. At the time, legal grounds for recourse were limited because homosexuality was illegal under state sodomy laws and public support was virtually non-existent. Even the American Civil Liberties Union wouldn't take an official stand on gay rights until 1967.[1]

The United States government also did its part to promote homophobia. As part of their Cold War campaign to protect the country from "subversives," homosexuals were classified as a serious threat to national security. In the early 1950s, a Senate subcommittee recommended the purging of all government-employed "sex perverts" because of their emotional instability, vulnerability to blackmailers, and "corrosive influence" on other employees.[2] In 1952, Congress enacted a ban that would remain on the books until 1990 which prevented gay and lesbian foreigners from entering the country. The next year, President Eisenhower issued an executive order prohibiting the employment of homosexuals by the federal government. Consequently, thousands lost their jobs and were dismissed from the military, while others were put under surveillance by the postal system and the FBI.[3]

Amidst the oppression and hostility, The Mattachine Society, ONE Inc., and the Daughters of Bilitis became important sources of collective support for gay men and lesbians. The strategies employed by these and other self-identified "homophile" organizations to combat intolerance and discrimination sharply differed from the tactics later employed by gay rights activists in the post-Stonewall era.[4] The central goal of these early organizations was to create a more enlightened, gay-friendlier society by educating the public about homosexuality and maintaining a positive public identity for homosexuals. Through public lectures and publications addressing medical, legal, and moral questions surrounding the homosexual's role in society, members were encouraged to assimilate into mainstream "straight" society by becoming responsible, respectable citizens.[5] Their respective monthly publications, the *Mattachine Review*, *One*, and Bilitis's *The Ladder*, provided gay men and lesbians around the country, many closeted and isolated, with a forum to share their feelings and experiences.

While the homosexual community was establishing its post-war identity, medical science was displaying a renewed interest in understanding "the homosexual." Since the late 1860s, homosexuality had been classified as a pathological condition. Despite the successful challenges against this position by psychoanalyst Sigmund Freud, German sexologist Magnus Hirschfeld, and many others, homosexuality was still regarded in American medical circles as a mental illness.

Then, in 1948, Dr. Alfred Kinsey published his bestseller, *Sexual Behavior in the Human Male*, which, along with his subsequent *Sexual Behavior in the Human Female* (1952), presented some startling, never-before-heard statistics regarding homosexuality. According to Dr. Kinsey, 4 percent of the white males he interviewed for his study identified themselves as "exclusively" homosexual, while 3 to 8 percent of the unmarried white females (between the ages of 20 and 35) labeled themselves as "primarily" or "exclusively" homosexual.[6] Even more shocking were the high percentages of men (37 percent) and women (13 percent) who'd had an overt homosexual experience to the point of orgasm.[7] On the basis of his data, Dr. Kinsey challenged the classification of homosexuality as a pathological behavior by conceiving human sexuality in terms of a continuum of behaviors, ranging, on a 0-6 scale, from (0) exclusively heterosexual to (6) exclusively homosexual.

Kinsey's findings sent shock waves not only through the medical community, but through all of heterosexual America. In the decades to follow, his controversial study would be refuted and supported, as researchers intensified their investigation into the etiology of homosexuality and, in some instances, even proposed possible cures. Although Kinsey and others offered evidence that homosexuality was not an illness and many homosexuals were, in fact, well-adjusted, the American Psychiatric Association included homosexuality on its official list of mental disorders in 1952, where it would remain for the next twenty years.[8]

"LET'S TALK ABOUT HOMOS!"

When the subject of homosexuality was first discussed on the still relatively new invention of television, it was in a medical context. In the mid-1950s, locally produced talk shows were the first programs to introduce the taboo subject into America's living rooms. The forerunners of *Donahue* and *Oprah*, early TV talk shows featured a panel of "experts," usually engaged in a round-table discussion on a specific topic or issue that was facilitated by a host/moderator.

In response to the increased visibility of homosexuals in the United States, homosexuality was initially discussed as a social problem. Panelists debated if and how the homosexual poses a threat to American society and, in the process, answered the many questions supposedly on every American's mind: *What makes someone a homosexual? Can he/she be cured? Is homosexuality immoral? Should it* [sodomy] *be legal?* The panel typically consisted of a legal expert, a clergyman, and a member of the medical community, often a psychiatrist, psychologist, or physician.

These early broadcasts most likely had both positive and negative effects on the public's attitudes. Without question, both TV and radio talk shows brought a complex and taboo issue, previously limited to closed-door discussions, into the public arena. However, the designation of homosexuality as a *social problem* (a term consistently appearing in program titles), combined with the bias of certain experts, may, in some instances, have done more to strengthen than to alleviate the public's growing fear. Therefore, homosexuality, as with any form of sexuality deviating from the so-called "norm" of consensual heterosexuality, became a prime target for exploitation and sensationalism by the media.

One of the earliest discussions of homosexuality on television was an April 1954 installment of the Los Angeles-based talk show *Confidential File*, entitled "Homosexuals and the Problem They Present." Host Paul Coates, a tabloid columnist for the *Los Angeles Daily Mirror*, explained at the onset that his goal was to bring "the *problem* out in the open," and not to offer any immediate solutions. After interviews with a psychiatrist and a police officer, who shed some light on the social aspects of homosexuality, Coates offered his viewers a never-before-seen glimpse into the lives of homosexuals living in Los Angeles. Viewers hoping to see Sodom and Gomorrah were probably disappointed by the footage of a Mattachine Society meeting, which showed men and women talking, drinking, coffee, and eating cookies in someone's living room.[9] Perhaps more revealing was a peek inside an actual gay bar, eloquently referred to in *Daily Variety* as a place where "sex deviates were known to hang out."[10] Coates himself supplied an added shock by holding a male physique magazine up to the camera (but not *too* close) as an example of a publication catering to male homosexual readers.

Daily Variety not only commended Coates for treating the issue with "taste and dignity," but suggested the program "could serve as a model for television's handling of touchy and important subjects."[11] By simultaneously playing to the curiosity and fears of its audience, *Confidential File* did, in many ways, become the model for the television talk show's approach to homosexuality. The sensationalistic titles alone, such as "Homosexuals Who Stalk and Molest Children" (*Confidential File*, 1955) and "Are Homosexuals Criminal?" (WTVS-TV, Detroit, 1958) certainly did their part in perpetuating negative stereotypes. The issues addressed on these programs became more specific over time, yet their primary concern remained the effects of the increased visibility of homosexuals on society, particularly on children.

The danger homosexuals posed to children was addressed by the New York-based talk show *Open Mind*, which devoted three shows to homosexuality during its 1956-1957 season. The first, an "Introduction to the Problem of Homosexuality," featured a debate over whether homosexuality is a crime to be punished or a problem to be treated. Attorney Florence Kelley, representing the Legal Aid Society, suggested homosexuality could be legalized if the medical community could guarantee the successful rehabilitation of the homosexual child molester. Psychologist Dr. Robert Laidlaw explained there are several factors which cause homosexuality (environmental, psychological, and predisposition to homosexuality) and emphasized how a homosexual's tendency to suffer from neurosis or psychosis is primarily a product of society's negative attitudes. In the end, the panelists agreed a well-conditioned upbringing in a good environment with two parents serving as positive heterosexual role models was important to insure a child would grow up straight as an arrow.[12]

The second installment, entitled "Homosexuality: A Psychological Approach," examined how a male child's relationship with one or both of his parents affects the formation of his sexual identity. A psychoanalyst and a pediatrician addressed the role of genetics (is homosexuality inborn?); the effects of a dominant and/or passive mother or father; the overall quality of one's family life; and the danger posed by the adult male homosexual seducer. One doctor went so far as to suggest that a father could divert his son's feminine tendencies by taking him to a baseball game. Rounding out the series was "Male and Female in American Culture," which consisted of a discussion between anthropologist Margaret Mead and *New York Post* columnist Max Lerner about how society institutionalizes gender identity through clothes, language, and stereotypes.

While the conflicting opinions expressed by medical professionals and other "experts" may have added to the confusion of some viewers, talk shows did allow actual, real-live gay men and lesbians to speak on their own behalf. Yet, even a self-identified homosexual appearing on television in the 1950s needed to take certain precautions because he/she risked losing his/her job, housing, family, and friends. The 1954 "Problem" episode of *Confidential File* included a conversation with the secretary of the Mattachine Society, who, appearing under the pseudonym Curtis White, had his face obscured by a black rectangle over the screen. White scored some points by characterizing himself as a "well-adjusted" homosexual and by challenging popular misconceptions about gay men. He knew he could lose his job by appearing on the program (in fact, he did), though his participation did not go unrecognized. The gay journal *One* devoted a full-page ad in their next issue commending him for his exemplary courage.[13]

At first, the discussion of homosexuality was limited to prime time or late night talk shows, but the subject made its way to daytime television. On the New York-based talk show *Showcase*, host Fannie Hurst (author of *Imitation of Life*) addressed the problems of the male homosexual in a reportedly well-rounded discussion which touched on a variety of issues (homosexuals as a recognizable minority, laws against homosexuality, possible cures, etc.). The panel included an officer of the New York chapter of the Mattachine Society, Gonzalo Segura, Jr., who, like Curtis White, concealed his identity, appearing with a hood over his head.[14] The Mattachines considered the show "a major breakthrough in public education" and publicly thanked the show's producers and participants "for the courage to pioneer in the task of public enlightenment on a too-often-beclouded subject."[15]

Another important milestone in the early discussion of homosexuality on television is the September 11, 1961 premiere of *The Rejected*, the first made-for-TV documentary on male homosexuality. Produced by San Francisco public television station KQED-TV, *The Rejected* offered the most comprehensive exploration of the subject to date. In his proposal for the hour-long film, under the working title *The Gay Ones*, writer John W. Reavis explained the documentary's central goal:

> The object of the program will be to present as objective an analysis of the subject as possible, without being overly clinical. The questions will be basic ones: who are the gay ones, how did they become gay, how do they live in a heterosexual society, what treatment is there by medicine or psychotherapy, how are they treated by society, and how would they like to be treated?[16]

Utilizing the talk show-style format, Reavis and director Richard Christian broke the subject down into subtopics. Each segment featured an expert or experts discussing homosexuality from a specific perspective (medical, anthropological, social, legal, etc.). The program's tone was established by an introduction by KQED manager James Day, who read this statement on behalf of Stanley Mosk, the Attorney General of the State of California:

> With all the revulsion that some people feel toward homosexuality, it cannot be dismissed by simply ignoring its presence. It is a subject that deserves discussion. We might just as well refuse to discuss alcoholism or narcotics addiction as to refuse to discuss this subject. It cannot be swept under the rug. It will not just go away...[17]

Equating homosexuality with other "social ills" (like alcoholism and drug abuse) was common in the 1950s and 1960s and no doubt provided a rationale for devoting an entire hour of public television to the topic. Although some of the negative myths of the period were reinforced, *The Rejected* was the most comprehensive and progressive television program to date.

The Rejected begins with an examination of homosexuality from both a cultural and a medical perspective. By means of an overview of the positive role homosexuality played in Ancient Greece and in Native American cultures, Margaret Mead demonstrated how it is society that stigmatizes homosexual behavior. Mead is

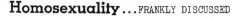

Homosexuality ...FRANKLY DISCUSSED

Research discloses that there may be as many as 15 million adult male homosexuals in the U.S. today. Shall we accept them in society, or will they continue to be...

"**THE**

HOUR-LONG TELEVISION DOCUMENTARY

REJECTED"

MONDAY EVENING--SEPTEMBER 11   9:30-10:30 pm

Introduction by **JAMES DAY**, Manager, KQED
FEATURED ON THE PROGRAM:
DR. MARGARET MEAD, Anthropologist, psychologist and author, New York
DR. CARL M. BOWMAN, Psychiatrist and former director, Langley Porter Psychiatric Institute
DR. ERWIN BRAFF, Director, VD Clinic
RT. REV. JAMES A. PIKE, Episcopal Bishop of California
RABBI ALVIN FINE, Temple Emanu-El, San Francisco
MORRIS LOWENTHAL, Attorney
J. ALBERT HUTCHINSON, Attorney, and formerly in Attorney General's Office
THOMAS LYNCH, District Attorney, San Francisco
AL BENDICH, Attorney and Lecturer
HAROLD L. CALL, Editor, Mattachine REVIEW
DONALD S. LUCAS, Executive Secretary, Mattachine Society
LES FISHER, Member, Mattachine Society

Homosexuals in America today...millions upon millions of them...a few satisfied with their condition, many of them desperately unhappy. This program will present a wealth of scientific knowledge, studied opinion and arguments calling for acceptance on the one hand and continued repression on the other.

THIS IS A MOST UNUSUAL TELEVISION PRESENTATION. IT SHATTERS THE CONSPIRACY OF SILENCE WHICH HAS SO LONG SHROUDED THIS PRESSING SOCIAL PROBLEM

"THE REJECTED" brings startling facts, evidence of changing attitudes, and a penetrating insight never before presented on a television screen. And perhaps, with more facts and more arguments, will come the beginnings of understanding. DON'T MISS IT!

CHANNEL **9**

A NATIONAL EDUCATION TELEVISION NETWORK PRESENTATION   **KQED 9**

Advertisement for *The Rejected* from the September 1961 issue of the *Mattachine Review,* a monthly publication from The Mattachine Society. (Art: *Mattachine Review*/KQED-TV)

followed by Psychiatrist Karl M. Bowman, former director of the Langley Porter Psychiatric Institute, who used the Kinsey Scale to explain why homosexuality is not a mental illness. Dr. Bowman expressed his skepticism about treating homosexuals as well as his support for legalization.

Providing the gay male perspective were representatives from the San Francisco chapter of the Mattachine Society, who concealed neither their names nor identities. *Mattachine Review* editor Harold Call explained how one of the major goals of the Mattachines was "to dispel part of this stereotyped picture" through "education, research, and social work...we are calling for a change of law because we know the number of homosexuals is large." Call also emphasized the Society's belief that the acceptance of male homosexuality is contingent on the male homosexual's ability to assimilate into straight society. "By and large, if these laws were changed, we might find that the homosexual is no different from anyone else," Call explained, "except perhaps in his choices of an object of his love."

The Rejected received a generally positive response from the press. *Daily Variety* praised the documentary for dealing with the subject in a "matter-of-fact down-the-middle manner, covering it quite thoroughly and, for the most part, interestingly."[18] Terrence O'Flaherty of the *San Francisco Chronicle* commended KQED for their courage in tackling "the most taboo of all subjects — homosexuality, the permanent underground."[19]

Viewer response was also positive. 97 percent of the letters received by the station favored the program, with many viewers asking for more like it on the topic. Almost four hundred requests were received for a transcript of the program, which was subsequently published by Dorian Book Service of San Francisco.[20] The *Mattachine Review* also reprinted the positive newspaper reviews of the program, which subsequently aired in Tucson, Los Angeles, Portland, and New York.[21]

"WHAT DO THEY MEAN BY LESBIAN?"

By the 1960s, the leaders of homophile organizations like the Mattachines and the Daughters of Bilitis were making the rounds on the radio and television talk show circuit. Lesbians started to participate on panels more frequently, though most programs continued to focus exclusively on the male homosexual because he was still perceived as the greater threat to children. In addressing this very issue on the Los Angeles talk show *Argument*, during a discussion entitled "Society and The Homosexual," Bilitis President Jaye Belle argued that there is a greater stigma attached to male homosexuality because the public is ignorant, or in denial, that lesbianism actually exists.[22]

The public's ignorance and denial was certainly reinforced by TV talk shows and documentaries, which consistently treated female homosexuality, if mentioned at all, as a secondary issue. As Reavis noted in his proposal for the exclusively male *The Rejected*, gay men and lesbians do not necessarily share the same experiences:

> Finally, and I would rate this strictly an optional segment, we can have an interview with a group of homosexual women — lesbians. Personally, I am against it for a number of reasons. First, the repugnance — or desire not to think about the problem — is even greater in society than that towards the problem of gay men. Second, the number of persons involved is much smaller — the rationale being perhaps one in seven or one in ten women homosexuals as against male homosexuals. Third, the problems are vastly different, as are the solutions. For example, promiscuity is much less, relationships apt to be bilateral, economic and social sanctions are less, and the ability to carry on a relationship of this sort is greatly simplified.[23]

Even when the subject of female homosexuality was discussed, as on an installment of the late night Chicago talk show *Off the Cuff* entitled "Homosexuality and Lesbianism," the "expert" panel was comprised entirely of men.[24]

The perception that lesbianism is less threatening than male homosexuality is perhaps the reason why the subject first received dramatic treatment on a prime time medical program. In the early 1960s, the NBC drama *The Eleventh Hour* capitalized on the popularity of psychotherapy in post-war America. Each week, psychiatrist Dr. L. Richard Starke (Ralph Bellamy), along with his colleague Dr. Paul Graham (Jack Ging), were "on-call" to help a patient through "the eleventh hour" — that moment when he/she is on the brink of a complete mental breakdown.

In "What Did She Mean By Good Luck?" Dr. Starke helps an unstable actress, Hallie Lambert (*As the World Turns*'s Kathryn Hays), who is trying to get her career back on track by appearing on stage in a romantic comedy directed by the tough, no-nonsense, Barbara Stanwyck-ish Marya Stone (Beverly Garland). During rehearsals, Marya is so critical of Hallie's work that the actress becomes convinced the director is deliberately tormenting her. In the "eleventh hour" — just minutes before the opening night curtain goes up — Hallie enlists Dr. Starke's help.

Dr. Starke previously diagnosed Hallie as having lesbian tendencies. As the doctor explains to the actress's overbearing mother, Gerry (Doris Dowling), Hallie's relationships with men have been "inhibited by unnatural impulses." Although it is natural to experience same-sex feelings at adolescence, Dr. Starke believes something or someone has prevented Hallie from making the "proper adjustment" to adult heterosexual relationships. When the doctor questions Gerry about Hallie's affection for her former high school drama teacher, Miss Aldrich, Gerry has a strong reaction and then denies ever meeting the woman. "It's wicked and disgusting," Gerry cries, "and I don't want to talk about it anymore!"

Hallie's off-stage emotional crisis begins to affect her performance, particularly in a pivotal "seduction" scene at the end of act two. Her character, a Holly Golightly-type ingenue, makes a pass at her co-star Simon Cole (Paul Burke), who's romantically pursuing Hallie off-stage. "Now this is such a simple scene for a good actress like you to play," Marya explains, "and it's topped off by a genuine warmth and a seductive moment, a moment that we must have or otherwise how's a man like that going to respond to it?"

On opening night, Marya, still displeased with Hallie's performance in the scene, instructs Simon to initiate the on-stage seduction. The actress becomes hysterical and accuses Marya of deliberately sabotaging her performance because she's jealous of her relationship with Simon. Shocked by the accusation, the director dismisses Hallie's outburst as opening night anxiety.

A desperate Hallie phones Dr. Starke, who rushes backstage for an eleventh hour therapy session. In the nick of time, Hallie suddenly realizes Marya reminds her of Miss Aldrich, who, she recalls, once slapped her in front of the entire class. The memory confuses Hallie because it contradicts the strong affection she still has for her former teacher. Hallie decides to perform opening night as scheduled, but when her director comes by to wish her "good luck" (shouldn't it be "break a leg?"), the paranoid actress asks Dr. Starke, "What did she *mean* by good luck?"

"You are also thinking that such a suspicion is foolish," Starke assures her. "Have faith in yourself. Trust yourself. You'll be fine."

At the end of act two, Hallie assumes the role of the "seducer" and, for the first time, performs the scene perfectly. During intermission, Hallie is nervous about Marya's reaction. As the director walks toward her, we suddenly see, from Hallie's point-of-view, Marya turn into her mother, Gerry, who raises her hand to slap her on the cheek. When her hand hits Hallie's face, Gerry turns back into Marya, who is only giving a playful slap for playing the scene so brilliantly. The director then admits to Hallie that she is jealous, not of her relationship with Simon, but of her talent. "Yes, you're right. I am jealous," Marya admits, "and I'm sorry I let it show."

After a successful premiere, Hallie reveals to Dr. Starke how the vision of her mother triggered a memory involving Miss Aldrich. When her mother arrived one afternoon to pick her up from school, she saw Hallie give Miss Aldrich an affectionate hug. Gerry later punished Hallie for having wicked and perverted feelings. Dr. Starke is now able to explain the connection between the childhood trauma and her extreme reaction to Marya:

> STARKE: Hallie, everyone at one time has a crush on a school teacher or camp counselor of the same sex. Most people grow out of it. But, because of what you have been through with your family, you haven't been able to make the adjustment. The impulses still upset you. To put it in simple terms, you defend yourself from the shame of having unnatural feelings by imagining you are being persecuted. It's as if to say, I couldn't possibly love Marya Stone. I hate her because she persecutes me.[25]

Upon discovering through psychoanalysis that her neurosis is the product of her deeply rooted guilt, Hallie is cured and can now enjoy a healthy, normal, heterosexual life.

Amid the episode's simplistic approach to a complex, yet rather convoluted, psychological problem, the possibility that Hallie is a lesbian is never even considered. Dr. Starke characterizes an adolescent's strong feelings toward a member of the same sex as normal. But for adults, those same feelings are "unnatural" impulses triggered by childhood trauma. Ellis Marcus's script subscribes to current popular medical theory surrounding the root of homosexual pathology; namely, the trauma of homosexual seduction of a youth by an adult and a dysfunctional relationship with one or both parents.[26]

Similarly, Gerry's misinterpretation of her daughter's display of affection for Miss Aldrich, and her subsequent hysterical reaction, are revealed through psychoanalysis to have hampered the actress's sexual development. Hallie disavowed the trauma, which ultimately affected her ability to assume the "seducer" role with men (both on-stage and off) and deal with female authority figures. The situation was no doubt exasperated by the unexplained absence of Hallie's father (who is never mentioned), which clearly strengthened her repressive mother's hold over her daughter.

When the episode first aired, Robin Richards, a critic for *The Ladder*, a lesbian publication, dismissed the show for dealing with lesbianism "on an adolescent level and in sophomoric language and platitudes. The handling of the subject was so poor it was embarrassing to watch...the only good angle was that Hallie has a so-so-happy ending instead of being dragged to the nut hatch." Richard's review also includes a short plot summary, in which she matter-of-factly states that *"Hallie actually loves Marya and doesn't want to admit it even to herself."*[27] What even Richards doesn't consider, however, is the possibility the feeling is mutual. Marya admits she's jealous of Hallie's talent, but *her* repressed psyche would certainly benefit from a few sessions with Dr. Starke. Then maybe we could have found out what Marya *really* meant by "good luck."

THE MAN BEHIND THE POTTED PLANT

The Eleventh Hour is an early example of the dramatic treatment homosexuality received on a prime time network television program. Yet through the mid-1960s, the subject was generally confined to talk shows. Then, in 1967, a network news organization finally addressed the topic in a special report.[28] Like *The Rejected*, *CBS Reports: The Homosexuals* attempted to answer the major moral, legal, and medical questions surrounding male homosexuality (once again, lesbianism is excluded). Hosted by *60 Minutes*'s Mike Wallace, the hour-long program consists of interviews with "experts" and profiles of several gay men, some well adjusted, others not so happy. In the *Confidential File* tradition, the producers also provide a touch of sensationalism by including film footage, shot in *cinema verité* style, of the inside of a gay bar; male prostitutes loitering on a Hollywood street corner; and, in the most disturbing sequence, a vice squad arrest of a 19-year-old man for public sex.

What little, if any, attempt made at "balanced" reporting is undermined by Wallace's shameless editorializing about what he characterizes as "the most despised minority group in the United States." The program does include interviews with self-assured, seemingly well-adjusted homosexuals, including Mattachine Society representative Harold Call, who explains the organization's rationale for the legalization of homosexual relations between consenting adults. But even Call's appearance is unable to counterbalance interviews with two gay men who share their self-hatred, shame, and guilt with the American public.

The first, an unidentified 30-year-old college instructor, lies on a psychiatrist's couch, his face obscured by his knee and hand. This tortured soul recites how his homosexuality isolated him from his family, who treated him, in his words, "like some wounded animal that they were going to send to the vet..."

The second is even more disturbing. A 27-year-old man sits in almost total darkness with his face obscured by a large potted plant. He characterizes himself as "not sick just sexually. I'm sick in a lot of ways...immature, childlike, and the sex is a symptom." Wallace explains the man, on probation after three vice arrests, is now celibate and undergoing therapy. The man behind the potted plant admits his hope of one day living a heterosexual life is still a "far away notion" because he's afraid of being intimate with women, which he believes stems from his fear of a domineering mother.

The fear and self-loathing expressed by both men is later reinforced when Wallace offers his "insights" into the male homosexual lifestyle. As we watch the footage shot inside a gay bar and on a Hollywood Boulevard corner, Wallace characterizes the "average" homosexual:

> WALLACE: They are attracted mostly to the anonymity a big city gives them. New York, Chicago, Los Angeles, San Francisco. The permissiveness and the variety of the city draw them. The average homosexual, if there be such, is promiscuous. He is not interested or capable of a lasting relationship like that of a heterosexual marriage. His sex life, his love life, consists of a series of one-chance encounters at the clubs and bars he inhabits. And even on the streets of the city — the pick-up, the one night stand, these are characteristics of the homosexual relationship.[29]

Wallace's narration — a string of gross generalizations and negative stereotypes — sounds as if it was scripted by Rev. Jerry Falwell. However, at one point Wallace does suggest all homosexuals are not alike by showing us a group of presumably gay men, nicely dressed in suits and ties, having a dinner party. The men are never given the opportunity to speak on their own behalf, but are used solely to illustrate Wallace's point that there are thousands of homosexuals "who deplore the tawdry image of the so-called gay life...men who lead quiet, unexceptional lives in towns and cities across the country."

"*There is just one thing,*" he adds, "*they share with their homosexual brothers.*"

Wallace's last statement serves as an introduction to Dr. Charles Socarides, the notorious New York psychoanalyst, who offers his professional opinion: "*Homosexuality is, in fact, a mental illness which has reached epidemiological proportions.*" The most outspoken advocate of homosexuality as a pathological condition during the 1960s and 1970s, Dr. Socarides expresses his views during an obviously staged question-and-answer session with his students at the Albert Einstein School of Medicine. Socarides believed male homosexuality is a *learned* behavior, the result of a disturbance during the child's pre-oedipal stage of development (before the age of three).[30] By forming an unnaturally strong tie with his mother, "normal" gender identity is disrupted and any attempt by the feminine-identified adult male to establish a heterosexual relationship triggers separation anxiety with the mother. Consequently, the homosexual, who turns to other men for his "fix" of masculinity, is typically neurotic or suffers from a serious pathological condition (schizophrenia, paranoia, etc.). All hope, however, is not lost. Dr. Socarides advocated psychoanalytic treatment as a cure and claimed personal success in turning even the most die-hard homosexuals into heterosexuals.

Wallace explains that Dr. Socarides's views aren't universally held, but adds "the thrust of diagnosis in any treatment in recent years has been along the line that Socarides details." No differing opinions are expressed, only an explanation of the etiology of homosexuality by psychiatrist Dr. Irving Bieber, professor of clinical psychiatry at New York Medical College, who also believed homosexuality to be a mental illness. According to Dr. Bieber, a boy's sexuality is rooted in an overprotective mother and a detached father. "I do not believe it is possible," he concludes, "to produce a homosexual if the father is a warm, good, supportive, constructive father for his son."

The response of the critics was mixed. Several papers, including *The New York Times*, the *Washington Star*, and the *Chicago Daily News*, applauded CBS for tackling the subject.[31] But not all believed the subject matter was suitable for television. In his review entitled "TV No Spot to Unload Garbage," the *Chicago Tribune*'s Clay Gowran accused CBS of doing a disservice to young, impressionable viewers."[32] Most critics did not acknowledge the program's obvious anti-homosexual bias. One exception was *The New York Times*'s George Gent, who suggested it would "have been better to give the minority viewpoint that homosexuals are just as normal as anyone else a chance to speak for itself."[33]

HOMOSEXUALITY AND THE PRIME TIME MEDICAL DRAMA

In June of 1969, the Stonewall Riots in New York ushered in the beginning of the modern gay-liberation movement, which made the homosexual community a more visible and viable political force. The initial strategy employed by the homophile organizations to gain acceptance through assimilation was replaced by a more in-your-face demand for equal rights and social justice.

Once the movement increased in size and gained political momentum, there were signs of progress. In 1973, the American Bar Association passed a resolution supporting the repeal of state sodomy laws, which had begun with Illinois in 1961 and resumed ten years later with Connecticut. The following year, homosexuality was finally removed (by a 54 percent majority) from the American Psychiatric Association's list of mental disorders. In 1974, a federal anti-gay discrimination bill (HR-14752) was introduced into the House of Representatives. Although it was ultimately defeated, similar measures passed in cities and counties around the country. Most importantly, gays and lesbians were building their own communities, complete with bookstores, community centers, music and publishing companies, synagogues, churches, and gay pride parades and celebrations in major cities across America.

The television medical drama, which gained a new popularity in the early 1970s with programs like *The Bold Ones*, *Medical Center*, and *Marcus Welby, M.D.*, "treated" homosexuality during this transitional period with a generally liberal, though ultimately misguided, attitude. Pity was advocated over condemnation, tolerance over total acceptance. Just as the discussion of homosexuality on early TV talk shows was a response to the viewers' presumed concern over the homosexual's increased visibility, the treatment of homosexuality by the medical dramas of the 1970s was a response to the burgeoning gay rights movement. By presenting the medical "facts" about homosexuality, medical shows took over the role of TV talk shows in alleviating the public's fears.

To avoid classifying homosexuality as a disease, 1970s medical dramas linked sexual confusion — or more specifically, "homosexual panic" — to a specific condition (ulcers, diabetes, a heart condition, etc.). Before a patient's condition could be treated, the confusion surrounding the patient's sexual orientation needed to be resolved. At the same time, television doctors battled a new, rapidly spreading disease: homophobia, the irrational fear and hatred of homosexuals brought on by scores of gay and lesbian doctors and nurses coming out of the closets. Once their sexual orientation was made public, these characters, generally confined to a single episode, found themselves in the center of a controversy. The homophobia they encountered from patients, the medical staff, and the hospital administration not only put their jobs in jeopardy, but also, inevitably, the lives of their own patients.

HOMOSEXUAL PANIC (AND THE PANICKY HOMOSEXUAL)

A 1972 episode of the NBC drama *The Bold Ones* entitled "Discovery at Fourteen" features child star and future Academy Award-winning director Ron Howard as Cory Melino, a troubled teenager suffering from a bleeding ulcer. His pediatrician, Dr. Amanda Fallon (guest star Jane Wyman), knows that something is bothering the boy.

"He mopes around like the weight of the world is on those 14-year-old shoulders," the doctor observes. "Cory's mask of indifference frightens me."

Dr. Fallon tries to find out what is wrong, but Cory's family isn't much help. His mother Dee (Lynnette Mettey), a divorcée, refuses to take her son to a psychiatrist because she believes it will only make matters worse. When Dr. Fallon questions her about Cory's father, Dee explains both Cory and his brother have no contact with him. The doctor becomes suspicious, however, when the boy's paternal grandfather, Peter Melino (*Dallas*'s Jim Davis), who lives with Dee and Cory, reveals he also never talks to his son.

When Cory purposely goes off his prescribed diet, making his ulcer bleed, Dr. Fallon decides to locate the boy's father. She tracks him to a neighborhood bar, "The Monanthous," a name derived from a botanical term meaning "one flower." Upon entering the dimly lit establishment, the good doctor doesn't find one "flower," but an entire garden of gay men, who silently exchange stares with the female intruder.

"May I help you, Miss?" the bartender politely asks.

The former Mrs. Ronald Reagan, looking as if she is recreating a moment from her Oscar-winning performance as a deaf-mute in *Johnny Belinda*, is speechless.

Dr. Fallon eventually finds Cory's father, Jack (Robert Hogan), at a nearby tennis court. After convincing him she is only there to discuss his son's health, Jack lets her in on Cory's secret. One night while Jack was entertaining some friends, Cory paid his father a surprise visit. "They [Jack's friends] were, I guess you would use the word *obvious*," Jack explains. "Kids aren't naive about homosexuals these days. I'm sure Cory knows about the whole gay scene." When Dr. Fallon later confronts Dee and Peter, they admit to hiding Jack's homosexuality from Cory.

"You'd think he [Jack] had two heads and warts on all four eyeballs," the doctor scolds, "Now we're not going to get any place until you crawl out of your Victorian caves! These are enlightened times!"

Realizing Cory is afraid he will grow up to be like his father, Peter, Dee and Dr. Fallon set him *straight*. After reading some books Dr. Fallon recommended, Peter decides to reconcile with his gay son because, as he explains to Cory, Jack's "attitude toward sex and marriage isn't something hereditary." Dee assures Cory that just because she compares him to his father, it doesn't mean he'll be *exactly* like him. Dr. Fallon also persuades Cory that although he and his father may have similar interests (like tennis), it is only a coincidence and not "some kind of genetic legacy."

> DR FALLON: It took evolution and I don't know how many thousands of generations to produce you, Cory. And yet the end result is one individual human being. An original with personality and beauty that's uniquely yours. Your virtues, your talents, your sins are peculiar to you. You alone have to shape your life. Alone. Remember that. Friends, family, environment, parents — these influence you. But you get to pick and choose. To make the decision to let us know just who Cory Melino is. You're not stuck with anything.[34]

In the final scene, Cory is clearly on the road to recovery. As Dee and Peter watch him play tennis, Dr. Fallon observes that "he doesn't see the game as something he inherited from his father. He's playing all his own."

Although she never actually utters the "H" word, Dr. Fallon's attitude toward homosexuality is, on the surface, generally progressive. The episode's gay-positive message is undermined, however, by the so-called medical "fact" that cures Cory's ulcer and Peter's attitude toward his gay son: homosexuality isn't genetic or environmental, it's a lifestyle, a *choice*. Peter earns points for reconciling with Jack, but isn't it suspicious he doesn't accept his son's homosexuality until he learns it's *not* genetic, but a personal choice? Perhaps he's just relieved that his genes are not to blame.

Dr. Fallon is one of the few TV doctors to take a position on the "nature vs. nurture" debate surrounding the origins of homosexuality. Her explanation is, however, puzzling, because she suggests homosexuality is ultimately an individual choice, yet downplays the influence of outside factors, like environment and child-parent relationships. Perhaps placing the emphasis on choice was a strategy — not only to alleviate parents' fears but make Dr. Fallon's gay-friendly attitude an easier pill to swallow.

This approach was not typical of late 1960s to early 1970s medical series, which, like *The Eleventh Hour*, usually linked a patient's homosexual tendencies to his/her dysfunctional relationship with one or both parents. Such is the case in "The Other Martin Loring," a controversial 1973 episode of the popular ABC series *Marcus Welby, M.D.* When Martin Loring (Mark Miller), an alcoholic and a diabetic, goes to Dr. Welby (Robert Young) for a checkup, the good doctor is concerned about Martin's weight gain and high sugar count. Martin assures Dr. Welby he's just under tremendous pressure at work. What he fails to mention is that his marriage is falling apart.

That evening, Martin's wife Margaret (Sharon Acker) informs her husband she's divorcing him and suing for full custody of their teenage son, Billy (played by Scott Jacoby, who won an Emmy for playing a homosexual's son in *That Certain Summer*). "The fact is you are not a fit parent," she sneers. "Now you ought to be the first one to admit that."

When he threatens to counter sue, Margaret vows not to hold *anything* back in court. Later that evening, after finishing his nightcap, Martin collapses. Dr. Welby arrives at the house, puts Martin to bed, and has a heart-to-heart with Margaret, who tells him their 20-year marriage is over. "It doesn't do much for a woman's self-esteem when she realizes her husband finds her undesirable," she admits. Assuming there's another woman, Dr. Welby suggests that infidelity can happen in the best of marriages. "I almost wish it were another woman!" she wails.

On the following day, Margaret serves her husband with preliminary divorce papers. After a quick drink and a shot of insulin, Martin goes for a drive, and smashes his car. He's charged with drunk driving, but Dr. Welby convinces the police that Martin was not intoxicated, just having a reaction to the mixture of insulin and alcohol.

Trying to understand why his patient is on a self-destructive path, Dr. Welby speaks to Martin's mother (Martha Scott), who characterizes her son as an excruciatingly shy child who never discussed his personal feelings. Mrs. Loring attributes Martin's unhappy marriage to the lack of love he received from his cold, unaffectionate, authoritarian father. "How could Martin be close to a wife or any woman when he never saw anything but distance between his two parents?" she asks. "How could he know what love is when he saw his own mother denied love?"

Dr. Welby does the arithmetic: one sensitive, lonely boy + one cold, distant father = one homosexual. He confronts Martin, who at first denies he has a "problem," but then finally confesses all:

MARTIN: Any kind of impulse in that direction, I suppressed it...then my father died and I felt an enormous sense of freedom. He was actually gone. With all that stifling, ultra-puritan morality. Then I let my guard down. And then I met a man. What really happened was that I picked him up in a bar. I just couldn't suppress my feelings anymore. I'd gone on seeing this man. I gave him a job, knowing what he was, tortured by the attraction I felt for him. You can't possibly imagine how powerful emotions like that can be. Or how *loathsome and degrading*.[35]

Martin admits his homosexuality "has always been there. *And that makes my whole life a cheap, hollow fraud.*"

Dr. Welby obviously doesn't always know best when he tells Martin he's *not* homosexual "in the true sense of the term."

MARTIN: What am I then?

DR. WELBY: Isn't it possible that you allowed the *fear* of homosexuality to make you feel unworthy and unwanted in your adult life because that's the way you felt as a boy? Have you taken your problems to a psychiatrist? Plenty of other men have —

MARTIN: What for? I may have homosexual tendencies, but I'm not crazy.

DR. WELBY: That's your father speaking. Don't you realize that?

MARTIN: So maybe it is. Just maybe he's right.

DR. WELBY: You don't believe that any more than I do.[36]

Dr. Welby's diagnosis only plummets his patient deeper into depression. Finally, after a failed suicide attempt, Martin reluctantly agrees to see a shrink. "Give it a try," Dr. Welby encourages him. "Perhaps if you can get rid of your self-hatred and repression, you can still learn to enjoy a *normal* marital relationship." Most importantly, Dr. Welby adds, he needs to do it for his son. "I think you are going to do it, Martin," adds Dr. Welby, "I think you are going to *win that fight.*"

Like Cory Melino, Martin is suffering from homosexual panic, but while Cory is just another confused, uninformed, heterosexual adolescent, the "other" Martin Loring is a repressed, self-hating, latent homosexual. The possibility that Martin *is* gay and *could* live a happy, healthy life is never considered. Instead, in his infinite wisdom, Dr. Welby pushes Martin deeper into the closet by suggesting that his *fear* of homosexuality, rather than his repressed homosexual feelings, is at the root of his neurosis. The homosexual desires of the "other" Martin are not something acceptable, let alone real, but a deep manifestation of his unresolved oedipal issues. Consequently, Dr. Welby, like Dr. Fallon, advises his patient to confront his fears. But while Cory's anxiety is alleviated by answering a few basic questions, Martin Loring will most likely be spending some quality time on his psychiatrist's couch.

"The Other Martin Loring" sparked a protest by gay advocacy groups who, in the early 1970s, "were beginning to see prime-time television as critical symbolic territory in their struggle to gain acceptance in the wider society."[37] In an effort to influence the portrayal of homosexuals on television, the Gay Activists Alliance (GAA), a group of activists at the forefront of the New York gay political movement since 1970, organized a protest against ABC to stop the network from airing the episode.

After reading the teleplay and attending an advanced screening, GAA news and media relations chief Ronald Gold publicly denounced the episode as "medically unsound, filled with quackery...defaming to homosexuals" and in violation of "ABC's own standards for dealing with minorities."[38] More specifically, the GAA objected to Martin's description of his feelings as "loathsome and degrading" and his life as a "cheap and hollow fraud." They also took issue with Dr. Welby's diagnosis of homosexuality as an illness and his advice to seek psychiatric help to repress his sexuality so he'll "deserve" his son's respect.[39] Interestingly, there never was any mention of the connection between Martin's latent homosexuality and his dysfunctional relationship with his father, probably because it was a generally accepted view at the time.

On February 13, 1973, Gold met with Grace Johnson, vice president in charge of standards and practices at ABC. Two days later, the network announced no changes would be made. On Friday, February 17, protesters picketed outside ABC's New York headquarters, while the GAA members inside occupied the 39th floor offices of ABC president Elton Rule and chairman of the board Leonard Goldenson. Network executives offered to meet with two members of the Alliance, but they declined, insisting all protesters must be present. Gold later remarked it was one of their biggest mistakes, but they "were afraid that we were going to get screwed over so we said no. That was foolish because we didn't get to talk to anybody. They thought we were crazy — and to a certain extent we were. But we were also justifiably paranoid."[40] Six members who refused to leave peacefully were arrested, but charges were later dropped when a judge ruled an ABC security guard had failed to identify himself properly to the protesters as someone authorized to toss them off the premises.[41]

In response to the protest, a spokesperson for ABC described the episode, which aired as scheduled, as:

> a sensitive and understanding dramatic presentation of the problems of a particular individual faced with a personal, emotional, and physical situation...It depicts a married man who, faced with divorce and alcoholic and diabetic problems, is concerned that he has homosexual tendencies and goes to Dr. Welby for advice.[42]

When the episode aired in February of 1973, the network reportedly did eliminate Martin's description of his homosexuality as something "degrading and loathsome" that made his "whole life a cheap and hollow fraud."[43] Although the deletions were made for the first-run telecast, the syndicated version of the episode, still running today in some markets, contains both statements.

The following year, *Marcus Welby, M.D.* was again a hotbed of controversy when it devoted an episode to the subject of child molestation. In "The Outrage," Ted Blakely (Sean Kelly) is sexually molested by his teacher, Bill Swanson (Edward Winter) while on a camping trip with his science class. Ted tries to hide the incident from his mother, Marian (Marla Adams), but when she finds blood on his bed sheets, she rushes her son to Dr. Welby. He examines the bruises and lacerations all over the teenager's body, but, ashamed and scared, Ted refuses to tell Dr. Welby what happened.

As Dr. Welby informs Marian her son has been molested, Ted slips out of the doctor's office and returns to school. When Mr. Swanson discovers Ted is dropping his science class, he confronts him in the gymnasium locker room. "Oh, I was afraid of this," Swanson says. "I was afraid you'd take it all wrong. Life is complicated." He touches his student gently on the shoulder, but when Ted pushes him away, the teacher warns him to keep quiet:

> SWANSON: Blakely, I thought you were ready to be a man. But I was
> wrong. I'll tell you this. You are ready to keep your mouth shut. Or else
> — because if you talk — do I have to draw pictures for you to know
> what other people are going to think about you? Huh? People are not
> that kind, Blakely.[44]

Ted agrees to keep quiet, but vows to kill his teacher if he ever touches him again. Meanwhile, Dr. Welby explains the situation to Ted's father George (Edward Power) and stepmother Leah (Gretchen Corbett). Advised to offer his son emotional support, George admits he never bonded with the kid and has always been "tongue-tied" talking to him. When Ted sees his father, he bursts into tears. George comforts him, but then asks accusingly, "Wasn't there something you could have done?" The guilt-ridden Ted becomes hysterical and locks himself in the bathroom.

On top of his fragile emotional state, Ted is diagnosed with acute peritonitis, requiring surgery to repair the internal injuries from the assault. Dr. Welby is equally concerned about his patient's mental health, but Ted's parents are so shocked and disgusted they offer little help. George admits he doesn't even have "the guts" to listen to the details of his son's assault.

Sergeant Buchanan (Patrick Wayne, the Duke's son), who is assigned to the case, knows what George is *really* worried about and assures him "*there is nothing homosexual about this. It's a case of violent child molestation.*" Buchanan characterizes the assailant as a married, middle-aged guy with a "crummy marriage and a crummier sex-life" suffering from severe mental problems. He also makes it clear the incident is not legally considered rape because, according to the penal code, rape is defined as a male assaulting a female. "I call it an outrage," Buchanan declares, "and that's why I'm here."

While Ted is recovering from surgery, Swanson is arrested on Venice Beach for attempting to molest a child. When Ted wakes up after surgery, he finally admits Swanson molested him and agrees to speak to a psychiatrist. Dr. Welby informs him the police already have his teacher in custody and he has been sent, by his own request, to a mental hospital. Everyone is relieved and, in a final moment, George affirms his son's masculinity: "Ted, you're a heck of a guy. You went through a nightmare, but you thought for yourself. *You acted like a man.*"

Before the program even aired, gay advocacy groups were the ones outraged by how the episode reinforced the stereotype of the homosexual male teacher as a child molester. In spite of statements made to the contrary, it is difficult not to think of what happened to Ted as anything but an act of violence committed by a gay man. When Ronald Gold, media director of the newly formed National Gay Task Force, received a copy of the script in July of 1974, he informed Richard Gitter, ABC's east coast director of broadcast standards and practices, of the script's unacceptability. Two weeks later, Gold discovered the episode had started shooting, so he spread the word to other activists around the country. He contacted Loretta Lotman, an experienced media advocate and the head of Gay Media Action, the nation's first local gay media advocacy group, to spearhead a grass roots campaign, involving everything from letter writing to demonstrations at ABC affiliates.[45]

Once again, the network refused to cancel the episode, but would consider script changes. According to *The Advocate*, the first set of changes included the deletion of the scene in which a character attempts to convince Ted he is still a man despite the attack. Another scene, in which Mr. Swanson tries to molest another boy and George's reference to the attacker as a "pervert," were also eliminated; the latter scene does appear, however, in the syndicated version.

In an article on the controversy dated September 11, 1974 (a month before the program's airing), *The Advocate* published the following excerpt from an undated script in which Sergeant Buchanan talks to Dr. Welby and Ted's parents:

GEORGE: I thought this was — the kind of thing that might happen in prison, or one of those bars — but —

BUCHANAN: Na — those "wierd [sic] bars" have got enough problems as it is — our garden variety homosexual, this isn't his game — let me tell you something.

Even as George winces at the dreaded word; the door opens and Marian, followed by Dr. Welby, enters.

GEORGE: Here they are. Marian — this is Sergeant Arthur Buchanan, Los Angeles Police. Sergeant, my ex-wife, Marian.

BUCHANAN: How d'y'do.

MARIAN: What were you going to tell him? Do I really want to hear?

GEORGE: Probably not.

BUCHANAN : (used to this kind of strife) We were talking about how this kind of assault takes place — and who commits it. This isn't something that happens because the assailant is homosexual — that's not the issue. This is a guy with severe mental and emotional problems — he's often married, middle-aged, with a crummy marriage and a crummier sex life or both.[46]

A copy of the revised script (dated June 27, 1974) in the International Gay and Lesbian Archives begins the same scene with Sergeant Buchanan offering George the following explanation:

BUCHANAN: — no, no, Mister Blakely, put your mind at rest. There is nothing "homosexual" about this, no homosexual involvement on your son's part. This is a case of violent child molestation, which is a lot more than bad enough — let me tell you —[47]

In the syndicated version, Buchanan offers George an even briefer explanation: "No, no, Mr. Blakely, there's nothing homosexual about this. It's a case of violent child molestation." Their conversation is interrupted by Dr. Welby and Marion's entrance. Buchanan then proceeds to characterize the assailant as a "a pedophile, a child molester."

The network believed the changes had remedied the problem. According to Gitter, ABC was standing by their decision to broadcast the episode because it "does not deal with homosexuality nor is any aspect of the program offensive in either content or viewpoint."[48] Yet, there are still gay overtones, particularly in that locker room scene where Swanson threatens Ted with public exposure.

In a letter to William Page of the Gay Human Rights League of Queens County, New York, Gitter, on behalf of ABC, explains the episode's social value:

The program explores the impact upon the family and a young boy who is the victim of a forcible sexual assault, and the physical and emotional problems which result from the attack...The presentation responsibly and unsensationally relates the problem of child molestation from both a physical and emotional point of view. It is made abundantly clear that this is not a matter of homosexuality, but rather, the result of the criminal actions of a child molester, sometimes known as a paedophile; such assailants are frequently married men, and that the importance of the script is to present to the public the problems of coping with such a tragic situation by the young assaulted victim. Not only is the physical damage to be repaired, but the mental damage involved in facing the assailant after the attack, reporting the incident to his family and authorities, pursuing prosecution through the judicial system and the return to emotional stability in facing his peers and his friends.[49]

Gay activists did not agree with the network's position. In a letter to legislators and a second addressed to all ABC affiliates, Dr. Bruce Voeller, Executive Director of the National Gay Task Force, explained how "The Outrage" reinforces the "greatest myth behind the fear and hatred of homosexuality...despite the fact that such a manifestation is statistically almost non-existent."[50] Legislators were encouraged to contact Elton Rule at ABC, while affiliate station managers were urged not to run the program:

> In urging you not to run this particular program we are not attempting in any way to censor you. As an oppressed minority in our society we would be the last to take such a position. What we *are* doing is trying to point out to you the incalculable damage that this program will do to the self-image and civil rights of millions of Americans."[51]

Activists indeed had reason to be concerned. "The Outrage" was scheduled to air around the time several gay rights bills were being considered by legislators around the county. The episode also foreshadowed the battle soon to be waged in California over the Briggs Initiative, which aimed to prohibit gays and lesbians from teaching in public schools. California voters defeated it in 1978 by a larger margin than had been expected.

Fortunately, the campaign gay activists launched against ABC was supported by the American Federation of Teachers, the AFL-CIO, and the American Psychiatric Association. Several major advertising sponsors — including Colgate-Palmolive, Shell Oil, Lipton, American Home Products, Breck, Sterling Drug, and Gillette — refused to buy time on the program.[52] A total of seventeen ABC affiliates, including two in major markets where gay civil rights legislation was pending in the city council (WCVB-TV in Boston and WPVI-TV of Philadelphia), refused to air the show.

A statement released by the management of WPVI argued the episode was "unsuitable for airing" because it presented a "false stereotype of homosexuals as persons who pursue and sexually molest young boys."[53] Although concerned about censorship, the station management expressed an equal concern "about the additional burdens of prejudice the airing of a shallow and facile treatment of such an explosive and confused subject area will doubtless lay upon a newly emerging minority in our society."[54] Although the show did air in most major markets, gay activists succeeded in sending a clear message to television producers and broadcasters that negative, malicious stereotypes would no longer be tolerated.

THE DOCTOR IS IN (AND OUT)

Several medical programs did deal more explicitly with the subject of homosexuality. The first episode of the long-running CBS medical series *Medical Center* to tackle the subject concerns a gay research scientist who becomes the target of a smear campaign. In an attempt to save the life of a young leukemia patient, Dr. Joe Gannon (Chad Everett) asks the hospital's permission to test a new drug developed by Dr. Ben Teverly (Paul Burke). The project is jeopardized when Dr. Gannon and Dr. Paul Lochner (James Daly), the hospital's chief of staff, receive an anonymous letter claiming Dr. Teverly is a homosexual.

"What kind of mind would put a lie like that on paper?" Dr. Gannon asks.

"A sick mind," Dr. Lochner explains. "Somebody out to get revenge."

The rumor spreads quickly around the hospital and, as a result, the medical staff refuses to approve the use of Teverly's experimental drug. Even Dr. Teverly's own supervisor, Dr. Oliver Garson (Andrew Duggan), gives it a thumbs down.

Dr. Gannon continues to defend both the scientist's drug and his hetero-sexuality, until Dr. Teverly verifies the rumor. "What does it take to get through to you?" he declares. "Why don't you face it? It's a fact! *I am a homosexual!*"

After getting over the initial shock, Dr. Gannon takes the liberal "I-don't-care-what-you-do-in-your-personal-life" attitude and continues to push for the drug's approval. When Dr. Gannon confronts Dr. Garson about his lack of support, the doctor explains how his "daughter's life was ruined because of one of those *deviants*...because of my limp-wristed son-in-law, my daughter has been in analysis for over a year!"

When a second vote is taken, Dr. Garson once again opposes the drug. Dr. Gannon manages to get the extra vote he needs by delivering a passionate speech about the danger of allowing bigotry to undermine treatment:

> DR. GANNON: You're willing to shelve a possible step toward the cure of leukemia just to satiate your own bigotry. Ollie [Dr. Garson], where does that leave us as human beings? Where does it leave us as doctors? Tomorrow, I tell a patient, "I can't treat your arthritis, you're psychotic." Or "Set your own broken arm Charlie, you're a junkie." "Sorry about your liver, Mac, but I'm against guys who booze it up." "Pardon me while I go dynamite the Sistine Chapel, I just heard it was a *homosexual* who painted the ceiling."[55]

Dr. Gannon's speech exemplifies a common contradiction of the era's medical dramas. Gannon doesn't believe homosexuality is an illness, although he equates it with psychosis, drug addiction, and alcoholism. He reprimands his colleagues for spreading "the sickness of intolerance," yet he pities the homosexual lifestyle.

"Look, I'm not defending homosexuality," Dr. Gannon admits privately to Dr. Garson. "I've seen it cause too much sadness."

Dr. Teverly is one of 1970s television's "safest" representations of a male

"A straight-acting, hard-working, closeted professional:" *Medical Center* guest star Paul Burke as gay research scientist Dr. Ben Teverly.

homosexual: a straight-acting, hard-working, closeted professional, who's neither neurotic, psychotic, or, in Dr. Garson's words, "limp-wristed." The producers also play it safe, however, by ducking the "gay" aspects of his personal life. The consequences of his "outing," particularly how it triggers Dr. Garson's homophobia — which, in turn, endangers Dr. Gannon's patient — suggests that it might have been better for everyone if Dr. Teverly had spent the rest of his career locked away with the labcoats.

Whether Dr. Teverly can actually be classified as a "closet case" is, however, debatable. Dr. Lochner reveals that Dr. Teverly admitted he was gay during his job interview because he was forced to resign from his last job after being outed. On the other hand, Dr. Teverly has been "playing it straight" by dating a colleague, Dr. Abby Whitten (Salome Jens). She has refused to believe the rumors, but when her attempt at seducing him fails, he finally tells her the truth.

"I'm a homosexual. Oh, not the *obvious* kind," he explains, "and for that I'm thankful."

Dr. Whitten is angry, but not only because he lied. She considered him husband material — the last salvation for a successful doctor who, at her age, couldn't possibly have a fulfilling life without a ring on her finger. "Don't you see? I'm *36 years old*!" she declares, "I'm alone! I saw an end to all this loneliness!"

Dr. Teverly wasn't the only member of the *Medical Center* staff outed during the series's seven-year run. "Impasse" features Lois Nettleton as psychiatrist Dr.

Annie Claymor, who assists Dr. Gannon with an emotionally disturbed heart patient, Tobi Page (Jamie Smith Jackson). When Tobi fails to take her heart medicine and refuses to have a life-saving heart operation, Dr. Claymor tries to figure out why she's lost her will to live. Tobi continues to have seizures, which seem to be triggered by phone conversations with her friend Sarah.

Meanwhile, Dr. Gannon, unaware that Dr. Claymor plays on a different team, puts the moves on her. She seems interested, though slightly distant. When Tobi's boyfriend Sam (Tim McIntire) discovers Dr. Claymor is a lesbian, he becomes convinced she is trying to "convert" his girlfriend. "Tobi doesn't need *that kind* of help," he tells Dr. Gannon, "Now if anybody needs help, she [Dr. Claymor] does!" When Dr. Gannon confronts Dr. Claymor about what he thinks is a "dirty, rotten, malicious lie," she tells him the truth. As with Dr. Teverly, Dr. Gannon refuses to believe her.

"Why not?" Dr. Claymor asks, "because I didn't bite you on the ankle when you asked me for a date? Because I let you kiss me and I enjoyed it?"

Dr. Gannon explains how her behavior is incompatible with being a lesbian because, as everyone knows, they hate men. "Oh, what an ignorant assumption. Who says I do?" she responds, "Listen, I put up with you, don't I?" Here we take a time-out so Dr. Claymor can clarify for Dr. Gannon and the viewers at home some of the common misconceptions about the sisters of Sappho:

> DR. CLAYMOR: I am a person. I am a woman. I am a psychiatrist. And I am a homosexual. And we are not all the same anymore than hetero-sexuals are all the same. I am not — I am not repelled by the opposite sex. But on a deeper level, any fulfillment comes with other women, that's all. Is that so hard to understand?...You think you are an enlightened man? Free of all prejudice. But somewhere, somewhere in your mind, there's a sneaking notion that a lesbian can't be trusted to live up to her professional vows and treat a patient of the same sex without pouncing on her....Lesbians are not a bunch of harridans consumed by a hatred of the opposite sex. Some are, yes, but that's too bad for them. People who hate whole chunks of the human race are sick, no matter what mode, what sexual preferences.[56]

Dr. Gannon gets the message, but he's still disappointed there won't be anything more between them than "just a good night kiss."

When Sam informs Tobi that Dr. Claymor is a lesbian, she phones her friend Sarah, who invites her to come over to "talk." A hysterical Tobi heads for the hospital roof, but Dr. Claymor and Dr. Gannon manage to talk her down to safety. Tobi finally admits she's afraid of being a lesbian (or of having the "disease" as she calls it) because after breaking up with Sam, Sarah "comforted" her. "We talked, she made me feel good, and I never had that kind of feeling with Sam," she explains to Dr. Claymor, who assures her she's not a lesbian, just confused because her sexual promiscuity contradicts what she really wants out of life:

TOBI: I want to fall in love with one man! Be his wife! Have his children. I want to be his woman and nobody else's. And I want him to love me. And not want to be anything but what I am. It was just a dream.

DR. CLAYMOR: Tobi, that's a dream that most women have. But you sold out, that's why you're so confused. Those aren't the words of a lesbian. Or a swinger. Or a fool. That's just the real Tobi Page. You don't have to pretend to be anyone but yourself. A sweet, honest, healthy girl with honest, healthy ideals. You don't have to hide them from yourself or anyone else. Don't you understand that?[57]

Just as Cory Melino is cured by understanding homosexuality is a choice, Tobi is on the road to recovery when she realizes one sexual experience with a woman doesn't qualify her as a lesbian. Her heart is now literally ready to be repaired.

In a variation on the themes explored in "Impasse," a 1972 episode of *The Bold Ones* entitled "A Very Strange Triangle" examines a young woman struggling with her sexual identity. Dr. Marty Cohen (Robert Walden) is excited when he's reunited with his former girlfriend, Valerie DeMarco (Donna Mills), a nurse who, unbeknownst to him, is in a lesbian relationship with an older woman, Eleanor (Hildy Brooks). Marty tries to rekindle their relationship, only to discover his competition wears a dress. He freaks out, because, as he explains to Dr. Paul Hunter (David Hartman), he had no idea Valerie was, *you know*. "I didn't have a single clue that anything was wrong until I took her home the other night and this *lesbo* [Eleanor] opens the door and tells me what the score is."

Reacting to the "L-word," Dr. Hunter is surprised how "unenlightened" his colleague is. Marty insists he has no problem with homosexuals, but admits Valerie's sexuality poses a threat to his masculinity ("If I can't spot a lesbian when I'm about to propose to her, what kind of shape am I in?"). The so-called liberal-minded, enlightened Dr. Hunter replies, "I would hope you'd think of it as a threat to her femininity."

"Triangle" subscribes to the myth that a homosexual chooses a same-sex partner to remedy his/her dysfunctional relationship with one or both parents. The older Eleanor is clearly a surrogate for Valerie's absent mother, a wealthy, alcoholic, self-involved actress. "Eleanor put it all together for me," Valerie explains. "I was finally able to break with my mother." According to Valerie, Eleanor not only helped her through nursing school, but increased her confidence level and cured her fear of being alone. Conveniently, Eleanor is earning her degree in clinical psychology and will soon be qualified to be Valerie's round-the-clock, presumabbly free-of-charge therapist.

During a session with her current shrink, Valerie discusses her feelings for Marty, whose first attempt at a reconciliation soured when he insisted Valerie leave Eleanor. "You mean you'd be willing to date me," he asks, "and live in the same place as *that*?" Marty then tries to win Valerie back by arriving unannounced at Eleanor's apartment to declare his love. Sounding more like a psychiatrist than a lover, Eleanor accuses Marty of destroying all the "good" her therapy accomplished by resurrecting Valerie's "guilts and doubts and fears." Recognizing the strong emotional hold Eleanor has over Valerie, Marty offers the nurse a chance to live a "normal" life:

ELEANOR: What is *normal*, doctor? What do you mean exactly?

MARTY: Something that isn't unnatural.

ELEANOR: That's exactly what I thought you meant. And you are going to introduce her to your normal way of life. And show her the error of her sick and perverted ways. Will you forgive her past sins doctor? Will you make her feel dirty and ashamed for the life she's lived with me? Huh?

MARTY: You're really going to slug it out, aren't you?

ELEANOR: No.

MARTY: I only want what's best for Val.

ELEANOR: As do I. We just disagree about what that is.[58]

The next day, Valerie moves out of Eleanor's house because she can no longer handle Marty and Eleanor fighting over her like a prize. She gives her resignation to the head of the hospital, Dr. Craig (E.G. Marshall), who, addressing her more like a patient than a nurse, attributes the hospital's failure to solve her personal problems to their failure to treat Valerie's mother's medical and psychological problems. Before leaving, Valerie tests the heterosexual waters for the first time by sleeping with Marty, but the next morning she admits the earth didn't move. "I think I just wanted to prove that I can do it," Valerie confesses. "I didn't make love to Marty Cohen last night. I made love to a man." Confused, yet knowing she has to be honest with herself, Valerie says goodbye to both Marty and Eleanor and leaves town to start a new life.

First telecast the night before the premiere of the groundbreaking made-for-TV movie *That Certain Summer*, "Triangle" caught the attention of the critics, who found its treatment of lesbianism both ridiculous and ambiguous. *The New York Times*'s John O'Connor suggested that if "taboo subjects" were going to be used on television "for little more than injecting titillation into inane plots, they should be left taboo."[59] While the episode thankfully doesn't subscribe to the myth that all a lesbian needs is one tumble with a man to straighten her out, it also plays it safe by never resolving the Valerie/Eleanor/Marty triangle. Instead, Valerie drives alone up the California coast in search of her sexual identity. Let's hope she stops in San Francisco.

HE IS A SHE (AND VICE VERSA)

The medical drama again broke ground in the mid-1970s when it took on an even more complex subject — transsexuality. A transsexual is an individual assigned the wrong sex at birth who elects to have sex reassignment surgery. In 1952, the controversial medical procedure captured national headlines when a former U.S. army sergeant, George Jorgensen, left for Denmark and returned as Christine Jorgensen. At the time, the public responded to the radical concept of changing one's sex with curiosity, disgust, and hostility. (In describing Jorgenson, one journalist quipped, "Jane Russell has nothing to worry about.")

As with homosexuality, medical shows provided the ideal dramatic context to introduce transsexuality to the American public.[60] They presented a generally sympathetic and sensitive portrait of the male-to-female transsexual by focusing on his struggle to get others (including the audience) to understand he feels like a woman trapped in a man's body. The stories typically concentrate less on the medical procedure itself and more on the reaction of the patient's family, friends, and colleagues.

In 1975, *Medical Center* became the first series to explore the subject in the two-part episode "The Fourth Sex." Robert Reed, best known as the father on *The Brady Bunch*, received an Emmy nomination for his guest starring role as Dr. Pat Caddison, a renowned vascular surgeon who returns to Los Angeles to undergo a sex change. In spite of the support he receives from his friend and colleague, Dr. Gannon, Dr. Caddison must surmount a series of obstacles before he can go under the knife, including a minor heart problem, the medical staff's objection to the procedure, and the hospital's fear of negative publicity. And then there are Dr. Caddison's estranged wife, Heather (Salome Jens), and teenage son, Steve (Gary Frank), who are less than receptive to the idea. The situation is complicated further because Heather's sister, Dr. Jessica Lambert (Louise Sorel), who also happens to be Dr. Gannon's girlfriend, vehemently opposes the procedure.

Part One focuses on Dr. Caddison's unexpected return to Los Angeles. He first breaks the news to Dr. Gannon, who notices that Dr. Caddison has become "thinner and —"

"Softer?" inquires Dr. Caddison.

He explains that "nature has played a ghastly joke" on him, so he is taking female hormones to begin the process of sex reassignment. Once Dr. Gannon is over the initial shock, he agrees to serve as his physician.

Unfortunately, Dr. Caddison's wife, Heather, who mistakenly thinks her husband has returned to solve their marital problems, is less sympathetic. Dr. Caddison begins by explaining that they should have never been married in the first place. Thinking she's the cause of their sexual problems, Heather offers to get professional help. But as Dr. Caddison explains, the problem is he's not attracted to her — as a woman:

HEATHER: Are you saying you're a homosexual?

In "The Fourth Sex," *The Brady Bunch's* Robert Reed is a famous surgeon who checks into *Medical Center* for a sex change.

DR. CADDISON: I'm a transsexual...I'm a male by the reason of my anatomy. But emotionally, I'm not. Emotionally, I'm just like you are. Emotionally, I'm a woman. I think that's why we were as close as we were. I understand your problems.[61]

Dr. Caddison isn't a homosexual, yet the question of his sexual orientation — or rather, which of the two sexes (or perhaps both?) he desires sexually — is never addressed. The differentiation between homosexuality and transsexuality is necessary (especially in 1975). Yet the producers may have believed it would have only created more confusion if Dr. Caddison were to elaborate any further.

Angry toward her brother-in-law for hurting her sister, Dr. Lambert advises the medical staff to oppose Dr. Caddison's sex change. She believes psychotherapy is the answer, but a staff psychologist disagrees and explains gender identification is established at the age of five. So Dr. Gannon begins Dr. Caddison's physical evaluation, only to discover an irregularity in his heartbeat which could postpone the operation indefinitely. Despondent over the news, Dr. Caddison drives his car off a bridge. He claims he wasn't trying to kill himself, but admits to Dr. Gannon it's an "attractive" idea.

In Part Two, Gannon tries to convince the staff that, despite the medical risks, it's imperative for the sake of his patient's mental health to go ahead with the operation. Once again, Dr. Gannon delivers a passionate speech to the medical staff about their inability to confront their own fears:

DR.GANNON: The issue here is and always has been sexual reassignment. If a man had come to us with an operative carcinoma or any other medical procedure which would have saved his life, nobody would have turned him down. Isn't that true?...But because the area is so fraught with taboo, because there's so little precedent, because what he wants offends us all so personally, we back away. We say, "it's too bizarre. We can't comprehend." I thought we were doctors. Scientists! If we can't look upon this human deviation or any other one with compassion, how can we expect the rest of the world to? The man is begging us for his psychological life because he can't bear to live trapped inside this physical purgatory.[62]

Unfortunately, Dr. Lambert steals Dr. Gannon's thunder. By asking the board to consider the effects on Dr. Caddison's family, she convinces them to reject the procedure.

Meanwhile, Dr. Caddison assists Dr. Gannon with a patient, a macho race car driver named Skip Daley (Dennis Cole), who has severely damaged his leg in an accident and may never walk again. When his surgery doesn't immediately bring back feeling in his leg, a sullen and bitter Skip is afraid he'll become a "vegetable."

"You're not a vegetable," Dr. Caddison assures him, "you're a man with a temporary problem."

Aware of his surgeon's upcoming operation, Skip snidely asks Dr. Caddison what he knows about being a man. Dr. Caddison tells him:

DR. CADDISON: Whether I am a man or a woman or anything in between, the only thing I know that should concern you is that I am a qualified surgeon. And a very good one. No less than a man is. Let me tell you there is more to it than driving cars at 200 m.p.h. And whether you drive again or you just push yourself along in a wheelchair, it doesn't qualify you for self-pity. And even if you lose your use of this leg, which is not going to happen, you won't lose your manhood. Your manliness, your virility, Mr. Daley, is all in your mind. It's in your head. If it's so important for you to be a real man, you better stop feeling sorry for yourself.[63]

Masculinity and femininity are a state of mind — a concept perhaps too radical for viewers to digest solely in terms of Dr. Caddison's transsexualism, but more palatable in the context of Skip's problem. Skip obviously was listening, because when he gets some feeling back in his leg, the big lug becomes teary-eyed and asks the nurse, "Have you ever seen a grown man cry?"

Dr. Caddison faces his greatest challenge in his son, Steve, who, distraught over his father's upcoming sex change, contemplates suicide. Instead, he decides to drown his sorrows in a six pack. "You're not my father. Maybe you're my mother," jokes a drunken Steve. "Maybe I've got two mothers." Like Cory Melino, Steve is afraid his father's transsexuality is hereditary.

"I'm no good at sports. I like to read a lot — poetry," Steve sobs. "Maybe I'm just like you."

"You're a man," Dr. Caddison assures him. "You always have been. And you don't have to fight to prove it."

Once Dr. Gannon gets both Steve and Heather's approval, Dr. Caddison has his sex change. Before Heather goes to see her ex-husband and say goodbye, Gannon prepares her (and us) for the shock.

"Pat's a woman now," he explains. "Very feminine. Hair. Clothes. Make-up. Not at all the Pat you know."

"Introduction to Transsexuality" is perhaps a more appropriate title for "The Fourth Sex," which gives viewers some insight into the subject from the perspective of both the patient and those affected by his decision. The story begins at the point where Dr. Caddison has already decided to have the operation, thus allowing writer Rita Lakin to devote sufficient time to his family and colleagues (and the audience) as they try to sort out their own feelings. Although the emotionally charged scenes involving Dr. Caddison and his family border on the melodramatic, Lakin's script handles the subject with sensitivity. Most importantly, the episode avoids sensationalism, even in the scene in which Heather (and the audience) see the post-operative Dr. Caddison, now fully transformed into a woman, for the first time.

A young post-op transsexual is the subject of an unusual episode of the short-lived medical series *Westside Hospital*, "The Mermaid."[64] After winning three gold medals in an international swimming competition in Los Angeles, East German swimming champion Niki Gunter (Betsy Slade) hits her head on the diving board. The teenager is rushed to the hospital, where Dr. Philip Parker (Ernest Thompson) performs emergency surgery. Dr. Parker wants Niki to remain for observation, but her coach, Kurt Hoffman (David Sheiner) demands she be released the next day.

Later, while Dr. Parker and his colleague, Dr. Janet Cottrell (Linda Carlson), are examining Niki, the young girl asks if they'll help her defect.

"They keep me like a prisoner," she cries. "Mr. Hoffman and the other coaches. I see no one, go nowhere without them."

When Dr. Parker checks Niki's X-rays, he thinks a mistake was made because Niki has male bone structure. He concludes Niki was born an anatomical male, but the East German government forced him to have a sex change in order to win medals and advance their political agenda. But as Niki reveals, she's the one who requested the operation after her parents died because, as a child, she felt like a little girl trapped in a boy's body. Now she's wondering if she made a mistake, since the East German government is preventing her from developing socially as a woman. Dr. Hoffman informs Niki she's got to go back home, but just before her release she sneaks out of the hospital and seeks refuge in Dr. Cottrell's apartment.

During a woman-to-woman talk with Dr. Cottrell, Niki explains how even though she's female on the outside, inside she feels like a "freak" because she doesn't know how to act around boys. Dr. Cottrell advises Niki to be honest with people. She starts by sharing her secret with Tom (Andrew Stevens), an American diver who is sweet on her. Tom doesn't know what to say, leaving Niki angry and even more confused.

When she begins to bleed internally, Niki is rushed back to the hospital. Once she's out of danger, a guilty Coach Hoffman agrees to loosen the apron strings. After a reunion with Tom, who apologizes for his behavior, Niki returns to what will hopefully be an improved life back home in East Germany.

The episode takes a unique approach to the subject of transsexualism by displacing a political issue — United States-East German relations — onto the issue of sexual identity. Niki wants to stay in the United States because the East German government controls the three major factions of her life — the political, the professional, and the personal. She's not seeking political asylum as much as *personal* asylum. The episode subscribes to the idea that while a person's sex is biologically determined (and can be surgically altered), gender, in terms of masculine and feminine behavior, can be learned. Sheltered by her coaches, Niki was never sufficiently socialized as a female. As she says to Tom, "I will make a good girl, but will you be my friend and help me find out?" In the end, the young swimmer really has no choice but to return to East Germany, but at least Coach Hoffman agrees to allow her to live fully as a woman.

An episode of *St. Elsewhere* ("Release") deals with a surgeon who refuses to accept his friend's decision to undergo a sex change. Airing eight years after "The Fourth Sex," "Release" reveals how society (or at least medical show fans) were perceived as more enlightened. Unfortunately, the same cannot be said for Dr. Mark Craig (William Daniels), a brilliant yet arrogant surgeon who is shocked when his college roommate, Bob Overland (Andy Romano), checks into St. Eligius for a sex change. Though Bob has the support of his understanding wife, Anne (Alice Herson), Dr. Craig is determined to change Bob's mind.

Dr. Craig can't believe his friend hid his secret from him during college, but Bob explains it would have ended their friendship. "It's taken me years to stop trying to be something I'm not," he admits, "Years of trying to be the best athlete, dating the most beautiful ladies, merely to compensate for my own strange feelings." When Bob refuses even to allow him to consult with his psychiatrist, Dr. Craig considers wielding his power as chief of surgery to halt the procedure.

"Well, you may have convinced your wife, but not me buddy," Dr. Craig snarls. "I know you too well to agree to anything so disgusting."

"Overland is gone," Bob declares. "He's dead."

In a way, transsexuality here serves as a metaphor for how rapidly our society

31

has changed over the years. Dr. Craig doesn't interfere with Bob's decision, but as he tells his drinking buddies, Nurse Helen Rosenthal (Christina Pickles) and Dr. Westphall (Ed Flanders), he wishes the world was the kind of place his father grew up in, where men and women assumed traditional male and female roles. His colleagues, however, aren't so sure that change is necessarily a bad thing.

The dramatic treatment of transsexuality in the 1970s and 1980s was not limited to medical shows. In 1986, CBS aired *Second Serve*, a made-for-TV movie based on the autobiography of Dr. Renée Richards, a male-to-female transsexual. A well-respected pediatric ophthalmologist and tennis pro, Richards made headlines when she was denied the right to compete as a woman in the 1977 U.S. Open Tournament. (A New York State Superior Court judge ruled in Richards's favor because, despite her high male chromosome count, her weight, height, and physique were comparable to a biological female.)

In yet another truly mesmerizing performance, an almost unrecognizable Vanessa Redgrave is equally effective in her portrayal of both Richard Raskin, who comes to terms with his gender identity; and a post-op Richards, who enters the national spotlight when she resumes her professional tennis career as a woman. Redgrave receives support from Gavin Lambert and Lisa Liss's sensitive script and the incredible make-up work of Peter Owen, an Academy Award winner for *The Lord of the Rings*. The result is an above average made-for-TV biography that takes an insightful, intelligent look at gender identity disorder from both a medical and a human perspective.

A DISEASE OF OUR OWN

On July 3, 1981, *The New York Times* ran an article on the back page with the headline "Rare Cancer Seen in 41 Homosexuals." The first major national newspaper story about AIDS, the *Times* article reported an outbreak of rare cancer — Kaposi's Sarcoma (KS) — among gay men in New York and the San Francisco Bay Area. Linking KS as well as Pneumocystis Carinii Pneumonia (PCP) to the gay male population, researchers gave the new disease a name — GRID (Gay-Related Immune Disorder). In 1982, GRID also began to show up in the heterosexual population, specifically in hemophiliacs, blood transfusion recipients, intravenous drug users, and the female sex partners of AIDS-infected men. No longer confined to the gay community, GRID was given a more neutral name — AIDS (Acquired Immunodeficiency Syndrome).

But for the American public, there was nothing neutral about the word and the disease, which became synonymous in the 1980s with male homosexuality. While children and blood transfusion recipients were labeled AIDS's "innocent victims," gay men and IV drug users were blamed for spreading the disease through their "immoral" behavior. In a demonstration of true "Christian" compassion, Moral Majority Leader Rev. Jerry Falwell declared that AIDS is God's wrath on homosexuals. The ignorant and hateful comments made by

Falwell and others, coupled with the many unanswered questions about the transmission of AIDS, only fueled the public's growing homophobia and hysteria.

The "gay plague" stigma was also the primary reason the Center for Disease Control and the federal government were slow in their response. To accuse the Reagan administration of negligence is an understatement. President Reagan waited until 1987 to give his first speech about AIDS. In that same year, 36,000 Americans were diagnosed with the disease, 21,000 had already died, and the numbers continued to grow.

In the 1980s, the AIDS crisis offered the television medical drama a context in which to address homosexuality — and homophobia. There was no longer a need to link homosexuality to an arbitrary medical condition like a bleeding ulcer, alcoholism, or heart disease. Finally, homosexuals had a disease of their own. So in addition to continuing to educate the public about homosexuality, medical dramas began to set the public straight about AIDS. In the process, they also openly criticized the American health care system for allowing the gay stigma attached to the disease to affect the quality of care being offered to AIDS patients.

Unfortunately, when AIDS became a front page story, there were few medical dramas on the prime time schedule. In terms of dramatic programming, television in the early 1980s was dominated by prime time soap operas (*Dallas, Dynasty, Knots Landing*) and detective/action shows (*Magnum, P.I., Simon and Simon*). Only two medical series enjoyed healthy runs during the 1980s — *St. Elsewhere* (1982-1988, six seasons) and *Trapper John, M.D.* (1979-1986, seven seasons). The subject of AIDS would eventually be addressed by other genres, including sitcoms, police dramas, and made-for-TV movies, beginning with the groundbreaking 1985 film, *An Early Frost*.

The first medical drama to tackle AIDS was the 1983 Christmas episode of *St. Elsewhere*, "AIDS and Comfort." A well-respected, up-and-coming 34-year-old Boston city councilman, Tony Gifford (Michael Brandon), is diagnosed with AIDS. His physician, Dr. Peter White (Terence Knox), is confused because Tony is heterosexual, not an IV drug user, and has never received a blood transfusion. Dr. White and Dr. Westphall are suspicious, so they enlist a friend of Tony's, hospital administrator Joan Halloran (Nancy Stafford), to find out the truth. Finally, Tony admits he's been having anonymous sex with men. Upon his release from St. Eligius, the councilman decides to go public with his illness and not resign from office.

Although Tony's diagnosis is the focus of the episode, the story devotes equal time to the reactions of the St. Eligius staff at having an AIDS patient under their care. The possibility of contracting AIDS through casual contact was still fresh in everyone's mind, no doubt thanks to a 1983 news release by the American Medical Association that erroneously made the very same suggestion. Dr. White is pressured by his wife to drop Tony as a patient. Nurse Billie (Rae Dawn Chong) doesn't want to handle his blood. Luther (Eric Laneuville), an orderly, leaves Tony's food tray outside his door. Someone even spray paints "AIDS!"

inside the hospital elevator. Fearing they could contract the disease by giving blood, members of the community and the hospital staff are reluctant to donate during a city-wide shortage.

As he contemplates going public with the disease, Tony shares with Dr. Westphall a passage from *The Decameron*, in which Boccaccio describes a plague that devastated 14th century Florence:

> It was the year 1348, Florence, lovely city of Italy, when the dreadful plague struck. The body was covered with purple spots. Those harborages of death. And the inevitable end was this — avoid those diseased and anything they had come near.

Later, Dr. Westphall, in a stirring speech, directly challenges the labeling of AIDS as a "plague" sent by God as punishment. At the same time, he emphasizes that the role of the medical community is to care for people who are sick, not to pass moral judgment:

> DR. WESTPHALL: Who am I? Why should any of us be penalized fatally for choosing a certain lifestyle? Especially when you realize it all boils down to chance anyway. And I tell you something, I don't give a damn for all this talk about morality and vengeful gods and all that. If you have AIDS, you're sick, you need help. And that's all that matters. And that's why we're here, right?[65]

Eighteen years later, Dr. Westphall's speech is still relevant when considering that PWAs (People With AIDS) continue to experience discrimination in areas such as health care, housing, and employment. Yet, we also now see how phrases like "choosing a certain lifestyle" and Tony's "secret" admission that he contracted AIDS through anonymous gay sex offered, at the time, a limited perspective of who is at risk. Tony's wife (Caroline Smith) is the only one who even questions whether her husband may have passed the virus on to her (Tony's doctors never even address the issue). The transmission of the virus through heterosexual sex would, in fact, become the centerpiece of the series's next AIDS story line.

During the 1985-1986 season, St. Eligius's resident Lothario, plastic surgeon Dr. Bobby Caldwell (Mark Harmon), learns he has AIDS. In "Family Feud," Dr. Caldwell is told the sore on his hand is a K.S. lesion. His blood tests positive for HTLV-III antibodies. (HTLV-III-human T-cell lymphotropic virus was the name given to the virus isolated by Dr. Robert Gallo in 1984. It was changed to human immunodeficiency virus, or HIV, in 1986.) Dr. Caldwell considers suicide, but instead moves to Los Angeles to work in an AIDS clinic. (Harmon actually left the series to pursue his film career.) Two years later, when the hospital receives word Dr. Caldwell has died ("Heaven's Skate"), the St. Eligius staff gathers for a memorial service.

During the same season, an episode of *Trapper John M.D.* ("Friends and Lovers") featured two intersecting story lines — the first about a gay man with AIDS and the second involving the hospital's "unofficial" admissions policy concerning AIDS patients. The episode begins with Nurse Libby Kegler's (Lorna Luft) reunion with her former fiancée, Terry Eliot (Robert Desidero), who broke off their engagement without an explanation. Terry is suddenly interested in getting back together, until a blood test reveals he has AIDS. Libby is, of course, distraught that her ideal man is not only sick, but gay. She's confused and seeks some answers ("What makes a person gay?," "I wonder if it means they'll be gay forever?") from Dr. Jackson (Brian Mitchell, better known today as Broadway star Brian Stokes Mitchell). Libby's naïveté surrounding homosexuality is unintentionally comical considering actress Lorna Luft is the daughter of gay icon, Judy Garland, and Liza Minnelli's half-sister.

Libby soon finds herself in the middle of a love triangle when Terry's ex-lover Brad (Terry Kiser) reenters the picture. She is ready for a fight, but when Terry admits he's still in love with Brad, she follows Trapper John's (Pernell Roberts) advice: "The reality is Terry is probably going to die. We are talking long term commitment here. If you are really willing to take that on, I want you to know. It is an emotional no-win. It takes a very special kind of love." So even though she still loves the guy, Libby helps Brad reunite with Terry.

In the episode's second story line, Trapper John goes up against the hospital administrator Catherine Hackett (Janis Paige) when he discovers that instead of admitting AIDS patients, San Francisco Memorial is transferring them to the AIDS unit at nearby Bay General Hospital. When Trapper shows her how many AIDS outpatients Memorial treats on a daily basis, Catherine successfully convinces the hospital board to open its own AIDS clinic.

A doctor's relationship with an AIDS patient is the subject of a multi-episode story arc during *St. Elsewhere*'s sixth and final season (1987-1988). Brett Johnston (Kyle Secor) is a gay PWA under the care of Dr. Seth Griffin (Bruce Greenwood), an ambitious physician short on compassion. Griffin allows his homophobia to affect his doctor-patient relationship with Brett, who finally confronts him. "To you," Brett tells Seth, "I'm only a queer dying of AIDS."

In "Night of the Living Bed," Dr. Griffin is forced to confront his homophobia when he accidentally pricks himself while drawing blood from Brett. The terrified doctor takes his anger out on the hospital's new chief administrator, Dr. John Gideon (Ronny Cox), by questioning why the hospital even bothers to treat AIDS patients. "There's no cure for AIDS! They're gonna die!" Griffin insists. "All we do is put off death. And expose other people in the process." Dr. Gideon and Ecumena, the conglomerate that owns St. Eligius, actually agree with Griffin. They've already turned down Dr. Westphall's proposal to open an AIDS hospice because it would not be in the best financial interest of the hospital ("Moon for the Misbegotten").

Meanwhile, Brett attempts to apologize to Dr. Griffin, but the doctor can't help but blame him for what happened. "If it weren't for you, I wouldn't be lying here worrying about what's left of my life..." Griffin says. "So get the message. I don't really care about you." Before Brett leaves, he explains how fear, not AIDS, poses the real threat:

> BRETT: I don't expect you to. I'm used to that. That's the way of the world. People reacting to their fears. Because of AIDS, we are still in danger of losing the comfort of human contact. Whether it's with gloves or condoms or a sterile mask covering someone's smile. We're pulling apart. Lines are being drawn.[66]

An Early Frost (NBC-TV)
November 11, 1985
Written by Ron Cowen
and Daniel Lipman
Story by Sherman Yellen
Directed by John Erman

Two years after *St. Elsewhere* was the first prime time series to feature an AIDS storyline ("AIDS and Comfort"), NBC aired this groundbreaking made-for-TV movie. Written by Ron Cowen and Daniel Lipman, creators of *Sisters* and the American version of *Queer as Folk*, *An Early Frost* combines a coming out story with an AIDS 101 film that aimed to educate viewers about the disease and shatter some myths surrounding the transmission of the virus.

Aidan Quinn stars as Michael Pierson, an up-and-coming lawyer who returns home to visit his parents, Katherine (Gena Rowlands) and Nick (Ben Gazzara). When he tells them he has AIDS and he is gay (in that order), Katherine begins educating herself about the disease, while Nick just gets angry. Nick finally starts facing the reality of his son's illness when Michael begins having seizures and the ambulance that arrives to the scene refuses to transport his son to the hospital. During his stay, Michael befriends a gay man named Victor (John Glover), who dies soon after Michael returns to his parents' house. A visit from Michael's boyfriend Peter (D.W. Moffett), who exposed him to the virus, is awkward for Nick, who refuses to accept his son's homosexuality. But when he prevents a depressed Michael from committing suicide, Nick is able to put his prejudices aside.

By today's standards, *An Early Frost* plays it fairly safe in its handling of both the subject of AIDS and homosexuality. Yet, the film's main purpose is to give viewers the facts about AIDS and, in the process, preach tolerance. As part of its promotional plan, NBC released a "Viewer's Guide" that included a plot summary and a list of discussion topics, such as "Fear of Contagion," "Responses to AIDS," "Support Services," and "Emerging Issues." The guide asks viewers to consider how they would react if someone they knew had AIDS and includes guidelines on how to prevent the transmission of the HIV virus (still referred to at the time as HTLV-III).

Unsure whether he was exposed to the virus or not, Dr. Griffin must now deal with being "in limbo."

Months later, Brett checks back into St. Eligius with pneumonia and discovers Dr. Griffin found God and become a Born Again Christian. He is more humane, yet terribly self-righteous — to the point of offering Brett unsolicited spiritual guidance to renounce his homosexuality and ask God for forgiveness ("Requiem For a Heavyweight"). In a moment of despair, the dying Brett wonders if Dr. Griffin is right — maybe he is going to hell. But as Griffin admits to a colleague the morning after Brett's death ("Split Decision"), he's the one who made the mistake:

> DR. GRIFFIN: I used to blame Brett for his disease. Hated him for what he was. I still don't understand why some people are gay. Or maybe I'm afraid of it. But the fact is, when I pricked myself with Brett's blood, we became equal. Two guys threatened by AIDS. And Brett's life isn't expendable because he's homosexual...[67]

In *An Early Frost* (1985), Aidan Quinn (right) tells his parents, Ben Gazarra (left) and Gena Rowlands (center), that he's gay and has AIDS.

The Dr. Griffin and Brett storyline was television's best to date about AIDS. By following an AIDS patient over the course of an entire season, the series's producers were able to give a realistic and accurate depiction of the unpredictable nature of the disease. More importantly, the series's perfectly counter-balanced the "clinical" with a powerful, heart-wrenching look at AIDS's emotional toll on the patient, the medical staff, and all the people — lovers, friends, family — who can only helplessly stand by, watching and waiting for a loved one to die.

AIDS IN THE NOT-SO-GAY 90S

In the Fall of 1994, the medical drama was resuscitated by two new series. *Chicago Hope*, created by David E. Kelley, followed the medical staff of a private Chicago hospital. Like *Medical Center*, the staff's professional and personal lives are examined in relation to the medical conditions of their patients. Also set in Chicago, *ER* follows a similar format, though the series tends to be faster-paced, grittier, and less melodramatic. In spite of their stylistic differences, both series picked up where *St. Elsewhere* left off by continuing to focus on the AIDS crisis, particularly the rapid rise of reported cases in the heterosexual population.

During *ER*'s first season, two gay men with AIDS passed through County General Hospital's emergency room doors. In "Long Day's Journey," Dr. Ross (George Clooney) treats a young, badly beaten street hustler named Terry (Alexis Cruz). He also has AIDS, but refuses treatment for his pneumocystis pneumonia (PCP). Dr. Ross lectures him about safe sex and gives him condoms, which Terry says he has no intention of using because "that's not what they [his customers] pay for."

In the series's first season finale ("Everything Old Is New Again"), Dr. Benton (Eriq LaSalle) treats Thomas (Jeff Seifer), a gay man in the final stages of AIDS. Thomas needs to have surgery to remove a bowel obstruction, but he has made it clear he'd rather die than endure another operation. Knowing his lover Jason (Charley Lang) would have difficulty carrying out his wishes, Thomas gave his power of attorney to his mother, Marjorie (Sylvia Short), who tells Dr. Benton not to operate. Jason respects her decision and understands it's time to let his lover go. "We already said our good-byes," Jason tells Dr. Benton, "but I guess you're never really ready."

Through their interaction with their respective patients, both doctors learn something about themselves. When Dr. Ross is unable to convince his patient to be treated for his pneumonia or even to practice safe sex, he questions how much he is really able to make a difference. Conversely, caring for a patient refusing treatment is a cathartic experience for Dr. Benton. Having recently lost his own mother, and feeling guilty he wasn't with her when she died, the usually unemotional Dr. Benton gets a second chance to say goodbye (at least in the metaphorical sense) by holding a late night vigil at his dying patient's bedside.

No doubt a sign of the times, the fact both AIDS patients are gay is never raised as an issue. However, this wasn't the case in a 1996 episode of *Chicago Hope*. In "Right to Life," Dr. Kronk (Peter Berg), a self-admitted homophobe, is assigned to treat an African-American female impersonator named Ms. Cherchez La Femme (Jazzmun), who collapses while rehearsing her new show. The antibiotics Dr. Kronk prescribed are not helping Cherchez, who's worried because his mother, who doesn't know he has AIDS, is coming to visit. Dr. Kronk is initially indifferent and uncomfortable around his patient, but he begins to understand that, like all the others he's treated, Cherchez deserves to be treated with kindness and respect. To make amends for his attitude, Dr. Kronk borrows a female staff member's make-up case so Cherchez can put on a healthier looking face for his mother's visit.

The episode marks a turning point for Dr. Kronk, who had something of a gender identity crisis himself ("Informed Consent") when he discovered his girlfriend Annie (Mia Sara) is a transsexual. He thought Annie was the sister of his childhood hockey buddy Andy, never suspecting Annie actually *is* (or was) Andy. Dr. Kronk admits he could have handled it if she was married or a criminal, but he finds the thought of having slept with someone who once had a penis to be revolting.

The following season, a desperate Annie turns to Dr. Kronk for help ("Women on the Verge") when her estrogen pills stop working. A cat-scan reveals the estrogen is causing her blood to clot, so she must stop taking the drug, which eventually will make her voice deeper and her facial hair regrow. The episode ends tragically when Annie commits suicide in her hospital room, leaving Dr. Kronk, already feeling guilty about the way he treated her, completely devastated.

The producers of both *Chicago Hope* and *ER* should be credited for not only treating gender and sexual identity issues with intelligence and sensitivity, but for keeping AIDS on the front burner. When both series first hit the airwaves, AIDS was shedding some of its stigma as a "gay disease," thanks in part to public figures like basketball player Earvin "Magic" Johnson, who announced that he was HIV positive in 1991. In 1994, the year *ER* and *Chicago Hope* premiered, the number of cases acquired through heterosexual contact was rising at an alarming rate (130 percent). AIDS was also the leading cause of death for American men between 25 and 44 (number four for women in the same age bracket).

The AIDS cases on both *ER* and *Chicago Hope* reflected this change. On the surface, the "heterosexualizing" of AIDS seemed problematic because gay AIDS patients (with few exceptions) seemed almost to disappear. Yet, these "new" AIDS episodes, involving heterosexual victims, still focused on the same two primary issues: the medical condition itself, and the "human side" of AIDS, particularly the physical and psychological effects of the disease on patients and their loved ones.

Medical series also started to address more specific social issues of AIDS patients. For example, the controversy surrounding the administering of marijuana for medicinal purposes is addressed in an episode of the short-lived series *L.A. Doctors* ("Under the Radar"). Dr. Tim Lonner (Matt Craven) is treating his childhood friend, a gay man dying from AIDS. The patient is having trouble eating and asks Tim if he could get him some marijuana to stimulate his appetite. Tim's a bit square, so he enlists help from his slick partner, Roger (Ken Olin), who sets up a meeting in downtown LA to score some weed. The pair get busted and thrown into jail. Dr. Cattan, who doesn't exactly shy away from the public spotlight, uses this as an opportunity to make a public statement supporting the legalization of marijuana for medicinal purposes.

Chicago Hope frequently addressed the ethical questions raised by experimental treatments. The series's third episode, "Food Chains," involved the battle over a baboon named Marty. Dr. Geiger (Mandy Patinkin) wants to transplant the lab animal's heart into his patient, John Lanier (Earl Billings). Dr. Thurmond (E.G. Marshall) wants to inject Dina Russell (Melinda Culea), a prostitute with AIDS, with Marty's bone marrow to revive her immune system. Both procedures are risky, the odds of them working are low, and the reality is both Lanier and Russell will eventually die. In spite of their experimental nature and protests by animal rights activists, Lanier gets his new heart and Russell a fresh supply of bone marrow. Their ultimate fates are never revealed.

An interrelated story examines how a physician's attitude toward an AIDS patient endangers her life and almost ends his career. When Dina Russell first arrives in the emergency room with severe stab wounds, she tells Dr. Nyland (Thomas Gibson) she has AIDS. He quickly moves on to a patient whose condition is less critical, leaving Dina almost to bleed to death. Dr. Nyland is reprimanded by Dr. Thurmond and he apologizes to Russell. He admits to her that because she's a prostitute with AIDS and maybe even an IV drug user, another patient's life seemed more worth saving. "I'll never owe a patient a bigger apology than I owe you," he tells her. She accepts his apology.

Toward the end of the first season, *Chicago Hope* introduced dedicated medical researcher named Dr. Diane Grad (Jayne Brook), who finds it difficult to keep an emotional distance from her subjects. In "Freeze Outs," she refuses to allow Dr. Hancock's (Vondie Curtis-Hall) patient, Charles Ellis (Obba Babatunde), to participate in her AIDS studies because there is no more room and Ellis is in the late stages of the disease. His death would also compromise the success of her study, which would put future grants in financial jeopardy. The issue poses an interesting dilemma: is the possibility of saving one life worth risking the potential saving of thousands of lives?

The experimental treatment poses another problem for both patient and hospital. Ellis's insurance won't cover the procedure, so chief of staff Dr. Watters (Hector Elizondo) refuses to give them permission, insisting it is too experimental and costly. They go ahead anyway when the hospital's legal counsel, Alan Birch (Peter MacNichol) is willing to look the other way if Ellis signs a liability release.

The long-suffering Ellis survives the treatment, but returns to the hospital a few episodes later ("Full Moon") with appendicitis. Dr. Hancock wants Dr. Bob Meriniak (Cotter Smith) to perform an appendectomy, but he refuses because the operation won't buy Ellis much time and the risk of him contracting AIDS is too great. With Dr. Grad's assistance, Dr. Hancock performs the operation, which prolongs Ellis's life long enough to grant his patient's last wish — to see the sun rise one last time. In a powerful ending, Dr. Hancock sits by Elllis's side as they watch the sun come up, at which instant Ellis takes his last breath.

As Dr. Grad continues her research, she also becomes involved with several HIV-positive patients. The list includes Ivy Moore (*American Beauty*'s Mena Suvari), a 15-year-old girl who refuses to take her medication ("Sympathy for the Devil"); and Mrs. Slater (Leslie Hope), who wants to get pregnant ("The Ties That Bind") even though she runs the risk of passing the infection on to her baby. Dr. Grad also finds out what it's like to be a patient herself when she's bitten by an HIV-positive lab ape named Bam-Bam ("The Ethics of Hope"). Luckily, she escapes exposure, though several seasons later she has another scare when she accidentally slices her finger during a C-section on Mrs. Slater. When Dr. Grad's first HIV test is inconclusive ("Teacher's Pet"), she repeats the test. Forty-eight hours later, she and her husband are relieved to find out that the results are negative.

ER has also featured several non-gay AIDS cases, such as the man who arrives in the emergency room with his fiancée looking for a cure for his hiccups ("Full Moon, Saturday Night"). Dr. Susan Lewis (Sherry Stringfield) treats him with Thorazinc, but his blood test reveals he's HIV positive. He claims he has never engaged in any risky behavior, but his fiancée tells Dr. Lewis she suspects her boyfriend may have been unfaithful to her. She gets tested, but her results are never revealed. The episode preaches a straightforward message about why practicing safe sex is a necessity and how the lack of honesty between two people can have catastrophic consequences.

Pediatric AIDS is the focus of another story ("Make of Two Hearts") involving an HIV-positive Russian baby girl, Tatianna, abandoned by her adopted mother. The mother does return, but only to explain to Nurse Carol Hathaway (Julianna Margulies) that her husband died two years earlier and she is afraid of getting too close to her baby, knowing she will die soon. Hathaway decides to adopt her, but her application is denied when a background check reveals she once attempted suicide.

Over time, the episodes involving AIDS continued to be more complex and, at times, heavy-handed. An episode of *ER* ("Flight of Fancy") involves a teenager named Trent (Blake Heron), who was never told by his grandmother (Joanna Miles) that he contracted AIDS from his late mother, a heroin addict. So Dr. Carter (Noah Wyle) takes it upon himself to inform Trent of his HIV status. Trent brings his girlfriend Emma in to get tested and the two have a fight, causing Trent to run out into the street and get killed by a car. Dr. Carter feels guilty and questions whether he did the right thing, but Dr. Kerry Weaver (Laura Innes) assures him he had no choice. The tragic, over-the-top ending, in which Trent crashes through a windshield, undermines the story's message about how shame and guilt continue to interfere with the treatment of AIDS.

A more realistic and highly disturbing *ER* episode ("Thy Will Be Done") involves a gay man, Jeff (Robert Beitzel), who comes in with a case of mononucleosis and asks Dr. Carter for an HIV test because he had unprotected sex with an infected partner. When Dr. Dave Malucci (Erik Palladino) gives Jeff and his significant other Sean (Noah Blake) the good news (he's negative), they're disappointed. Dr. Malucci asks if Jeff is a "bug chaser," a slang term for someone trying to contract AIDS. Apparently Jeff wants to get infected because Sean is HIV positive and, in Sean's words, "they're together in everything." When a second test comes back negative, Dr. Malucci counsels the patient by explaining that even though people with HIV are living longer, AIDS can still kill you. The February 2001 episode is a powerful response to the recent rise of HIV infection among young gay men, who health officials fear are abandoning safe-sex practices because recent medical advancements have improved the quality of life for people living with HIV.

The most complex and longest ongoing AIDS story line on *ER* involved physician's assistant Jeanie Boulet (Gloria Reuben). She contracts AIDS from her husband Al (Michael Beach), who tests positive for the HIV virus when he comes to the emergency room for the flu ("Take These Broken Wings"). Jeanie is eventually forced to disclose her HIV status to Dr. Weaver when she's unable to remove glass from a patient's chest, fearing she may cut herself and infect the patient ("Don't Ask, Don't Tell"). Jeanie also reveals her HIV status to hospital administration, which has developed strict work guidelines for HIV positive employees. However, she finds it increasingly difficult to adhere to them and is eventually reprimanded by Dr. Weaver for violating policy ("When the Bough Breaks"). Jeanie's job later gets downsized, but when she learns a new RN has been hired for the ER, and Dr. Weaver recently received a salary increase, she threatens the hospital with a lawsuit. Weaver is forced to rehire Jeanie, even though Weaver believes she is only using her HIV status to get her job back.

In subsequent episodes, Dr. Weaver becomes Jeanie's ally and even puts in a good word for her when Jeanie decides to adopt an HIV-positive baby ("Greene With Envy"). When actress Gloria Reuben left the series in 2000 (to sing back-up for Tina Turner!), her character marries Officer Reggie Moore (Cress Williams) and they're given temporary custody of the baby.

CODE PINK: DOCTORS AND PATIENTS IN THE 90S

Although gay men may have been conspicuously absent from these AIDS story lines, the medical shows of the 1990s did pick up where 1970s series left off by featuring gay and lesbian doctors, hospital staff members, and, of course, patients. Some of the same issues, such as homophobia and sexual confusion among teenagers, continued to be addressed. However, beginning in the mid-1980s, medical dramas started to reflect some of the changes in society's attitudes toward homosexuality.

The shift in attitudes is first evident in a 1984 episode of *St. Elsewhere* entitled "Girls Just Wanna Have Fun." When a reputable medical researcher named Dr. Christine Holtz (Caroline McWilliams) visits St. Eligius, Dr. Cavanero (Cynthia Sikes) invites her to stay with her. Dr. Holtz later comes out to Dr. Cavanero, who is extremely uncomfortable around her lesbian houseguest. When she shares Dr. Holtz's secret with members of the hospital staff, the rumor rapidly makes its way around the corridors. People even begin to talk about Dr. Cavanero, who, as one character puts it, "never really had a relationship with a man."

Dr. Holtz hears about the rumor from one of her patients, Mr. Millstein (Harold Gould), who believes lesbians don't really exist ("it's just media hype"), though he does have a nephew who "can't even tell the Celtics from the Bruins." Mr. Millstein claims he doesn't care if the doctor who saved his life is a lesbian, but when Dr. Holtz admits it's true, he doesn't believe her.

That night, she confronts Dr. Cavanero about betraying her confidence. She says she assumed it wasn't a secret, but when she shares her true feelings about Dr. Holtz's sexuality, it's clear she did have an ulterior motive:

> DR. CAVANERO: What you do is perverted. Sex between two women is unnatural...Ever since you told me you were gay, I don't know how to treat you. I was taught women shouldn't have those feelings and if you do, it's wrong. It's just wrong.

Although the writers try to redeem Dr. Cavanero by having her apologize, they thankfully resist trying to make us believe she is suddenly cured of her homophobia:

> DR. CAVANERO: Chris, I stayed up thinking last night. I'm sorry.

> DR. HOLTZ: People don't change overnight. Listen, I don't try to hide

the fact that I'm a lesbian, but it's not the first thing I tell people. Especially colleagues. It's hard enough being accepted in this profession as a woman, let alone as a gay woman. All I wanted was to be friends. And you made that friendship suspect. Automatically assumed I was interested in you romantically.

DR. CAVANERO : I hope we can still be that.[68]

AIDS EPISODES, TV-MOVIES, AND SPECIALS

Andre's Mother (PBS)
March 7, 1990
Written by Terrence McNally
Directed by Deborah Reinisch

A presentation of *American Playhouse*, this first-rate drama from gay playwright McNally explores a gay man (Richard Thomas) and his deceased lover's mother (Sada Thompson), both trying to come to terms with Andre's death. Thomas and Thompson are superb, as is McNally's script, making it one of the best original AIDS dramas produced for television.

"Steve Burdick"
Lifestories (NBC-TV)
December 18, 1990
Written by Richard Gollance
Directed by Aaron Lipstadt

D.W. Moffet, who co-starred in *An Early Frost*, stars as Steve Burdick, a closeted news anchor who breaks down on the air the day his lover dies of AIDS. After revealing to the public he is HIV positive, Steve decides to do a series of first-person news reports on the disease. Loosely based on San Francisco newscaster Paul Wynne, who died of AIDS in 1990, "Steve Burdick" is a touching story that exposes the media's failure to provide adequate and necessary coverage of the disease.

Our Sons (ABC-TV)
May 19, 1991
Written by William Hanley
Suggested by the documentary
Too Little, Too Late
Directed by John Erman

While it would seem like every gay boy's fantasy to have Julie Andrews or Ann-Margret as their mother, this made-for-TV film is a disappointment. Andrews plays a successful businesswoman who never

bonded with her gay son, James (Hugh Grant). His live-in lover, Donald (Zeljko Ivanek), is dying. James asks his mother to convince Donald's mother (Ann-Margret), a gum-chewing barmaid who thinks homosexuality is a sin, to see her son before he dies. This sappy, well-intentioned film tries hard to say something about love, compassion, and acceptance, but despite a stellar cast, it misses the mark.

"Incident on Main"
Life Goes On (ABC-TV)
January 10, 1993
Written by Scott Frost
Directed by R.W. Goodwin

Chad Lowe won a much-deserved Emmy for his portrayal of Jesse McKenna, an HIV positive teenager. During the show's fourth season, Jesse's health begins to decline steadily and both he and his girlfriend Becca (Kellie Martin) are forced to come to terms with his inevitable death. In this episode, Jesse is beaten up outside of a hospice by a group of Neo-Nazis who assume he's gay. When Becca tries to help him, she gets his blood on her hands, though thankfully her HIV test comes up negative. This underrated series broke new ground in its dramatization of a teenager living with AIDS.

Roommates (NBC-TV)
May 30, 1994
Written by Robert W. Lenski
Directed by Alan Metzger

Eric Stoltz and Randy Quaid are a mismatched pair of AIDS patients. Stoltz is an educated, privileged gay man, while Quaid is a straight, homophobic ex-convict who contracted AIDS through a blood transfusion. Despite their differences, they develop a close friendship.

"A Mate For Life"
Beverly Hills 90210 (Fox Network)
September 4, 1995
Written by John Whelpley
Directed by Burt Brinckerhoff

In a storyline similar to *Sisters*, Kelly (Jennie Garth) is sentenced to community service at an AIDS Hospice, where she befriends a gay man, Jimmy (Michael Stoyanov), who has only a few days to live. Not as effective as the *Sisters* storyline, but Stoyanov is terrific.

"A Sudden Change of Heart"
Sisters (NBC-TV)
January 6, 1996

The first episode of a storyline in which Reed (Noelle Parker) is sentenced to community service at an AIDS Hospice, where she befriends a transvestite named Chardonnay (K. Todd Freeman). Reed later asks her Aunt Teddy (Sela Ward), Chardonnay's favorite designer, to design her burial dress. When Reed reluctantly returns to the Hospice after Chardonnay's death, she finds comfort in speaking to her ghost. A well-executed storyline with some terrific moments between Parker and Freeman.

"The Violin Lesson"
Touched By An Angel (CBS-TV)
December 22, 1996
Written by Glenn Berenbeim
Directed by Peter Hunt

Angel Monica (Roma Downey) serves as an apprentice to a violin maker, Jordan (Peter Michael Goetz), whose son, Tony (Lawrence Monoson) returns home for the holidays to tell his family he's gay and has AIDS. Fortunately, Monica and fellow Angel, Tess (Della Reese), are able to reunite father and son before Andrew, the Angel of Death (John Dye) whisks Tony away. The highlight of this moving episode is Tony's encounter with Angel Tess. He thinks God hates him because he's gay and has AIDS. "What you've heard has been someone else's words," Tess explains, "words of hate and confusion. God is not the source of confusion. God's love is perfect."

The episode breaks new ground because, unlike the blatantly homophobic characters on *Medical Center* and *The Bold Ones*, Dr. Cavanero is a series regular. Nor is she painted, like *Medical Center's* Dr. Garson, as a villain. Instead, Dr. Cavanero is someone who has believed a certain way about homosexuality her whole life. Now, through her friendship with Dr. Holtz, those beliefs are being challenged and possibly re-evaluated.

Like most lesbians on television, Dr. Holtz checked into *St. Elsewhere* for only two episodes. It would take five more years before the first lesbian would be introduced on a prime time series as a regular. In 1989, ABC's medical drama *Heartbeat* included a lesbian, nurse-practitioner Marilyn McGrath (Gail Strickland), among its ensemble cast. Divorced and estranged from her daughter, Marilyn works at a women's clinic, Women's Medical Arts, and has been in a relationship for four years with her lover Patti (Gina Hecht), a recurring character on the series.

Marilyn is a breakthrough character because her lesbianism is a non-issue. As Anne Lewis of the gay newspaper, the *Washington Blade*, observed in February of 1989, Marilyn is depicted "as a wholesome, well-adjusted individual who just happens to be Gay."[69] Like other medical dramas, the focus of each episode of *Heartbeat* shifts between the characters' professional and personal lives. In comparison to her female and male colleagues, who all seem to have relationship and/or sexual problems (i.e. impotency, jealousy, divorce), Marilyn is the most stable character on the show.

The two-part finale of the series's initial six-episode run looked at Marilyn's reunion with her daughter Allison (Hallie Todd), who's returned to California to get married ("To Heal a Doctor"). Allison makes it clear she doesn't want her mother to bring Patti to the wedding. "I don't think it would be a good idea for you to bring her," she tells her. "A lot of my friends don't know about you." Patti understands and encourages Marilyn to take care of "the biggest piece of unfinished business" in her life and talk to her daughter.

Their conversation reveals why Allison resents her mother:

ALLISON: It's not that you're a lesbian. That's not what bothers me. It's — why did you marry Dad?

MARILYN: I thought I could make a life with your father. I wasn't in love, but I liked him and I wanted children. And I decided I could keep those different feelings buried deep within in me.

ALLISON: But you left me.

MARILYN: I didn't have a choice. It was the hardest thing I ever did, but believe me it would have been more devastating for you if I had stayed.[70]

Allison is concerned she might also turn out to be a lesbian, but after Marilyn assures her that won't happen, mother and daughter finally reach an understanding.

Patti does attend the wedding, but as Marguerite J. Moritz points out in her insightful critique of the two-part episode, Marilyn and Patti are only shown twice during the wedding ceremony ("The Wedding"). In fact, the mother of the bride has only one line. ("I think I'm going to cry.") After the ceremony, they virtually disappear, which is absurd considering all of Marilyn's colleagues are in attendance. What Moritz finds even more problematic is how the heterosexual characters all resolve their relationship problems during the reception in scenes involving "overt sexual exchanges in which the men exert their virility and dominance over the women in their lives."[71] Patriarchy and heterosexuality are ultimately affirmed:

While the heterosexual couples exhibit an outpouring of desire as the wedding reception plays out, the lesbians are politely kept from view, never intruding on the show's vision of what it is to be a couple or to be in a romantic relationship...The overall effect is to reaffirm the patriarchal order and to tell the world what really counts goes on in the heterosexual world, the arena of passion, desire, and drama.[72]

Moritz raises an important question regarding the non-stereotypical representation of homosexual characters on television. Even when gay characters are portrayed positively, we must examine how they're represented in context. In their analysis of *Heartbeat*, Darlene M. Hantzis and Valerie Lehr find the depiction of the lesbian couple problematic because it is completely nonsexual. While the heterosexual characters are shown making love (one couple even do it in an office), Marilyn and Patti were not even permitted by the network to touch. Hantzis and Lehr conclude that ultimately many so-called "'positive' portrayals serve as mechanisms to perpetuate hetero/sexism even as they appear to display the 'good will' of various producers, directors, and writers toward lesbian and gay issues."[73]

Still, *Heartbeat* did usher in an era in which sexual orientation on medical dramas was becoming less of an issue. Now when a regular, recurring, or guest character comes out, it is in a matter-of-fact fashion. Dramatic speeches about the "sickness of intolerance," which once echoed through *Medical Center*'s boardroom, have been replaced by more casual conversations in front of the water cooler.

In a *Chicago Hope* episode aptly titled "Sexual Perversity in Chicago," a male resident, Dr. Robert Lawrence (Mark Benninghofen), who is interested in specializing in neurosurgery, volunteers to assist Dr. Shutt (Adam Arkin) with a research project. Dr. Shutt is interested in working with him, until Dr. Lawrence, who thinks Dr. Shutt is gay, impulsively straightens his colleague's tie and puts his hand against his cheek. A very surprised Dr. Shutt flips out, but later realizes he may have overreacted.

Six months later, Drs. Shutt and Lawrence finally begin their project ("Liver Let Die"). This time around, they become close friends and even share intimate details about their lives. Dr. Lawrence even encourages the hard-working Dr. Shutt to do something about his lack of a personal life. In one of television's rare honest exchanges between a gay and a straight man, they discuss the respective challenges each faces in maintaining a relationship. By working so closely with Dr. Lawrence, Dr. Shutt's homophobia slowly begins to dissipate.

Another gay member of the *Chicago Hope* staff, the passionate and outspoken Dr. Hancock, is continually at odds with HMOs, the other doctors, and the hospital administration, all of whom he fights to ensure minority patients receive the care they deserve. The politically minded doctor runs the hospital's clinic and at one point even considers pursuing a career in politics. In comparison to the other characters on the show, little is known about Dr. Hancock's personal life, though he often finds himself in the middle of a crisis. (a bomb goes off in his clinic, he's shot by his brother-in-law, etc.)

No doubt some of these character traits were factors when producers made the decision to have Dr. Hancock, who'd been a regular for nearly two and a half seasons, come out to Dr. Shutt in the fourth season ("The Lung and the Restless"). His disclosure during his conversation with Dr. Shutt is integral from a thematic standpoint to the respective personal conflicts both characters are experiencing in the episode. Dr. Shutt is having an identity crisis because a brain aneurysm has left it impossible for him to perform surgery. Forced to slow down,

Viewers discovered *Chicago Hope*'s Dr. Dennis Hancock (Vondie Curtis-Hall) was gay when he came out to a colleague in November 1997.

he begins to realize he has sacrificed his personal life to pursue his career. Dr. Hancock is disillusioned when he discovers his political mentor, Bill Burke (Lawrence Pressman), wants to keep his black ancestry a secret to protect his political career when his daughter tests positive for the sickle cell gene. In the final scene of the episode, they are watching surgery in the observation deck when Dr. Shutt poses a question: "You know who you are outside of being a doctor?"

"I'm a guy who does charity," Dr. Hancock replies, "restores antique cars, jogs ten miles a day, collects first editions, I'm gay."

Dr. Hancock's disclosure makes Dr. Shutt realize he hasn't been paying enough attention to the world around him. "Wow. I really have not been at the party, have I?"

"No, but you're here now. Welcome to it," Dr. Hancock replies.

Like Dr. Hancock, *ER*'s Dr. Maggie Doyle (Jorjan Fox) was not one of the series's original characters (she was introduced as a new resident during the third season). Opinionated, competitive, sometimes to the point of being abrasive, she admits she has trouble dealing with authority. When she catches Dr. Carter's eye, she shares her love of firearms by taking him to a shooting range ("Who's Appy Now?"). During shooting practice, Dr. Doyle points out her "girlfriend" in the next stall, an ex-cop who is extremely jealous. Dr. Carter is mostly taken aback by the news she is gay and accidentally shoots out one of the lights. GLAAD media director Chastity Bono was more eloquent than Dr. Carter in her response to Dr. Doyle's revelation, which she hoped would develop into a "strong plotline."[74] Unfortunately, Bono didn't get her wish. Dr. Doyle's sexuality was never fully explored and like many gay and lesbian characters, she inexplicably disappeared from the series during the fifth season.

ER has featured a few other gay characters. The first was paramedic/EMT Raul Melendez (Carlos Gomez), the partner of Nurse Hathaway's boyfriend, Ray "Shep" Shepherd (Ron Eldard). Raul's sexuality is first revealed when desk clerk Randi Fronczak (Kristin Minter) comments to Hathaway and Shep that Raul is cute ("Dead of Winter"). Hathaway politely tells her she's not his type. Shep's response is far less subtle: "Ever dress up like a lumberjack? Longshoreman? Greco-Roman wrestler?" Shep's kidding aside, it was refreshing to see a straight man and a gay man have a professional and personal relationship with the sexuality of the latter never being an issue.

Shep's devotion to his partner is evident when Raul tragically dies after being burned over 90 percent of his body ("The Healers"). Shep blames himself for what happened because, instead of waiting for the fire department to arrive, he led Raul into the burning building to rescue three children. In an emotionally charged scene, a guilt-ridden Shep stays at his dying friend's bedside and repeatedly tells him he's sorry. Raul's death leaves Shep with emotional scars that lead to his nervous breakdown, which puts an end to his relationship with Nurse Hathaway.

Another gay *ER* character is nurse Yosh Takada (Gede Watanabe), who for a time was the only gay Asian male on television. He's a minor character, but like the other members of the *ER* nursing staff, he's ever-present. He's also subject to the occasional homophobic comment. In "Split Second," a patient refers to him as a Chinese fag. ("Japanese," says Yosh matter-of-factly). An obnoxious E.M.T. refers to him as the "Cookie Fairy," as he munches on the cookies Yosh baked for the doctors ("Hazed and Confused"). The E.M.T. later explains to Dr. Greene he doesn't mind if the guy is a "bone smoker. I was just joking with him like I would with anybody."

In the Fall of 2000, *ER* introduced a strong storyline that lead to the coming out of Dr. Kerry Weaver. Like Dr. Hancock, Dr. Weaver's personal life had always been something of an enigma. Although her abrasive, efficient, and at times patronizing manner continues to alienate people, her character has been softened since she debuted at the start of the second season. Weaver is finally given a personal life when she enters a lesbian relationship with psychiatrist Dr. Kim Legaspi (Elizabeth Mitchell). In "Rescue Me," they go to dinner, which Dr. Legaspi mistakes as a "date." Dr. Weaver tells her she is not gay, but it's clear she is attracted to her. At the very least, it's an honest portrayal of a woman who, by all accounts, is exploring the possibility of entering a physical relationship with another woman. She does eventually become involved with Dr. Legaspi, but they get off to a rocky start. Dr. Weaver is not totally comfortable being involved with a woman, and certainly not with going public about it. When Dr. Legaspi is falsely accused of sexual misconduct with a young, suicidal patient who caused a rail accident ("Witch Hunt"), Dr. Weaver, fearing their personal relationship will be revealed, doesn't come to her defense. Dr. Legaspi has no choice but to break it off with Dr. Weaver.

In the wake of society's (and television's) changing attitudes, homosexuality was no longer being "treated" via the guise of a medical condition, like alcoholism, ulcers, or heart problems. Living in a more enlightened TV age, not only are doctors more prepared to "treat" their gay patients, but the patients themselves are more self-aware than their late-1970s counterparts in recognizing the "symptoms" (i.e. sexual attraction to other men). The patients are typically teenagers, who are worried that other people, particularly their families, will find out they're gay.

In "It's Not Easy Being Greene," *ER*'s Dr. Ross checks out a teenage jock named Ray (Jonah Rooney), who comes in complaining of headaches. Dr. Ross can't find anything physically wrong with him. Finally, Ray breaks down and admits he is gay. Instead of talking to the confused teenager himself, Dr. Ross lets someone from the psych unit handle it. When Nurse Adams (Yvette Freeman) asks him why he didn't talk to the boy himself, Dr. Ross claims it's outside his expertise; he also resents the implication he's homophobic. The psychiatrist never arrives and when his father shows up, Ray pretends his headaches are from doing his math homework. Realizing he should have spoken to Ray himself, Dr. Ross tells the teen he'll be around if he ever needs to talk.

In terms of Dr. Ross's character, the point of the story is a little unclear. At first it seems Dr. Ross may indeed be a little uncomfortable dealing with the subject because he gets very defensive when he is questioned by Nurse Adams. On the other hand, there was never any indication in prior shows that he is homophobic. His professionalism is certainly not in question. Dr. Ross is constantly putting his job on the line by refusing to follow procedures if it is in the patient's best interests. Perhaps the situation means to demonstrate how some doctors are unable to handle certain cases.

An even more complicated case awaits psychiatry intern Dr. Shutt when a 19-year-old Hasidic Jew, Jacob (Michael Goorjian) is admitted to Chicago Hope for obsessive-compulsive disorder ("Austin Space"). According to Dr. Shutt's supervisor, Dr. Webber (Christine Tucci), Jacob's compulsive behavior (he paces back and forth and tells bad Jewish jokes nonstop) can be found in young people from strict religious backgrounds. At first, Dr. Shutt assumes Jacob doesn't want to follow in the footsteps of his rabbi father (Arthur Rosenberg). On the contrary, Jacob wants nothing more than to be a rabbi, but he is afraid if he tells his father he's gay, he'll be rejected. When Jacob finally comes out, his father slaps him and begins lecturing Dr. Shutt about the Bible's position on homosexuality. Dr. Shutt advises the rabbi not to allow religion to come between him and his son. The rabbi eventually comes around and agrees to seek family counseling. The episode's religious angle on an otherwise familiar storyline is noteworthy because religion isn't the villain. Once again, it simply becomes a matter of an individual

In between saving lives, *ER* Chief Dr. Kerry Weaver (Laura Innes) came out of the closet during the show's seventh season.

trying to accept something which strongly defies his traditional beliefs.

Some kids have an even worse time of it. While riding with paramedics, *ER*'s Dr. Greene (Anthony Edwards) saves a badly beaten male prostitute ("Stuck on You"). 16-year-old Kevin Delaney (Chad E. Donella) suffers from blood clots due to a protein "s" deficiency in his blood, but he refuses to take his blood thinner because if he were to get hurt on the streets, he could bleed to death. The teenager is extremely flirtatious with Greene, suggesting he join him in the shower and making remarks like "You're cute when you're angry." "Is that the only way you can relate to me," Dr. Greene asks, "by turning me into a john?" Dr. Greene takes a genuine interest in the teen's welfare, so when he discovers there's a warrant out for his arrest, he gives him $50, his pager number, a list of shelters, and puts him in a cab.

In "The Domino Heart," Dr. Greene once again takes a personal interest in a gay patient. Michael Mueller (Justin Louis) arrives in the ER after a car accident caused by a seizure while driving. Michael's lover Curt (Hank Stratton), who was in the passenger seat, has only a minor cut on his forehead. Greene determines that Michael's seizure was caused by an overdose of theophylline, which he takes to control his asthma. Dr. Greene suspects the overdose was intentional. Soon,

Michael admits Curt has been beating him up over things like forgetting to pick up the dry cleaning. Each time Curt promises to never to do it again. Dr. Greene's attempt to intervene fails and the two men leave the hospital.

Towards the end of the episode, they return. But this time it's Curt who got hurt while loading bags into the back of the car and Michael "accidentally" put it in reverse. Dr. Greene manages to clear Michael's name with the police. "I guess you got what you wanted," Michael tells Dr. Greene. "I'll be safe at home tonight." Michael still refuses to talk to a social worker, but thanks Dr. Greene for his support.

CHILDREN AND GENDER IDENTITY CONFUSION

Another medical issue that has gained national media attention in the past five years is intersexuality, a condition involving the "congenital anomaly of the reproductive and sexual system."[75] An intersexed individual is born with sex chromosomes, external genitalia, or an internal reproductive system that is not considered "standard" for either a male or a female. An estimated one out of every 1,500 infants born is intersexed, though the number is higher "if we include all children with what some physicians consider cosmetically 'unacceptable' genitalia."[76]

Serious ethical and medical questions have been raised regarding the so-called "treatment" of intersexed individuals. Cheryl Chase, executive director of the Intersex Society of North America (ISNA), estimates nearly one of every 2,000 infants is subjected to cosmetic genital surgery. In the majority of cases, the procedure is "unnecessary. Outcomes are poor in functional, cosmetic, and emotional terms. Surgeries are often repeated, sometimes over a dozen times."[77]

The main goal of the procedure, which is typically followed by hormonal treatments, is to assign a newborn with either a male or a female identity. Yet, the question remains: is the surgery in the child's best interest or, as the ISNA claims, merely "a policy of pretending that our intersexuality has been medically eliminated?"[78]

> This "conspiracy of silence" about intersexuals exacerbates the predicament of the intersexual adolescent or young adult who knows that s/he is different, whose genitals have often been mutilated by "reconstructive" surgery, whose sexual functioning has been severely impaired, and whose treatment history has made clear that acknowledgment or discussion of our intersexuality violates a cultural and a family taboo.[79]

In 1997, intersexuality received unprecedented media coverage in newspapers and magazines around the country.[80] Network news magazine shows devoted segments to the subject, such as *Dateline NBC*'s "Gender Limbo" (1997), which features an interview with Chase, and ABC's *Prime Time Live*'s "Boy or Girl?"

(1997). The media's interest in the topic was in part generated by the formation of the ISNA, which has raised society's awareness of intersexual people by gaining the support of individuals in and outside the medical community, including activist groups like Transsexual Menace, GLAAD, and the National Gay and Lesbian Task Force.[81]

Prime time medical dramas like *Chicago Hope* and *ER* also responded with storylines about intersexual individuals. One of the earliest is a 1996 episode of *Chicago Hope* ("The Parent Rap") in which a baby with ambiguous genitalia is born to a couple, Bob and Gail Broussard (Paul McCrane, Cynthia Lynch). Complications during delivery force the surgeon to perform a hysterectomy to save Gail's life. Consequently, she will not be able to have other children. This upsets Bob, who wanted a son to carry on the family name.

So the Broussards consider their options. Constructive surgery can be performed, but only to give the infant female genitalia because the procedure to make the baby a male is too risky. Another possibility is to simply wait until the child develops rather than pre-determining its gender. The distraught couple also consider a third option — giving the baby up for adoption. In the end, they elect to go ahead with the surgery and make their child a female.

The episode effectively dramatizes the dilemma parents of intersexed infants face, though for dramatic purposes the writers throw some complications into the plot (the mother cannot have more children; surgery to make the infant a male cannot be performed) in order to limit their options. Still, the ISNA would not agree with the Broussards' decision because they believe "no surgery should be performed unless it is absolutely necessary for the physical health and comfort of the intersexual child. We believe any surgery…should be deferred until the intersexual child is able to understand the risks and benefits of the proposed surgery and is able to provide appropriately informed consent."[82]

The remaining episodes do not focus on newborns, but older children; typically the child who is unaware he or she is intersexual. On *ER* ("Masquerade"), Dr. Benton performs exploratory surgery on an 11-year-old girl and discovers she has "testicular feminization," meaning she is genetically a male but developed external female sex organs, yet has no ovaries or uterus. The parents are referred to a genetics counselor and the fate of the child's gender is unknown.

Chicago Hope went one step further than the *ER* story line with an episode that explores intersexuality from the patient's point-of-view. In "Boys Will Be Girls," Dr. McNeil (Mark Harmon) discovers his female patient, Deborah (Mae Elvis), was actually born a boy. Deborah's mother (Christine Estabrook) reveals to Dr. McNeil that a doctor botched her son's circumcision. The hospital convinced the couple that the best course of action was to raise their son as a girl. Now Deborah, who never received female hormones when he reached puberty, is a confused teenager who wants to be a boy and doesn't know why.

When Deborah learns the truth, he is happy, especially when Dr. McNeil and Dr. Hanlon (Lauren Holly) tell him there's a procedure that can be performed to reconstruct his penis. But his parents object, so Chicago Hope is forced to take them to court.

On the stand, Deborah explains she could "never be the daughter that her parents always wanted." The judge rules in his favor, but Deborah hesitates about going ahead with the procedure for fear his parents will reject him. The parents eventually consent and Deborah's dream finally comes true.

GLAAD praised "Boys Will Be Girls" for its "uncommonly sophisticated and nuanced look at gender identity and sexual orientation." Although the organization felt that the episode "overstates the ease with which Deborah's male physiology is restored," they considered it a "ground breaking" look at gender reassignment.[83]

The episode also exemplifies how much progress has been made since the days Dr. Welby and Dr. Gannon were doing hospital rounds, in both the medical field and the medical drama, and in regard to cases involving gender identity and sexual orientation.

CHAPTER TWO

"JUST THE FACTS, MA'AM"
HOMOSEXUALITY AND THE
"LAW AND ORDER DRAMA"

The medical dramas of the 1970s delivered a series of mixed messages. On the one hand, homosexuality was no longer being treated as an illness or a disease. Gay, lesbian, and transgender doctors were depicted as healthy, stable, and productive members of society. However, some of their patients were still very confused about their sexual identity. Fortunately (or unfortunately), doctors were able to reaffirm their patients' heterosexuality, through the miracle of modern medicine, by simply dispensing a few basic "facts" (i.e. homosexuality isn't hereditary, one homosexual experience does not a gay make, and so on).

Consequently, series like *The Bold Ones* and *Medical Center* served a dual function. They advocated tolerance by telling their presumably hetero audience "gay is O.K." (and homophobia isn't). Yet, in response to the increased visibility of homosexuals in American society, they also aimed to educate viewers, particularly parents, who presumably needed to be reassured their child's heterosexuality wasn't at risk.

Like the 1970s medical shows, detective, police and courtroom dramas (or, more simply, "law and order dramas") also conveyed contradictory messages about homosexuality. Beginning in the late 1960s, series such as *N.Y.P.D.*, *The Bold Ones*, *Dan August*, *Police Story*, and *Police Woman* simultaneously reinforced and challenged negative stereotypes by featuring gay characters on both sides of the law. On the one hand, homosexuals were portrayed sympathetically as victims of blackmail, violence, and murder. Yet, gay men, lesbians, and drag queens were also depicted as deranged, knife-wielding, gun-toting psychopaths whose sexuality was considered as "deviant" as their criminal behavior.

This, of course, was nothing new. As Vito Russo demonstrates in *The Celluloid Closet*, there is a long tradition of gay and lesbian villains in Hollywood cinema.[1] According to Russo, the preponderance of gay killers in films and on television in the post-Stonewall period was part of the cultural backlash against the increased public visibility of homosexuals.[2] And although media watch groups, like the Gay Activists Alliance and the Gay Media Task Force, continued to actively challenge the three major networks in the early 1970s, they would by no means put an end to negative gay stereotypes.

Even in the so-called enlightened 1980s and 1990s, crimes continued to be committed by (and against) homosexuals. The one major difference was that the gay killers had the same motives (greed, ambition, jealousy, etc.) as their heterosexual counterparts. Yet, with such a limited number of gay characters on television, it is undoubtedly difficult even today for some viewers not to think of a homosexual who murders people as a *gay* killer, rather than as a killer who happens to be gay.

Beginning in the mid-1970s, gay men and lesbians were also appearing on law and order dramas as detectives and police officers. The majority of the long-running police and detective series of the 1970s and 1980s (*The Streets of San Francisco, Starsky and Hutch, Hill Street Blues,* etc.) featured one or more episodes about a gay cop or detective who comes out of the closet. In most instances, an off-duty police officer or detective (usually male) witnesses a crime inside or outside a gay bar. As soon as the officer files his report, the rumors begin to circulate around the precinct, thereby thematically linking the hatred and anti-gay violence on the streets to the officer's personal struggle against homophobia. These storylines focused primarily on male cops and detectives. However, the sexual orientation of several female TV police officers was called into question in the 1970s when they were falsely accused of molesting a female prisoner.

Far more progressive than police and detective series have been the courtroom dramas, which are generally critical of the justice system for its failure to protect the civil rights of gay, lesbian, and transgender Americans. Popular series, such as *L.A. Law, Law and Order,* and *The Practice* drew from actual court cases to examine a wide range of issues, including discrimination against gay people in areas such as employment, adoption, child custody, marriage, and health care. As with police and detective series, gay characters are on both sides of the law as defendants, defense attorneys, plaintiffs, prosecutors, and judges.

"EVERYBODY RUN! MISS BRANT'S GOT A GUN!"

The gay killer would become a 1970s stock character on law and order dramas, but a few choice gay (and gay-coded) psychopaths were on the prowl as early as 1961. One of the first (and most bizarre) is a lesbian sniper who shoots young women in an episode of *The Asphalt Jungle,* a short-lived police drama based on the popular 1950 film.

In the opening scene of "The Sniper," a young woman is shot while sitting in a parked car with her boyfriend in Lover's Lane. The mysterious sniper has already claimed three victims, who, according to Deputy Police Commissioner Matthew Gower (Jack Warden), are all young, pretty, and with their boyfriends at the time of the shooting. The only suspect is Lonnie Peterson (Leo Penn), a 34-year-old man who is found roaming around one of the crime scenes. Lonnie admits to killing the women when the police question him, but he is sketchy about the details. His employer, Miss Brant (Virginia Christine), who owns and operates a local teenager hangout, the Paradise Diner, rushes to his defense. She claims Lonnie, who is mentally slow, is incapable of murdering anyone. The one thing that is clear is that Lonnie is enamored of Miss Brant, who, unlike his hateful mother (Ellen Corby), treats him with kindness and understanding.

The police are forced to release Lonnie due to the lack of evidence. Soon afterwards, the sniper strikes again. First, a bullet fired through the diner window grazes Miss Brant's shoulder. Then another girl is shot while necking on the steps of her apartment building. The police once again suspect Lonnie, but his rifle is too old and rusty to have been fired. Lonnie finally admits he was trying to protect the real killer — Miss Brant. The police track the lady sniper down at the local drive-in just as she is about to shoot one of her waitresses, Susie (Natalie Trundy), who is on a date with her boyfriend. When Miss Brant is finally caught, she explains her motives for murdering all "those girls:"

> MISS BRANT: Those girls! Carrying on like that! They had to be punished! I told them! They shouldn't kiss, hug like that with the boys! They wouldn't listen to me! Wouldn't listen! Those girls! Those stupid girls!...I never meant to do any of this! It just came over me and I couldn't hold it back![3]

Miss Brant confesses that she murdered her female victims because they made themselves sexually available to men. Overcome by a twisted sense of morality, she believed it was her duty to punish them for exhibiting overt sexual behavior. The "L-word" is never uttered, but you don't need a degree in psychology to understand Miss Brant is a repressed lesbian compelled to kill pretty young women because they arouse her repressed sexual desires. The fact she shoots her victims during or after they engage in a little prime time foreplay is all the more telling.

Miss Brant's affinity for young women is also obvious when she interacts with Susie. She dotes on the young waitress, and in one scene even fixes her blouse and suggests she wear her pink one next time because she looks prettier in it. ("All the customers think so," Miss Brant assures her.) When the sniper strikes again and Susie admits she's afraid to stay alone, Miss Brant insists she move in with her. She also does not hide her disapproval when Susie goes out on a date. Although Miss Brant assumes the role of the good mother with Lonnie, she is more authoritative with Susie, to the point of being controlling.

Another early example of a gay-coded psychopath is a transvestite who terrorizes nurses in "An Unlocked Window," a chilling 1965 episode of *Alfred Hitchcock Presents*. On a dark and stormy night, two private nurses, Stella (Dana Wynter) and Betty Ames (T.C. Jones), are caring for a sickly man in a remote old house. The women are on edge because a killer who is targeting nurses is reportedly on the loose in the area. When the killer phones and tells Betty he's been watching them, Stella becomes hysterical. Suddenly, Stella hears a man laughing in the front hallways, so she goes downstairs to investigate. She is shocked to discover the laughter is coming from Betty, who is actually a man in a nurse's uniform. As he strangles Stella to death, the killer compliments her on being "such a pretty nurse."

Betty is played by professional female impersonator T.C. Jones (and by Bruce Davison in the 1985 remake for the series revival). Jones played a similar dual role in a memorable 1967 episode of *The Wild Wild West*. In "Night of the Running Death," Jim (Robert Conrad) and Artemus (Ross Martin) are on the trail of a murderer named Enzo who, like Nurse Betty, strangles his victims to death. In hope of tracking Enzo down, Jim and Artemus join a wagon caravan carrying Enzo's girlfriend, Miss Tyler. What they don't know is that Miss Tyler is actually Enzo — in drag!

There is a clear link in both "The Sniper" and "An Unlocked Window" between sexual perversion and murder. While Miss Brant reveals her motives, twisted as they are, for killing young women, Betty the killer nurse is just your run-of-the-mill transvestite/psychopath. The reason why he kills nurses is never revealed, though one can speculate he suffers from some sort of gender identity disorder. Or maybe he just likes how he looks in white.

SHAKEDOWN AND BREAKDOWN

The first law and order drama to directly address homosexuality is the 1967 premiere episode of the police series *N.Y.P.D.* "Shakedown" opens with Det. Jeff Ward (Robert Hooks) and Det. Johnny Corso (Frank Converse) arriving on the scene of an apparent homicide. An out-of-towner named Huntington Weems has been found dead in the bathroom of his hotel room. Their subsequent investigation uncovers a homosexual blackmail ring operating within the hotel. Apparently, a man working for the blackmailers picks up gay men in the hotel bar, brings them up to a hotel room, and robs them. The blackmailers threaten to use the information in the victim's wallet to tell his family and employer he is gay unless he pays them off. With the cooperation of one of their victims, a closeted construction worker named Gaffer (James Broderick), the detectives manage to break the ring.

When Ward, the African-American detective, first meets Gaffer, he encourages him to help them catch the blackmailers, even if it means coming out of the closet. Gaffer is hesitant because he knows if he comes out, his troubles will be far from over:

WARD: Mr. Gaffer, nobody's troubles are over.

GAFFER: Very easy for you to say.

WARD: Why, because I can't hide what I am anyway?

GAFFER: I'm sorry. I didn't mean that.[4]

The link between the oppression of homosexuals and African-Americans in this brief exchange is acknowledged once again in the final scene.

After convincing Gaffer to cooperate, Ward seems less sympathetic toward the victim's situation than the other two detectives. Corso thinks Gaffer is a "gutsy guy" for volunteering to help the police catch his blackmailers. Ward questions whether it is really so "gutsy" because if they are caught, he'll no longer have to pay them off. Corso tells Ward to take it easy because the man has "a real problem." "The world is full of problems," Ward retorts.

Once the blackmailers are apprehended during a sting operation, Gaffer knows he'll have to come out publicly when he testifies. "You go tell people you're different," Gaffer tells Ward, "they don't like it."

"That's the way it is, Mr. Gaffer," Ward says with a quick smile. Gaffer flashes a slight smile back.

This subtle, yet somewhat ambiguous exchange acknowledges that Ward and Gaffer do in fact have something in common. Rather than dismissing Gaffer's problem, Ward is instead expressing, albeit subtly, that he does understand. Yet, Ward also seems to resent Gaffer's attitude because by the very color of his skin, Ward doesn't have the choice of keeping what makes him different a secret.

The conversation between Ward and Gaffer did catch the attention of several television critics. *Variety* observed that the fact "Hooks [Ward] is a Negro allows for some obvious but well-directed social comment, as when he counterpoints the homo on the matter of being 'different' in society."[5] George Gent of *The New York Times* was more critical of the exchange, noting that the "use of a Negro officer to persuade a homosexual that life is easier if one concedes being different from others was a very embarrassing grafting of different sociological concerns."[6]

The episode also features a character who acts as a "representative" of the gay community, an openly gay businessman and activist named Charles Spad (John Harkins). Det. Lt. Haines (Jack Warden) asks Spad if he knew Weems, who the police discovered was not murdered, but committed suicide because he was afraid his blackmailers would expose his homosexuality. For one brief moment, this "straight-acting," intellectual homosexual displays a little gay attitude when he makes it clear that "just because I'm homosexual...doesn't mean I know every other one in the country."

But when Haines explains he needs some information, Spad succinctly characterizes the kind he's looking for:

SPAD: [Information] about an area of human activity feared and abominated by our pluralistic, moralistic, straighter-than-thou — forgive the expression — body politic. So dedicated to hypocrisy that they do their own secret things and call it having a little fun and what someone else does they call perversion.[7]

Besides serving as the gay "expert" who leads the detectives to Gaffer, Spad's function in the story is to point out society's hypocrisy in condemning homosexuality, while at the same time engaging in sexual practices outside the so-called "norm" of heterosexual monogamy. Although Spad is certainly sympathetic toward Gaffer and Weems, the gay activist's view of the world is more cynical than optimistic. In reference to Weems's suicide, he laments, "I think if he's homosexual, it's not hard to think of reasons why he might commit suicide."

In addition to the gay blackmail story, the episode breaks new ground in its depiction of the two male homosexual characters, Gaffer and Spad, who are anything but stereotypical — something American viewers were not used to seeing in 1967. *Variety* even praised the casting of Broderick (the late father of actor Matthew Broderick) as one of the "virile third-sexers," but was quick to note the actor "shaded the rugged construction worker with just enough of that fey quality to make the point."[8]

The following season (1968-1969), *Judd, for the Defense* tackled the subject of homosexuality in "Weep the Hunter Home." The episode contains no negative gay stereotypes, largely because it has no homosexual characters. Almost 30 years after it first aired, "Weep" was rebroadcast on Nick at Nite's TVLand on September 21, 1997, as part of the Museum of Television and Radio Showcase.

The plot concerns a wealthy college student, Larry Corning (a young Richard Dreyfuss), who, along with his best friend, Don Daniels (Peter Jason), play a practical joke for "kicks" on Larry's conservative father, Lawrence Corning, Sr. (Harold Gould).

Pretending to be kidnappers, young Larry and Don call Corning to tell him they have his son. Don then shows up at Corning's house with a phony ransom note demanding $15,000 he claims was given to him by the kidnappers. Corning tells his lawyer and friend, Clinton Judd (Carl Betz), he's suspicious because Don is involved. He doesn't hide his disdain for his son's friend, who he refers to as a "queer" and an "aberration." "You can see for yourself," he tells Judd, "what he is...those tight pants, the way he walks, the way he talks. Don't you read in the papers and the magazines what's going on with young people?"

When Corning finds evidence in his son's room proving Larry wrote the ransom note himself, he decides to take matters into his own hands. With a gun in his pocket, Corning hunts down Don and Larry. During a scuffle, Corning is shot. He claims Don shot him, but at the trial, Larry, who was standing behind his father with a gun, admits to shooting him to prevent him from killing Don.

Somewhere within this muddled story there is supposedly a message about homophobia. Corning hates Don because he's a homosexual who he fears is trying to convert his son. If one or both of the young men were actually gay, the episode would have certainly made a statement, particularly back in 1968. But instead, the homosexual issue is displaced onto a generational conflict. As Larry explains to Judd, his father thinks he's gay because "You people [meaning the older generation] don't groove the way we do." Don is more specific and explains that when the older generation becomes suspicious of two men who like to spend time together, "they get called *fags*."

In the end, Corning is forced to make a decision. Should he let the boys go to jail or tell the judge that Larry and Don were just playing a joke and never intended to keep the money? We never find out, though in the final scene Judd makes his position clear to Corning, whom he blames for falling victim to the media hype surrounding the teenager's lack of morality:

> JUDD: You read that every sixth male in the United States is a homosexual, just as you read that most college girls rely upon the pill, and that practically all young people smoke pot and take LSD. And all this legalized libel stuck in your mind. I call it libel because you can also read about studies showing that the morals and mores of college students today are not that much different from their parents. I read one like that, but I accidentally found it on the back page. If you believe just what you read on the front pages, you'll have to think that all young people today are going to hell in a handbasket. And you might be tempted into the idiocy of trying to stop them with a gun.[9]

In the end, "Weep the Hunter Home" delivers a mixed message. Corning's temporary mental breakdown, which almost drives him to commit murder, is caused by his irrational hatred of homosexuals. But instead of chastising him for being homophobic, Judd criticizes him for assuming the worst about Larry, Don, and their generation. The episode ultimately reinforces the notion that homosexuality is a vice topping the list of contemporary social evils. In the end, the real issue here — homophobia — is never sufficiently addressed.

ATTACK OF THE KILLER GAYS!

In the 1970s, law and order dramas reached an unprecedented popularity with American audiences. On almost any night of the week, channel surfers could tune in to a police or detective series. Consequently, the gay killer became a stock character. Some, like Miss Brant, were suffering from severe sexual confusion or internalized homophobia. Others were self-admitted homosexuals who killed anyone — homosexual or heterosexual — who stood in their way. Even when a killer had a specific motive for committing murder (wealth, power, love, etc.), there was still the implication that their criminal behavior was linked to his or her deviant sexuality.

Surprisingly, one of the earliest was another episode of *N.Y.P.D.* entitled "Everybody Loved Him." On the opening night of his new film, Arnold Eliot, a successful producer, is murdered in the bathroom of his high rise apartment. To prevent word about Arnold's homosexuality from getting around town, his sister Freida (Leora Dana) hires a sleazy detective, Jerry Jameson (Jack Somack), to protect her brother's good name. Jameson first slips a fin to the doorman, who tells Jerry that Arnold used to bring young men ("tough guys with tattoos") up to his apartment. He then bribes the elevator man, Nick (Walter McGinn), who helps Jameson sneak into Arnold's apartment so he can swipe some incriminating photographs from his wall safe. When he finds Nick's photograph among them,

Jameson accuses him of being one of "Arnold's boys."

Meanwhile, Lt. Haines is interviewing their prime suspect, Arnold's "right-hand man," an effeminate actor named Wade Hansen (Ted van Griethuysen). The police discover Hansen is bitter because Arnold led him to believe he was going to make him a star, but the only role he ever played was that of Arnold's flunky. They had a fight the night Arnold was murdered, but Hansen claims he left the apartment and, when he returned, Arnold was dead.

Wade is only a red herring. The killer turns out to be Nick, the building's psychotic elevator man. During his confession, Nick describes how since his childhood, homosexuals have been bothering him. That night, Arnold invited him up to his apartment. "He smiled," explains Nick, "and then I wiped that smile off his face." Ward and Corso sit in silence, which causes the paranoid Nick to freak out. "What are you guys looking at? I killed that guy, and you still think..." He then suddenly screams, "*What do I have to do, anyway?*"

Like Miss Brant, Nick is a closet case suffering from acute internalized homophobia, which has —naturally — turned him into a psychotic killer. While Miss Brant targets the young women she desires, the paranoid Nick is disturbed not only by homosexuals (like Arnold) who objectify him, but heterosexuals like Jameson, Ward, and Corso, who he assumes are *thinking* he is a homosexual.

As in "Shakedown," the episode encourages blackmail victims to seek help from the police. When Jameson reveals he has worked for Freida in the past to lean on blackmailers threatening to expose her homosexual brother, Det. Lt. Haines chastises him for not going to the police for assistance. "All you had do is call us. You know we would never release information on his private affairs..." Haines explains. "You would have had a happy client with no risk at all."

The following season (1969-1970), the first in a long line of homosexual killers left his mark in an episode of *The Bold Ones: The Lawyers* ("Shriek of Silence"). Gubernatorial candidate Stephen Patterson (Craig Stevens) is framed for the murder of one of his campaign workers, Ellen Sherman. When he finds her dead in his apartment, he panics, stashes her body in his car, and parks it outside her apartment building. Instead of calling the police, Patterson seeks advice from his lawyer, Walt Nichols (Burl Ives). Meanwhile, a witness named Paul Mitchell (Richard Van Vleet) comes forward and testifies he saw Patterson moving the victim's body. During the trial, Nichols confronts Mitchell with a discrepancy between his testimony and the physical evidence. According to a police report, the victim's blood was found in the trunk, not the front seat. Mitchell finally admits he is testifying on behalf of a "friend" and simply repeating what he told him he saw.

The "friend" turns out to be the killer, Barry Goram (Morgan Sterne), Patterson's old college chum and a former member of his campaign committee. When Patterson discovered Goram was a homosexual, he forced him to resign to avoid a scandal. Goram was not pleased, so he sought revenge by framing Patterson for murder.

Donning a pair of color-tinted eyeglasses, Goram is one of those cool, calculated homosexual killers. Like the murdering duo in Hitchcock's *Rope*, he has an air of superiority about him when being interrogated. He is so brazen he even attends Patterson's trial. Goram's motive is clearly revenge. Yet, before getting her throat slashed, Ellen implies Goram is really in love with the heterosexual Patterson and is bitter because the feeling isn't mutual. Goram never responds to her accusation and, consequently, he remains a one-dimensional character.

Discrimination against a gay employee by the federal government is at the center of a 1971 episode of *Dan August*. In "Dead Witness to a Killing," Det. August (Burt Reynolds) investigates the murder of the wife of Frank Devlin (Monte Markham), an assistant district attorney with a less than exemplary reputation. Ambitious, opinionated, and hot-tempered, Devlin is a prime suspect because he and his late wife were having marital problems. Devlin also beats up a witness, a cab driver named Norman Sayles (Martin Sheen), who claims to have seen him running from the scene. The case gets even more complicated when Sayles is hospitalized for chest pains and then assassinated by a sniper through his hospital room window. Unfortunately, poor Devlin can't clear his name because his alibi dies before admitting he was with him the night of his wife's murder. Yet, August still believes there's a missing piece to the puzzle. He finds it, of all places, in a gay bar.

Reynolds turns a few heads when he strolls into Logan's Place (he also gets an "oink," a familiar anti-cop jeer in 1971) and demands some straight answers from Logan, the cooperative gay proprietor, who quips "I'll be as straight as I can." August discovers Sayles was the lover of Devlin's brother-in-law, Arthur Coleman (Laurence Luckinbill). As Coleman later explains in his confession, his late sister Joyce disapproved of his lifestyle. When he was appointed as a special consultant to the President's cabinet, she refused to lie for him when the government conducted his background check. So to insure he didn't lose his high-level government job, he not only killed his own sister, but his lover/accomplice, Sayles, who he was afraid was going to crack under pressure:

> FRANK: She was my sister. I loved her...she knew about me. She knew I was homosexual. She wished I could be what she called normal. But she could live with the fact as long as it didn't affect her life. I was discreet. I never embarrassed her. But when I got that job in Washington, I knew I was going to be investigated. And I went to Joyce and I begged her not to say anything about me. And she said she couldn't lie for me. Well, I worked for fifteen years for that job. It was the culmination of my life...I did love her. But I couldn't let her expose me. You see, I deserved that job! I earned that job! And I was the best man for it! The best man![10]

At the end of his confession, Coleman breaks down and starts weeping. Like Barry Goram, Coleman will stop at nothing to get what he wants. He considers himself a victim of society's homophobic attitudes, so he'll go as far as to murder his own *sister* and *lover* to get a job as a consultant — to the Nixon administration!

In the early/mid-1970s, the representation of gay men as ruthless killers gained the attention of gay activists, who were at times asked to serve as consultants on scripts. According to *The Advocate*, three members of the Gay Media Task Force — clinical psychologist Newt Dieter, Pat Rocco, and a woman identified only as "Country" — were consultants on a 1974 episode of *Police Story* entitled "The Ripper." The team were reportedly "active consultants on script revisions and authenticity of performances by actors and actresses playing gay characters, with the full cooperation of NBC and the production company, Screen Gems."[11]

"The Ripper" follows two Los Angeles detectives, Matt Hallett (Darren McGavin) and his younger partner, Doug Baker (*The Mod Squad*'s Michael Cole), on the trail of a serial killer who is murdering gay men in Los Angeles. Baker is an opinionated homophobe who freely uses words like "fag" and thinks lesbianism is a "waste." He would even prefer to handle cases involving only heterosexual victims, but as Hallett explains, it should make no difference because all murders come down to "the murdered and those who murder." While they're enroute to inform Mrs. Bannister (Pat Carroll), the mother of the ripper's latest victim, of her son's untimely passing, Hallett contemplates how difficult it must be for a mother to lose her son. Baker suggests it must be especially difficult "when the only one you have is a dead *fag*."

Hallet is quick to correct him. "A dead *son*," he says.

When they meet the loud and overbearing Mrs. Bannister, Baker decides she must have been the cause of her son's homosexuality. "Home like that, no wonder the kid ended up a fag," he says. "She wouldn't mother a child, she'd smother a child."

Baker also assumes the ripper is "one of them" (meaning gay), but Hallett suggests the killer may be a homophobe, which he defines as "somebody who's convinced himself that he hates homosexuals and that hate allows him to carve them up afterwards. Of course, on the other hand, he could be a latent homosexual."

Hallett's first guess was correct. The killer turns out to be Abbott (Peter Mark Richman), the homophobic owner of a fashion modeling agency (talk about picking the wrong profession!) who enticed his victims with the chance of a modeling career. Abbott has no difficulty rationalizing the killing of homosexuals and others on the margins of so-called "normal" society:

> ABBOTT: You're arresting me, but you leave the streets full of those people whose continued existence offends purity of nature. Narcotic addicts, homosexuals, prostitutes...I see the sick vanity, the cheap desire for easy money. When I suggested to him [his victim] that he might be able to live without even the need for modeling, his eyes lit up. I know decadence when I see it, sergeant.[12]

With a little prodding from Hallet, Abbott adds he'd also include on his hit list "the lame and the blind," who would all be eliminated as "painlessly as possible of course."

Even though members of the Gay Task Force served as consultants, the gay press's reaction to the episode was less than favorable. *The Advocate*'s Harold Fairbanks characterized the plot as "clichéd," the characters as "cardboard," and the episode as catering to "the lowest mentality of the viewer." Fairbanks admitted he was the wrong choice to review the episode because he was not an avid fan of network programming. He believed public, rather than commercial television, to be the more suitable forum for "positive gay thought" because of its greater innovation and willingness to treat controversial subject matters accurately. "Authentically gay drivel," Fairbanks concluded, "is just as unstimulating as homophobic drivel."[13]

Wayne Jefferson of the *Gay People's Union Newsletter* identified some positive aspects of the episode. He liked how the gay characters "look refreshingly like non-gays, which is good not because we see 'respectable' images or put down flaming types, but simply because that's the way it is realistically."[14] The same goes for the gay bar scenes, though he notes that only lesbians are shown same-sex dancing.

Jefferson also uncovers the episode's major contradiction within the subplot involving Hallet and his fiancée Sheila (Kathie Browne), who are contemplating having children. In describing why he is hesitant about bringing a child into a troubled world, the supposedly gay-friendly Hallet puts gay people on his list of undesirables that also includes addicts, pushers, hookers and thieves — a list similar to the one recited later by Abbott in his confession. On a more positive note, Jefferson acknowledges the significance of having Baker emerge from the case more enlightened, if not sympathetic, to homosexuals, though it is never made clear in the end why "some persons have queer-fear and others not have it?"[15]

Meanwhile, up north, *The Streets of San Francisco* are being terrorized by a killer in a 1974 episode aptly titled "Mask of Death." John Davidson guest stars as a successful female impersonator named Ken Scott, who is best known for his imitations of Carol Channing and a fictitious actress named Carole Marlowe. When a tired and overworked Scott allows Marlowe to take over his personality, "she" begins stabbing men to death with a large hat pin.

Inspector Keller (Michael Douglas) applies some basic textbook psychology to figure out how Scott chooses his victims, who are all out-of-town salesmen. According to her biography, the legendary Miss Marlowe blamed all of her problems on her absent father, a traveling salesman. A psychiatrist who treated Scott confirms the possibility that his former patient is suffering from "psychic dualism," which allows him to imagine he feels exactly what the person he is imitating would feel. In fact, Scott may not even be aware of what his alter ego is doing. Luckily, Keller and his partner, Inspector Mike Stone (Karl Malden), manage to move in on Marlowe before he/she claims another victim. The predictable plot aside, the episode is memorable if only to see Davidson doing a pretty decent Carol Channing impression (with a singing voice supplied by professional female impersonator, Jim Bailey).

Two years later, Bailey took the spotlight as a female impersonator receiving death threats on an episode of *Vega$* ("The Man Who Was Twice"). Bailey plays Las Vegas headliner Jeremy Welles, who hires private investigator Dan Tanna (Robert Urich) to find a stalker, a man with a gravelly voice who identifies himself only as Martin. Jeremy receives a copy of his own 8 x 10 glossy head shot with "DIE" written across it and a doll-like replica of his head, which tumbles out of his refrigerator. Later, he is attacked in his dressing room. Then, while singing "The Man That Got Away" onstage dressed as Judy Garland, the lights go out and he is nearly stabbed to death. Even Dan starts receiving death threats from the mysterious Martin, warning him to drop the case.

So who is Martin? Welles's tough-as-nails manager (Darleen Carr)? His ex-manager (Dick Dinman) who may be holding a grudge? His devoted make-up man Kirk (Bill Fletcher)? None of the above. The answer is Welles himself, who, like Ken Scott, is suffering from a split personality. He created an alter ego, Martin, to cope with the sudden death of his sister, with whom he'd had a love-hate relationship. In the climactic scene, Dan stops Jeremy from taking a plunge off a catwalk. Holding him in his arms, Dan offers the entertainer some comforting words: "Jeremy, don't give up. What will happen to Judy or all those wonderful performers if you give up?" Apparently the show must and does go on. In the next scene, Jeremy is back on stage belting 'em out. Jerry's manager assures Dan he'll be getting psychiatric treatment. Good idea. And some time off from performing might help too.

Interestingly, Jeremy's alter-ego, unlike *Streets*'s Ken Scott, is a man rather than a woman. Perhaps this was writer Judy Burns's strategy, to separate Jeremy's "problem" from his being a female impersonator, as if to suggest his pathology has absolutely nothing to do with performing six shows a week dressed as a woman. Still, neither Scott nor Jeremy's sexual orientation really factors heavily into the story. Scott seems to be straight, but the nature of his relationship with female friend Lori (Marianne McAndrew) is ambiguous. As for Jeremy, we never see any aspect of his personal life beyond his professional relationships.

Killer drag queens barely raised an eyelash compared to the fury surrounding the depiction of homosexual child molesters. Since the controversial 1974 airing of the *Marcus Welby, M.D.* episode, "The Outrage," the National Gay Task Force kept close watch on TV series dealing with the subject of child molestation. In October of 1976, the Gay Task Force issued a "media alert" for an episode of *Kojak* ("A Need to Know") in which a foreign agent, Carl Dettro (*Chicago Hope*'s Hector Elizondo), is accused of molesting two young boys. Dettro is captured by the police, but they are forced to let him go because he has diplomatic immunity.

According to the gay newspaper, *The Blade*, the Task Force issued the alert because they were concerned the character "would be interpreted by a large segment of the public to be about homosexuality, thus perpetuating the common misconception that gays are child molesters."[16] The article continues by stating there were no references to the word "homosexual," yet "a detective called the molester a 'fruitcake' and a psychologist said he had problems dealing with women."[17] Washington D.C.'s CBS affiliate, WTOP-TV (now WUSA-TV 9), was the only station to insert a disclaimer at the beginning of the episode to "clarify that the program deals only with the subject of child molesting, not homosexuality."[18]

Prior to its broadcast, members of the Task Force viewed the episode and recommended some edits. A copy of the shooting script was sent to the NGTF's Production Consultant, who said he'd have approved the script with a few minor changes. According to Richard L. Kirschner, Vice President of Program Practices at CBS, the broadcast wasn't edited or delayed because there were "sufficient comments about molesting 'children' (meaning both male and female) rather than just boys." A member of the National Gay Task Force also agreed with CBS that the "fruitcake" remark "was a reference to a lunatic rather than a gay."[19]

Three years later, *Baretta* tackled the subject of child molestation within the context of teenage prostitution. In "The Sky Is Falling," Det. Tony Baretta (Robert Blake) befriends 14-year-old street hustler Tommy (Barry Miller), who witnesses the brutal murder of his friend, Jeff (John Herbsleb), by a john named Harding (James Ray). Baretta discovers both boys ended up on the streets because they were physically and mentally abused. Tommy was raped in reform school and Jeff kicked out of his home by his mother (Jadeen Barbor), a religious fanatic who claims "an evil force got hold of her boy." Although it is never actually stated, the "evil force" she is referring to is obviously homosexuality. When she claims the "hand of God" killed her boy, Baretta doesn't mix words when he tells her *she* is responsible for his death.

Harding and the men who frequent the arcade where the hustlers hang out are characterized by Baretta as pedophiles and "chicken hawks" (a slang term for a man who seeks out boys as sexual partners). Their "partners" in this case are not unsuspecting children, but teenage boys who solicit men for sex. Fortunately, there is no direct connection made between these men and adult male homosexuals. The well-intentioned episode is rightfully more concerned with exposing teen prostitution as a social problem by dramatizing the sad and often tragic lives of homeless teenage boys forced to sell their bodies to survive.

Not all gay killers on television in the 1970s were drag queens or chicken hawks. And not all series were sending a serious social message. On an episode of *Harry-O* ("Coinage of the Realm"), a pair of hit men, Joe Heston (David Dukes) and Fred Lassiter (Granville van Dusen), are hired by the "big boss" to kill a man holding incriminating evidence. The fact Heston and Lassiter are lovers has absolutely nothing to do with the plot. While no one can accuse the producers of stereotyping, depicting professional killers as homosexuals is probably not what gay activists had in mind in their fight for equality.

Lesbians also did their share of killing in the 1970s. In November of 1974, NBC aired "Flowers of Evil," an episode of *Police Woman* that became one of the decade's most controversial TV hours. Premiering a few weeks after *Marcus Welby, M.D.*'s "The Outrage," the episode concerns three lesbians — the super butch Mame (Faye Spain), the bitchy Gladys (Lorraine Stephens), and her femme lover Janet (Lynn Loring) — who own and operate The Golden Years Retirement Home. The police suspect the trio of murdering their elderly female residents and stealing their pension checks. To expose their operation, Sgt. Suzanne "Pepper" Anderson (Angie Dickinson) gets out her white hat and shoes and goes undercover as a nurse.

Before it even hit the airwaves, the episode generated protests from the National Gay and Lesbian Task Force. Consequently, NBC postponed the episode's original scheduled telecast (on October 22, 1974) so it could be re-edited. According to an NBC spokesman, the program dealt with lesbianism in a "somewhat sensationalized and insensitive manner."[20] Producer Douglas Benton described the changes as "mostly cosmetic cutting," which according to the *Los Angeles Times* included explicit references to lesbians, shots of hands touching, a lesbian's "lascivious glance" at Pepper while she's undressing, and Gladys giving Janet a kiss on the forehead.[21] The editing only seemed to create more controversy because it tried (and failed) to conceal the sexual orientation of the murderers. Although it is never directly stated that "they are lesbians" (Pepper's line stating just that was excised), the characters are such gross stereotypes it'd be difficult to think otherwise.

Mame, the surly, flannel-outfitted ex-Marine, described by Lt. Bill Crowley (Earl Holliman) as looking like "she should be driving a diesel truck," is the most problematic. In his review of the episode, John O'Connor of *The New York Times* describes her as "a hostile 'My Favorite Martian' with mussed hair.[22] Faye Spain, the actress who plays Mame, even admitted in an interview that "the Lesbians in this show have no redeeming virtues. I'm surprised the gay libs haven't protested."[23]

After 40 minutes of lesbian-bashing, "Flowers of Evil" shifts gears with a scene involving Pepper, who tries to reach out to the younger lesbian, Janet. While Pepper claims not to condemn Janet for being what she is, she also implies lesbian love is unhealthy and leads to nothing but unhappiness.

> PEPPER: She [Gladys] must be very special to you. How long has it been? Ten, twelve years. You have nothing to hide from me. I knew it the minute I saw you two together. I don't condemn you. Not at all. I've known what a love like yours can do to a person. I've lived with it. I don't think I've ever told anybody else. In college I had a roommate who meant a great deal to me. But I meant even more to her. I watched what a love like yours can do to a person. I watched her suffering. And I couldn't help her. I guess what I'm trying to tell you is don't protect Gladys. Don't destroy yourself.[24]

Pepper seems to be saying she doesn't condemn Janet for being a lesbian. But in the next breath, she states she knows "*what a love like yours can do to a person.*" By a "love like yours," what exactly does she mean? Lesbian love? Or an obsessive

Police Woman Sergeant Suzanne "Pepper" Anderson (Angie Dickinson, left) goes undercover as a nurse to catch killer lesbian Gladys (Lorraine Stephens, right) in the controversial "Flowers of Evil."

kind of love which makes you lose all sense of yourself and be an accomplice to murder? The analogy between Janet's love for Gladys and Pepper's lesbian roommate's unrequited love for her is confusing. The implication, whether intentional or not, is that there is a correlation between obsessive love and lesbian love. Janet does finally come to her senses and fingers Gladys for the murders, yet in the next breath she pleads, "Just don't hurt her please! She's all I ever had!"

NBC had originally planned to air the edited version on November 15, but decided at the last minute to move the airdate up to November 8. Activists disliked what they saw. Members of the Lesbian Feminist Liberation staged a sit-in inside an NBC executive's office, while protestors rallied outside of the building. Gay activists eventually met with NBC executives, who agreed not to rerun the episode.[25]

What is puzzling is why producer David Gerber didn't have the foresight to consult Newton Dieter and other gay media activists as he did previously on "The Ripper." According to the *Los Angeles Times*, Gerber believed there was no need to get expert advice because the lesbian overtones were minor. Also, since the premise was based on an actual case, he didn't think there was a need for consultants to question the facts.[26]

"Flowers of Evil" remains one of the most blatant examples of negative stereotyping on television. By today's standards, the episode is so outrageously offensive it borders on camp. One scene in particular, in which Gladys interviews Pepper for a nursing job, oozes with sexual innuendoes:

> GLADYS: I have been looking over your application. There seems to be one small matter. You've never worked in a retirement home before.

PEPPER: Should that be such a drawback, Miss Conway? I don't think there is a thing you couldn't teach me.

GLADYS: Perhaps. But why should I choose you above a qualified practical nurse?

PEPPER: Because I learn quickly and I'm willing.

GLADYS: Yes, I think you are.[27]

"Flowers of Evil" did not put an end to lesbian killers on television. *The Streets of San Francisco* ("Once a Con...") featured a lesbian college student named Jackie Collins (yes, Jackie Collins!) who murders her lover's best friend. Jackie (Devon Ericson) confesses to killing Mary because she was jealous. "I didn't mean to," she explains to her lover Tina (Joanne Nail), "It was an accident. I only meant to scar her because she was so beautiful." Tina is horrified, yet still embraces Jackie and assures her that she and Mary were only friends. Too bad they didn't have this conversation sooner.

As law and order dramas moved out of the 1970s and into the Reagan era, greed would become the number one motive for crimes committed by and against gay men and lesbians. Two episodes of *Hunter* — "The Fifth Victim" and "From San Francisco With Love" — feature characters who kill strictly for the cash.

"The Fifth Victim" begins with a manhunt for a serial killer of eleven gay male victims. When the psycho is nabbed, he admits to killing all of the men except one — victim number five, an architect named Sanger. Det. Sgt. Hunter (Fred Dryer) and Det. Sgt. Dee Dee McCall (Stepfanie Kramer) are able to track down the second killer when they discover the detective in charge of the case, Sal Drasso (Bill Smith), revealed confidential details about the serial murders to his friends. An associate of Sanger's, Sedgwick (William Joyce), used the information to commit a copycat killing. He murdered Sanger because he knew Sedgwick was skimming money off the top of a construction project. The episode also includes the by now familiar subplot involving a closeted gay detective, Frank Buchanan (Rick Giolito), who is forced to come out while helping Hunter. Fortunately, he receives support from the gay-friendly Hunter and their boss, Captain Devane (Charles Hallahan).

In "From San Francisco With Love," Hunter assists an attractive San Francisco detective, Valerie Foster (Laura Johnson), in her investigation of the murder of a millionaire and the subsequent murder of his son. After sleeping with Valerie, Hunter becomes suspicious — she seems too preoccupied with the case and suspects she faked her orgasm during sex (the possibility that Hunter may have been the cause is never considered).

Once again, Hunter's instincts are right on the money. He and McCall discover that Valerie plotted both murders with her lesbian lover, Casey (Philece Sampler), the millionaire's young wife. Now that her husband and stepson are dead, Casey stands to inherit $80 million. Hunter and McCall foster friction between the lesbian couple, which culminates with a little face slapping before Casey turns Valerie over to the police. Once again, lesbianism is reduced to something cheap and tawdry — the dirty little secret which needs to be uncovered in order to catch the killer.

Deception, greed, and murder are also in ample supply in an episode of *The Rockford Files*. In "The Empty Frame," a wealthy gay man, John (Richard Seff) and his lover Jeffrey (Paul Carr), hire Jim Rockford (James Garner) to retrieve their entire art collection, which has been stolen from their seaside mansion by an armed group of ex-Berkeley radicals (!?!). When Jeffrey is murdered shortly after the heist, Rockford discovers he was actually the thieves' inside man. Despite his lover's betrayal, John still pays for his funeral.

"I don't know why he did what he did," he explains to Rockford. "I probably will never understand that. But for fifteen years, he was my devoted friend. I can't forget that. And I won't."

Rockford understands his reasons and respects his decision. The 1978 show is noteworthy because the couple's gayness is never an issue. More remarkably, none of the usual homophobic jokes, quips, or comments are tossed off by the other characters at their expense.

Heterosexuals have also been known to commit a murder or two in their quest for financial security. On *Kate Loves a Mystery* ("Feelings Can Be Murder"), newspaper reporter Kate Callahan (Kate Mulgrew) investigates the murder of a bisexual married woman, Claire (Shannon Wilcox), who belonged to a sexual consciousness raising encounter group. The list of suspects includes the psychologist with fake credentials, the group's self-proclaimed ladies man, and the victim's closeted (and married) lesbian lover. In the end, Kate discovers the killer is the deceased's own husband, Peter (Rudy Solari), who admits to bumping off his bride because she was planning to divorce him and run off with half his business.

A similar motive is behind the murder of a wealthy gay couple on an episode of the delightfully cheesy *Silk Stalkings*. In "Compulsion," Det. Sgt. Tom (Chris Potter) and Det. Sgt. Cassy (Janet Gunn) suspect the deceased's business partner, Rikki Rivers (Erika Anderson). But the murderer turns out to be Rikki's ex-husband, Chance (*The Blue Lagoon*'s Chris Atkins), who, before killing the couple, cuts a deal with them that would bequeath to him their portion of the business.

Another *Silk Stalkings* mystery ("Pumped Up") involves a bisexual vixen named Roxy (Kimberly Patton) murdered in her own health club after a session of hot, steamy lesbian sex (no doubt for the benefit of the series's male heterosexual viewers). Once again, there are the usual suspects: Roxy's fiancée Harmon Lange (Patrick Wayne), who recently caught her with another woman; her ex-business partner, Nino Cunetto (Anthony Addabbo); and her sexual playmate, a mystery woman named Angel who Roxy picked up in a sex club. The whodunit reaches a rather anti-climactic climax when we discover Angel is actually

Harmon's daughter, Taylor (Belinda Waymouth). Apparently Taylor was afraid she would lose her portion of her father's business to Roxy, so she pretended to be a lesbian to seduce and kill her. ("It was more fun than I thought," Taylor admits.)

The Practice featured a gay psychopath named Joey Heric (John Larroquette) who, on two separate episodes, kills his ex-lover and his current lover in exactly the same fashion (a knife through the chest). The smug, narcissistic Heric knows he is the smartest person in the room, so he has no trouble getting his lawyer, Bobby Donnell (Dylan McDermott), to help him get away with murder. (Isn't that a lawyer's job anyway?).

In "Betrayal," Heric accuses his current lover, Marty Adleman (Stephen Caffrey) of murdering his ex-boyfriend. Heric is given immunity in exchange for his testimony, but when he takes the stand, he shocks everyone by confessing to the crime. His immunity thus prevents him from being prosecuted.

The following spring, Heric murders Marty ("Another Day") and is once again not guilty. He initially claims it was self-defense, but when assistant district attorney Helen Gamble (Lara Flynn Boyle) manages to unnerve him on the stand, he testifies that Marty committed suicide. A psychiatrist expert witness for the defense claims Heric took credit for the crime because he suffers from an acute narcissistic disorder which drives him to come out on top in any situation (including the trial, as Helen so rightfully points out). The jury buys the psychiatrist's testimony and Heric gets off, even though Helen, Bobby, and the viewer *know* he is guilty.

Like the gay-coded killers who graced the silver screen in Hitchcock's *Rope* (1949) and *Strangers On a Train* (1951), Heric revels in his intellectual superiority. He demonstrates no remorse for committing murder and is proud he can manipulate the legal system. But unlike Robert Walker in *Strangers* or Farley Granger in *Rope*, he is able to get away with committing not one, but two murders. Although characters such as Heric don't exactly give homosexuals a good name, when played so deliciously by character actors like Larroquette, who won an Emmy for his performance, they're undeniably entertaining.

Far more disturbing than Heric is a pair of killers in an episode of the short-lived American version of the British crime series, *Cracker*. In "Best Boys," a homeless teenager named Bill (Jared Rushton), on probation for car theft, befriends his boss, Mitchell Brady (Peter Firth). When Brady's landlady thinks something is fishy about her tenant's relationship with Bill, she threatens to call the police. Afraid of getting the police involved, Bill, with Brady's help, kills her. But there's more trouble for the duo when Bill begins to terrorize his former foster parents and then kills his social worker when he threatens to turn him into the authorities.

Fitz (Robert Pastorelli), a psychiatrist who works as a consultant for the L.A. Police Department, discovers both Bill and Brady have abandonment issues. Brady's a suicidal ex-Marine who lost his "friend" while serving in the Middle East. Bill was emotionally scarred by his foster family's decision not to adopt him when the couple got pregnant after years of trying. With Fitz's help, Brady gets

Bill to surrender by telling him he loves him. But what kind of love is it exactly? Their relationship is ambiguous because there is a homoerotic subtext (at one point they almost kiss, but are interrupted), yet there is also a definite father-son dynamic. Brady is clearly gay. Bill seems willing to do anything to be loved.

OUR GIRLS IN BLUE

In 1972, *Owen Marshall, Counselor at Law,* opened its second season with a provocative segment about a champion college diver accused of molesting a young girl. In "Words of Summer," athlete Ann Glover (Meredith Baxter) seeks help from Owen Marshall (Arthur Hill) when she is stripped of her amateur diving status. Ann discovers Louise Carpenter (Barbara Rush) told the International Diving Committee she accepted cash for giving her daughter Ardis (Denise Nickerson) diving lessons the previous summer. The money, which was forced onto her by Ardis's father, Julian (Craig Stevens), becomes a secondary issue when Louise's real motive for writing the letter is revealed: Ardis claims Ann sexually molested her. As evidence, Louise shows Marshall photographs of Ann being affectionate with Ardis and a letter Ann wrote to her daughter containing a suggestive quote from Lord Byron: "Come lay thy head upon my breast and I will kiss thee into rest."

Proving Ann's innocence becomes more challenging for Marshall when her former roommate for two years, Meg (Kristina Holland), is forced by the prosecution to take the witness stand and admit she is a lesbian. Meg is a soft-spoken young woman who writes for a lesbian publication under a pseudonym because she is not out to her family. The prosecutor (played by *Gilligan's Island*'s Professor, Russell Johnson) points out the publication is entitled *The 12th Letter,* as in the letter L, for Lesbos. But Meg isn't ashamed of being a lesbian. "I am what I am..." she testifies, "I guess I always have been."

During her testimony, Meg states under oath that her relationship with Ann has always been platonic. She also offers a sympathetic account of how Ann stuck by her and insisted she not move out when rumors began to circulate the two were lovers. The sensationalistic nature of the case aside, the scene is important for two reasons. First, viewers are introduced, perhaps for the first time on television, to a stable, self-identified, politically minded lesbian secure in her sexual identity. Second, and equally rare for early 1970s television, is the characterization of a heterosexual as a supportive ally of her gay friend.

"Words of Summer" was clearly going for something bold and daring, but as *Variety* points out, the theme of false accusations around lesbianism was handled more effectively in Lillian Hellman's play (and film), *The Children's Hour.* (Of course, one major difference is one of the women commits suicide at the end of Hellman's play.) *Variety* was also not terribly impressed by Meg's testimony, which they unfairly dismissed as "the expected speech about how hard it is to be out of step with community sexual mores."[28] The review concludes that the term "the new daring," which was being tossed around at the time in reference to the mature themes currently being addressed on television, is "a proclamation that looks increasingly more exploitative than informative or sensitive."[29]

What *Variety's* cynical critic failed to recognize is that the episode's real problem lies not in Meg's testimony, but in the implication, at least from the prosecution's perspective, that there is a correlation between lesbianism and child molestation. By implying Ann is a lesbian, even if only by association with Meg, the prosecution is suggesting Ann is more likely to be guilty. Even Meg is aware of this when she testifies they were never more than close friends, then adds, "either way, it doesn't do much for Ann, does it?" Fortunately, Ardis finally admits she lied because she felt abandoned when Ann returned to school and resented her younger sibling for getting all her mother's attention.

Lesbianism and molestation are once again equated in several episodes involving female police officers who are falsely accused of molesting female prisoners. Law enforcement is a male-dominated field, particularly on 1970s television, so most episodes dealing with homophobia on the police force concern gay male police officers. The few exceptions involve female police officers forced to prove they're not lesbians, and, therefore, innocent of molestation. Whether the episode, in total or in part, is promoting or critiquing the feminist movement and its support of women working in traditionally male occupations is not always clear.

In the mid-1970s, two series, *Bronk* and *Police Woman*, featured episodes about female police officers accused of molesting female prisoners. In *Bronk* ("The Deadlier Sex"), a 1975-76 series created by Carroll O'Connor, the first police woman assigned to Lt. Alex "Bronk" Bronkov's (Jack Palance) department of Ocean City, California, is accused of attacking a female prisoner, Eleanor (Jaime Lyn Bauer). According to a story that appeared in *The Advocate*, "the policewoman [Sara, played by Julie Sommars] is horrified at the accusation, but eventually her heterosexual reputation and good name are restored."[30] To protest the airing of the episode, in which, according to National Gay and Lesbian Task Force media director Ginny Vida, "negative implications about lesbianism abound," a list of the show's advertisers was published.[31]

A year after the "Flowers of Evil" debacle, *Police Woman* featured yet another lesbian-themed episode. This time around, the producers were smart enough to consult the Gay Media Task Force on the script. In "Trial By Prejudice," Pepper is falsely accused of molesting Nina Daniels (Carol Lynley), a warehouse-robbery suspect. While sitting alone with Pepper in a squad car, a screaming Nina jumps on Pepper and pretends to resist her sexual advances. The robbery charges are dropped due to lack of evidence, but internal affairs is forced to investigate Nina's accusations against Pepper.

One name that comes up during the investigation is Marlena Simpson (Pat Crowley), an ex-police officer who was Pepper's police academy roommate. (Marlena is the "college roommate" Pepper referred to in her speech to Janet at the end of "Flowers of Evil.") When her superiors begin to question Pepper about her relationship with Marlena, she refuses to answer and turns in her gun and badge. Meanwhile, two more female prisoners arrested by Pepper come forward to accuse her of propositioning them.

In an attempt to clear Pepper's name, Lt. Crowley speaks to Marlena, who reveals Pepper is trying to protect her. When she and Pepper roomed together at the academy, Marlena came out to her. Pepper thought it would be best for both of them if she moved out. (While never stated, the implication is Marlena had feelings for Pepper.) Marlena was later forced to resign from the police force when they discovered she was living with a woman. Now a successful business-woman, Marlena knows if she comes to Pepper's defense, she could jeopardize her professional reputation.

The case gets even more complicated when Pepper follows Nina to her accomplices' hideout. There is a struggle, during which she accidentally shoots and kills Nina. On the day of Pepper's hearing, Crowley and his fellow officers prove the two female prisoners are lying about Pepper's advances. They also find one of Nina's accomplices, who vouches for Pepper's innocence. Just as Marlena is about to testify, Pepper hands her resignation in to the board. When Crowley produces his witness, Pepper gets her job back and Marlena doesn't have to testify. Marlena thanks Pepper for her willingness to sacrifice her career to protect her. "You know something Pepper," Marlena says, "you are one special friend."

Speculation surrounding a female cop's sexual orientation was acceptable as long as it was limited to the *other* characters on the series. This theory was put to the test when CBS decided to recast the role of Chris Cagney on the feminist-oriented crime drama, *Cagney and Lacey*. The two female detectives were first introduced in a highly rated 1981 made-for-television movie starring Loretta Swit and Tyne Daly. Swit was still appearing on *M*A*S*H*, so the network cast Meg Foster.

According to a *TV Guide* article, Foster was then replaced because, in the words of one unnamed CBS programmer, the characters on the show are "too tough, too hard and not feminine."[32] (Daly would remain in the role of Mary Beth Lacey "because she was less threatening.") As the CBS executive explained further, CBS wanted to make them less aggressive because they feared the duo would be seen as feminists and dykes:

> They were too harshly women's lib. The American public doesn't respond to the bra burners, the fighters, the women who insist on calling manhole covers people-hole covers. These women on *Cagney and Lacey* seem more intent on fighting the system than doing police work. We perceived them as dykes.[33]

Even Richard Rosenblum, one of the series's producers, admitted the women could be perceived as gay because they were working in a male-dominated profession. He believed the stigma is "unfair and unfortunate and had absolutely nothing to do with show..." especially because "two guys, Starsky and Hutch, or

Redford or Newman, aren't considered fags or homos."[34]

In response to the *Cagney and Lacey* controversy, Lucia Valeska, Executive Director of the National Gay and Lesbian Task Force, stated that if *TV Guide's* story is accurate, CBS is "once again guilty of perpetrating an unseemly and damaging view of both women."[35] Valeska also points out that the firing of Foster violates CBS's own internal hiring practices which prohibit discrimination on the basis of sexual orientation. More specifically, she found CBS's actions objectionable on several grounds, including:

a) the implication that if the characters *were* Gay, that would be unacceptable to CBS's programs and practices;
b) the derogatory use of the words "dyke," "fags," and "homos," and;
c) the implication that Lesbians are not feminine and that feminine women could not be Gay.[36]

Apparently, the Gay Media Task Force were also displeased with Foster's replacement, actress Sharon Gless. Quoting a line from *All About Eve*, the Task Force snidely described her as "from the 'Copacabana School of acting,' very kittenish and feminine."[37] They must have been surprised when Gless, who'd later go on to star in Showtime's gay miniseries, *Queer as Folk*, received two consecutive Emmys (1985-1986, 1986-1987) for her performance as Chris Cagney.

In all, *Cagney and Lacey* was no doubt a casualty of the wave of conservatism ushered in by Reagan's landslide victory in 1980. With the defeat of the Equal Rights Amendment by Congress in the Spring of 1982, the Reagan administration was also responsible for the renewal of time-honored, God-honest, old-fashioned, traditional American values, like patriarchy, sexism, and homophobia. Yet, even though CBS canceled the series after the 1982-1983 season due to low ratings, the record number of letters CBS received, coupled by Tyne Daly's Emmy (her first of four) in September 1983, convinced the network to give it a second chance. The series returned in March of 1984 and managed to retain some of the pilot's feminist edge, as well as tackle many controversial issues during its healthy seven-season run.

The late 1980s exhibited definite signs of progress when *Hill Street Blues* featured an episode reminiscent of *Bronk* and *Police Woman*. In "Look Homeward Ninja," a female officer, Kate McBride (Lindsay Crouse), is falsely accused of sexual harassment by a prostitute, Jackie (Ren Woods). Jackie is lying to protect her pimp, Maurice (Larry Fishburne), who is accused of shaking down her johns. McBride's partner, Sgt. Lucy Bates (Betty Thomas), defends her partner's heterosexuality to Captain Furillo (Daniel J. Travanti). But when McBride admits she is a lesbian and did, as Jackie charges, sit alone with the suspect in the squad car, Bates doesn't know what to think. McBride still maintains her innocence, claiming she was only questioning her witness.

As in *Police Woman*, McBride and Bates produce a witness to the shakedown

"Too tough, too hard, and not feminine:" After only a few episodes of *Cagney and Lacey*, CBS replaced Meg Foster (above, with Tyne Daly) in the role of Chris Cagney with the more feminine Sharon Gless (right photo, left).

operation. This allows them to bargain with Maurice, who admits he told Jackie to lie about McBride molesting her. McBride's lesbianism is only raised as an issue within the context of the false accusations. More importantly, when McBride comes out to Bates, the sergeant turns out to have a "different strokes for different folks" attitude about her partner's sexual orientation.

In the 1990s, *N.Y.P.D. Blue* featured two lesbian story lines, the first involving Det. Adrienne Lesniak (Justine Miceli) and the second, Officer Abby Sullivan (Paige Turco). Both women are forced to disclose their sexual orientation when one of their co-workers takes a romantic interest in them.

The least developed of the stories involves Lesniak, who is transferred from the Bronx because she had an affair with another officer, Det. Abruzzo (Bruce Nozick), who'd become obsessed with her. One day he pulls a revolver on her in the squad room ("Simone Says"), but he is apprehended and shipped off to Bellevue. Lesniak is understandably not interested in getting into a romantic relationship, particularly with a co-worker. So when she discovers Det. James Martinez (Nicholas Turturro) has his eye on her, she asks his partner, Det. Medavoy (Gordon Clapp), to tell him she is a lesbian ("One Big Happy Family"). Without thinking, an upset Martinez tells someone in the precinct, who, of course, starts spreading the word ("Heavin' Can Wait"). When the precinct's gay PAA (Principal/Police Administrative Assistant), John Irvin (Bill Brochtrup), hears the news, he invites Lesniak to a Gay Officer Action League (GOAL) meeting ("Dirty Laundry"). She admits to Irvin she only wanted to get Martinez off her back.

So is Lesniak a lesbian? The answer is sort of, but not really. Lesniak lied to Medavoy and Martinez, but she later admits to Det. Russell (Kim Delaney) she *is* questioning her sexuality ("Curt Russell") and did attend a GOAL meeting, but didn't feel comfortable. It is unclear whether the writers changed their minds about Lesniak's sexuality midstream or, perhaps, like Lesniak herself, couldn't decide.

The story begins to fall apart when Lesniak reveals she is questioning her sexuality because she's been in a series of bad relationships with men. The idea that she's sexually attracted to other women (considered by many a prerequisite for being a lesbian) is never really addressed. Lesniak does eventually become romantically involved with Martinez ("The Nutty Confessor"), but he eventually breaks up with her when she gets too clingy. At the end of season three, her character is written out of the series ("Auntie Maimed").

At the start of the following season, a real live, 100 percent, bona fide lesbian police officer named Abby Sullivan (Paige Turco) is introduced. Perhaps as a way of remedying the quasi-lesbian story line from the previous season, there is no waffling about Abby's sexuality. She comes out when Medavoy asks her out on a date ("Unembraceable You"), although Martinez wonders if she could be lying like Lesniak. But her sexual orientation is confirmed by Medavoy when he joins Abby and her lover Kathy (Lisa Darr) for dinner ("A Wrenching Experience"). The couple think Medavoy is a great guy, and so they later ask him to be a sperm donor for their baby. He agrees and when the fourth season opens, Abby is pregnant.

The Medavoy-Abby-Kathy story line had great potential because it had none of the trappings of the Lesniak plot's hangups. Abby was not pretending to be a lesbian, nor was she the victim of a failed heterosexual relationship. Furthermore, Abby and Kathy are a happy, stable lesbian couple. This would all soon change ("Three Girls and a Baby") when a man enters the couple's apartment and guns down Kathy. The detectives grow suspicious because there is no apparent motive and, at one point, they actually begin to suspect the pregnant Abby of killing Kathy during an argument. While the circumstances around the murder are suspicious, the idea that Abby would be considered a suspect is implausible because she had no motive and it would have been way too out of character.

The killer turns out to be another lesbian, Abby's psycho ex-lover Denise (Ashley Gardner), who hired a killer to rub out Kathy so she can be reunited with Abby. During questioning, Denise explains she tore up Abby's car "in the fit of love" and shows no remorse for hiring a gunman to kill Kathy. As Medavoy explains to Abby, Denise crossed the line of understanding the difference between right and wrong. The same line was transgressed by the series's writers, who were too quick to counteract positive lesbian characters with a tired old stereotype like the unstable, deranged lesbian. The following season, Abby, like Lesniak, disappeared. We're informed she moved upstate, where she has her baby. No doubt her character is safer living away from New York (and the show's writing staff).

N.Y.P.D Blue struck out a third time ("Thumb Enchanted Evening") with the brief introduction of another lesbian character, Lt. Dalto (Denise Crosby).

Reassigned from the "rat squad" (officers and detectives in the Internal Affairs Bureau), Dalto was called in to replace the departing (and recently promoted) Capt. Fancy (James MacDaniel). Before she even walks through the door, Irvin "outs" her by telling the rest of the squad she is a member of GOAL (and therefore a lesbian) and a real by-the-book "ball buster." His description is accurate because when she meets her squad for the first time, she is terse, dismissive, and condescending. She comments on the female detectives' inappropriate footwear, immediately considers rearranging the detectives' partner assignments and desks, and tells Sipowicz to remove his fish tank and John a tchotchke from his desk. As Sipowicz says, she's never going to change; no one will dare tell her to because "she's a lesbian woman, got that double minority clout, no one's going to risk getting in front of that." The following week ("Flight of Fancy"), Fancy, realizing Dalto is the wrong choice for his successor, calls in a favor and has her reassigned. She is angry, but Fancy points out she has succeeded in alienating an entire squad of detectives in 48 hours.

There is no question that Dalto was the wrong choice to supervise this somewhat unorthodox team of detectives, but why did the writers make her a lesbian? The implication — in this case it's difficult to believe it was not intentional — is that her "ball-busting" managerial style is intrinsic to her sexual orientation. Just as troubling was the decision to have the only other gay character on the show "out" her and smear her name. Her "castrating" nature is further compounded by a subplot line involving a man who is literally, albeit partially, emasculated when a male hustler named Shorty (Terence L. Bloom) bites off part of his penis for shorting him the agreed fee. (The remaining part of his member is later found at an ATM machine.) Surprisingly, Dalto is not considered a suspect.

OUR BOYS IN PINK

While female officers on shows like *Bronk* and *Police Woman* were falsely accused of being lesbians, 1970s series like *Streets of San Francisco* and *Starsky and Hutch* featured actual gay male policemen and detectives. Gay men working in such a high testosterone profession often find it difficult to keep their private lives private. Once a gay cop goes public, he must contend with his homophobic superiors, co-workers, and partner, who is usually the last to know and the hardest hit. He typically "outs" himself because he's being blackmailed or has witnessed a hate crime (a shooting in a gay bar, gay bashing, etc.). Coming out is therefore not a personal choice, but a professional and moral obligation.

One of the earliest examples contains all the major story elements, later repeated by other popular law and order dramas. On *The Streets of San Francisco* ("A Good Cop, But..."), a gay detective, Inspector Lambert (Barry Primus) must come out of the closet to convict a drug kingpin. An attempt by one of the kingpin's men to blackmail him backfires when Lambert tapes their conversation

Two men who spend 75 percent of their time together: Det. Ken "Hutch" Hutchinson (David Soul, left) and Det. Dave Starsky (Paul Michael Glaser, right).

and agrees to play the recording in open court. His partner, Ernie (Robert Walden), who had no clue, feels betrayed and immediately puts in for a transfer. But when Ernie hears Lambert's brave testimony during the trial, he has a change of heart.

Not all gay detectives are so lucky. On *Starsky and Hutch* ("Death in a Different Place"), John Blaine (Art Fleming) picks up a hustler, Nick Hunter (Gregory Rozakis), who drugs the detective, accompanies him back to his seedy hotel room, and robs him. While in the lobby of the hotel, Blaine sees a crooked narc named Lt. Corday (Don Gordon) making a drug deal. So after Nick robs Blaine, who has by now passed out, Corday murders him. With a reluctant Nick's help, Starsky (Paul Michael Glaser) and Hutch (David Soul) manage to catch Corday. The gay angle ultimately has little to do with the otherwise familiar corrupt cop plot, except for providing the perfect milieu for the final scene — a seedy gay bar called The Green Parrot.

The series's final tag does include a funny, self-reflective exchange between Starsky and Hutch in which they acknowledge the homoerotic undertones of their relationship:

STARSKY: A man preferring a man is not casual like someone having a bad cold...I'm not taking a position for or against it. But it is something to contend with. It's not your usual, everyday thing.

HUTCH: Starsky, would you consider a man who spends 75 percent of his time with another man has got certain tendencies?

STARSKY: 75?...you mean three quarters?...Yeah, sure, why not? You mean this case between John [Blaine]...?

HUTCH: No, that's the case between you and me...[He figures out how much time they spend together.]...75 percent of the time we spend together and you are not even a good kisser.

STARSKY: How do you know that?[38]

There's definitely chemistry between Starsky and Hutch (or should I say Soul and Glaser?) and the producers enjoyed having the duo go undercover, particularly when it involves a stereotypically gay profession. In "Dandruff," Starsky and Hutch pose as hairdressers, Mr. Marlene and Mr. Tyrone, at a hotel salon to uncover a jewel heist. In "Tap Dancing Their Way Into Your Hearts" (directed by Fernando Lamas!), they pose as dancers in a Hollywood dance studio to break an extortion ring. Although the heterosexuality of both characters was repeatedly affirmed, usually by the obligatory shot of one or both detectives checking out a beautiful woman, it will always be difficult to imagine Starsky without Hutch (and vice-versa).

Gay cops were not just limited to detective series. The newspaper drama *Lou Grant* tackled the subject in a compelling episode ("Cop") about a series of unrelated gay murders which claim the life of Grant's neighbor and five people who perish in a gay bar fire. Grant (Ed Asner) and reporter Joe Rossi (Robert Walden) realize one of the policeman investigating the case, Mike Tynan (Joe Penny), is gay. However, he's kept his sexual identity hidden from the force, including his partner Robert Denahay (Ed Winter). When Denahay finds out, he puts in for a transfer because he feels Tynan is unfit to be a police officer. But when Tynan saves his life during a shootout, Denahay changes his tune.

"Cop" is an outstanding episode that raises ethical questions surrounding the press's obligation to report a story vs. the people's right to know. The issue is first raised when Grant insists the *Tribune* publish the names of the five men who died in the gay bar fire. Consequently, they would all be labeled gay, which is problematic if they were married and/or not out to their families. "If the newspaper doesn't print the names this time," Grant asks, "how can the public know that we're not withholding other information from them in the future?" The *Tribune*'s owner, Mrs. Pynchon (Nancy Marchand), eventually agrees. (The story was based on a real-life incident in which eight people perished in a fire in a gay film club in Washington, D.C.[39]) The decision ties back into the Tynan plot when the *Tribune*, in keeping with their philosophy, doesn't report the officer is gay because it has no relevance to the capturing of the murder suspect.

Trapper John, M.D. ("Straight and Narrow") combined elements of a medical drama with a whodunit plot in which a gay cop is, ironically, shot during a gay rights rally. Joey Santori (Joseph Cali), San Francisco's first openly gay policeman, is partially paralyzed after being shot in the head. His partner, Sam (Charles Hallahan), blames the gay community for what happened to Joey. "Some fag shot my partner," Sam tells Dr. Gonzo Gates (Gregory Harrison), "...they want power. There's already too much fag power in San Francisco!"

When the gay-friendly Gonzo gets a tip that the gunman was a cop, he announces to the press that Joey can identify his assailant. With Sam's assistance, Gonzo traps the killer, a police detective (Frank Martin), who explains he did it because the police force was being "contaminated." "You didn't want fags on the force any more than I did," he tells Sam, "I had to keep the poison from spreading, from destroying the force." (Airing the same year as *The New York Times* article about AIDS, words like "contaminating" and "spreading" would soon become standard homophobic rhetoric in America.)

In addition to the "Who shot the gay cop?" plot, there are several gay-related subplots. The first involves Joey's relationship with his father (Harold J. Stone), who hasn't spoken to his son since he came out ten years earlier. The second involves the hospital's homophobic administrator Arnold Slocum (Simon Scott), who realizes that if a cop could be gay, so could a member of his staff. "The problem is that it's too difficult to tell," he explains to Dr. Riverside (Charles Seibert). "It's usually a person you least expect." (In a *San Francisco* hospital? That's difficult to believe.) The third story involves a drag queen named Judy (played by *Outrageous* star Craig Russell), who tries to cheer up a lonely, severely depressed patient, Mrs. Gelgood (Janet Brandt) by bringing some much needed gay sunshine into her life.

There's plenty going on in this well-intentioned episode, which goes to great lengths to demonstrate how homophobia can take many forms: from the homophobic detective/killer, to the father who rejects his gay son, to the homo-hunting hospital administrator. The subplot involving Judy and Mrs. Gelgood is less integral, except perhaps to show acceptance shouldn't be limited to handsome, seemingly straight gay cops, but includes drag queens as well.

Unlike the *Lou Grant* and *Trapper John, M.D.* episodes, most story lines centered around police officers either targeted by rumors or outed by circumstances out of their control. On *Cagney and Lacey* ("Conduct Unbecoming"), the sexual orientation of a detective assisting the female duo on a weapons case is questioned when his photograph turns up in a gay magazine. On *L.A. Law* ("Outward

Bound"), a gay cop sues a journalist who outed him without his permission. Questions regarding a closeted married police officer's (Paul Carhart) honesty are raised during a murder trial on *The Practice* ("We Hold These Truths") when the defense discovers he has been living a lie. On *Hill Street Blues* ("Here's Adventure, Here's Romance"), a married, off-duty cop, Art Bradley (Lawrence Pressman), who is the only witness to a massacre in a gay bar, decides to come out to his boss Captain Frank Furillo (Daniel J. Travanti). On *Law and Order: Special Victims Unit* ("Bad Blood"), a closeted gay cop (Peter Rini) who attends a gay birthday party provides key evidence in a murder case.

The gay police officer plot is also used to examine issues such as hate crimes and gay bashing. On *The Commish* ("Do You See What I See?") a gay police officer witnesses a gay bashing outside a gay bar. Officer Hank Ranavich (John Brennan) is forced to step forward and file a report. When his fellow officers find out he is gay, he is verbally harassed. Even his partner, Jon Hibbs (Ian Tracey), wants nothing to do with him, until Ranavich is bashed by the same men, who ironically work for a charity organization. Hibbs goes undercover at the organization as a gay man and is almost bashed himself, but luckily Commissioner Scali (Michael Chiklis) arrives just in time to rescue him.

When a straight cop like Hibbs finds out his partner is gay, he can only accept his friend's sexual orientation by becoming personally involved in the case himself (and in some instances emerge as a hero). While Hibbs's heroism is a way for him to redeem himself for rejecting his gay partner, it also suggests that acceptance is contingent on empathy. Unfortunately, not every gay police officer has a member of the force on his side. Consequently, homophobia within the force itself can produce tragic results.

On a memorable episode of *Law and Order* ("Manhood"), a gay cop is badly wounded in a shootout. Back-up is called but arrives too late and the officer dies. The detectives assigned to the case are suspicious and question the dead cop's partner, Craig McGraw (Adam Trese), who shows them an anti-gay flyer that circulated around the precinct. One of the suspects, Officer Weddeker (Sam Rockwell) eventually breaks down and admits, "they just wanted to scare him. They didn't think he was going to die!"

The district attorney decides to prosecute Weddeker and the two other officers for intentionally leaving a fellow cop to die. The D.A. loses his case because the defense puts a psychiatrist on the stand who states that heterosexual men's hatred of homosexuals is pathological and therefore uncontrollable. The episode makes a point that homophobia, or any form of bigotry for that matter, can be legitimized when it involves a group. As D.A. Adam Schiff (Steven Hill) and Executive Assistant District Attorney Ben Stone (Michael Moriarity) lament in the final scene, "four cops let him die and twelve citizens did it again. And they voted their indifference." The episode, directed by Ed Sherin and written by Robert Nathan (from a story by Nathan and Walon Green), received a 1993 GLAAD/LA Award for Outstanding Dramatic Television Episode.

With so many gay cops on television, one would think it was only a matter of time before a police drama would include one as a series regular. Still, long-running law and order dramas like *Hill Street Blues*, *Law and Order*, and *N.Y.P.D. Blue* have never included gay male cops and detective as regular or recurring characters. However, there are some notable exceptions.

The first is *Hooperman*, a dramedy starring John Ritter as a San Francisco police detective. The series was created by Steven Bochco, the man behind *Hill Street Blues* and *N.Y.P.D. Blue*. Among the police officers at the Hooperman's station is Rick Silardi (Joseph Gian), a handsome, openly gay cop who is forced to remind his man-hungry partner, Officer Maureen "Mo" DeMott (Sydney Walsh) he is not (and will never be) heterosexual. Even her not-so-subtle flirting with Vinnie Corral (Geoffrey Scott), a movie star who rides along with her and Silardi to research an upcoming film role, is all in vain ("Don We Now Our Gay Apparel"). DeMott may have her eye on Corral, but he's only interested in Silardi, who he asks out on a date.

As Silardi's homosexuality is generally known and accepted in his division, the homophobia he faces usually comes from outside, including his macho twin brother, Bob (Gian in a double role), who is also a cop. In "Surprise Party," Bob is ashamed his brother is gay and blames him for causing their parents grief. "You should have stayed in the closet," Bob sneers. Bob's homophobia eventually gets him into trouble when he attacks a gay deputy district attorney, who, thinking he is Rick, mistakenly tries to make a date with Bob. Bob goes ballistic and lands in jail. After some convincing from a sympathetic Hooperman, Rick convinces the D.A. to drop the charges and the two brothers reconcile.

A far more complex character is *Homicide: Life on the Street*'s bisexual detective Tim Bayliss (Kyle Secor). Sensitive and intelligent, Bayliss first demonstrates interest in men while investigating the recent murder of a gay man, whose body is found in a gay restaurant's dumpster ("Closet Cases"). The owner of The Zodiac, Chris Rawls (Peter Gallagher), leads Bayliss and his partner Det. Pembleton (Andre Braugher) to the killer, a hunky hustler named Peter Fields (Brian Van Holt). Fields agrees to confess only if Bayliss admits he finds him attractive (and loves his "nice, hard, ass.") Bayliss obliges and Fields gives a full confession, claiming he killed the "faggot," but he himself isn't gay. ("I am a normal, red-blooded, heterosexual man.") Bayliss later accepts Rawl's dinner invitation, which confuses Pembleton, particularly when Bayliss begins to take an interest in Det. Laura Ballard (Callie Thorne) in the next episode ("Sins of the Father").

Bayliss officially comes out as a bisexual in October of 1998 when he asks Det. Renee Sheppard (Michael Michele) out on a date ("Just an Old Fashion Love Song"). She asks him about the rumor going around the precinct that he is gay. Bayliss admits he slept with a guy recently (a couple of times) and labels himself "bi-curious." Renee admits she's bi-curious also and has dated bisexual men.

Another aspect of Bayliss's private life is introduced on "Homicide.com," in which a murder is staged over the internet. The killer advertises his next murder on www.inplainsite.com, Bayliss's anonymous website that features information on "Buddhist Perspectives on Bisexuality" (Bayliss is a Buddhist). Word spreads

Homicide: Life on the Street's bisexual Buddhist, Detective Tim Bayliss (Kyle Secor)

that Bayliss is the owner of the website ("Truth Will Out"), which kills his romantic chances with Sergeant Roger Fisk (Michael Ford). Fisk stands Bayliss up for dinner because he's afraid he'll be outed (and never promoted) if he associates with him. When Bayliss tries to talk to him about it, Fisk shouts "leave me alone or I'll kick your faggot ass," loud enough for everyone in the squad room to hear. From that point on, poor Bayliss considers celibacy.

The issue surrounding Bayliss's sexuality eventually subsides as the series winds down. In the series finale ("Forgive Us Our Trespasses"), the internet killer, Luke Ryland (Benjamin Busch), is set free on a technicality. Bayliss is angry and quietly leaves his job, but not before he warns the killer he'll be watching him. At the end of the episode, Ryland turns up dead. In the two-hour follow-up to the series, *Homicide — The Movie*, Bayliss admits to Pembleton he murdered Ryland, but the bi-curious detective's fate is never revealed.

Unlike most bisexuals in films and on television, Bayliss is neither sexually confused nor a sex maniac who is trying to get it from anyone he or she can all the time. His sexual interest in both men and women is presented, like heterosexuality and, more recently, homosexuality, as quite natural and normal. Turning Bayliss into a murderer in the end was no doubt unsettling for the show's devoted fans. Fortunately, his actions are consistent with a character who was clearly reacting, albeit irrationally, to a faulty legal system, rather than being driven by some sort of oedipal problem or repressed sexual rage.

THE SUPPORTIVE SUPPORTING PLAYERS

Most regular and recurring gay characters on law and order dramas still appear in supporting roles as friends, family members, co-workers, and informants. For example, *The Profiler*'s Violent Crimes Task Force team includes a top-notch gay computer hacker, George Fraley (Peter Frechette). *Hollywood Beat*'s detectives, Nick McCarren (Jack Scalia) and Jack Rado (Jay Acavone), hang out at the Frolic Room, a cocktail lounge owned by a very big gay man named George Grinsky (ex-pro football player John Matuszak). And Chris Cagney has another shoulder to cry on when her handsome gay neighbor, Tony Stantinopolis (Barry Sattels), moves in across the hall ("Rights of Passage").

The issue hits closer to home for *The Division*'s Inspector Jinny Exstead (Nancy McKeon), who supports her gay brother, a fellow police officer, when he comes out of the closet ("Don't Ask"). In "Knockout," detective *Nash Bridges* (Don Johnson) not only finds out his sister Stacy (Angela Dohrmann) is a lesbian, but she is dating his ex-girlfriend. But it's not an issue for Nash who is so comfortable in his own sexuality that he and his partner, Joe (Cheech Marin), pose as a gay couple to retrieve a stolen Super Bowl ring for a gay ex-pro football player ("The Counterfeiters").

Nash and Joe's masquerade continued in the 1998-1999 season when the duo open a gay detective agency. Their first client is a Cher impersonator ("Imposters") who hires them to retrieve her wigs, stolen by her understudy. In a later episode ("Girl Trouble"), Joe finds himself in an embarrassing situation when he starts corresponding with a mystery woman over the internet. His cyber gal turns out to be none other than Pepe (Patrick Fischler), the agency's gay office manager, who thinks Nash and Joe have been a couple for 20 years. Luckily, Nash manages to rescue Joe without hurting Pepe's feelings.

While there have been regular and recurring lesbian characters on Steven Bochco's numerous series, with the exception of *Hooperman*, most gay male characters on his shows are relegated to the role of the boss's faithful assistant. *Cop Rock*'s corrupt mayor, Louise Plank (Barbara Bosson), had the loyal Ray Rodbart (Jeffrey Allan Chandler) at her side. *Murder One*'s law offices were managed by the efficient Louis Heinsberger (John Fleck).

And then there's *N.Y.P.D. Blue*'s John Irvin (Bill Brotchup), the embodiment of the limited perception some heterosexuals have of gay men.[40] Efficient, emotional, and fey to the point of being a little frail, Irvin's involvement in story lines is limited. Most of his screen time is spent sitting behind his desk, like a spectator, silently observing the action. Until recently, we knew very little about his personal life, though in one early episode ("The Bank Dick"), he is dating a police officer, Paul Caputo (Paul D'Ambrosio). The couple, who are never shown together on screen, are gay-bashed by two kids paid off by cops in Paul's precinct. Irvin elicits help from Det. Simone (Jimmy Smits), who counsels the closeted Paul and warns the two homophobic cops from Paul's precinct to lay off.

On occasion, Irvin is actually involved in a story line. He tries to reach out to his friend and fellow PAA, Dolores Mayo (Lola Glaudini), when she gets involved in prostitution and drugs ("What's Up Chuck?"). When Dolores turns up dead ("Voir Dire This"), Irvin feels guilty he wasn't able to help. He has subsequent misgivings about not stopping her father, Jimmy Mayo (Bob Glaudini), from avenging her death by gunning down Assistant District Attorney Sylvia Costas, a.k.a. Mrs. Andy Sipowicz (Sharon Lawrence).

In "Welcome to New York," Irvin offers his "expertise" on gay relationships to help the detectives solve the murder of a man involved in a gay love triangle. In the episode's final scene, Irvin offers his emotional support to the victim's ex-lover, a sweet southerner named Blake (Misha Collins):

> JOHN: I hope you won't give in to despair. That's what I want to tell you. It's so hard making sense of our lives...making our lives sensible in a strange city. We begin a different lifestyle completely. Maybe not exactly sure inside if the changes we are choosing are right necessarily. Even if they are right for us. It's so easy to become confused. It's so hard to love ourselves and to find what's good for our lives. And then to experience something like you just experienced. I want you to know it's possible to make your way and that happiness, friendship, the sun rising and setting, the birds in the wind at the harbor, they are all here too, Blake. As much for you as for anyone else in the world.[41]

Not even a good actor like Brotchup can make a bizarre speech like this work. Irvin talks about himself, Blake, and other gay men who move to New York as if they were visitors from another planet. While one can appreciate Irvin's attempt to counsel this gay man whose ex-lover was just murdered by his current lover, his monologue only confirms the series's limited perception of gay men. Furthermore, we have no idea what Blake is thinking because he just silently listens and then, at the end, politely thanks him.

Irvin's character would be more palatable if there was some balance in terms of the other gay male characters on the show. Over the years, *N.Y.P.D. Blue*'s roster of gay (and gay-related) victims and killers have included a Truman Capote look-alike whose Oscar (for Best Screenplay) is pinched by a hustler ("Oscar, Meyer, Wiener"); a crackhead transvestite ("Jumpin' Jack Fleishman"); a New York University professor who picks up hustlers and is killed by a mentally ill student ("Head Case"); and, as discussed above, a stiffed hustler who severs part of a john's johnson ("Thumb Enchanted Evening").

The writers also like to add a little touch of decadence to cases by having the detectives conduct their investigation in a gay bar (on drag night in "Don We Now Our Gay Apparel"). In "The Man With Two Right Shoes," a gay out-of-towner is stabbed and castrated by a hustler because the john kissed him. The detectives' investigation leads them, in Sipowicz's words, to a "fairy bar" frequented by the victim. The scene in which the detectives apprehend the suspect in the bar goes to great lengths to emphasize Sipowicz's hostility and disgust for what he sees (like the bartenders' bare buttocks, which no doubt is an inside joke on the series's more infamous behind-barings). While Sipowicz would have used words like "fairy bar," "queer moron," and "fruits," in the show's first few seasons, you'd think he would have grown more tolerant over the years — at least enough to think twice before using derogatory terms. Even GLAAD, which applauded the series for featuring a gay male character in a recurring (and now regular) role, believed "work still needs to be done to avoid gratuitous language and inconsistencies in characterizations when depicting gay themes."[42]

Another example involves Sipowicz, now a single father, trying to find a last-minute babysitter for his son Theo ("Writing Wrongs"). Irvin offers to sit, but Sipowicz is reluctant to leave Theo alone with a gay guy. His partner, Danny Sorenson (Rick Schroeder), tells him he is being irrational and explains Irvin is gay, not a pedophile. "I would trust my life with him," Sorenson says. Sipowicz asks him to sit with Theo and he becomes his regular babysitter.

In the context of Sipowicz's character, the situation makes little sense. Even though the child involved is his own son, an experienced, street smart detective like Sipowicz knows the difference between a homosexual and a pedophile. He has also known Irvin for several years. The situation confirms there is no place in the world of *N.Y.P.D. Blue* for a gay man beyond fulfilling his role as the "gay other." Instead of having any semblance of a personal life (or even a relationship), Irvin can only do the things all gay men are good at, like babysitting and cutting hair (which he graciously does again for Sipowicz before his big date).[43]

The transgender community doesn't fare much better on *N.Y.P.D. Blue*. Transvestites and transsexuals, usually hookers, are either witnesses to or victims of crimes. In "Unembraceable You," two prostitutes, Angela (Alec Mapa) and Peaches (Jazzmun), who Det. Russell knew from her days as a vice cop, prove to be helpful witnesses to a homicide. Both characters return later that season ("I Love Lucy") when Angela is beaten up by her low-life boyfriend, Jimmy (Clifton Gonzalez-Gonzalez). Jimmy later kills her because she refused to have a risky sex-change operation. In an equally disturbing episode ("A Hole in Juan"), a crack addict leaves her baby for four days with a transsexual named Inez (Erik Dellums). Inez in turn leaves the baby alone for a few hours. When she returns, the infant is dead, so she puts the body in a dumpster.

Surprisingly, producer Steven Bochco's previous police drama, *Hill Street Blues*, was less sensationalistic when it came to gay characters and issues. Like the 12th Precinct, Hill Street Station also had to contend with the usual murderers, thieves, and gang-related crime. Gay characters on the whole were treated more sympathetically than on *N.Y.P.D. Blue*, sometimes to the point of being conde-scending. In the opening of the third season ("Trial By Fury"), undercover detective Michael Belker (Bruce Weitz) befriends a gay male prostitute named

Eddie Gregg (Charles Levin), who affectionately refers to Belker as "Mick." Eddie is sad-eyed, childlike, and very needy. He is the perfect counterpart for Belker, who has a gruff exterior but is a softie deep down.

Belker also becomes Eddie's defender and protector. When Det. LaRue (Kiel Martin) begins imitating Eddie, Belker tells him off. "You make me sick. Just because a guy is different. What the hell is it to you?" he shouts. "He's just a poor, scared guy trying to get through the day." In "Phantom of the Hill," Eddie becomes Belker's snitch and is forced to inform on a lover involved in a homicide. Belker feels disappointed and betrayed when Eddie lets his emotions get the best of him and almost prevents the police from capturing the killer. Before Eddie leaves town, he thanks the detective for being his friend and gives him a kiss on the cheek.

Three years later ("Slum Enchanted Evening"), Belker runs into Eddie, who tells him he has "it" (in 1986, "it" meant AIDS). Once again, Belker plays good Samaritan and buys him ice cream. He later returns to his tenement with groceries, only to find out Eddie has died. To the series's credit, the Eddie-Belker story line broke new ground in exploring the relationship between a straight and a gay man. What was disappointing is that the producers fell into the trap of characterizing an adult gay man as a pathetic mess. As a result, Belker's interest in Eddie comes across as slightly patronizing.

Law and order dramas have also featured lesbian and bisexual lawyers and judges. In November of 1990, *L.A. Law* introduced a bisexual attorney (she preferred the term "flexible") named C.J. Lamb (Amanda Donohoe). In a highly controversial episode ("He's a Crowd"), C.J. plants a kiss on one of her colleagues, Abby (Michele Green). *The Hollywood Reporter* characterized "what might be the first lesbian kiss on network television as rather chaste."[44] Some of the advertisers pulled their ads, but they were quickly replaced with no financial loss to NBC.[45] The episode indeed broke new ground, though by today's standards the lip lock between Abby and C.J. would barely register on the Kinsey scale. (And, just for the record, if a bisexual woman kisses a heterosexual woman, is it really a "lesbian" kiss?)

C.J. may have paved the way for television's first lesbian African-American judge. On the short-lived *Courthouse*, Jenifer Lewis plays Rosetta Reed, a single mother who left her husband to live with her female lover Danny (Cree Summers). Danny is upset that Rosetta is afraid to show any public affection in front of her colleagues ("Order on the Court"), though the judge claims she doesn't want to give up everything she worked for so they can walk down the hallway holding hands. The issue creates tension in their relationship, particularly when Rosetta asks Danny to go to a hotel when her parents come to visit ("Fair-Weathered Friends"). The first African-American lesbian couple to be regularly featured on a television series, Rosetta and Danny's relationship was never given the chance to develop because CBS closed *Courthouse*'s doors after only nine episodes.

Following in Rosetta's footsteps is *100 Centre Street*'s lesbian Judge Atallah Sims (La Tanya Richardson). Known as "Atallah-the-Hun," the feisty Judge Sims

She prefers the term "flexible:" *L.A. Law*'s Amanda Donohoe as bisexual lawyer C.J. Lamb.

is outed by the press ("The Bug") when she defies the mayor to help a fellow judge, Joe Rifkin (Alan Arkin). As with *Courthouse, 100 Centre Street* explores the challenges faced by women and racial minorities in traditional male power positions, particularly when their personal lives become front page news.

DON'T ASK, DON'T TELL, DON'T BASH

In 1993, the Clinton administration issued a new policy regarding gays, lesbians, and bisexuals serving in the United States military. The current version of the policy, now known as "Don't Ask, Don't Tell, Don't Pursue, Don't Harass," prohibits military commanders from 1) questioning service members about their sexual orientation; 2) pursuing an inquiry into someone's sexual orientation, except if they already have credible information; and 3) harassing or tolerating the harassment or violence against any service member for any reason. Harassment includes verbal and physical assault, anti-gay graffiti, comments, and slurs.

The "Don't Tell" portion of the policy prohibits gay, lesbian, and bisexual service members from engaging in "homosexual conduct," a broad term which includes 1) stating "I am gay;" 2) engaging in a "homosexual act," which, in addition to sexual relations, includes touching for the purpose of sexual gratification, kissing, hugging, and holding hands with someone of the same gender; and 3) marrying, whether it is legal or not, a member of the same sex.[46] While the policy was supposedly designed to *protect* the rights of homosexuals in the military, it has had adverse effects. After its implementation, the number of homosexuals discharged rose at the alarming rate of 92 percent over a five-year period. In 1998, a record 1,145 people were dismissed, 414 from the Air Force alone (271 of whom were stationed at the Lackland Air Force Base in San Antonio, Texas). C. Dixon Osburn, co-director of the Servicemembers Legal Defense Network, characterizes the Pentagon's assertion that the rise in discharges is due to the increase in the number of homosexuals voluntarily coming out as "disingenuous."[47] What the Pentagon considers so-called "voluntary statements" have included conversations with psychotherapists, personal diary entries, answers to illegally asked questions, and admissions made through intimidation, coercion, and violence.[48]

Clinton's policy, which he himself admitted in 1999 is "out of whack," failed to protect homosexuals and men and women perceived as homosexual from being the targets of verbal harassment and physical assault. Consequently, in December of 1999, Secretary of Defense William Cohen ordered an investigation into how much "harassment of Service members based on perceived or alleged homosexuality" and "disparaging speech or expression with respect to sexual orientation" occurs and is tolerated.[49]

The renewed interested in Clinton's flawed policy was sparked by the brutal murder of Private First Class Barry Winchell at Fort Campbell, Kentucky in July of 1999. While Winchell was asleep in his barracks, his head was bashed in with a baseball bat by a fellow soldier, Private Calvin Glover. Trial testimony revealed Winchell had been harassed prior to the incident because he was labeled gay, but no action was taken to protect him. Glover was sentenced to life in prison and a second soldier, Spec. Justin R. Fisher, was sentenced to twelve and a half years as an accessory.

In conducting their investigation, the Defense Department distributed 70,000 surveys to servicemen. The results indicate a high percentage of respondents have heard offensive speech (80 percent); believed such comments were tolerated (85 percent); and witnessed or experienced such behavior they would consider harassment based on perceived homosexuality (78 percent).[50]

As long as "Don't Ask, Don't Tell" is in effect, the military will no doubt continue to be, as it has been for centuries, a breeding ground for homophobia. Even if homosexuals were allowed to openly serve, a patriarchal institution such as the military, which subscribes to and promotes certain ideals of masculinity regarded as antithetical to homosexuality, would certainly not change overnight.

Consequently, the military is the ideal setting for addressing the subject of homophobia and exposing the contradictions of the "Don't Ask" policy. Ironically, law and order dramas continually sidestep the issue of anti-gay violence by suggesting gay bashing occurs in the civilian world, but not on military compounds. While the assailants are typically servicemen, their victims are usually civilians. Another strategy is to set the story in a military school or college. The military's policies are thereby indirectly critiqued by exposing the homophobia that underlies the school's teachings about honor and manhood.

A prime example is an episode of *21 Jump Street*, in which Officers Tom Hanson (Johnny Depp) and Doug Penhall (Peter DeLuise) are forced to go undercover as cadets ("Honor Bound"). Hanson befriends three cadets who enjoy taking a ride into town for a little queer bashing. The cadets justify their late night "search and destroy" missions as part of their military training.

The meaning of the word "honor" is called into question when the cadets' company commander, Sgt. Major Jackson (Manfred Melcher), covers for his fellow cadets when they sneak out. Even when Penhall reveals he's a cop, Jackson still refuses to cooperate with the investigation because turning in a fellow cadet is a violation of the "unwritten" code of honor.

One of the cadets, Richard (Dean Hamilton), participates in the "search and destroy" missions for personal reasons. He's ashamed of his gay older brother and worries he'll turn out to be gay too. But when Richard realizes one of their victims was his brother's friend (and could easily have been his brother), he finally understands the consequences of his actions. In the end, he and the other cadets do the right thing and turn themselves in.

A military school is also the setting for a controversial episode of *Quantum Leap*. In "Running for Honor — June 11, 1964," Sam (Scott Bakula) leaps into the body of Tommy York, a cadet commander in a naval prep school. Tommy is class valedictorian and star of the school's track team, which is preparing for an upcoming meet with a rival school. Sam (as Tommy) also discovers his former roommate, Phillip Ashcroft (Sean O'Bryan), was recently thrown out of school for being gay. Phillip wants Sam/Tommy to help him expose The C.H.A.I.N (Cadets Honoring an Ideal Navy), a gang of five anti-gay cadets who, as Sam and his "observer," Al Calavicci (Dean Stockwell), know, will be responsible for Phillip's death by hanging in two days' time. But what Sam and Al don't know is that Phillip is actually planning to commit suicide and blame his death on The C.H.A.I.N. Meanwhile, Sam is also confused about Tommy's sexual orientation. The issue becomes irrelevant because as soon as Tommy comes to Phillip's defense, he is labeled gay by The C.H.A.I.N.'s leader, Ronnie Chambers (Anthony Palermo).

The controversy surrounding this episode began when *Variety* reported that NBC wanted Universal Studios, the series's producer, to bear financial responsibility if advertisers pulled out. NBC spokeswoman Sue Binford said that although there had been discussion about "potential advertiser concerns," the network never asked Universal to pay for advertiser fallout.[51] Richard Jennings, executive director of GLAAD, then erroneously revealed alleged changes made to the script, including the addition of a positive gay character and the implication that the character Sam leaps into is gay. The series's executive producer, Donald P. Bellisario, responding in a *Los Angeles Times* editorial, claimed *Variety* and GLAAD's allegations were false. According to Bellisario, the controversy broke out during the third day of shooting and the only changes made in the final shooting script involved raising the characters' ages because the network didn't want to depict a teenager contemplating suicide.[52]

In October 1991 (four months before the episode aired), a GLAAD press release reported Jennings's reaction to the script:

> According to Jennings, who read drafts of the script, the portrayal of a gay ex-cadet is negative and unbalanced, since he is shown as being someone too willing to commit suicide to get others in trouble and as planning to reveal the sexual orientation of other cadets. The dialogue between the show's two major characters is full of offensive, stereotype-based "jokes" that are never responded to or balanced by accurate information about gays and lesbians. Moreover, the graphic portrayal of a suicide in the script is a serious network concern, since similar portrayals in the past have sparked "copycat" suicides and copycat attempts.[53]

TEN-HUT! BASED ON A TRUE STORY

Sgt. Matlovich vs. the U.S. Air Force (NBC-TV)
August 21, 1978
Written John McGreevey
Directed by Paul Leaf

Brad Dourif stars as Sergeant Leonard P. Matlovich, who received a dishonorable discharge from the U.S. Army when he decided to contest the military's anti-homosexual policy and come out of the closet. The court case is more interesting than the flashbacks of his childhood and early military career, which reveal little about his "personal" life. In the end, Matlovich, a recipient of the Purple Heart who served three tours of duty in Vietnam, was given a general discharge. Dourif is excellent as the very honorable Matlovich, but this docudrama is surprisingly uninvolving.

Serving in Silence: The Margarethe Cammermeyer Story (NBC-TV)
February 6, 1995
Written by Alison Cross
Directed by Jeff Bleckner

Colonel Margarethe Cammermeyer, a 26-year decorated Army veteran, was discharged from the service when she admitted to being lesbian during a security-clearance check. Glenn Close is terrific in this Award-winning telefilm as the Colonel who fights to be reinstated, but must also contend with the personal toll her legal battle against the Army is taking on her children, ex-husband, and lover, played by Judy Davis. In spite of the 1993 "Don't Ask" rule, Cammermeyer was reinstated in 1994 and made an unsuccessful bid for a congressional seat in the state of Washington in 1998.

Any Mother's Son: The Dorothy Hajdys Story (Lifetime)
August 11, 1997
Written by Bruce Harmon
Directed by David Burton Morris

In October 26, 1992, Petty Officer Allen Schindler, 22, was beaten to death in Japan by two of his Navy shipmates, Airman Apprentice Terry M. Helvey, and Airman Charles E. Vins. Schindler was reportedly so badly disfigured his mother could only identify him by the tattoos on his arms. Helvey was sentenced to life in prison. Vins, his accomplice, served only 78 days and was released from the military. This powerful made-for-TV movie features another terrific performance from Bonnie Bedelia as Schindler's mother, Dorothy Hajdys, who overcame her personal feelings about her son's homosexuality and took on the U.S. Navy, which unsuccessfully tried to conceal details about the case.

What the media release does not mention is the episode is set in the year *1964*, not 1991. This is central to understanding the episode's message that the same homophobic reasoning used for decades to keep homosexuals out of the military still exists. Both Al, a former military man himself, and Admiral Spencer (John Finn), the head of the academy, think homosexuals are a security risk who lack the military's required leadership qualities. Sam disagrees and tries to convince both Al and the Admiral that an individual's sexual preference has nothing to do with his/her ability to lead.

According to GLAAD, "offensive, stereotype-based 'jokes'" between Sam and Al are "never responded to or balanced by accurate information." Actually, they're being made for the very purpose of demonstrating they're offensive. Sam isn't sure whether the cadet he has leapt into is gay (he's a virgin, shy with his girlfriend, etc.), yet Al starts to make homophobic comments about how Sam crosses his legs when he sits, stands with his hands on his hips, and drinks tea instead of coffee. Each time Al makes an offensive remark and begins explaining why homosexuals should not be allowed in the military, Sam vehemently challenges his opinions. And while the school, of course, doesn't change its policy, Al does change his views after witnessing Phillip's suicide attempt.

Luckily, Sam rides to the rescue with the school's track coach, Coach Martz (John Roselius), who talks Phillip out of hanging himself by admitting he's gay and knows all about "the guilt, the shame, and fear." He assures Phillip he "has nothing to be ashamed of." The scene, in which a closeted gay military man reaches out to a desperate young gay man, is highly emotional and very effective. Jennings suggests the "graphic portrayal of a suicide" (perhaps Phillip does kill himself in another version?) could spark copycat suicides. But Phillip doesn't commit suicide because he has received support from another gay man, who delivers the most important message of all — *you're not alone.*

Homophobia is also central to an episode of the legal drama, *J.A.G.* (an acronym for the Judge Advocate General Corps of the United States Navy). In "The People vs. Gunny," Gunnery Sgt. Victor "Gunny" Galindez (Randy Vasquez), who serves in the J.A.G. Corps, is charged with assault when he becomes involved in an altercation outside a gay bar. Galindez's friend, Master Sgt. Manny O'Bregon (Jesse Corti), starts making disparaging remarks to a gay man, Edward Proxy (Jamison Jones), when the civilian accidentally bumps into him. The three men exchange words and begin to brawl. Petty Officer Tiner (Chuck Carrington), who also works for J.A.G., walks out of a nearby gay bar and starts defending Proxy. As Tiner is about to throw a second punch, he realizes he's about to hit Gunny, his work supervisor.

Gunny is tried for assaulting a civilian, yet refuses to give up Manny's name because his friend is close to being released from the military. According to Gunny's testimony, he wasn't gay-bashing Proxy, but coming to his friend's defense. Tiner only saw the very end of the scuffle, so in his mind Gunny and Manny were beating up Proxy. The incident makes for a complicated case because it all comes down to what actually happened (which the viewer sees in its entirety) versus what each individual believed happened. Furthermore, as Tiner admits on the stand, he knows Gunny isn't the type who'd bash gays.

The convoluted plot also addresses the "Don't Ask" policy. Tiner is seen coming out of a gay bar, so his co-workers assume he's gay and begin treating him accordingly. But because of the military's policy, no one can *ask* him if he is gay. Finally, Tiner takes the stand and Adm. Chegwidden (John M. Jackson), acting as Gunny's lawyer, asks him the big question (which he can do because it's in a civilian court). Tiner says no, and explains Proxy is his half-brother and they were in the gay bar celebrating his birthday. He now understands how his brother has felt his entire life because once his colleagues thought he was gay, everything he said and did suddenly seemed to have double meaning. During his testimony, Tiner takes a clear position against the "Don't Ask" rule:

> TINER: I want to be a J.A.G. lawyer some day, sir. But if I were gay, I would be kicked out of the Navy. And for what? I'm the same person. Ed [Proxy], me, we all acted stupidly that night. Let's just forget it and go home.[54]

As in *21 Jump Street*, the larger issue surrounding gays in the military is once again resolved by displacing it onto a personal story, which coincidentally also involves two brothers.

But what about Manny? The detectives investigating the case were never able to track him down? Why doesn't Proxy make any attempt to identify the man who started the incident? Proxy fingers Gunny as his attacker, but why not Manny? In the end, Gunny, who knows Manny is homophobic, follows the unwritten code of the military. He refuses to give up the name of his friend, who actually did start harassing Proxy (the writers try to even the score by having Proxy hurl insults back and take a punch at Manny while Gunny holds him back). But isn't Gunny condoning Manny's actions by his silence? Gunny is fined for refusing to give Manny's name on the stand, but this simply reinforces the idea it is the unwritten "code of silence" keeping homophobia alive in the military. The episode ultimately sidesteps the issue by putting Gunny on the stand instead of Manny, and using the trial to air some sympathetic, yet very familiar, rhetoric.

Since the 1980s, law and order dramas have responded to the growing number of reported hate crimes. "Fag bashing" is certainly not a phenomenon of the last twenty years. Gays, lesbians, and transgender people have been the targets of violent attacks for centuries. But it has only been recently that the general public has become aware of the issue, in part because of the media attention given to certain cases, such as the brutal murder of Matthew Shepard.

Gay activists continue to fight for laws which will protect everyone — homosexuals and heterosexuals — from violence, for one does not necessarily have to be gay to be a victim. On *L.A. Law*, one of the firm's partners, Douglas Brackman, Jr. (Alan Rachins) is gay bashed ("Do the Spike Thing") while coming out of a gay restaurant where he has just had dinner with a friend. He's initially afraid to prosecute because the publicity from the trial will give the public the impression he's gay (which he is not). In the end, he realizes he must do the right thing and press charges.

In a compelling episode of *Homicide* aptly titled "Hate Crimes," a young man is beaten to death by a group of skinheads at a bar in Baltimore's gay section. Bayliss and his partner Pembleton talk to the victim's distraught father, Bailey Lafeld (Terry O'Quinn) who becomes belligerent when the detectives imply his son was gay. "He was no queer," Lafeld insists. "Queers are sick, perverted animals, diseased, unnatural." LaFeld kicks the detectives out of the house and tells them, "If what you say is true, it's better he's dead."

Throughout the episode, Bayliss and Pembleton have an ongoing discussion about homosexuality. Neither character is entirely clear how he feels; particularly Bayliss, which, in retrospect, suggests that the detective's latent bisexuality was beginning to emerge.

At the conclusion of their investigation, Bayliss admits to Mr. LaFeld that he was mistaken — his son was not gay. The father becomes emotional and bursts into tears. "Thank God," he cries.

"Hetero, homo, what does it matter?" Pembleton later asks Bayliss. "He's dead."

"That is the worst part," Bayliss replies. "It shouldn't matter, but it does."

Not all officers are as open-mined as Bayliss and Pembleton. Sometimes it takes the death of someone you know before your eyes are opened. On *Street Justice* ("Bashing"), Malloy's (Charlene Fernetz) gay brother Danny is gay-bashed and later dies from his injuries. The search for his killers gives Police Sgt. Adam Beaudreaux (Carl Weathers), the former partner of Danny and Malloy's father, the opportunity to come to terms with his own homophobia. Danny was rejected by his late father because of his homosexuality and "Uncle Adam" never offered Danny his support, even after his father's death. Adam admits he's ashamed he never reached out to Danny, so he tries to make up for it by catching his killers.

Some series have tried to put their own spin on the subject of gay bashing. In an episode of David E. Kelley's short-lived detective series, *Snoops* ("Constitution"), a man hires Glenn (Gina Gershon) to find out if his future son-in-law is gay. What she discovers is the exact opposite —he's a gay-basher. On *The Big Easy*, Mitchell Teague is murdered at his own bachelor party by his friend, Fairchild (Taylor Nichols), who found out Mitchell was sexually involved with a drag queen named Tawny ("Cinderfella"). Fairchild, sickened by the idea that Mitchell lived a deviant lifestyle and was soon going to marry a woman he was in love with himself, ironically dons drag to pin the crime on Tawny. Before hitting the streets to catch a transvestite-basher ("Javelin Catcher"), *Nash Bridge*'s Inspector Evan Cortez (Jaime P. Gomez) gets some fashion tips from drag queen Simone DuBois (RuPaul). The sting is a success and they catch two men hired by a land developer trying to clean up the area. Coincidentally, dressing in drag also perks up Cortez's love life. The detective, who was having trouble pleasing his girlfriend in the bedroom, discovers she gets turned on seeing him in a dress.

Gay-bashing received more realistic treatment on episodes of *Third Watch* and *Law and Order*. *Third Watch* ("32 Bullets and a Broken Heart") opens with a bloodbath at a gay Valentines Day wedding. According to witnesses, a gunman entered the church and opened fire during the ceremony, killing several people. The gay community is understandably upset and feels the police aren't doing enough to catch the killer. When the gunman strikes again, some gay men start taking matters into their own hands by forming a vigilante group. At one point, the overzealous group starts harassing a man they mistakenly believe to be the assailant. The episode concludes with the police apprehending the killer, but not before the vigilantes nearly beat him to death.

As in *Homicide*, the crimes provide the series's regulars the opportunity to share their respective views about homosexuality and gay rights, all of which have a familiar ring to them. Carlos (Anthony Ruivivar) compares the struggle of homosexuals as a minority with the struggle of African-Americans. His African-American partner, Doc (Michael Beach) resents the comparison between the struggle up from slavery and the struggle for sexual preference. The bigoted Bosco (Jason Wiles) tells his partner Yokas (Molly Price) that gays are only asking for it by assembling together in public. She finds his racist and homophobic remarks offensive.

The writers seem to be bending over backwards to offer multiple viewpoints, by using the characters as mouthpieces. The episode is also equally critical of the gay vigilante group, who are depicted as distrustful of the police. Of course, it's hard to blame them after we overhear homophobic officers like Bosco expressing opinions about "fags" and "queers."

Gay political activists with a lynch mob-mentality are also featured in a compelling episode of *Law and Order* ("Pride"). The murder of San Francisco City Councilman Harvey Milk in 1978 by fellow ex-City Councilman Dan White provides the basis for this story about a gay city councilman, Richard Durban, murdered by an ex-cop-turned-right-wing-councilman, Kevin Crossly (Daniel Hugh-Kelly). Crossly claims that, despite their strong public policy differences, he and the deceased were actually friends.

But Crossly's defense team argues their client is being accused of murder solely because of his anti-gay views, which is what Crossly planned to do to hide his real motive. As Harvey Milk did to Dan White, Durban had managed to get Crossly voted off of the city council, so Crossly sought revenge. Although the evidence, largely circumstantial, makes it clear Crossly killed Durban, the jury's deadlocked. The conclusion (or lack of one) is in perfect sync with the episode's criticism of politicians who take certain ideological positions to win votes, as well as political groups that are too quick to rush to judgment.

Perhaps the DA's office should have used the same strategy they employed a few seasons later to convict a man of murder. In "Phobia," a gay man is beaten to death in broad daylight and his adopted baby snatched. The baby's mother, Celia (Catherine Kellner), an ex-junkie who gave it up for adoption, had notified the child's natural father, Robert Kelly (David Vadim) about his son. Kelly was upset his child was being raised by a gay couple, so he and Celia seized an opportunity to take the child. In the process, he beat the child's adopted father to death shouting "Faggot! Faggot!" The prosecutors are able to add a hate crime to the other charges and get a conviction, thanks mostly to Celia's testimony, offered in exchange for immunity. "Phobia" broadens the definition of hate crimes by demonstrating how they are the motivation for other criminal acts.

LIVE AND LET LIVE

In October 1998, 22-year-old Matthew Shepard was brutally beaten and left to die in a field on the outskirts of Laramie, Wyoming. Two locals, Aaron McKinney and Russell Henderson, pistol-whipped and robbed the gay University of Wyoming student before tying him to a cattle fence. Eighteen hours passed before his blood-drenched body was found. He never regained consciousness and died in a hospital five days later.

The murder and subsequent trial received national media attention because of the horrific nature of the crime that was so clearly motivated by hate. Henderson pleaded guilty to charges of kidnapping and felony murder. McKinney also entered a guilty plea, but his lawyers were prepared to argue that he was inebriated and under the influences of methamphetamines when Shepard allegedly came on to him, which triggered his childhood memories of being sexually abused. Judge Barton Voigt of the Second Judicial District Court of Wyoming barred McKinney's lawyers from using the "gay panic" defense because it was a form of temporary insanity or diminished capacity defense, neither of which are allowed under Wyoming law.

Henderson is currently serving two consecutive life sentences. McKinney was found guilty of first-degree felony murder and second-degree murder. He faced the death penalty, but in an impassioned speech to the judge, Matthew's father, Dennis Shepard, speaking on behalf of his family, recommended his son's murderer not be put to death.

"Mr. McKinney, I am going to grant you life, as hard as it is for me to do so, because of Matthew," Mr. Shepard said. "Every time you celebrate Christmas, a birthday, the Fourth of July, remember that Matt isn't."[55]

Shepard's life and death is the subject of three made-for-TV movies, beginning with *Anatomy of a Hate Crime*, which debuted in January 2000 to kick off MTV's year-long campaign, "Fight for Your Rights: Take a Stand Against Hate Crime." *Anatomy* is a well-intentioned, yet heavy-handed account of the events surrounding Shepard's murder. The first half focuses on Matthew (Cy Carter), who is portrayed as a sensitive, intelligent, and politically minded college student. He also suffers from bouts depression, is HIV positive, and has problems with intimacy, which is apparently linked to being raped by three men in Morocco. Unfortunately, the film doesn't have the time to examine any of these issues in any detail, so their significance in relation to Matthew's death is ultimately unclear.

Like many made-for-TV movies, *Anatomy* tries to cover too much territory and show the events leading up to and following Shepard's murder from the perspective of Shepard, his executioners, and their girlfriends, who help Henderson (Ian Somerhalder) and McKinney (Brendan Fletcher) hide the evidence. Serving as the film's narrator, Matthew reappears at the conclusion of the trial to reflect on whether his death accomplished what he had aspired to do with his life. It's an effective device, yet marred by the final moment — a touch of unnecessary theatricality — in which Shepard, walking near the site of his murder, turns to the camera and says "Don't forget me."

Following the film, MTV's John Norris hosted a discussion on hate crimes with two guests: Matthew's friend, Romaine Patterson and Jim Andersen, a representative of the Gay, Lesbian, Straight Education Network (G.L.S.E.N.). The segment serves as an introduction to an unprecedented television event. For next 17 hours, MTV interrupted its usual programming with a continuous loop of the first names of hate crime victims (including "Matthew") and a short description of the crimes committed against them. It's an extremely powerful strategy, even more than the preceding film, for spreading the word about the prevalence of hate crimes in a country where there is still no national Hate Crimes bill protecting all Americas on the basis of gender and sexual orientation.

In March of 2002, two made-for-TV movies about the Shepard case debuted one week apart. The first, NBC's *The Matthew Shepard Story*, doesn't stray too far from the TV movie formula. John Werrick and Jacob Krueger's well-crafted teleplay interweaves Matthew's life story with his parents' struggle to cope with their loss. More specifically, the story focuses on the decision Judy and Dennis Shepard must make regarding McKinney's fate. Should they ask for the death penalty or allow one of their son's murderers to live out the remainder of his life in a prison cell?

In a series of flashbacks that cover Matthew's high school years through the events leading up to his murder, we slowly come to understand Matthew (nicely played by Shane Meier), who is portrayed as an amiable but somewhat discontented young man. Matthew feels like an outsider, in part because he is gay, but also because in comparison to his peers, he never feels like his life has any real purpose. His anxiety is compounded by a traumatic incident: while on a school trip in Morocco, he is gang-raped by three men. The film suggests his emotional scars from the rape were the cause of his lack of direction during his teen years. Ironically, he is beginning to feel his life is just starting to have a purpose when it is suddenly cut short on that tragic October evening. As he explains to his best friend, Romaine (a superb Kristen Thomson), he enrolled in the University of Wyoming so he could "major in political science, become a diplomat, travel around the world, help people, and make the world a better place."[56]

As the Shepards, Stockard Channing and Sam Waterson are, as always, terrific, conveying a mixture of pain, grief, and anger. For a film produced with the cooperation of the Shepard family, it is surprisingly critical of the couple, who, over the course of the film, slowly recognize their limitations as parents who never fully understood what Matthew experienced as a gay man in a homophobic world. More importantly, they come to realize how, despite his daily encounters with homophobes (like the neighbor who hurls derogatory remarks at him and writes "fag" on his door), he had a touch of the idealist in him because he trusted people to a fault and was always able to see the good in them. "You are going to think the whole world hates you," he advises a friend who is about come out of the closet, "but you will be surprised who's standing in your corner." Thus, when the two narrative threads — Matthew's and his parents' — come together, we understand that the Shepards spared McKinney's life because it is what Matthew would have done.

Ironically, neither Matthew nor the Shepards are central characters in the second film, *The Laramie Project*, which premiered at the 2001 Sundance Film Festival before its March 2002 debut on HBO. The docudrama is based on interviews with residents of Laramie, who share their feelings and opinions about Shepard's murder, the trials, and their effect on the sleepy Wyoming town. The transcripts of the interviews, conducted by Moises Kaufman and members of the Tectonic Theatre Program, formed the basis of a stage play that received critical acclaim when its debuted in Denver in 2000, followed by a short run in New York and a national tour.

In adapting their play for the small screen, director Kaufman and his team of co-writers have crafted a powerful portrait of a community that brought closer together as the result of tragic events. *Laramie* gives the townspeople a voice — an opportunity to respond to the murder and the trials that put them in the national spotlight by the media, which many people felt painted Laramie and it residents as intolerant, ignorant, and homophobic. A few knew Shepard personally, while others, like the cyclist who found his body and the officer who arrived on the scene, were connected to him only through his death.

Their words are translated and interpreted by an impressive amalgam of actors from television, films, and the stage: Dylan Baker, Steve Buscemi, Nestor Carbonell, Kathleen Chalfant, Jeremy Davies, Peter Fonda, Joshua Jackson, Terry Kinney, Laura Linney, Amy Madigan, Camryn Manheim, Christina Ricci, Frances Sternhagen, and Lois Smith. Although the use of recognizable actors could have been distracting, in this case it proves to be an asset. These diverse actors offer uniformly subtle performances as they each take their turn on screen to offer their characters' perspectives.

There are some definite stand-outs: Jackson as the guilt-ridden bartender who served Matthew his last drink in the bar where he met McKinney and Henderson; Buscemi as a limo driver who befriended Matthew when driving him to Denver so he could go out to the bars; Linney as a polite, homophobic housewife who doesn't quite understand why so much attention is being paid to Shepard's death; and Davies as an enthusiastic drama student who defies his parents by playing a gay man in the U of W's production of *Angels in America*.

Out of respect for the grieving family, the writers decided not to interview the Shepards, though they appear as characters in a recreation of trial. The talented Kinney, a Chicago stage actor best known for his work on *Oz*, has the

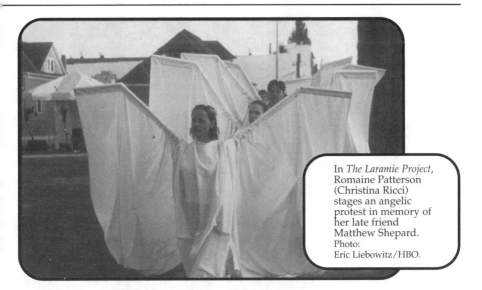

In *The Laramie Project*, Romaine Patterson (Christina Ricci) stages an angelic protest in memory of her late friend Matthew Shepard. Photo: Eric Liebowitz/HBO.

privilege of delivering Dennis Shepard's speech. Compared to Waterston, who, perhaps after all these years on *Law and Order* is too adept at addressing the court, Kinney's rendition rings truer because its less polished and theatrical.

The one character who does not appear in *The Laramie Project* is Matthew himself. Kaufman's choice not to include and/or recreate his image or voice reinforces Shepard's role as the film's structuring absence. In this case, it's not necessary because it is evident through the words of the people of Laramie that the effect he has had on their, and all of our lives, will endure.[57]

KILLER AIDS

In 1988, the television drama *Midnight Caller* featured a controversial episode about a bisexual, HIV-positive man deliberately exposing his male and female sexual partners to the virus. In "After It Happened," Jack Killian (Gary Cole), an ex-cop who hosts a late night radio talk show in San Francisco, is reunited with his ex-girlfriend, Tina (Kay Lenz). She asks Killian's help in tracking down a one-night stand, a man named Mike Barnes (Richard Cox), who got her pregnant and infected her with HIV. During his search, Killian meets Barnes's other victims: his ex-lover, Russ (J.D. Lewis), who Barnes abandoned when he became ill; and another one-nighter (Kelly West), who Killian advises to get tested. Killian finally locates Barnes, who feels no remorse for intentionally infecting his partners. "Why can't you understand? It's my life..." Barnes explains. "I have to live my whole life in one hundred nights."

Knowing he has no legal right to stop Barnes, Killian warns people about him on his radio show. Barnes hears the broadcast and threatens to sue him for

Talk show host Jack Killian (Gary Cole) tries to track down the man who knowingly infected his ex-girlfriend with the AIDS virus in "After It Happened," a controversial episode of *Midnight Caller*.

defamation. Their heated conversation is interrupted by Kelly, who, having discovered she's HIV positive, pulls a gun on Barnes. When Killian manages to talk her out of shooting him, a grateful Barnes asks why he saved his life. "Because your life is worth saving," Killian explains. (In an alternate ending to the script, Kelly reportedly wastes him.)

As the episode was going into production, the script for "After It Happened" was leaked to San Francisco AIDS activists. "Getting Screwed By NBC Is Not Safe Sex" was the headline of a leaflet inviting everyone to attend a protest march and rally on October 25 starting at the corner of Market and Castro Streets and ending at City Hall. The flyer accused NBC and Lorimar Production of issuing "shoot to kill orders" against anyone who's HIV positive:

> With 42,000 dead from AIDS in this country alone, HOW DARE THEY come to San Francisco to stir up violence and hatred against us. In the name of bringing big Hollywood bucks to S.F., the show's producers and the city's liason [sic] to the film company are willing to set up the gay, lesbian, and other AIDS-impacted communities as targets for continued violence. Because ACT UP successfully shut down filming on October 20th, the producers are trying to use the courts to silence our outrage..."Midnight Caller" will encourage a vigilante atmosphere that says it's O.K. to murder people with AIDS and those perceived to carry the virus (gay men, IV drug users and people of color). Both are dangerous and unacceptable.

Despite the court order Lorimar won to keep protestors away, filming around the city was disrupted.[58]

The protests didn't end when production wrapped on the episode. On the evening "After It Happened" aired (December 2, 1988), protestors stormed the offices of KRON-TV, NBC's affiliate in San Francisco, and demanded the station run a disclaimer during each commercial break. The station refused, but the following disclaimer did appear at the opening of the show:

> Tonight's episode of *Midnight Caller* deals with the topic of AIDS. San Francisco is a role model in AIDS education and has set the standard for effective and humane public policy. If you have any questions about this disease and want to learn more about AIDS, volunteers at the San Francisco AIDS Foundation are standing by to take your call at 800-FOR-AIDS.

The protest was the top story on KRON-TV's 11 o'clock news. Live coverage of the protest was followed by several AIDS-related stories, including a report on the AIDS quilt, which was on view at the Moscone Center; advancements in AIDS testing; and a new study on the development of the HIV virus in children.

Immediately following the news, KRON-TV aired a live, half-hour special news report entitled *Midnight Caller: The Response*, which gave San Francisco officials and community leaders the opportunity to air their concerns about the episode. Among the guests was Terry Beswick of ACT-UP San Francisco, who discussed how the series's producers ignored the organization's concerns about the episode's content. Dr. David Werdegar, San Francisco Director of Public Health, voiced his objections to how "After It Happened" presents vigilantism, rather than health education, as a legitimate response to the AIDS crisis. Werdegar also stressed how the episode inaccurately reflects the San Francisco gay community's response to the AIDS crisis. For example, there's no evidence of a support system for people with AIDS like Barnes's abandoned ex-lover, Russ.

The protestors' concerns were indeed legitimate. The episode clearly exploits the AIDS crisis by characterizing HIV as this mysterious, evil, unknown "other" lurking around dark street corners, rather than what it is — a disease transmitted by a virus from which we can protect ourselves by taking certain precautions. Furthermore, having the show's protagonist literally hunt down Barnes certainly legitimizes vigilantism as a response to people known to be HIV-positive.

Far more problematic than *Midnight Caller* is the premiere episode of Chris Carter's *Millennium*. The supernatural detective series from the creator of *X-Files* focuses on an ex-FBI agent, Frank Black (Lance Henriksen), who has the ability to see through the eyes of a killer. In the series's pilot, he helps track down a serial killer he characterizes as a man confused about his sexuality. Black believes the killer is fulfilling prophecy by trying to end the great plague (AIDS), which can only be "avenged by the blood of a just man." In one grisly scene, they discover one of his victims, a gay man buried alive in a coffin. Apparently the killer takes the blood of his victims then buries them alive before testing it for HIV. If the captive tests HIV positive, he dies.

Like Carter's other series, the long-running *X-Files*, *Millennium* is dark, moody, and intellectual. The clues left by the killer contain references to the Bible, Nostradamus's prophecies, and Yeats's poem "The Second Coming." Yet scripture and poetry can't mask what the episode is really about — a serial killer who hunts down gay men to rid the world of AIDS. Black doesn't actually say the killer is gay, but when he characterizes him as confused about his sexuality, the implication is clear enough. Due to his "confusion," his victims include women. GLAAD was certainly not pleased with the episode, which they argued "relied on out-dated stereotypes about gay men by presenting a violent gay serial killer...[who] hates women and thus murders a stripper and then kills a gay man in a public cruising area in Seattle because he is so ashamed of his own sexuality."[59]

Fortunately, most law and order dramas take a more humanistic approach to AIDS. In *The Equalizer*'s 1987 Christmas episode ("Christmas Presence"), Robert McCall (Edward Woodward) protects a six-year old boy, Mickey Robertson (Corey Carrier), from a neighbor who doesn't want the boy around. On *21 Jump Street* ("A Big Disease With a Little Name"), Det. Hanson goes undercover to protect an HIV-positive teenager, Harley Poolish (Philip Tanzini). Harley, a hemophiliac who supposedly contracted the virus through a blood transfusion, has been the target of death threats. He grows closer to Hanson and finally admits he's not a hemophiliac. He reveals, without actually using the "G word," that he is gay by comparing his father to Anita Bryant. The 1988 episode isn't only cautious in how it handles the gay issue; it also fails to mention that the HIV virus can be transmitted through heterosexual as well as homosexual sex.

Courtroom dramas like *L.A. Law*, *Law and Order* and *The Practice* have addressed legal issues — usually based on actual cases — that have been raised since AIDS was declared a national health crisis (as opposed to just being "that gay disease"). *L.A. Law* first approached the issue in 1985's "The Venus Butterfly." Deputy district attorney Grace Van Owen (Susan Dey) is forced to prosecute a gay man, Christopher Appleton (Peter Frechette), accused of mercy-killing his dying lover. Van Owen is clearly moved by Appleton's testimony, in which he describes the pain and suffering his lover endured, but feels obligated to enforce the law. When he is found guilty, Van Owen helps out his lawyer, Mark Gillian (Stanley Kamel), with their appeal ("Fry Me to the Moon"). She gives Gilliam information he can use for Appleton's retrial, which is granted when Gilliam admits to the judge that he wasn't prepared to defend his client and is therefore incompetent. Ironically, Appleton ends up thanking Van Owen, the woman who successfully prosecuted him, for her help.

Mercy killing is also the focus of *Law and Order*'s third episode, "The Reaper's Helper." Bobby Holland is found shot dead in his apartment and after questioning the victim's lover, they track down an acquaintance of Holland's named Jack Curry (once again, Peter Frechette). Curry admits to mercy-killing

Holland and other men with AIDS in San Francisco and Los Angeles. Executive Assistant District Attorney Ben Stone (Michael Moriarity) decides to prosecute, only to regret his decision when he finds out Curry has AIDS. But when a copy-cat killing occurs, he has no choice but to continue the trial. So Stone asks Dets. Greevy (George Dzundza) and Mike Logan (Chris Noth) to find a piece of evidence to help him dismiss the trial. Curry's lawyer learns about Stone's instructions to the detectives and uses the information as part of his client's defense. In a variation on the *L.A. Law* episode, Curry is acquitted and it is revealed Stone was actually the one who provided the defense attorney with the information that exonerated him.

Both of these shows question whether people who commit euthanasia should be prosecuted as criminals, even when they have the consent of their victims. Grace Van Owen and Ben Stone are both torn between following their moral conscience and enforcing the law. Their respective resolutions find a middle ground by having both DAs fulfill their legal obligations to serve the public yet work within the boundaries of the law to aid the defendants.

A series that took a more sensationalistic approach to the same topic is *New York Undercover*, created by *Law and Order*'s Dick Wolf. In "Without Mercy," a married bisexual man with AIDS poisons himself after infecting his wife with the virus. His former male lover, Hector (Vincent Laresca) doesn't believe he'd have committed suicide. So when a man treated by the same clinic dies from the same type of poison, Eddie (Michael DeLorenzo) goes undercover at the clinic as an intravenous drug addict with AIDS. When he starts asking around the clinic about where he can get some poison, someone slips something into his food, landing him in the hospital. Meanwhile, another patient, Judd Dawes (Charles Malik), despondent over being disowned by his family, admits to a clinic counselor, Jane Simmons (Amy Povich), he doesn't want to live. When Dawes is poisoned and goes into a coma, Eddie realizes Jane is killing AIDS patients because she didn't want them to suffer like her daughter, who she also poisoned. In the end, Jane fatally poisons herself.

"Without Mercy" takes an otherwise serious issue — mercy killing — and trivializes it by turning it into a motive for a paint-by-numbers whodunit. GLAAD was particularly critical of the episode because as in *Midnight Caller*, it perpetuates negative stereotypes about bisexuals: they spread AIDS to hetero-sexual women; they can only get AIDS through sexual contact with gay men, who are the "carriers of the virus to the rest of society;" and they're "deceptive, promiscuous" and have relationships with both sexes simultaneously.[60]

DISCRIMINATION SUITS

During *L.A. Law*'s eight-year run, the law firm of McKenzie, Brackman, Chaney, and Kuzak handled several discrimination cases. Some of the institutions, com-panies, and individuals targeted have included an insurance company that denies coverage to a lawyer with AIDS ("Since I Fell For You"); a doctor who refused to perform emergency surgery on an accident victim with AIDS ("Blood, Sweat, and Fears"); a cosmetics company who fired a model because she is a transsexual ("Speak, Lawyers for Me"); and the parents of a gay man dying of Lou Gehrig's disease who refuse to allow their son's lover to visit ("Smoke Gets in Your Thighs").

David Kelly, a former writer/producer on *L.A. Law*, continued to present gay-related cases on three of his subsequent series, *Picket Fences*, *The Practice*, and *Ally McBeal*. A job discrimination case on *The Practice*, reminiscent of the feature film *Philadelphia*, involves a childhood friend of lawyer Jimmy Berluti (Michael Badalucco) accused of discriminating against one of his employees with AIDS ("Honorable Man"). Peter Hines (Tom La Grua) is charged with violating Wayne Mayfield's (Jim Pirri) privacy by circulating a memo around the office stating that Mayfield has AIDS. Hines argued he did it to protect himself in case another employee had to administer emergency medical treatment to Mayfield without knowing his HIV status. Berluti agrees, until he realizes Hines really is a homophobic bigot, a point the lawyer implies in his closing statement. Mayfield wins the case, but Hines is only fined $25. The episode demonstrates quite clearly how homophobia can in fact be protected under the law, yet the small amount demonstrates what little importance is placed on the issue.

Something positive does comes out of the trial. Berluti picks up the telephone and calls his mother, who came out of the closet in an episode from a few seasons prior ("The Civil Right"). Berluti has had mixed feelings about his mother's lesbianism, particularly when she asks him to represent her in her attempt to legally marry her lover. The phone call suggests his experience with Hines has made Berluti reexamine his own prejudices about his mother's homosexuality.

Another David Kelly series, *Ally McBeal*, has featured several cases involving transgender clients. In "The Oddball Parade," John Cage (Peter MacNicol) defends four clients — an obese woman, a man who obsessively claps his hands and has verbal tics, another man described as "scary looking," and a cross-dresser, Matthew Vault (Anthony Anderson) — who are all fired from their jobs at a graphic design company because of their appearance. Cage, feeling like an oddball himself, decides to take the case. The humor on *McBeal* becomes suspect when it is derived from characters considered outside of the so-called "norm" of its neurotic, heterosexual world. Matthew, who returns in a later episode ("Prime Suspect") when his boss is murdered, and the other oddballs are treated sympathetically. At the same time, they become targets of McBeal and company's snippy quips.

This was particularly evident in a three-part episode involving a transvestite named Cindy McCauliff (Lisa Edelstein), who hires Fish (Greg Germann) and Ling (Lucy Liu) to represent her in a lawsuit against her employer for requiring her to have a physical exam ("Girl's Night Out"). As an anatomical male living like a female, she feels the exam violates her privacy. The problem comes when the lawyers' colleague, Mark (James LeGros), falls for Cindy. His colleagues aren't allowed to tell him she is anatomically a he because of lawyer-client confidentiality.

When Mark begins to date her ("Two's a Crowd"), he becomes the butt of jokes around the office, though he eventually finds out the truth when she presses up against him on the dance floor. The fact that Cindy is a man doesn't change Mark's feelings for her, until the next episode ("Without a Net"), in which Mark tries to deal with the situation by convincing Cindy to join a support group for odd couples.

Although Cindy is a well-developed, three-dimensional character, her central purpose seems to be to give the other characters the opportunity to crack cheap jokes, which GLAAD found problematic:

> Bigoted comments by every regular character on the show go unchallenged, and every character ended the storyline as transphobic as they began. (Nell hysterically claimed that Mark's relationship was a "circus act" that was "embarrassing for the entire firm." Fish gargled and used mouth spray because a transgender person kissed him. Cage called Cindy "it.")

GLAAD wrote a letter to Kelley requesting a meeting, which never happened. The organization's media director, Scott Seomin, did speak to the writers, who were planning to bring Cindy's character back. She appears briefly in "Love on a Holiday," in which the homophobic Fish participates in a male auction. Cindy gets revenge by having gay men bid on him. Seomin felt the episode, in his words, "sort of misses the point by 45 degrees. We want the transgender character to be treated with respect, not to seek revenge."[61]

Cindy finally receives the respect she deserves when she returns for her third appearance in "Hats Off to Larry." She wants Fish to represent her in her suit against the Commonwealth of Massachusetts, who won't let her marry her new boyfriend (Todd Eckert). Although some homophobic comments are still bandied about, as Bill Roundy of the *Washington Blade* observes, there is a definite shift in the way the other characters treat Cindy, who is now referred to as "she." Mark, who clearly still has feelings for Cindy, also comes to his ex-lover's defense, while Fish agrees to officiate at their non-legal wedding ceremony. Although they lose their case, Fish unloads a passionate trial speech in which he points out that "sex offenders can marry, murderers, cannibals can take vows — but two Gay people...Woah! There goes the sanctity." Roundy concludes that the episode "almost manages to erase memories of the earlier, offensive stories...showing characters growing out of their reflexive trans-phobia."[62]

CHAPTER THREE

DRAMA QUEENS
HOMOSEXUALITY AND DRAMATIC SERIES, MINI-SERIES, AND MOVIES OF THE WEEK

By the mid-1970s, the prime time closet door was wide open and homosexuality was the *issue du jour* on medical, police, detective, and courtroom dramas. But television's treatment of gay themes was not limited to these genres. Around the same time, other types of dramatic programming, such as prime time soaps, made-for-TV movies, and mini-series, started to feature gay and lesbian characters and deal with gay-related issues. Like the dramatic genres previously discussed, they aimed to educate viewers about homosexuality. Sometimes they succeeded, yet, like the other genres, their message was often muddled and riddled with contradictions.

As in the real world, television characters reside in a predominantly heterosexual world. When gay, lesbian, bisexual, and transgender TV characters visit Planet Hetero — either in a regular, recurring, or single episode capacity — they are often treated like alien invaders. TV programming is produced for a presumably heterosexual audience, so when a gay character is introduced, the focus is usually on the straight character (a parent, child, sibling, or friend) who has the greatest difficulty accepting a loved one's homosexuality. In the end, he or she (and the viewer as well) understands the importance of treating a gay family member or friend with kindness and respect.

In the 1970s through the mid-1980s, this scenario is the basic framework for single gay-themed episodes, multi-episode arcs, and central storylines for several dramatic series. Then, in the late 1980s, "quality" series like *thirtysomething*, *Northern Exposure*, and *Relativity* broke new ground by featuring characters that were treated less like outsiders and more like integral members of the show's ensemble cast. When the homosexuality of adult characters became less of an issue, the coming out stories shifted to teenagers and young adults, first in made-for-TV movies in the mid-1980s and then teen dramas in the 1990s.

THAT CERTAIN MADE-FOR-TV MOVIE

On November 1, 1972, ABC aired the first made-for-television movie about the subject of homosexuality. In *That Certain Summer*, 14-year-old Nick Salter (Scott Jacoby) visits his father, Doug (Hal Holbrook), a gay man living in the San Francisco area with his lover, Gary McClain (Martin Sheen). Not yet totally comfortable with his homosexuality, Doug isn't ready to tell Nick the real reason

In *That Certain Summer* (1972), the first made-for-TV movie about homosexuality, 14-year-old Nick Salter (Scott Jacoby, left) discovers his dad (Hal Holbrook, right) is gay.

he divorced his mother, Janet (Hope Lange), three years earlier. So Gary temporarily moves out of the house, yet still spends time with Doug and Nick, who is understandably confused about the nature of his father's close friendship with another man.

Over the course of the weekend, Nick grows increasingly suspicious. Then he finds his father's watch and reads the inscription on the back: "To Doug, With Love, Gary." An upset Nick telephones his mother, who senses there's something wrong and hops on the next plane. Nick spends the day wandering around the streets of San Francisco. When he returns to his dad's house, Doug has no choice but to tell have that certain father-and-son talk.

> DOUG: A lot of people, most people I guess, think it's wrong. They say it's a sickness, that it's something that has to be cured. I don't know. I do know it isn't easy. If I had a choice, it's not something I'd pick for myself. But it's the only way I can live...I lied to myself for a long time, why should I lie to you?...The hardest time I ever had was accepting it myself. Can you at least try to understand, please? Nick, I love you.[1]

Upset and confused, Nick packs his bags and goes home with his mother without even saying goodbye. "Give him a little time," Janet tells Doug. After they leave, Doug starts to cry. The final images, which also appear during the opening credit sequence of the film, are from home movies that depict a much happier Doug and a younger Nick playing together.

A somber yet powerful drama, *That Certain Summer* boasts an intelligent script by veteran TV scribes Richard Levinson and William Link and superlative performances by Holbrook, Sheen, Lange and young Jacoby, who received a supporting Emmy for his work. The film is essentially an adult coming out story. But instead of focusing on the obvious, like Doug leaving Janet for another man, which would have been difficult to explore in the film's 75-minute running time, Levinson and Link wisely chose a simpler and ultimately more interesting route.

When the story opens, Doug is already living with Gary but not yet completely out of the closet. He doesn't tell a flirtatious female client he's gay and doesn't approve of public displays of affection between men. When he sees Nick watching two gay men holding hands in the park, he expresses his disapproval to Gary, who questions whether his reaction is really coming from the part of him that's still ashamed about being gay. "It takes some of us a while to come all the way out," Gary explains. What Gary is implying is that Doug isn't all the way out because he hasn't told his son the truth. The overly protective Doug thinks Nick is too young to understand. As we soon see for ourselves, the teenager is not emotionally ready. But when he discovers the truth on his own, Doug has no choice but to have that certain father-and-son talk.

Doug's coming out speech to Nick was criticized by some gay activists who objected to the father telling his son "some people think it's [homosexuality] a sickness" and "If I had a choice, it isn't something I'd pick for myself." According to Levinson, ABC insisted those lines be inserted:

> Their feeling was somewhere in the script we had to introduce a character...who would give voice to prevailing public opinion. Meaning that they were reflecting a corporate concern over the fairness doctrine. They felt that we were taking a pro-homosexual stand and that the opposing view had to be aired. We strongly resisted, disagreeing with them totally, but finally we decided to have the homosexual himself, rather than some bigot imposed on the story, tell his son the harsh truth, that some people think homosexuality is a sickness — some people do — and that if he had his choice, he would not be a homosexual. We justified this in our mind by feeling that in a racist and bigoted society, it is simply more comfortable being rich, white and straight than poor, black, or gay.[2]

There's no doubt Levinson and Link's hearts and minds were in the right place. If only the latter part of Link's statement (about how it's more comfortable to be straight than gay in a bigoted society) was included in Doug's speech to clarify what the character meant by "*it's not something I'd pick for myself.*" To complicate matters more, the network wouldn't permit any on-screen physical contact between the two men, making them seem more like roommates than lovers. Of course, Doug does object to public displays of affection and the two men are seldom alone together, which makes it difficult for them to engage in even a little on-screen foreplay.

According to *The New York Times*'s television critic John J. O'Connor, one version of the script contained an alternate ending in which Nick admits to his mother at the airport that he "should've said goodbye to him." Cut to Doug, who is watching home movies, but isn't crying. O'Connor preferred the ending that was used because there was a more "subtle indication of an eventual reconciliation" which "was preferable in the over-all dramatic context."[3] What O'Connor also found preferable was how the film generally treated the subject matter in comparison to "A Very Strange Triangle," an episode of *The Bold Ones* that aired the very same week, which he characterized as "inane" and "superficial." "There is a need for the exceptional level of quality found in *That Certain Summer*," O'Connor suggests, "but that type of intelligence and sensitivity is essential for all television, from situation comedies to news specials."[4]

That Certain Summer broke new ground by portraying homosexuals as real people, rather than one-dimensional stereotypes. How honestly and accurately the film reflected gay life in America is certainly debatable, but there's a more important question: who exactly is the film's "intended" audience? Clearly, it was not gay male couples living in San Francisco, but heterosexuals who have never met a gay person (or so they think) that hopefully gained some new insight into gay male relationships and the emotional struggle many gay people endure as they seek acceptance from loved ones.

Since the early 1970s, TV has continued to offer viewers advice on how to (and how not to) treat their son, daughter, parent, and friend when he or she comes out of the closet. The trauma of coming out would continue to be a source of dramatic conflict, especially for teenagers, even as dramatic series and made-for-TV movies could then begin tackling other gay-related issues, such as homophobia, discrimination, and AIDS.

LATHERING UP

In 1964, ABC, the lowest-rated and most innovative of the three networks, successfully transported the daytime serial format to prime time with the premiere of *Peyton Place*. Based on Grace Metalious's bestseller, which was adapted for the big screen in 1957 (followed by a 1961 sequel), the series was set in a small New England coastal town. In addition to launching the careers of newcomers Mia Farrow and Ryan O'Neal, *Peyton Place* broke new ground on television with its treatment of what were considered "mature themes," such as adultery, pre-marital sex, illegitimate children, and suicide. The show's popular and healthy five-year run (at its peak, ABC ran three new episodes a week) insured the genre — which, for a long time, had been considered synonymous with daytime television — a future on prime time. As far as we knew, there were no homosexuals living in Peyton. In fact, homosexuality would remain one of the last of the great taboos for both daytime and prime time soap operas until the late 1970s.

The first bona fide non-heterosexual character introduced on a daytime soap opera was in 1977. *Days of Our Lives*'s Sharon Duval (Shelly Stark), an unhappily married bisexual, fell in love with one of the show's central characters, Julie Williams (Susan Seaforth Hayes), who made it clear she had no romantic interest in her (or any woman). Like many prime-time lesbian/bisexual characters on television in the 1970s, Sharon was confused and deeply troubled. After two unsuccessful suicide attempts, she was hospitalized and upon her release, she and her husband left Salem permanently.

Days opened the closet door — albeit in a not very flattering way — but it would take a long time for daytime soaps to work up enough nerve to take on the subject of homosexuality and feature gay, lesbian, and bisexual characters on a regular basis. Although not all gay characters are as fragile as Sharon, homosexuality would still generally be approached as an "issue," usually in the form of a big secret that would eventually be uncovered. Once their storyline drew to its conclusion, gay characters typically disappeared, though starting in the 1990s certain soaps, like *All My Children*, have let their gay characters stick around.

Around the same time that Salem's resident lesbian was having her nervous breakdown on *Days*, *Executive Suite*, a prime time CBS soap, introduced a similar character. Like *Peyton Place*, the series was based on a bestseller that had been a successful feature film in 1954. The short-lived drama focused on the professional and personal lives of executives working for the fictitious Cardway Corporation. In the tenth episode ("Re: The Sounds of Silence"), Julie Solkin (Geraldine Brooks), who's being physically abused by her husband Bernie (Norman Fell), admits to her best friend Leona (Patricia Smith) she is a lesbian. Bernie shares his suspicions about his wife's friendship with Leona with her husband, Andy (William Smithers). When Leona later admits to her lesbian friend that she does have feelings for her ("Re: What Are Patterns For?"), Julie follows an upset Leona into the street and is hit by a truck. At the funeral ("Re: The Identity Crisis"), Bernie blames Leona for his wife's death, causing a guilty and confused Leona to have a nervous breakdown.

It's no coincidence that all three women had troubled marriages: *Days*'s Sharon is unhappy with married life, while *Executive*'s Julie Solkin is being battered and Leona's husband is cheating on her. Lesbianism and bisexuality are thus positioned as alternatives to heterosexuality. So poor Julie must be killed off after awakening Leona's repressed lesbian tendencies that, in combination with her guilt over her friend's death, eventually turn her into a catatonic.

The only other non-heterosexual characters to appear on a nighttime soap opera in the late 1970s were featured on what were essentially parodies of the genre. *Mary Hartman, Mary Hartman* (1975-1977) followed the trials and tribulations of an off-the-wall suburban housewife (Louise Lasser) and her equally loopy family and friends. Among the residents of Fernwood, Ohio, was a bisexual named Annie "Tippeytoes" Wylie (Gloria DeHaven) and the Hartmans' neighbors, a gay couple who posed as the sons of fortune teller Betty McCullough (Vivian Blaine). When Mary's husband Tom Hartman (Greg Mullavey) temporarily moves in with Howard (Beeson Carroll) and Ed McCullough (Lawrence Haddon), he walks in on what he believes are the two brothers kissing.

The truth about Howard and Ed eventually gets around Fernwood and at one point, the couple even consider tying the knot.

Producer Norman Lear attempted to repeat the success of *Mary Hartman* with *All That Glitters* (1977), another syndicated soap set in corporate America, but with one major twist: traditional male-female roles are reversed, so it's the women who helm Globatron Corporation, while the men are either at home where they belong or taking dictation (when not being chased around the boss's desk). The cast featured a pre-*Dallas* Linda Grey as Linda Murkland, a male-to-female transsexual model.[5] The very presence of a transsexual character exposes the absurdity of a patriarchal (or in this case, matriarchal) male-female power structure that is, at its very core, rooted in biology. The series lasted only five months, perhaps because the sex-role reversal gimmick wasn't enough to sustain an entire series. Of course it may have been a matter of poor timing, considering *All That Glitters* aired in 1977, when the backlash against the feminist movement was in full swing and the defeat of the Equal Rights Amendment (in 1982) was on the horizon.

GAY/LESBIAN/BISEXUAL/TRANSGENDER CHARACTERS ON DAYTIME SOAP OPERAS (1977–)

ALL MY CHILDREN (1970–)

Dr. Lynn Carson (Donna Pescow) (1983): lesbian doctor who worked at Pine Valley Hospital.

Michael Delaney (Chris Bruno) (1995-1998): ex-Marine who taught history and coached basketball at Pine Valley High School. The school board unsuccessfully tried to fire him for being gay.

Kevin Sheffield (Ben Jorgensen) (1995-1998): gay teenager disowned by his parents.

Dr. Bradford Phillips (Daniel McDonald) (1996-97): orthopedic surgeon who fell in love with Michael Delaney.

Rudy (Lance Baldwin) (1995-1998): production assistant at local TV station WRCW.

Bianca Montgomery (Eden Riegel) (2000 -): daughter of Erica Kane (Susan Lucci) who eventually came out to her mother when she returned from boarding school.

Sarah Livingston (Elizabeth Harnois) (2000-2001): Bianca's lover in boarding school.

Mary Francis "Frankie" Stone (Elizabeth Hendrickson) (2001): the object of Bianca's affection who was murdered in December of 2001.

AS THE WORLD TURNS (1956–)

Hank Elliot (Brian Stracher) (1988-1989): designer who worked briefly with Barbara Ryan (Colleen Zenk Pinter), but left town to take care of his off-screen lover Charles, who was dying of AIDS.

THE CITY (1995-1997)

Azure C. Lee/Chen (Carlotta Chang) (1995-1996): male-to-female transsexual supermodel engaged to a clueless Bernardo (Phillip Anthony).

DAYS OF OUR LIVES (1965–)

Sharon Duval (Sally Stark) (1976-1977): bisexual woman who suffered a nervous breakdown.

THE DYNASTY DECADE

Daytime soap operas traditionally feature middle to upper middle-class characters, most of whom are white-collar professionals (doctors, lawyers, corporate executives, etc.). In addition, there are typically one or two super rich families under the thumb of a ruthless patriarchal figure, like *All My Children*'s Palmer Cortlandt and Adam Chandler, Sr.; *One Life to Live*'s Victor Lord and Asa Buchanan; *General Hospital*'s Edward Quartermaine; and *Days of Our Lives*'s Victor Kirakis. These men wield their power over the other characters because they control the family fortune. They have *some* good qualities, like loyalty when it comes to their families and an occasional pang of philanthropy when the local hospital needs a new wing. Still, most of the rich white old men who reside in TV towns like Pine Valley, Llanview, Port Charles, and Salem usually act out of their own self-interest or misguided paternalism, which frequently puts them at odds with their loved ones.

In the 1980s, the effects of wealth and power on the nuclear family became a familiar theme on daytime soap operas as well as the decade's new crop of prime

---

Harold (Ryan Scott) (2001-2002): friend of Princess Greta Von Amberg (Julianne Morris) who was hot for Jack Devereux (Matthew Ashford), when pretended he was gay.

GENERAL HOSPITAL (1963-)

John Hanley (Lee Mathis) (1994-1996): gay man with AIDS who helped pal Lucy Coe (Lynn Herring) with the annual Nurses Ball, an annual AIDS fund-raiser. Mathis died in 1996.

Ted Murty (Patrick Fabian) (1997-1998): teacher who Elizabeth Webber (Rebecca Herbst) mistakenly accused of rape, only to discover he's gay.

Elton Freeman (Loren Herbert) (2001-): flamboyant wedding planner who became Laura's (Genie Francis) campy, officious executive assistant.

ONE LIFE TO LIVE (1968-)

Billy Douglas (Ryan Phillipe) (1992-1993): gay high school student who turned to Rev. Andrew Carpenter (Wortham Krimmer) for advice, which started a scandal in Llanview.

Jonathan Michaelson (Bruce McCarty) (1992-1993): the lover of Rev. Carpenter's late brother, William, who died of AIDS. Jonathan made William's panel for the AIDS quilt, which was displayed in Llanview.

Rick Mitchel (Joe Fiske) (1992-1993): gay waiter who befriended Billy Douglas.

SANTA BARBARA (1984-1993)

Channing Capwell, Jr. (Robert Wilson) (1984-1985): character who was shot to death in a flashback in the soap's first episode and would be seen again in subsequent flashbacks.

THE YOUNG AND THE RESTLESS (1973-)

Kay Chancellor (Jeanne Cooper) (1973-) & Joann Curtis (Kay Heberle) (1975-1978): In 1977, Kay has a pseudo-affair with Joann, who had recently divorced her husband Jack. Kay become extremely possessive of Joann to the point where her son Brock fears his mother is turning Joann against men. Kay eventually admits she has feelings for her, but the storyline is dropped due to negative viewer reaction.

time soaps. The "fun" was put back into dysfunctional with the premiere of *Dallas* in April of 1978, and continued with the success of *Dynasty* and *Falcon Crest*. All three series benefitted from the change in America's economic climate during the 1980s, a period of prosperity the country hadn't seen since the Eisenhower era. As middle and upper-middle class Americans were transformed into a race of conspicuous consumers, those who were really, truly rich became even richer. As for the rest of us, who were denied the luxury of driving up the stock market to the breaking point (on October 17, 1987, a.k.a. Black Monday), we could live tele-vicariously through the Ewings and the Carringtons.

As on daytime soaps, the patriarchs who resided over prime time had the family's fortune and good name to protect. Even the slightest blemish on the family name could put the family's reputation and social standing in jeopardy. So what better blemish on the family name than a son who's not exactly "the marrying kind?" (Though, as we'll see, that's never enough to prevent a guy on a soap opera from getting married.)

Gay characters were conspicuously absent during *Dallas*'s 14-season run, but a plotline during the show's first season (1978-1979) did feature a minor gay character, the very handsome Kit Mainwaring (Mark Wheeler), who was briefly engaged to Lucy Ewing (Charlene Tilton), niece of the nasty J.R. (Larry Hagman). J.R. approves of the marriage, which he regards as more of a merger, because it will unite two of the city's most powerful oil families ("Royal Marriage"). Unfortunately, Kit is a closeted homosexual, a tidbit J.R. ironically uses to blackmail him into marrying his niece. Kit decides to come out to Lucy, who protects him from J.R. by pretending to break off the engagement because of Kit's insane jealousy. Much to J.R.'s dismay, the marriage and the merger are called off.

Although the situation is hardly original, both Lucy and J.R.'s brother Bobby (Patrick Duffy), who Kit turns to for help, are surprisingly sympathetic. When Kit tells Bobby he's gay, Bobby is of course concerned about Lucy getting hurt. However, he makes it a point to tell Kit he respects him for having the courage to come out. (Lucy puts on a brave front, but she is so traumatized by the break-up she turns to pills.) Bobby confronts J.R. about his scheme and tells him Kit has "a lot of guts" and is more of a man than him. Surprisingly, J.R. displays no signs of homophobia. His motives are, as always, purely financial; he is simply treating Kit the way he does anyone who stands between him and a fortune.

Kit is afraid to come out because he's a member of a wealthy, prominent family that is unlikely to accept his homosexuality. *Dallas* fans never actually find out what happened to him, but there was another rich gay kid waiting in the wings, ready to disgrace his family's name. When *Dynasty* premiered on January 12, 1981, with a three-hour episode, America received their first introduction to the Carringtons, another rich and powerful TV family who reside in a modest 48-room mansion in Denver, Colorado.

The premiere centers on the wedding of the Carrington family patriarch, Blake (John Forsythe), and his second wife, Krystle (Linda Evans). The pilot also introduces viewers to Blake's 23-year-old son, Steven (Al Corley). When Steven returns home for the big event, Blake tells his globe trotting son he wants him to start working at Denver-Carrington. But Steven, a liberal Democrat, disapproves of his father's business practices. (He accuses him of selling out the country by conspiring with the Arabs to fix oil prices.) Their ideological differences are not the real issue, however. Blake knows Steven is gay and, although at first he appears to have some insight into what he refers to as his son's "sexual dysfunction," it's soon clear he's not open to the possibility of having a gay son permanently.

> BLAKE: Steven, I am about as Freudian as you can hope for in a capitalist, exploiter of the working classes. When I am not busy grinding the faces of the poor, I read a little. I understand about sublimation. I understand how you can try to hide sexual dysfunction behind hostility toward a father. I'm even prepared to say that I can find a little homosexual experimentation acceptable just as long as you didn't bring home with you. But don't you see son, I'm offering you the chance to straighten yourself out.

> STEVEN: *Straighten myself out?* I'm not sure I know what that means. I'm not sure I could if I wanted to. And I'm not sure if I want to.

> BLAKE: Of course, I forgot. The American Psychiatric Association have decided it's no longer a disease. It's too bad, we could have endowed a foundation. The Steven Carrington Institute for the Treatment and Study of Faggotry.[6]

Blake's disdain for his son's lifestyle culminates in the accidental death of Steven's lover, Ted Dinard (Mark Withers). Upon walking in on Steven giving Ted a goodbye hug, an outraged Blake pushes Ted, who hits his head on the fireplace and dies. The season concludes with Blake's trial and the entrance of the prosecution's star witness, whose identity is revealed in the second season opener as Blake's ex-wife, Alexis Morrell Carrington Colby (Joan Collins).

In the second season, the producers proceeded to "soften" Blake, who receives two years probation for Ted's "accidental" death. The senior Carrington is still a ruthless capitalist, but when the five o'clock whistle blows, he turns back into a loving, caring husband and father. Unfortunately, he still disapproves of his son's "lifestyle," so he has no choice but to do the right thing and cut him out of his will and take him to court to gain custody of his grandson, Steven's son Danny. It would take the death of Steven's lover, Luke Fuller (*Once and Again*'s Billy Campbell) — in the bloody massacre that put a crimp in sister Amanda's (Catherine Oxenberg) Moldavian wedding — for Blake to start accepting his son's homosexuality.

Steven had the potential to be TV's first bisexual series regular, but instead of being sexually attracted to both sexes, he seems to be in a perpetual state of sexual confusion. Steven is also continually deceived, blackmailed, and victimized by his father, brother Adam (Gordon Thomson), and ex-wife Sammy Jo (Heather Locklear). While he is capable of committing the occasional act of heroism (like rescuing the family from Krystle's ex-lover), his character, on the whole, is far too passive and bland to sustain viewers' interest (including the gay ones).

If audiences, particularly gay men, continued to tune in to *Dynasty* (in the 1980s, Wednesday was *Dynasty* night in most gay bars around the country), it had more to do with Steven's mother, America's numero uno rich bitch, Alexis, deliciously played by Collins. Alexis became a bona-fide gay icon because everything about her was excessive and over-the-top, particulary her wealth, thirst for power, and wardrobe.

It's not surprising the three networks tried to capitalize on the success of *Dallas* and *Dynasty* by adding more soaps onto their prime time line-up. Only two series found an audience: *Falcon Crest* (1981-1990), starring Oscar-winner Jane Wyman as the owner of a family vineyard; and *Knot's Landing* (1979-1993), the long-running spin-off of *Dallas* about the lives of California suburbanites. Although neither series featured gay characters, several of the short-lived clones included a regular or recurring gay male character, typically a friend and confidante of the series's heroine.

The success of the 1982 miniseries *Bare Essence* spawned a short-lived series in the spring of 1983 starring *General Hospital*'s Genie Francis as perfume maven and heiress Patricia "Tyger" Hayes. Every heiress needs a gay friend, and Tyger has Robert Spencer (played by Morgan Stevens in the miniseries, Ted LePlat in

TEN REASONS WHY GAY MEN LOVED DYNASTY

1. Alexis vs. Krystle, particularly the cat fights involving mud or water.

2. Their gowns (and those shoulder pads!) designed by Nolan Miller.

3. The characters had names like Dex, Fallon, Caress, Kirby, and Dominique. Just like real people.

4. During its nine-season run, the cast featured Helmut Berger (Peter de Vilbis), Ali McGraw (Lady Ashley Mitchell), George Hamilton (Joel Abrigore), Diahann Carroll (Dominique Deveraux), and Rock Hudson (Daniel Reece) in supporting roles.

5. Even the producers were the first to admit when the show started to go too far (i.e., the Moldavian Massacre of 1985).

6. All imitations paled in comparison.

(Remember *Bare Essence*? *Berrenger's*? *Flamingo Road*? *The Colbys*? *King's Crossing*? *The Hamptons*?)

7. The Carrington Mansion, the exteriors of which were shot in two different California locations (San Francisco and Pasadena).

8. When roles were recast, no one seemed to notice that Fallon (Pamela Sue Martin) disappeared and returned with a British accent (Emma Samms); Amanda lost her British accent when Catherine Oxenberg was replaced by Karen Cellini; and Steven (Al Corley) grew two feet when he had plastic surgery and was replaced by Jack Coleman, only to look again like Al Corley for *Dynasty — The Reunion*, the 1991 ABC miniseries.

9. The jewelry! The jewelry!

10. Big hair. Lots of it.

the series), who dates a professional football player named Tim (Jim Negele). *Paper Dolls* (1984), another miniseries spin-off set in the model and fashion industry came complete with its very own gay hairdresser, Conrad (Jeffrey Richman). Gay male characters fulfilled similar roles in other miniseries. In *Sins* (1986), Joan Collins plays Helen Junot, a French woman who runs a fashion magazine empire and seeks revenge on a man who destroyed her family during the Nazi occupation. Helen befriends a Black American photographer named Jacques "Jake" Danvers (William Allen Young), whose photography contributes to her success. As Keith Howes, author of *Broadcasting It*, observes, even though his main purpose is to help "set the heroine's career in motion...it is rare for a black gay character — 'escaping from a number of prejudices' — to be presented in such a debonair, positive way."[7] Howes also points out that Jake not only has his own theme music but an off-screen sex life, with a member of his laboratory staff and possibly with his "sexy assistant, played by Timothy Wood."[8]

Lesbians were also included in the fun. One of the most provocative made-for-television movies of the 1970s, *In the Glitter Palace*, has enough decadence, vice, and violence for an entire season of *Dynasty*. The two-hour film stars *Medical Center*'s Chad Everett as Vincent Halloran, a lawyer hired by his ex-girlfriend, Ellen Lange (Barbara Hershey), to defend her lesbian lover, Casey Walker (Diana Scarwid). Casey is falsely accused of murdering Norma Addison (Gloria LeRoy), who is blackmailing Casey and several other lesbians. In addition to Ellen and Casey, the film contains an assortment of lesbian characters, including Daisy Dolon (Carole Cook), a gay-club entertainer; Ricky (Lynn Marta), a mother hiding a child she lost to her husband in a custody battle; Grace Mayo (Tisha Serling), who is paid by Norma to seduce her victims; and Kendis Winslow (Salome Jens), a judge also being blackmailed by Norma.

In a feature article in *The Advocate*, Newt Dieter, who consulted on the film with fellow Gay and Lesbian Media Task Force member Sheila Bob, outlined their role in working on the script from its initial conception to the production:

> We point out things that are wrong. We try to put some life into a piece of work from a gay perspective. We try to help non-gay writers, producers, directors, actors and actresses understand a bit of what it means to be gay, to walk in our shoes...Our principal goal is our own elimination. There should be no need for a Gay Media Task Force. If we're successful, there won't be.[9]

Los Angeles Times critic Kevin Thomas was apparently impressed with the Task Force's work. In his review, he described the lesbian characters in this "standard melodrama" as "recognizable humans." They come from all walks of life and then range from saints to sinners, from the successful to the tragic — just like everyone else." He argues the film's "virtue" lies in the fact that "it has the effect of raising consciousness about the plight of gay people without being unduly preachy."[10]

According to the press release from the Columbia Pictures Television publicity department, the film aimed to take a "sincere, serious and non-sensational look at lesbianism and how it affects the lives of several people." Yet not all critics agreed. Writing in *NewsWest*, Terry deCrescenzo lambasted the film for depicting lesbian life as all about "murder, blackmail, violence, sick relationships, victimization, despair, prison, disaffected homes, insanity and, of course, bars and drugs."[11]

In the *Dynasty* Decade, the threatening lesbian characters that inhabited the television movies of the 1970s were replaced by their more chic, stylish sisters. These women posed a different kind of danger, particularly to inexperienced young women who were trying to find themselves in the cruel, cold world. The 1981 television miniseries version of Jacqueline Susann's *Valley of the Dolls* (which unfortunately lacked the camp quality of the original 1967 film), featured a Parisian lesbian artist, Vivienne Moray (Camilla Sparv), who befriends a down-on-her-luck Jennifer North (Veronica Hamel). Poor Jennifer has no man, no job, no friends, and a drug problem. Vivienne paints her portrait and the two become lovers just long enough for Jennifer to be "rehabilitated" back to a "normal" (meaning heterosexual) life. Jennifer is grateful to Vivienne, who she describes as an "incredible woman." Keith Howes describes the lesbian love in the film "as a glamorous retreat, a cleansing, a halfway house, a necessary but temporary stopping-off point before returning to the basics of everyday life."[12] But not all women are rescued from the clutches of their lesbian benefactors. In *Scruples* (1980), fashion editor Harriet Toppingham (Gene Tierney) keeps a tight leash around ambitious actress Melanie Adam (Kim Cattrall), as she introduces her to fame, alcohol, and drugs.

Lesbianism was also presented as an option for lonely heterosexual women in search of some companionship. In the made-for-TV movie, *My Two Loves*, widow and single mother Gail Springer (Mariette Hartley) befriends an executive, Marjorie (Lynn Redgrave), who she later discovers is a lesbian. Gail said she had no idea because Marjorie doesn't look gay. "We don't all wear black leather and ride a Harley Davidson," Marjorie explains. Their friendship turns into an affair, much to the dismay of Gail's mother (Sada Thompson) and her old friend, Ben (Barry Newman), a male chauvinist who is romantically pursuing her. The premise of this 1986 made-for-TV movie, co-written by lesbian author Rita Mae Brown (*Rubyfruit Jungle*), bears a striking resemblance to the 1972 "Very Strange Triangle" episode of *The Bold Ones*. They also share a similar ending. Gail, who must decide between Marjorie and Ben, chooses neither. Again, her choice seems to be between lifestyles, not individuals. Like Gail, television was still not ready to commit either way.

LATHER, RINSE, REPEAT

While most attempts to imitate *Dallas* and *Dynasty* were short-lived, producer

Aaron Spelling successfully adapted *Hotel*, Arthur Hailey's best-selling novel, for the small screen. Like two other successful Spelling series, *The Love Boat* (1977-1986) and *Fantasy Island* (1978-1984), *Hotel* (1983-1988) featured a new batch of guest stars each week that checked into the St. Regis Hotel with their suitcases and emotional baggage. They were greeted by the staff and the hotel's owner, Mrs. Victoria Cabot (Anne Baxter), who took over the St. Regis when her sister-in-law, Laura Trent (Bette Davis) took an extended vacation that lasted the entire run of the series (any resemblance to *All About Eve* was most likely intentional). When they were not busy dealing with their own mini-dramas, Mrs. Cabot and her staff never hesitated to get involved with their guests.

For a swanky hotel located in the heart of San Francisco, the St. Regis ironically played host to a steady stream of homophobic and "gay-nervous" guests. The gay-themed stories featured early in the show's five-season run were conventional "coming out" plotlines. In "Faith, Hope, and Charity," a playwright, Zan Elliot (Carol Lynley) invites her best friend, Eileen Weston (Barbara Parkins) to town for the premiere of her new play. Eileen freaks out when she finds out Zan is a lesbian, but once she reads what she has to say about friendship in her play, all is well. In "Transitions," Maggie (Deirdre Hall), wife of TV sportscaster Larry Dawson (Robert Reed), gets an even bigger shock when she finds her husband in the arms of another man, his director, Biff Henry (Granville van Dusen). In "Mistaken Identities," Ed Curwin (Steve Kanaly) tries to get closer to his introverted son, Ron (Lance Kerwin), whom he fears is gay. But when Ron's plan to set his son up with a hooker is foiled by a vice-cop, it drives them even farther apart.

These stories were neither original nor groundbreaking in their approach to topics like bisexuality and homophobia. Yet, just as the new crop of television dramas that debuted in the mid-1980s (*St. Elsewhere*, *Hill Streets Blues*, and *L.A. Law*) were zeroing in on more specific gay-related issues (like gay bashing, discrimination, and AIDS), *Hotel* started to feature more issue-oriented story lines.

For example, a 1986 episode ("Scapegoats") examined the relationship between a gay hotel waiter, Joel (Leigh McCloskey) and a homophobic bartender, Frank (Ken Kercheval). When Frank discovers he has AIDS, he's convinced he contracted the disease from Joel, who is actually HIV negative. Upon hearing the news, Frank's ex-wife, Sheila (Rita Taggart), is horrified because in her mind, if he has AIDS, he must be gay. "How could you do that to us, Frank?" Sheila asks, "You have a son! What are you going to tell him? That his father is a character out of *Boys in the Band?*" But when his son Elliot (*Melrose Place*'s Doug Savant) hears the news, he assumes his father is a member of another high risk group — IV drug users.

When Frank collapses from pneumonia, it's the understanding Joel who rushes to his side and manages to reunite his sick friend with his family. The "mystery" surrounding Frank's HIV status is solved (he contracted the virus through a blood transfusion), but as Joel explains to Sheila, "even if he had been fooling around with guys, no one deserves a disease like this. It's not God's punishment, Sheila. It's a virus! It kills little kids too!" The thought that it kills gay men alone was apparently still not enough to elicit sympathy from viewers in 1986.

"Scapegoats" also raises some important questions about AIDS and the workplace. When the hotel management staff learns Frank is in the early stages of AIDS, they wonder what action they should take, if any. They agree not to get caught up in the AIDS hysteria, yet General Manager Peter McDermott (James Brolin) suggests asking Frank to take a medical leave. But as his assistant Christine (Connie Sellecca) points out, that would be the same as asking him to quit. The management never has to take any action because Frank is suddenly hospitalized with pneumonia. Upon hearing the news, Mrs. Cabot takes a personal interest in Frank's welfare and decides to put him on medical leave with full salary and benefits. As she explains, it's not out of kindness, but what any loyal employee deserves.

The three remaining episodes touch slightly on issues that would receive national attention in the 1990s. In "Undercurrents," a U.S. Army officer, Nick Hauser (Jan-Michael Vincent) gets a much-needed lesson in tolerance when he discovers best friend and fellow officer, Roger Gage (Boyd Gaines), is gay. The truth comes out when Roger is gay-bashed by a gang, but he can't report it for fear it will end his military career. The St. Regis's bellhop, Dave Kendall (Michael Spound), who coincidentally happens to be Roger's old friend, tries to talk some sense into Nick. The same gang of gay-bashers, who mistake Nick and Dave for a gay couple, interrupts their conversation. Doing his part to keep the streets of San Francisco safe, Nick kicks their homophobic butts. Afterwards, Nick commends Roger for his courage, but tells him he has to end their friendship because he can't accept his homosexuality ("It's how I was brought up"). Roger decides to come out and press charges against the bashers, even if it means a dishonorable discharge.

Hotel also tackled the issue of gay parenting. In "Rallying Cry," 11-year-old Jodi Abbott (Missy Francis) is left by her late mother to a gay couple, Dr. Michael Vaughn (Doug Barr) and his lover, Alex Halpern (Michael Sabatino). Jodi wants to live with Michael and Alex, but her aunt and uncle, Nora (Marion Ross) and Cameron Wheeler (Lloyd Bochner), don't believe homosexuals should raise a child. So they take Michael and Alex to court and are granted custody. When an unhappy Jodi runs away to be with Michael and Alex, Mrs. Cabot intervenes and brings both couples together. Nora, who's concerned for her niece's happiness, manages to convince Cameron to let them live with Alex and Peter. Cameron gives in, but he is still unhappy.

The final gay episode also revolves around a legal matter. In "Contest of Wills," a young woman named Joanne Lambert is killed in an accident. When Joanne's father (Dick O'Neill) arrives to claim the body and her belongings, he discovers his daughter was a lesbian and had been living with Carol Bowman (Christopher Norris), the hotel's catering manager. Mr. Lambert tries to get Carol fired from the St. Regis and then demands she return a family heirloom

Joanne gave to Carol. But when the two start going through Joanne's possessions, they start to bond. In the end, Carol accompanies her "father-in-law" back to Maine for the funeral.

Gay-bashing, gays in the military, and custody suits are complex issues. While there is certainly limited time an hour episode to give them the attention they warrant (especially when an episode contains not one, but two or three plots), the producers of *Hotel* deserve credit for addressing topical issues that are important to the gay community. Of course the basic conflict is always resolved in the end, thanks to a meddling member of the hotel staff, yet the writers demonstrate some restraint and never completely sugarcoat the resolution. For example, although his wife has a change of heart, Cameron Wheeler still disapproves of his niece being raised by two gays. After going a few rounds with gay bashers, Nick admits no one deserves to be victimized, but he still ends his friendship with Roger.

For the 1984-1985 television season, *Hotel* ranked twelfth in the overall ratings. *Dynasty* and *Dallas* were, respectively, first and second in prime time, while *Knot's Landing* came in ninth. The following season, *Dynasty* and *Dallas* lost their top slots to a pair of situation comedies — *The Cosby Show* (#1) and *Family Ties* (#2) — and dropped down, respectively, to seventh and sixth. The ratings of the other prime time soaps, though still respectable, were slipping (*Knot's Landing* #17, *Hotel* #22, Falcon Crest #24). Meanwhile, the highly publicized *Dynasty* spin-off, *The Colbys*, which debuted in November of 1985, didn't even make the top thirty. Although the series was renewed for another season, the spin-off never found an audience, so ABC spun it off for good in March of 1987.

Why the sudden, steady decline in the popularity of prime time soaps? Perhaps viewers had had enough of the increasingly ridiculous plots: *Dynasty's* violent royal wedding massacre in Moldavia; Bobby Ewing's return from the dead via the shower, which meant the entire 1985-1986 season was his wife Pam's (Victoria Principal) bad dream; Fallon's abduction by aliens in *The Colbys's* second season finale and her return to earth in the Mojave Desert in the Fall 1987 *Dynasty* season opener. Or maybe the American public was no longer impressed with the lifestyles of the rich and overly dressed, particularly when greed became a dirty word following the stock market nosedive of October 1987.

The Carringtons did survive through the 1988-1989 season, when it sunk to 71 in the ratings during its final months. The cast was reassembled one last time for a four-hour miniseries, not surprisingly entitled *Dynasty: The Reunion*, in November of 1991. Al Corley resumed the role of Steven Carrington, who is now living happily ever after in Washington D.C. with Bart Fallmont (Cameron Watson). In the miniseries, Steven's relationship with his father has greatly improved. He even helps Blake get his company back after a hostile takeover by an international business consortium that brainwashes Krystle and orders her to shoot Blake.

4616 MELROSE PLACE

It was only a matter of time before a prime time soap as sensationalistic and trashy (but in a fun way) as *Dynasty* would sneak back onto the prime-time schedule. During its seven season run (1992-1999), *Melrose Place* was never a ratings success, but it did develop a cult following. In the 1990s, it was the show everyone was watching, though most fans were too embarrassed to admit it (including Jerry Seinfeld, who, on a memorable *Seinfeld* episode, fails a polygraph test he is forced to take when he tells the female cop he's dating that he's never watched the show).

Created by Darren Star, who spun the show off his other series, *Beverly Hills, 90210*, *Melrose Place* follows a group of twentysomethings living in the trendy Melrose district of Los Angeles. The original eight residents included a medical student and his wife, an aspiring actress, a motorcycle mechanic, a receptionist, a writer, and a handsome gay social worker named Matt Fielding (Doug Savant). Despite its over-hyped premiere in the summer of 1992, the show failed to find an audience, but was saved from cancellation by switching to a serial format (in the early episodes, the plot lines didn't continue). The other major change was the addition of three new bad girls: advertising executive Amanda Woodward (played by *Dynasty*'s Heather Locklear), the devious Sydney Andrews (Laura Leighton), and the resident psychopath, Dr. Kimberly Shaw (Marcia Cross).

There was more partner switching at *Melrose Place* than at a square dance, yet the writers and producers had no idea what to do with their lone homosexual. Like Steven Carrington, Matt has a moral conscience, which is dangerous in soap opera land because it makes you an easy target for blackmailers, homophobic employers, abusive boyfriends, and psychos (see page 127 for a comprehensive comparison of Steven Carrington and Matt Fielding). It's not just that bad things happen to Matt. Whenever he appeared to have found Mr. Right, the Fox Network immediately put the brakes on any display of physical affection between the two men. Meanwhile, the heterosexual characters were free to play musical beds.

The network's hypocrisy was challenged when Fox insisted the producers cut a scene of Matt and another guy kissing. In "Till Death Do Us Part," Matt discovers he has something in common with Billy's (Andrew Shue) best man, Rob (Ty Miller). Billy doesn't know Rob is gay until he sees his two friends locking lips in the courtyard. Unfortunately, the audience doesn't get to see the kiss because Fox, concerned about the loss of advertising revenue, forced the producers to cut away before their lips touch. GLAAD criticized the decision and asked, "What are the censors afraid of in a simple kiss? Why can't Matt be a full human being like the rest of his heterosexual counterparts?"[13] GLAAD also took a full page ad out in *Daily Variety* (May 10, 1994) which read: "Fox — Censorship Is Un-American. Don't Censor the Creative Community and Don't Censor Our Lives." Co-creator/producer Darren Star also voiced his objections and insisted the producers received letters from both gay and non-gay viewers urging them to further develop Matt's character. "The viewers are more sophisticated," said Star, "than advertisers, or than advertisers...give them credit for."[14]

GLAAD raised the issue once again when in a November 1996 episode Matt asks his current squeeze, Dan (Greg Evigan), to spend the night ("Farewell Mike's Concubine"). Dan wants to take it slow, so slow that the scene ends with the couple giving each other a goodnight *hug*. GLAAD offered Matt some good advice: "If you don't feel comfortable kissing someone good night you probably shouldn't invite them in for a sleepover."[15] At a time when gay characters are so visible in films and on television, it's no longer sufficient to simply *tell* us Matt is gay. We expect him to have some semblance of a gay life on screen. The double standard is blatant, particularly on a hyper-hetero show like *Melrose Place* that requires a flow chart to keep track of who is sleeping with whom.

In the sixth season opener ("Brand New Day"), Matt gets custody of his late brother's daughter, Chelsea (Katie Wright) and moves north to San Francisco. But the producers were not content with letting Matt live happily ever after. One year later, the residents of Melrose Place learn Matt was killed in a car crash ("The World According to Matt") while visiting Los Angeles. Matt's mom gives Amanda her son's diary, which is chock full of gossip about his former neighbors. Amanda begins reading ("It's like reading a trashy novel, except you know all the people.") and discovers Kyle (Rob Estes) has a brother, Michael (Thomas Calabro), who works as a male stripper in a Chicago club, Jane (Josie Bisset) slept with her college friend on the eve of her wedding, etc. (Of course Matt's journal revealed little about its author because he was never allowed to have a life.) In the end, his death was nothing more than a cheap plot device used to put some spark back into a series that was on its last legs. Ironically, it seemed an appropriate farewell for a character that never got his fair due.

Matt and his string of troubled boyfriends were not the only gay characters on the show. When Matt departs, the series's "gay slot" is filled by a lesbian named Connie Rexroth (Megan Ward), a friend of Billy's fiancée, Samantha Reilly (Brooke Langton). Connie tries to create friction between the couple by getting a drunk Billy to kiss her. Only Billy gets a tip from Samantha's ex that it's really Connie who Samantha is after. GLAAD acknowledged that many viewers might welcome a "wild gay character," especially on a show full of "hypersexual heterosexual psychos." But they were also concerned that people might see "this portrayal of a scheming psycho lesbian in the tradition of *Basic Instinct*" problematic.[16] Fortunately, the situation never goes that far because when Billy confronts Connie, she apologizes and scrams.

Melrose Place was a cult hit in the 1990s, yet it was the only post-*Dynasty* soap done in the same "over the top" 1980s style to enjoy a long, healthy run. In fact, *Melrose*'s many imitators, including a cheesy spin-off, *Models, Inc.* (1994-1995), and Darren Star's more "upscale" *Central Park West* (1995-1996), barely lasted a season each. Even Aaron Spelling, one of the most successful television producers of all time, made several ill-fated attempts to revive the prime time soap. His list of casualties include *2000 Malibu Road* (1992), *Savannah* (1996-1997), *Malibu*

	DYNASTY'S STEVEN CARRINGTON (1958-)	*MELROSE PLACE'S* MATTHEW FIELDING (C. 1967-1998)
FATHER	Blake Carrington	Matthew Fielding, Sr.
MOTHER	Alexis Morell Carrington Colby Dexter Rowen	Constance Fielding
SIBLINGS	Adam, Fallon, Amanda, and Krystina	Luke (deceased)
WORK HISTORY	Political Activist President, Denver-Carrington Manager, pro football team Executive, Colbyco Laborer, oil rigs in Colorado and Indonesia	Doctor, Wilshire Memorial Medical student Social worker, Wilshire Memorial & L.A. Halfway House for Teens
MALE LOVERS	Bart Falmont, Washington lobbyist Luke Fuller, executive assistant in Colbyco public relations dept. (deceased) Ted Dinard (deceased)	Dan Hathaway, physically abusive rehab doctor Alan Ross, closeted actor Paul Graham, framed Matt for wife's murder Jeffrey Lundley, closeted naval officer
HETERO MARRIAGES	Claudia Blaisdel, married in 1983, divorced in 1986 Sammy Jo Dean, married in 1982, divorced in 1983	Katya Petrova, Russian doctor who married Matt in October 1993 to stay in the U.S.; returned to Russia in December 1993
CHILDREN	Danny Carrington, son with Sammy Jo	Stepfather to Katya's daughter, Kiki, who returns to Russia in December 1993 Legal guardian to Luke's daughter, Chelsea
VICTIM	Father accidentally kills his brother; cuts him out of his will for being gay; tries to gain custody of Danny Harassed by oil rig workers for being gay; falsely accused of sabotage; injured in rig explosion Hits his head and almost drowns in Carrington swimming pool Arrested for beating up blackmailer	Gay bashed by three thugs and subsequently fired from teen center for being gay; donates $10,000 settlement to gay legal defense fund Assaulted by men hired by Kimberly because he refused to alter her psychiatric evaluation Fired from hospital by homophobic doctor Develops pill addiction, enters rehab, and gets involved with abusive rehab doctor Fights with ex-sister-in-law for custody of his niece; he loses the case, but she gives her to Matt anyway

Familiar gay faces from prime time: *Dynasty*'s troubled son, Steven Carrington (Al Corley, left) and *Melrose Place*'s resident victim, Matt Fielding (Doug Savant).

Shores (1996), and *Titans* (2000). The failures of these and other *Dynasty/Melrose Place* clones were due in part to a shift in the viewing publics sensibility in the 1990s toward dramatic series with less glitz and more grit, like *ER*, *Law and Order*, and *N.Y.P.D. Blue*. The character-driven dramas of the 1990s, including those not set in a high school, hospital, or police station, were also more, for want of a better word, realistic. Like their prime time predecessors, they did retain some of the elements of daytime serials: continuing story lines; characters dealing with family, relationships, and work-related problems; and the occasional tragedy or crisis. Yet, the characters were not, like the Carringtons and the Ewings, in the top income bracket, but rather, in the tradition of daytime serials, white collar professionals from middle or working class families. Furthermore, every conflict was not reduced to a battle between good and evil. Instead, prime time dramas in the 1990s, shows like *thirtysomething*, *Sisters*, and *Relativity*, emphasized their characters' emotional struggles.

KEEPING IT REAL

To expose the hatred, fear, intolerance, and ignorance at the root of homophobia, dramatic series and situation comedies generally approach homosexuality as an issue. When a series like *Dynasty* and *Melrose Place* included a gay character as a series regular, sustaining the character's homosexuality as an "issue" challenged producers. Consequently, characters such as Steven Carrington and Matt Fielding were never developed to their full potential. Steven was essentially a hetero-curious homosexual, while Matt became a professional victim who landed in a series of unhealthy relationships. The limitations placed on both characters were imposed to some degree by the producers, often in response to the network, whose primary concerns were, as always, ratings and advertising revenue.

The shift to a more realistic style had a profound effect on how prime time dramas both represented and utilized gay characters. The sexual orientation of a gay or lesbian character was no longer an ongoing problem, nor the only aspect of his or her character. Consequently, gay characters were not only more three-dimensional, but no longer had to be treated as a stand-in for an entire sexual minority.

One of the first and best was *thirtysomething*, a slice-of-life character drama about seven yuppies — two couples and their three single friends, two of whom marry during the show's four season run. In *Television's Second Golden Age*, Robert J. Thompson includes *thirtysomething* in his discussion of "quality television" programs of the 1980s. Thompson lists the attributes that set series like *L.A. Law*, *Cagney and Lacey*, *Northern Exposure* (1990-1995), *Twin Peaks* (1990-1991), *Picket Fences* (1992-1996), and *thirtysomething* (1987-1991) apart, such as:

1. appeal to young, upscale urban viewers
2. have a large ensemble cast and characters that develop and change over time
3. are literary and writer-based
4. are willing to tackle controversial issues, including homosexuality
5. create a new genre by mixing old ones (i.e., a dramedy like *Northern Exposure*) or take a traditional genre and transform it (i.e., *Hill Street Blues*, *thirtysomething*, *Moonlighting*)
6. are self-conscious, particularly in terms of allusions to high and popular culture, including television
7. aspire toward "realism"[17]

Thompson recounts how the critics and the public were split over *thirtysomething*'s seven main characters. Apparently, many people felt they were nothing more than whiny yuppies. Fans of the show, which garnered several awards, including the Emmy for Best Drama Series in its first year, praised it for emphasizing character over plot and taking its time to examine the minutiae of everyday life.

In the second season, photographer Melissa Steadman, wonderfully played by Emmy winner Melanie Mayron, befriends an artist, Russell Weller (David Marshall Grant), who she concludes is gay upon overhearing his phone conversation about a friend recently diagnosed with AIDS ("Trust Me"). Although Russell is only featured in five episodes and his appearances are spread out over the course of seasons two through four, we're led to believe his friendship with Melissa has evolved off-screen. White, handsome, articulate, and upscale, Russell is by all appearances cut from the same cloth as the seven main characters. The fact he is gay, the mark of difference that marginalized characters like Steven Carrington and Matt Fielding, is entirely incidental. The producers assumed that was just fine with their viewers, so there was no need to include the standard "gay is O.K." speech.

In a memorable and, at the time, controversial episode ("Strangers"), Russell has a one-night stand with Peter Montefiore (Peter Frechette), who works for the same advertising agency as Melissa's cousin, Michael (Ken Olin). In the introduction to his publicized teleplay, writer Richard Kramer responded to all those who believed it was politically incorrect to have Russell and Peter sleep together on their first (and only) date. "That may be," Kramer explained. "I was trying to write people and not role models."

The fact that Peter and Russell have a one-night stand was not the issue. The controversy stemmed from a scene in which the pair are shown in bed together having a post-sex conversation about their first girlfriends, the friends they lost to AIDS, and the Italian translation of Peter's last name (Montefiore means "mountain of flowers"). Kramer had intended to conclude the scene with the men embracing, but ABC already had sponsors pull their ads to the tune of $1.6 million (nixing any rerun over the summer), so the scene contains no physical contact.

But "Strangers" should be remembered for what it does show — Russell and Peter lying in bed talking, just like Michael and Hope (Mel Harris), Elliot (Timothy Busfield) and Nancy (Patricia Wettig), and Melissa and her boyfriend Lee (Corey Parker). Kramer saw Russell and Peter as a mirror for Melissa and Lee, who have entered that stage in their relationship when one partner starts to have doubts. In this case, it's Melissa, who thinks her friends are judging her for going out with someone much younger. Her fears come to life in a series of embarrassing vignettes, in which Lee meets her friends for the first time. Eventually, Melissa realizes it's her own self-judgment that is distorting how others perceive their relationship. She starts questioning whether they should be together for the same reason Russell never phones Peter back after their first date: the fear of letting someone get too close to you — so close you expose your true self to them.

The episode breaks new ground in terms of how gay characters are fully integrated on a thematic level into the storyline without homosexuality being "the issue." Nor are the gay characters "heterosexualized" to the point of bleaching their gayness out. In addition, "Strangers" and a subsequent episode in which Peter discovers he is HIV positive ("Closing the Circle") also demonstrate how the prevailing straight male mentality is either oblivious or paternalistic to the "gay other." For example, Michael initially had no idea Peter was gay until Melissa told him, which is interesting considering that Michael is his boss. Furthermore, Peter tells Russell during their pillow talk session that he doesn't want to make his co-workers uncomfortable (liberal Michael Steadman hardly seems the kind to care), yet he does make the point of saying he won't lie to take a day off from work to attend a friend's funeral.

The issue is raised once again during the show's fourth season in an episode written by Kramer and Pulitzer Prize-winning writer Paul Monette, who died of AIDS in 1995. "Closing the Circle" focuses on Michael's inability to let go of his friend Gary (Peter Horton), who is killed in an accident. Michael feels obligated to "fix" everything, though the people he is trying to help don't want it. He assists Susannah (Patricia Kalember) with settling her late husband's estate, but she doesn't want or need Michael's financial or emotional support. Michael becomes equally frustrated when Peter baits the agency's owner, Miles Drentell (David Clennon) into firing him when they disagree over how to handle an account. When Michael rushes to the rescue, he finds out the real reason why Peter is upset — he's HIV positive. He tries to counsel him as one friend to another, but as Peter rightfully points out, their friendship is limited to the office — Michael doesn't really know anything about him or his life. In the end, Peter actually does follow Michael's advice and returns to the agency because he needs his health insurance benefits.

Following the cancellation of *thirtysomething* in 1991, series creator Marshall Herskovitz and Ed Zwick branched out into feature films. Their production company, Bedford Falls, remained active in television and produced several subsequent quality hour dramas, such as *My So-Called Life* (1994), *Relativity* (1996-97), and *Once and Again* (1999-2002). Despite the critical attention all three received, only *Once and Again* survived longer than one season.

Created by *My So-Called Life* writer Jason Katims, whose other credits include the teen alien drama *Roswell* (2000-2002), *Relativity* included among its regulars a young lesbian named Rhonda (played by the terrific Lisa Edelstein, who later played a pre-op transsexual on *Ally McBeal*). The series stars an attractive couple, Isabel (Kimberly Williams) and Leo (David Conrad), who meet and fall in love in Italy and continue their romance at home in Los Angeles. The situation is complicated by Isabel's existing engagement to straight-laced boyfriend Everett (Randall Batinkoff).

In the second episode ("Just One More Thing"), a parallel is made between Isabel's break-up with Everett and Rhonda's break-up with her lover Sylvie (Kathryn Morris). As in *thirtysomething*, the fact Rhonda's a lesbian isn't an issue. She's a strong-minded, slightly neurotic woman who maintains a strong emotional bond with her brother, who offers her his love and support (and even accompanies her to a lesbian bar to spy on Sylvie).

In the same episode, there is a memorable scene in which Rhonda and Isabel share Leo's bed (he gets the couch). In a rare moment of female bonding that transcends the usual heterosexual-homosexual boundaries, Rhonda and Isabel lie together, discussing and sharing their feelings about ending their respective relationships. The scene even caught the attention of GLAAD, who commended the producers for making Rhonda a "full, complex, and realistic character" and presenting "a fair and accurate look at the life of a lesbian..."[18]

GLAAD also took notice when a January 11, 1997 episode featured a full, honest-to-God, on-screen kiss between Rhonda and her new girlfriend Suzanne

(Kristin Dattilo), an earthquake expert. The scene was fully integrated into the episode, which also contained a love scene between Leo and Isabel in which he asks her to marry him — a proposal that catches both of them off-guard.

Rhonda was not the only lesbian character featured on a 1990s prime time drama. *Sisters* is an old-fashioned nighttime soap about the lives of the four Reed sisters (a fifth was added in April of 1993) who live in the small town of Winnetka, Illinois. Among its large ensemble cast is a straight-talking, no-nonsense gay TV producer played by *Saturday Night Live* veteran Nora Dunn. Norma Lear (as opposed to Norman) is a perfect match for Alex (Swoosie Kurtz), the oldest, wealthiest, and certainly the most colorful member of the family, who gets her own local talk show, *Alex Live!*

Initially, she has difficulty warming up to Norma, who is abrasive, ambitious, and resentful of Alex landing her own show (the previous host had a heart attack on camera and Alex, who was his guest, was forced to take over). Once they clear the air and open up to one another, Norma reveals she is a lesbian. Of course, Alex misinterprets Norma's sudden change in attitude as a romantic overture (Alex even feels uncomfortable getting undressed in front of her). When Alex's mother Bea (Elizabeth Hoffman) hears about Norma through the Reed sister grapevine and brings up the subject to her daughter, Alex doesn't want to discuss it because she thinks her mother doesn't even know what a lesbian is. But Bea knows more from Alex because her best friend (who Alex refers to as "Aunt Evelyn") is a lesbian. As Bea explains, once she came out to her, it brought them closer together. Alex gets the message and apologizes for her behavior. Norma assures her she's only interested in her as a friend and colleague. Their friendship is sealed.

Although the situation is hardly original, it's a bit of a stretch to think Alex, who seems smart and worldly, as least by Winnetka standards, would jump to the conclusion Norma is interested in her. Within in the context of the series as a whole, the episode ("Something in Common") serves as a starting point for their friendship, A gay-straight friendship between two women or men is rare on television. So despite the show's heavy-handed and, at times, maudlin treatment of subjects like divorce, breast cancer, and euthanasia, the producers are to be commended for allowing us to see Norma and Alex's friendship develop, even though Norma's homosexuality is still occasionally an "issue."

In subsequent episodes, Norma is forced to come out to her parents, Ben (John Lehne) and Gladys (Elizabeth Franz) when Alex arranges a surprise visit without Norma's knowledge so they can see their daughter win an award ("Life Upside Down"). Norma tries to remedy the situation by convincing Alex's brother-in-law Mitch (Ed Marinaro) to pose as her husband. But Norma comes to her senses and puts an end to the charade, even though she runs the risk of losing her parents. Ben tells his daughter he is proud of her, but Gladys is less receptive. When Norma gives birth to her daughter ("Deceit"), Gladys attempts to sue her daughter for custody. If anything, Norma adds some much needed spice to the series, created by Ron Cowen and Dan Lipman, who'd go on to adapt the British miniseries *Queer as Folk* for American television.

OFF THE BEATEN PATH

In his analysis of "quality television" in the 1990s, Robert Thompson asserts that the "shocking iconoclasm for its own sake became more associated with 'quality' than solid stories told in more traditional ways."[20] "Quirky" is the word critics used most often used to describe dramas like *Twin Peaks, Northern Exposure,* and *Picket Fences,* all of which featured off-beat characters living in a small, remote town where surreal and inexplicable events often occur. The respective settings of each series — Twin Peaks, Washington; Cicely, Alaska (*Northern*); Rome, Wisconsin (*Picket*) — seem tailor-made for characters that live off the beaten path and are considered, for whatever reason, to be on the margins of the heterosexual mainstream.

OSCAR AND WALT

Two important figures from gay literary history, playwright Oscar Wilde (1854-1900) and poet Walt Whitman (1819-1892), take center stage in two unusual 1990s TV westerns.

"Oscar"
Ned Blessing: The Story of My Life
(CBS-TV)
September 8, 1993

Ned Blessing was a notorious bandit sentenced to hang for his crimes. Each episode of this short-lived CBS western begins with Ned (Brad Johnson) in his jail cell writing his memoirs. In "Oscar," Ned recalls meeting Oscar Wilde (Stephen Fry) during his American tour. Fry, who later portrayed the writer in the 1998 bio-pic *Wilde*, described his role as "a small cameo, more of a ring than a brooch...It wasn't an insult to Oscar, however: it showed a knowledge of his kindness and physical strength and did nothing to perpetuate the idea prevalent in some people's heads that he was a mimsy, brittle sort of creature with crimped hair, an enormous buttonhole, and a smart line in self-satisfied repartee."[19] Wilde's homosexuality isn't addressed in the episode, except for Ned's final-scene reference to Wilde's imprisonment for indecency. Having known a few indecent men in his time, Ned considers Wilde to be one of the decent ones.

This wasn't Wilde's first appearance in a television western. He also appears as a character in a 1958 episode of *Have*

Gun, Will Travel ("The Ballad of Oscar Wilde"), in which gunslinger Paladin (Richard Boone) is hired to protect the playwright (John O'Malley), who is kidnapped and held for ransom.

"The Body Electric"
Dr. Quinn, Medicine Woman (CBS-TV)
April 5, 1997
Written by Christine Berardo
Directed by Gwen Arner

Walt Whitman (Donald Moffat) pays a visit to Colorado Springs, Colorado, in this intelligent episode about homophobia in the Old West. When word gets around town the poet is "the kind that prefers the company of men," his poetry reading is canceled. Dr. Mike (Jane Seymour), a good liberal at heart, comes to his defense, but must deal with her own homophobia when her young son Brian (Shawn Toovey), an aspiring journalist who wants to interview Whitman for the local newspaper, starts spending time alone with him. She realizes her fears are unfounded and organizes a poetry reading outside town. Moffat's splendid as Whitman in this well-crafted tale set in the 1860s, with a timeless message about not only accepting, but appreciating our differences.

In a world in which everything and everyone is a little bit off, gay and transgender visitors often feel right at home. When D.E.A. Agent Dennis/Denise Bryson (David Duchovny) arrives in Twin Peaks to investigate drug theft allegations against Special FBI Agent Dale Cooper (Kyle MacLachlan), he's wearing a dress. Bryson explains that while posing as a transvestite during a sting operation, he realized wearing women's clothing relaxes him. Cooper is amazed by Bryson's discovery and is completely supportive of his lifestyle choice.

Another fictional town that lies far to the northeast of Twin Peaks is Cicely, Alaska, the setting for the CBS drama, *Northern Exposure*. In the pilot episode, a young New York doctor, Dr. Joel Fleischman (Rob Morrow), arrives in Cicely to fulfill his service to the state of Alaska, which picked up his $125,000 med-school tab. Fleischman has difficulty adjusting to living in a small town, particularly one that's in the middle of nowhere and inhabited by a group of eccentric characters, such as the strong-minded Maggie O'Connell (Janine Turner), a bush pilot from Grosse Point; the philosophical Chris Stevens (John Corbett), the local disc jockey who served time for grand theft auto; and the enterprising Maurice Minnifield (Barry Corbin), an ex-astronaut with a $68 million fortune who wants to turn Cicely into a tourist mecca.

When Ron (Doug Ballard) and Erick (Don R. McManus) arrive in Cicely ("Slow Dance") and offer to transform an abandoned building on Maurice's property into an inn, he's glad to sell it to them. He's also pleased to discover he has so much in common with his new neighbors — they're also ex-Marines who love antiques, gourmet cooking, and show tunes (Maurice's collection includes the complete Mitzi Gaynor and a bootleg Ethel Merman). What he doesn't know is they're a gay couple, which sends homophobic Maurice into a tizzy. When he discovers the truth, he gives Chris his show album collection, soufflé dish, and fondue pot. Chris warns him about overreacting, because men who freak out about homosexuals usually have tendencies themselves. But Maurice still doesn't want Cicely overrun by "nancy boys," so he backs out of his offer. Erick and Ron think he's just using the "no fairies" rule to jack up the price. They make Maurice a higher offer, which he can't refuse because it wouldn't be wise to let his personal feelings interfere with a business deal.

With the exception of Maurice, Erick and Ron are completely welcomed in Cicely because it's a town where people from different social, cultural, ethnic, and economic backgrounds peacefully co-exist. In the episode's final scene, a slow song is playing on the jukebox at the Brick, Cicely's main (and only) hangout. Everyone is slow dancing to the music, including Ron and Erick, though nobody seems to notice or care that the two men are dancing together. Then again, they're not the first same sex couple to dwell in Cicely (see pg. 134).

Maurice is also the only voice of dissent when the couple decides to tie the knot after eight years. The whole town is invited to the wedding, which Maurice has no intention of attending; even though, according to Erick's mom (Joyce Van Patten), her son looks up to Maurice as a father figure. When Erik has a fight with Ron over the wedding arrangements, he tells Maurice he's leaving town.

Maurice finds himself convincing Erick to go ahead with the wedding because he and Ron seem as "happy as a couple of cuckoo birds" and it'd break his mother's heart (which Maurice points out he did once already with his "proclivities"). So the Reverend Chris Stevens, who obtained his divinity degree through an ad in the back of *Rolling Stone*, pronounces the couple "married."

"I Feel the Earth Move" is typical of the series, which often centers on an event that brings the Cicely community together. Producer Diane Frolov describes Cicely as a "non-judgmental universe...[where] a gay marriage is a natural part of the fabric of this place."[21] Unfortunately, two CBS affiliates in the deep south, KNOE-TV of Monroe, Louisiana and WTVY-TV of Dothan,

"Cicely"
Northern Exposure (CBS-TV)
May 19, 1992
Written by Diane Frolov and Andrew Schneider
Directed by Rob Thompson

This remarkable episode, which tells the tale of the founding of the show's fictional setting — Cicely, Alaska — was the highlight of the 1991-1992 television season.

We learn about the town's early history from one who was there, 108-year-old Ned Svenborg (Roberts Blossom), who returns to Cicely one day for the first time in eighty-three years. We flashback to 1909 and meet a nameless town's inhabitants (played by the series regulars), that is under the control of the evil Mace Mobrey (the turn-of-the-century counterpart to Cicely's current resident millionaire, Maurice Minnifield). While Mace is out of town, the kind-hearted and beautiful Cicely (Yvonne Suhor) arrives with her lover Roslyn (Jo Anderson). The women plan to transform the community into the "Paris of the North" — a utopian society rich in art and culture. The women begin by holding a salon featuring a modern dance performance by Cicely and a poetry reading by Ned.

But the women's dream is soon shattered when Cicely falls ill and Mace returns to reclaim the town. Roslyn attempts to make peace with Mace, but when one of his trigger-happy gunmen tries to shoot her, Cicely steps in front of her and is shot. She dies in Roslyn's arms. The tragedy puts an end to all the feuding in the town, which is named

Cicely in her memory. Afterwards, Roslyn remains in Cicely, where she lives as a recluse for several years. One day, she suddenly leaves and is never heard from again.

The story of Cicely and Roslyn, which is alluded to early in the series (Maurice insists their relationship was strictly platonic), reveals not only the origin of the town's name, but the ideals on which Cicely was founded: a sense of community and the deep appreciation and respect of individuals' differences. Lesbian couples are still rare on television, and even rarer is the depiction of a female couple with such intelligence and tenderness as Roslyn and Cicely, wonderfully played by Anderson and Suhor. "Cicely" is a truly remarkable hour of television.

Alabama, believed there was nothing natural about two men getting married, and chose not to air the episode. In addition, the Nestlé Corporation withdrew sponsorship at the last minute. Still, CBS stood by the episode and accused the two affiliates, in the words of one spokeswoman, of "condemning a program they haven't seen, and we think the program is in good taste."[22] Meanwhile, The Rev. Donald E. Wildmon, president of the American Family Association, referred to CBS's decision to "give the homosexual lifestyle such warm approval" as "tragic."[23] He accused the networks of caving in "to pressure from the radical wing of the homosexual movement."[24]

On the other end of the spectrum, GLAAD/LA Executive Director Lee Werbel criticized the episode for not showing the couple kissing: "Stripping of a big part of an important aspect of any individual's life is rude, insensitive, and sends a clear message to society that gay people are very different...[it's a] real kick in the face to lesbians and gay men, and non-gay people across the country."[25]

"Don't mess with Cicely:" the founders of *Northern Exposure*'s Cicely, Alaska, Roslyn (Jo Anderson, seated) and Cicely (Yvonne Suhor).

According to Frolov, the producers decided not to turn Erick and Ron's marriage into an issue, which they knew would happen if the two men kissed. "The things the show is really about will get lost if all people are focusing on is the idea of two men kissing," Frolov explains, "That's what happened with *Roseanne*. The episode ["Don't Ask, Don't Tell" with Mariel Hemingway] wasn't even about that kiss."[26] Is the absence of a kiss at the end of the ceremony noticeable? While I understand Frolov's rationale, have you ever been to a wedding where the couple didn't kiss at the end of the ceremony?

PUBLIC (INCLUDING HOMOSEXUALS) TELEVISION

CBS, as well as the other networks, make programming decisions based on the potential appeal of a series, TV movie, or special to a mainstream audience. When more people are watching, the ratings are higher, which translates into increased advertising revenues and more money in the pockets of the network and their shareholders. The networks don't necessarily shy away from trying something new or dealing with controversial subject matter, particularly if it will attract viewers. They have also renewed some "quality series" that received critical acclaim but didn't score high ratings, like *Picket Fences* (four seasons) and *thirtysomething* (three seasons). Both shows did, however, have strong appeal among 18- to 34-year-old men and women.[27]

Some of the most innovative and original programming dealing with the subject of homosexuality has aired on the Public Broadcasting System (PBS) and cable television, which includes both commercial channels (Lifetime, MTV) and pay channels (Home Box Office, Showtime). These three alternatives to the major commercial networks — public TV, commercial cable, and pay cable —

make programming decisions based on their respective target audience and the means by which they generate revenue or, in the case of public television, private or public funding.

PBS has certainly been the leader in presenting both fictional and non-fictional gay-related programming. As the chief importer of British television in the United States, PBS introduced American audiences to such gems as *The*

WAY OFF THE BEATEN PATH

In *Sexual Generations: Star Trek: The Next Generation and Gender*, Robin Roberts examines how science fiction has been used to critique social attitudes toward gender and feminist issues, including sexual orientation.[27] Science-fiction series set in the distant future or in a galaxy far, far away provide the perfect setting for showing homosexuality as anything but alien. The following episodes give us a glimpse of what the future may hold:

"The Host"
Star Trek: The Next Generation
May 13, 1991
Written by Michael Horvat

Dr. Beverly Crusher (Gates McFadden), the Enterprise's Chief Medical Officer, falls in love with Odan (Franc Luz), who is being transported by the Enterprise for a peace conference. Odan's a Trill, a human parasite who lives inside a male or female human host body. When Odan is injured, the Trill temporarily enters Commander Riker (Jonathan Frakes) until a replacement body arrives. While inhabited by Odan, Riker and Beverly make love. The body arrives and the transfer is made. Dr. Crusher is shocked because Odan is now a woman. A female loving another female is completely natural for Odan, but not for Beverly. "Maybe someday our ability to love won't be so limited," confesses Beverly. Before saying goodbye, the Trill says "I will never forget you."

"The Outcast"
Star Trek: The Next Generation
March 16, 1992
Written by Jeri Taylor

Soren, a member of the J'naii, an androgynous race, seeks help from Commander Riker to rescue the J'naii's lost space shuttle. Soren admits having "female tendencies" to Riker, which are considered deviant by the J'naii. Soren and Riker fall in love, but when her tendencies are discovered, she is put on trial. Riker's

efforts to save him/her fail, and even though Soren is a hero, he/she is brainwashed back to a "normal" androgynous state. As Roberts points out, the episode, particularly the military-style courtroom scene, "emphasizes the parallel between Soren's situation and that of gay and lesbian members of the armed forces."[28]

"Rejoined"
Star Trek: Deep Space Nine
October 28, 1995
Written by René Echevarria
Story by René Echevarria and Ronald D. Moore

When a team of Trill scientists arrives to conduct experiments, the group includes Lenara Kahn (Susanna Thompson), who, in a previous host, was the wife of Dax's (Terry Farrell) host, Torias. According to Trill law, society forbids reassociation between loved ones of a past host. Dax and Lenara fall in love and although he is willing to risk everything, she'd rather not be exiled from her homeworld.

"Racing Mars"
Babylon Five
April 24, 1997

Posing as a newlywed couple, Dr. Stephen Frank (Richard Biggs) and Marcus Cole (Jason Carter) travel to Mars to infiltrate the planet. The episode treats same-sex relationships in a very matter-of-fact manner as the two men show affection and bicker about their in-laws — just like a few gay couples I know.

Naked Civil Servant (1979), starring John Hurt as writer Quentin Crisp, who defied social convention by living openly and unapologetically as a homosexual in England from the 1930s through the 1960s; *Brideshead Revisited*, a superb, faithful adaptation of Evelyn Waugh's novel about a British army captain (Jeremy Irons), who recalls his "special relationship" with a rebellious aristocrat (Anthony Andrews) and his oppressive family; *An Englishman Abroad* (1984), based on the friendship between actress Coral Brown (who plays herself) and gay British spy Guy Burgess (Alan Bates) during her trip to Moscow in 1953; and *Breaking the Code* (1997), a fascinating portrait of mathematician Alan Turing (Derek Jacobi), who cracked the Nazi's military code and subsequently struggled to live his life openly as a gay man after being declared a national hero.

One trait these British dramas share is how homosexuality and gender issues are linked to social and political themes, particularly class relations and national identity. Although they contain gay characters, homosexuality isn't *the issue*, but rather an integral part of a larger critique of the oppression in a patriarchal Britain. By comparison, American television series and made-for-TV movies only began to integrate gay characters into story lines in the late 1980s/early 1990s. Even now, television in the U.S. rarely comes close to addressing social and political themes with the same complexity as the British.

One definite sign of progress was the six-hour PBS miniseries version of Armistead Maupin's *Tales of the City*, presented by PBS's *American Playhouse*. The novel originated in serial form in the *San Francisco Chronicle* back in 1976, and featured an assortment of colorful and loopy characters — gay, straight, bisexual, transsexual — living in San Francisco in the 1970s. Like Maupin's book, the miniseries captures the vitality and spirit of gay life in the pre-AIDS era as it follows the intersecting lives of over a dozen characters. The action centers on an apartment house at 36 Barbary Lane, home to new-girl-in-town Mary Ann Singleton (Laura Linney), bohemian Mona Ramsey (Chloe Webb), her gay soul-mate Michael "Mouse" Tolliver (Marcus D'Amico), and their landlady, the free-spirited Mrs. Anna Madrigal (Olympia Dukakis), who harbors a big secret.

Tales originally aired on PBS in two-hour installments on three consecutive nights. The miniseries format provided writer Richard Kramer (*thirtysomething*) ample screen time to introduce, develop and intertwine each character's story line, an impossibility in a two-hour theatrical film or made-for-TV movie.

In Maupin's world, characters that are traditionally marginalized on the basis of their gender identity and/or sexual orientation are at the center of the narrative. At the same time, they're not relegated to some "sexual ghetto," for the richness of Maupin's book derives from the way a wide variety of characters — from Mary Ann's conservative boss Edgar Warfield Halcyon (Donald Moffat), to straight liberal ex-lawyer Brian Hawkins (Paul Gross), to black model D'Orothea/Dorothy Williams (Cynda Williams) — occupy the same world.

The miniseries was produced by Channel Four Films, Britain's commercial television station, which over the years has produced, co-produced, and aired a long list of gay-themed fictional and non-fictional features and miniseries, including *My Beautiful Laundrette* (1985), *Maurice* (1987), *The Celluloid Closet* (1995), *Hollow Reed* (1996), *Bent* (1997), *Like It Is* (1998), *Paragraph 175* (1999), and *Metrosexuality* (2001). Like these and other Channel Four productions, there is explicit "gay content," particularly in bedroom scenes between Michael and his new beau John (Billy Campbell). Unlike the "Strangers" episode of *thirtysomething* (also penned by Kramer), they are permitted to actually touch and even kiss. While a scene such as this is nothing new for British audiences, a few red flags were raised in the States before the program even aired.

Several PBS affiliates received phone calls from irate viewers, who demanded that the station not broadcast the miniseries. WTCI-TV in Chattanoga,

---

RIGHT-WING TARGETS

Over the years, PBS has been the target of right wing religious and conservative groups, who have objected to their funding and presentation of non-fictional programming that addresses social and political issues affecting our daily lives. Here are two examples:

Tongues Untied July 15, 1991 Directed by Marlon Riggs.	*It's Elementary: Talking About Gay Issues in School* June 1999 Directed by Debra Chasnoff.

Riggs, who died of AIDS in 1994, describes his 55-minute video as "a nationwide community of voices — some quietly poetic, some undeniably raw and angry — which together challenge society's most deeply entrenched myths about what it means to be black, gay, a man, and above all, human."[30] When *P.O.V.* decided to program the piece, nearly half the PBS affiliates decided not to air it, and some that did were the subject of indecency complaints filed with the Federal Communications Commission. Right wing groups seized the opportunity to lobby Congress and the FCC because both Riggs and *P.O.V.* received government funding through the National Endowment of the Arts. Conservative newspapers also had a field day. Dick Williams of the *Atlanta Constitution* denounced *Tongues* as "without a doubt the most explicitly profane program ever broadcast by a television network."[31] The *Washington Times*'s Don Kowet concurred, suggesting that the film belongs "in the bawdy leather bars that litter such gay havens as Castro Street in New York, but not on public television. Unless the 'P' in PBS now stands for "Pornographic."[32]

Academy Award-winner Debra Chasnoff (*Deadly Deception: General Electric, Nuclear Weapons, and Our Environment*) directed this controversial documentary that explores how educators can address gay and lesbian-related issues, such as prejudice, discrimination, and, depending on the age group, violence against gay, lesbian, bisexual, and transgender people. Right wing religious organizations such as the American Family Association and the Family Research Council spearheaded a campaign to stop PBS affiliates from airing the piece. In Idaho, Frank Vandersloot, owner of a beauty products company (!), put up 25 billboards lambasting public television for promoting the homosexual lifestyle to children. When the Idaho state legislature threatened to cut funding for public television, Governor Dirk Kempthorne screened the video and requested that stations air it after 11 p.m. and precede it with comments from a member of the state board of education. Both Idaho Public Television and the stage legislature approved the compromise.[33] Visit the film's website at www.womedia.org/elem/.

Tennessee, received a bomb threat, prompting them to cancel *Tales* an hour before the series's scheduled debut.

Anticipating such reaction, PBS offered an edited version. But apparently that wasn't enough. Even after an Oklahoma PBS station aired the edited version, the Oklahoma State legislature passed a bill stating that "no monies shall be expended herein for program material or content which promotes, encourages, or casts in a favorable light homosexuality or any activity violative of state law."[34] The Lieutenant Governor of Georgia also threatened to cut $20 million of the state's allocated funding, even though he admittedly had not seen the program.

Tales also gave right wing groups like Rev. Donald Wildmon's American Family Association, the Family Research Council, and other "bastions" of morality plenty of reason to go after the Corporation of Public Broadcasting, which allocates government money to PBS projects, for funding, in the words of the Research Council's Robert Knight, "a slick of piece of gay propaganda."[35]

Fortunately, they were in the minority. The critics praised the show, which

---

TWO GOOD REASONS WHY YOU SHOULD SUPPORT YOUR LOCAL PUBLIC TV STATION

Reason #1: *In The Life*

Over 130 public television stations around the country air this gay and lesbian public affairs/new magazine program devoted to gay and lesbian issues and culture. Each hour episode includes six to eight stories on topics ranging from youth and education, health and AIDS, arts and culture, the workplace, families and relationships, and global issues, such as the continuing struggle for gay rights around the world. A national membership network and the H. Van Amerigen Foundation provide funding for the program. Visit their Web site at www.inthelifetv.org.

Reason #2: *P.O.V.*

Since 1988, this series has showcased some of the best gay, lesbian, and transgender-themed documentaries. In addition to Tongues Untied, works that have aired under the *P.O.V.* banner include:

"Absolutely Positive" (June 18, 1991) Directed by Peter Adair.
A moving portrait of eleven HIV-positive men and women, gay and straight, who candidly tell their stories.

"One Nation Under God" (June 15, 1994) Directed by Teodoro Maniacia and Francine Rzeznik.
A disturbing look at the controversy over attempts to "cure" homosexuality with shock therapy, 12-step programs, and beauty makeovers for lesbians.

"The Transformation" (July 9, 1996) Directed by Susan Aiken and Carlos Aparicio
Profile of a former homeless transvestite and his transformation with the help of a Dallas ministry into married churchgoer.

"License to Kill" (June 23, 1998) Directed by Arthur Dong
A candid, insightful examination into the minds of prisoners who have murdered and committed violent acts against homosexuals.

"Golden Threads" (June 8, 1999) Directed by Lucy Winer and Karen Eaton.
Profile of Christine Burton, founder of Golden Threads, an international network for older gay women.

"Scout's Honor" (June 19, 2001) Directed by Tom Shepard
Insightful and informational look at the campaign led by 12-year-old Steven Cozza to overturn the Boy Scouts of America's ban of gay scouts and leaders.

garnered PBS's highest ratings ever for a dramatic series. In San Francisco, *Tales* even beat out the network competition. The series received a George Foster Peabody Award (1994), was awarded "Best Miniseries" by the National Board of Review, a GLAAD Media Award for best miniseries, and two Emmy nominations.

So with all the critical acclaim, record-breaking ratings, and awards, why did PBS decide not to produce the sequel, *More Tales of the City*? PBS claimed they didn't have their share of the $8 million dollars that Channel Four, which financed most of the first series, demanded. *The Advocate's* Steve Greenberg suggests the reason the *Tales* sequel was dumped has more to do with one man, PBS President Ervin Duggan. A former George Bush appointee to the Federal Communications Commission, Duggan "was backed by the National Association of Evangelicals and campaigned for 'decent family values.'"[36]

PBS's decision did not go unnoticed. *San Francisco Chronicle* TV critic John Carman characterized "PBS's pullout from a *Tales* sequel" as "either a case of rank stupidity or cringing cowardice."[37] Frank Rich of the *Times* went after Duggan, stating that "PBS can hardly afford a president who recklessly tells both the gifted creators and discerning audience of the most successful prime-time drama in years to get lost."[38] Duggan indeed did, but fortunately Showtime stepped in and the saga of Mary Ann, Mouse, Mona, and Mrs. Madrigal resumed on pay-cable.

GAY FOR PAY

The two leading pay-cable networks, Home Box Office and Showtime, have also produced original, groundbreaking comedy and drama series featuring gay characters.

Both were originally launched as movie channels (HBO in 1973, Showtime in 1978) that showed, via satellite, feature-length films without commercial interruption. Unlike commercial TV networks and their affiliates, which generate a profit through advertising revenues, pay cable stations make money by charging subscribers a monthly service fee. Initially, HBO and Showtime attracted new subscribers by programming films that had already been released theatrically but had not yet aired on television. With the boom in the home video market in the 1980s and pay-per-view in the 1990s, pay cable channels were no longer the only means to see a film in its entirety before it fell victim to a broadcast network's editing-room chopping block.

HBO and Showtime tried to hold onto their subscribers adding new series to their respective schedules. Most of the early comedy and drama series were low-budget versions of network shows, particularly sitcoms: HBO's *First & Ten* (1984) and Showtime's *The Boys* (1988); and anthology dramas: HBO's *The Hitchhiker* (1983-1985) and Showtime's *Red Shoe Diaries* (1992-). Both networks also started taking full advantage of not being obliged to affiliates or advertisers in regards to program content. Therefore, it wasn't uncommon for the producers to "pepper" an episode with a little blue language or the occasional glimpse of frontal female nudity.

IT'S NOT HETERO, IT'S HBO

Home Box Office is the most successful pay-cable channel, with the number of subscribers hitting the 28 million mark in September of 2001. Over the years, HBO has earned a reputation for its high quality original programming, which includes hip, offbeat comedies (*The Larry Sanders Show* (1992-1998), *Sex and the City* (1998-)); dark, edgy dramas (*The Sopranos* (1999-), *Oz* (1997-), *Six Feet Under* (2001-)); and big-budget made-for-cable movies and miniseries. In 2001, HBO's programming budget exceeded $400 million. The network reportedly spent $125 million alone on the ten-hour World War II miniseries, *Band of Brothers* (2001).

With a larger subscriber base to retain, HBO has been generally less aggressive than Showtime in targeting specific demographics. Although HBO has yet to create a gay series like Showtime's *Queer as Folk* (some believe *Sex and the City* comes pretty darn close), the network's original series and made-for-TV films are not lacking gay content.[39] Over the years, HBO has remained committed to social, political, and historical issues, such as racism, the women's movement, abortion rights, and various gay-related issues, particularly AIDS.

In addition, HBO has showcased some of the best gay-themed documentaries. In 2001, HBO aired the award-winning *Southern Comfort*, a moving portrait of male-to-female transsexual Robert Eads, who has been diagnosed with ovarian cancer. Eads is a witty, insightful individual who lives with his girlfriend Lola Cola in a small Georgia community (which he refers to as "Bubba Country"). In celebrating Eads's power and spirit, director Kate Davis challenges our preconceived ideas of transgender people and the Deep South. More importantly, the filmmaker treats Eads as an individual, rather than an oddity.

HBO also co-financed several documentaries by filmmakers Robert Epstein and Jeffrey Friedman, including *Common Threads* (1989), a moving tribute to five AIDS victims and their loved ones; *The Celluloid Closet* (1995), an entertaining and informative look at the history of homosexuality in Hollywood based on Vito Russo's groundbreaking study; and *Paragraph 175* (1999), a harrowing account of the persecution of homosexuals as told by a few remaining gay survivors of the Nazi concentration camps. Epstein and Friedman are skillful filmmakers who tackle complex social, historical and political issues affecting the lives of gay people around the world. In the process, they give their subjects, whether they be people with AIDS or Holocaust survivors, the opportunity to tell their stories.

Their Academy Award-winning *Common Threads* opens our eyes to the emotional toll AIDS has taken on the family and friends of its victims. The filmmakers also challenge our preconceived ideas about P.W.A.s and the disease itself by focusing on five very different individuals (a young hemophiliac, a drug addict, an Olympic medalist, an entertainer, and the lover of gay author/activist Vito Russo), who are all commemorated by panels on the AIDS quilt.

Around the time *Common Threads* premiered, the commercial TV networks started to produce a series of made-for-TV bio-pics about public figures and celebrities who died of AIDS or whose HIV status was the subject of a national news story (see inset). The majority were "doubly closeted" gay men who hid their illness as they did their sexual orientation. These films expose how homophobia is at the root of the American public's indifference toward people with AIDS.

HBO produced two of the best: *Citizen Cohn* (1992), starring James Woods as the closeted conservative attorney Roy Cohn, who served as chief counsel to Senator Joseph McCarthy during the Communist witch hunts; and *Gia*, starring Angelina Jolie in her Emmy-winning portrayal of supermodel Gia Maria Carangi, one of the first public figures to die of AIDS. Both films have an edge most commercial network films lack because they concentrate on the complex personalities of their title characters, rather than on the disease that ended both their lives in 1986.

Cohn was a maniacal, self-loathing, closeted Jewish homosexual who made a career of destroying the lives of known and suspected Communists and other "subversives." Significant moments in Cohn's life are seen through flashbacks, including his early success as the prosecutor who sent Ethel and Julius Rosenberg to the electric chair; his association with McCarthy and J. Edgar Hoover; and his disbarment and financial downfall in the 1980s. In a remarkable performance, Woods captures the essence of a walking contradiction. Although *Citizen Cohn* doesn't go deep enough into certain aspects of his story, such as his sex life, it ultimately makes no apologies for the son of a liberal Jewish judge who was vindictive, self-serving, and responsible for smearing the names and ruining the lives of many innocent people.

While Cohn hid his insecurities and self-hatred behind his vengeance, Gia followed a more self-destructive path, which the film suggests stemmed from her abandonment by her mother (Mercedes Ruehl) at an early age. Novelist Jay McInerney (*Bright Lights, Big City*) and the film's director/co-writer Michael Cristofer trace the model's meteoric rise to stardom, her tumultuous relationships with both men and women, and her battle with heroin and AIDS. Jolie manages to embody the rebellious beauty who knew how to push everyone's buttons, yet deep down was a frightened child.

HBO's most ambitious project to date about AIDS is *And the Band Played On*, a two-hour-plus adaptation of Randy Shilts's best selling account of the AIDS crisis. The project had been in development for several years, passing through the hands of two major networks (ABC and NBC) and several directors. Once the producers added some stars to the cast list (Richard Gere, Lily Tomlin, and Steve Martin), the $8 million dollar project finally received a green light. Director Roger Spottiswoode and writer Arnold Schulman approached the events leading from the earliest cases to the discovery of the virus as a detective story with government virologist Don Francis (Matthew Modine in a terrific performance) in the "Sam Spade" role.

The roadblocks Francis and his associates at the Centers for Disease Control encounter are numerous: bureaucratic red tape, lack of funding, an apathetic

Reagan administration, a self-serving medical researcher, and members of the gay community, who fought the closing of the bathhouses in San Francisco in the name of sexual freedom. *Band* demonstrates how homophobia and greed were the underlying reasons why it took so long for public and private institutions to take action to prevent the spread of the virus. In one standout scene, Francis meets with representatives of the major blood supply companies, who object to spending money on testing the blood supply because only a few people received contaminated blood. "How many people will it take?" Francis asks. "Give us a number, so we can stop bothering you."

With its large ensemble cast and multiple story lines, *Band* was an ambitious undertaking. The docudrama effectively links a series of events (some occurred simultaneously) that preceded and, in some instances, lead to the discovery of the virus. But the dramatic tension is somewhat diminished when the film pauses to focus on one of the many minor characters, like a successful choreographer (Richard Gere), who, upon learning he's sick, utters one of the film's memorable lines, "The party's over!" Another subplot involves AIDS activist Bill Krause (Ian McKellan), who jeopardizes his relationship with his lover Kiko (B.D. Wong) by devoting all his time and attention to his work. When characters, relationships, and situations like these are not sufficiently developed, certain moments never achieve their intended emotional impact. Consequently, Krause's death from AIDS at the end of the film is overshadowed by the powerful final montage, which intercuts clips of the media's early coverage of the disease and the faces of those lost over the years.

According to Raymond Murray, author of *Images of the Dark*, *Band* was also criticized for promoting "the general perception that it took the intense work of a group of straight men and women to come to the rescue of the helpless gay community."[40] Apparently Shilts and members of the gay community were displeased with Spottiswoode's cut of the film because it didn't present the gay community in a positive enough light. HBO fired Spottiswoode, who kept his name on the film, but publicly expressed his dissatisfaction with the final edited version, which he felt was "sanitized." "It was supposed to be a tough film," he remarked, "but equally tough on everyone."[41]

And the Band Played On is not a perfect film, but like Shilts's book, it is a powerful indictment of the individuals and public and private institutions who failed to respond to the crisis during its infancy, out of apathy, greed, fear, and homophobia.

In addition to fact-based dramas, HBO has also produced fictional works about families preparing for or dealing with the death of a loved one. One early entry was *Tidy Endings* (1988), an adaptation of actor/playwright Harvey Fierstein's one-act play (originally presented on stage as part of a series of one-acts under the title *Safe Sex*). Fierstein stars as Arthur, who has just buried his lover, Colin, after a long battle with AIDS. Grief-stricken over his loss, Arthur is in no mood to contend with Colin's ex-wife Marian (Stockard Channing), who still has unresolved feelings about losing her husband to another man.

Both Fierstein's writing and performance capture the anger, frustration, and isolation many people feel after losing a loved one, particularly to a debilitating disease like AIDS. Marian is a bundle of mixed emotions, all of which the terrific Channing unleashes as she attempts to bring closure to her relationship with her ex-husband and make amends with Arthur. The result is a subtle, well-crafted drama that explores why we need to turn to others to gain the strength we need to move on with our lives.

Unresolved feelings are also at the center of *In the Gloaming* (1997), a sentimental drama starring Robert Sean Leonard as a gay man with AIDS who returns to his parents' home to die. Danny spends his remaining months getting reacquainted with mom, Janet (Glenn Close), who feels guilty for keeping her son at a distance. We witness Danny's rapid deterioration over the next few months, but also see someone coming to terms with his own mortality. Leonard and Close are terrific actors and their exchanges, in which, for the first time, they share their thoughts on everything from movies to sex, are touching and nicely written by Will Scheffer, who based his teleplay on a *New Yorker* short story by Alice Elliot Dark. First time director Christopher Reeve is effective at creating an atmosphere that grows increasingly more tranquil and serene as Danny prepares for the inevitable. Some moments, like an outburst from Danny's yuppie sister (Bridget Fonda), who is jealous of the attention her dying brother is receiving from Mom and Dad, don't ring quite as true. Still, *In the Gloaming* exemplifies the type of original programming that has earned HBO its reputation for quality drama.

Over the past five years, the network has introduced several critically acclaimed dramatic series. At the top of the list are *Oz*, a provocative prison drama that takes an inside look at life behind bars, and *Six Feet Under* (2001-), an offbeat drama about a family-owned funeral home. Both series, to varying degrees, deal with mature themes and contain adult language, nudity (frontal female and male), and graphic violence. In terms of gay content, both *Oz* and *Six Feet Under* feature gay male characters in their respective ensemble casts and deal with gay-related issues, such as homophobia, AIDS, rape, and anti-gay violence.

Oz paints a dark, realistic portrait of prison life from the inmates' point-of-view and, to a lesser extent, of the prison staff and administration. Oz, short for Oswald Security Penitentiary (and renamed Oswald State Correctional Facility in the third season), houses an experimental cellblock known as Emerald City. The inmates assigned to "Em City" are required to follow a regimented schedule that includes physical exercise, work detail, classes, and drug and alcohol counseling. The cell block's diverse population consists of tightly-knit groups of Muslims, Italian wise guys, White Aryan Supremacists, Bikers, and Latino and Black "gangstas," who resort to violence, murder, and rape to gain and maintain control.

All three vices come into play in one of the series's central storylines involving Tobias Beecher (Lee Tergesen), a corporate attorney sentenced to fifteen years for killing a woman while driving drunk. Beecher enters Oz as a mild-mannered, heterosexual male with a wife and children. Over the course of four seasons, we witness his transformation into a hardened killer who develops a deep, obsessive love for another inmate, Chris Keller (Chris Meloni).

In the series's premiere ("The Routine"), Beecher arrives at Oz and is befriended by Vern Schillinger (J.K. Simmons), an inmate who, unknown to Beecher, is the sadistic leader of the White Aryans. Schillinger forces poor Beecher to be his "slag" (slang for slave) and subsequently brands a swastika on his ass and rapes him. Consequently, Beecher grows increasingly unstable and suffers a breakdown.

At the start of season two, Beecher starts to fight back, first by biting the tip off of the penis of an aggressive cellmate, James Robson (R.E. Rodgers), when he makes the mistake of demanding oral sex. He then shares a "pod" (slang for cell) with a new prisoner, Chris Keller, who pretends to hate the White Arayans, but is actually helping Schillinger seek revenge on Beecher for nearly blinding him. To complicate matters more, Beecher falls in love with Keller. In a conversation with one of the prison's resident spiritual advisors, Sister Pete (Rita Moreno), he tries to sort out his feelings:

BEECHER: Two men shouldn't love each other. They can't feel the same things a man and a woman feel. I mean, if a guy has a lot of bad shit happen to him and another guy comforts him, I mean, that's all it is, right? I mean, that's not love, right?

SISTER PETE: Well, some of the men here are homosexual and some need sex...

BEECHER: I'm not talking about sex. I'm talking about love. I had sex with Schillinger. It was brutal, hardly loving. This is different.

SISTER PETE: Tobias, are you in love with another man?

BEECHER: I think so, yeah.[42]

At the end of season two ("Escape From Oz"), Schillinger makes his move and with Keller's help, breaks Beecher's arms and legs. Keller starts to feel guilty because he murdered several homosexual men after having sex with them, scared that people would find out he's a closet case. He confesses to Father Ray (B.D. Wong), who refuses to absolve him of his sins until he confesses to the authorities ("A Word to the Wise").

Beecher and Keller are eventually reunited, though it's difficult enough having a relationship in the outside world, let alone behind iron bars. They are occasionally seen sharing an intimate moment, but their history and respective shifting alliances within the various groups vying for power makes it difficult. Consequently, most of their time is spent launching accusations at each other, seeking revenge, and then trying to win the other back. In prison, candy, flowers, or a simple "I'm sorry" won't do. You have to show it. Keller eventually wins his way back into Beecher's pod by going after Schillinger just as he's about to finish off Beecher. In the end, Keller makes the ultimate sacrifice by taking responsibility for the murder of Schillinger's brother to protect Beecher, who was accused of the crime. Consequently, Beecher is forced to say adieu to his lover when Keller is transferred to a Massachusetts prison.

Beecher and Keller aren't the only friends of Dorothy living in Oz. The population includes a group of self-admitted homosexuals who play integral roles in some of the major storylines. In the show's first season, Billie Keane (Derrick Simmons), an African-American gay man, was badly beaten by the Italians. Billie's brother, Jefferson (Leon), who was head of the Gangstas, avenged his death. When Jefferson becomes a Muslim, he rejects his brother because Islam doesn't accept homosexuality. But before Jefferson is executed, he makes amends to Billie, who is subsequently written out of the show.

Islam's views of homosexuality are again raised when another gay inmate, convicted murderer Jason Cramer (Rob Bogue), asks Said (Eammon Walker), a Muslim, to serve as his lawyer for his appeal. Apparently one of the jurors was overheard making anti-gay remarks. At first, Said has no interest in talking to him. ("Oh, you mean, cause I'm queer and you Muslims consider homosexuality an abomination?" Cramer asks.) Empathizing with a victim of prejudice, Said reconsiders and takes the case. His Muslim brothers object, including Rebadow (George Morfogen), who has a dream that Cramer could be let free on his appeal. Said is confident that won't happen, until a detective on Cramer's case admits to tampering with the evidence. Said's conscience catches up with him and he removes himself from the case; but as Rebadow predicted, Cramer is set free.

In the merry old land of Oz, homosexuality isn't approached in a made-for-TV fashion as a single, isolated issue. Like Billie Keane and Jason Cramer, homosexuality may be a label society has assigned to you. Or in the case of Beecher and Keller, sexuality is but a single strand within a large, complex nexus of social relations. As Sister Pete states, there are some men who are homosexual and some who need sex. Oz remains one of the most provocative shows on television because characters like Beecham and Keller occupy a place somewhere in between.

Another HBO hit, Six Feet Under, is an unpredictable and, at times, surreal drama that features David Fisher (Michael C. Hall), a gay undertaker who runs the family funeral home with his brother Nate (Peter Krause). David is romantically involved with an openly gay police officer, Keith (Michael S. Patrick), but he's still conflicted about his homosexuality as well as afraid to come out to his brother; neurotic mother, Ruth (Frances Conroy); and misunderstood younger sister, Claire (Lauren Ambrose). Ironically, David's family members either know or suspect he's gay and don't have a problem with it. Over the course of the first season, we follow David as he goes through a coming out process, which is fully integrated into the series's story lines.

Along the way, David receives guidance and counsel from an unusual source. The series occasionally employs an inventive narrative device involving the

Fisher Funeral Home's latest client, who comes back to life to converse with one of the characters. In two such episodes, David's interaction with the dearly departed have a significant impact on his relationships with Keith and his mother and on his willingness to come to terms with his homosexuality.

In "Familia," David and Keith have an argument over an encounter in a parking lot. An impatient guy waiting to take their space makes the mistake of calling them "fags." Keith grabs the guy out of the car and identifies himself as a cop. "Next time you call someone a fucking fag," Keith warns, "you make sure that fag isn't a LAPD police officer." Back in their car, David suggests Keith over-reacted, prompting Keith to reply, "Do you hate yourself that much?"[43]

Later, while preparing the body of a 20-year-old murder victim, Manuel "Paco" Bolin (Jacob Vargas), a gang member, David starts complaining to the deceased about Keith being too self-righteous. But Paco points out the guy called him a fag also and he didn't say or do anything. Paco urges him to stop being a "pussy" and apologize to "your boy Keith;" otherwise he's just "born a bitch." David's conversations with Paco not only help him resolve his problems with Keith, but empower him to stand up to a representative from the funeral conglomerate that starts pressuring the Fishers to sell their business.

In a later episode ("A Private Life"), a 23-year-old gay man, Marc Foster Jr. (Brian Poth) is brutally murdered by two gay-bashers. David meets Marc's parents, who reveal their son never came out to them. Mr. Foster blames Marc's death on his sexual orientation. "It is the only reason," he exclaims. "If he wasn't, he'd be alive today." The situation parallels David's relationship with his own mother, who repeatedly tries to get her son to come out to her. When Ruth brings up the subject of Marc's murder, David doesn't take the bait because he's still uncomfortable discussing that aspect of his private life.

When Marc's ghost later appears to David, our expectations are once again subverted. Instead of encouraging David to come out, the dearly departed turns out to be a self-hating homosexual who regrets giving into the sickness and not having the faith in God to live a "normal life." David finds himself in the position of arguing for the other side. He points out that living a heterosexual life would have been a lie because homosexuality is not a choice. "That's just liberal propaganda to justify your own depravity," Marc responds, "...No matter how nice you fix me up, I'm still going to Hell, and you know it — 'cause you're going there, too."[44]

Meanwhile, Ruth has a similar conversation when she asks her co-worker at the flower shop, Robbie (Joel Brooks), about his experience coming out to his parents. Robbie admits he never did because he knew his father would never speak to him and his mother would go insane.

ROBBIE: A child knows what his parents need him to be. My mother is one of those women that never did anything but raise children, so if you came out wrong, like in the opposite of what she was trying to make you into, then, you know, her whole life is a failure.

RUTH: I'm not like that.[4]

At Marc's funeral, there's a group of protestors at the cemetery holding signs reading "No Fags in Heaven" and "Homos in Hell." Keith, who has since broken up with David, has been assigned to keep the crowd under control, which proves difficult when David, in a rage of anger, lunges after one of the protestors. Keith rescues him and David apologizes for the way he acted when they were together. But David still has doubts and admits to Keith that part of him agrees with the protestors.

DAVID: But you know that you're right. That you're a good man. For me, it's like I agree with them, you know? Like it is my fault and I should be able to fix it.

KEITH: There's nothing to fix.[46]

David is convinced his father would have hated him if he knew, but as Keith points out, he did know. The mistake David made is never talking to him about it.

He finally gets the opportunity by telling his mother, though in the process he doesn't hide his resentments toward his parents for never really opening up to him. Instead of the usual mother-son coming out scene, writer Kate Robin once again takes us in a completely different direction. David accuses Ruth of only loving him because it's her duty as a mother, but she explains that it's much more difficult to play the maternal role with him now that he's older. He asks that she let him take care of himself. Later that evening, Marc reappears and continues to taunt him about going to hell. David drops to his knees and asks God to take away his pain and to help him "fill this loneliness with your love."

Despite the series's surreal quality, the episode approaches the subject of self-hatred and homosexuality with honesty and without quick answers. A network television series would never have turned homosexuality into such a complex issue. Instead of David having a sudden realization and accepting his homosexuality or a tearful heart-to-heart talk with his mother (two devices not uncommon to commercial network series), David's internal struggle continues. He's no doubt learning along the way, but Alan Ball and his writing staff clearly understand that coming to terms with your true self is a process, rather than something that can get resolved in the big scene before a commercial break.

SHOWTIME: NO LIMITS (NO KIDDING)

In 1984, Showtime produced the first situation comedy for pay cable TV. Created by David Lloyd (*Cheers*), *Brothers* focuses on the relationship between three very different siblings: Lou (Brandon Maggart), a conservative working-class man's man; Joe (Robert Walden), an ex-pro football player who owns his restaurant; and their baby brother Cliff (Paul Regina). In the pilot episode, Cliff is about to get married, but calls off the wedding at the eleventh hour and makes a shocking announcement — he's gay. His brothers aren't exactly thrilled, especially when they meet Cliff's best friend, Donald (Phillip Charles MacKenzie), a sharp-tongued swishy queen who's proud of it. (When Joe calls Donald a "fairy," he retorts, "actually we prefer the term 'hobgoblin.'") Joe is offended by Donald and tells Cliff, "If that's the kind of friend you want, if that's the kind of person you want to be, you're no brother of mine." But it's a sitcom, so a few scenes later, Joe and Lou are giving Cliff their support.

TRUE-LIFE AIDS STORIES

Liberace (ABC-TV)
1988,
Written by William Hale
Directed by Anthony and Nancy Lawrence

Liberace: Behind the Music (CBS-TV)
1988
Directed David Green
Written by Gavin Lambert

In October of 1988, two made-for-TV movies aired on the life of Wladizu Valentino Liberace. ABC's *Liberace*, made with the cooperation of his estate, stars Andrew Robinson as the flamboyant entertainer. The bio-pic focuses on his professional and personal life, including his close relationship with his mother (Rue McClanahan), and the palimony suit brought on by his ex-assistant/lover Scott Thorson. One week later, CBS aired *Liberace: Behind the Music*, with Victor Garber in the title role. The critics favored this "unauthorized version," which deals more explicitly with the master show-man's life and death from AIDS in 1987.

The Ryan White Story (ABC-TV)
1989
Written by Phil Penningroth and John Herzfeld
Story by Penningroth
Directed by Herzfeld

A moving telefilm about the midwestern youth who contracted AIDS from a blood transfusion. The film exposes how all people with AIDS, gay and straight, can become the target of the public's fear, ignorance, and bigotry. Judith Light, who, in real life, has done tremendous work in the fight against AIDS and homophobia, gives a terrific performance as Ryan's mother, Jeanne. White, who died in 1990 at the age of 18, appears in the film as Ryan's friend Chad.

Rock Hudson (ABC-TV)
1990
Written by Dennis Turner
Directed by John Icholla

Hudson look-alike Thomas Ian Griffin stars as the closeted, handsome movie star in this paint-by-numbers biography. The film focuses on two aspects of Hudson's life: his marriage to Phyllis Gates (Daphne Ashbrook), whose book, *My Husband, Rock Hudson*, served as the basis of the teleplay; and his relationship to Marc Christian (William R. Moses), who won a civil suit against Hudson's estate three years after his death for Hudson's failure to disclose his illness.

Breaking the Surface: The Greg Louganis Story (USA Network)
1996
Written by Alan Hines
Based on the book by Greg Louganis and Eric Marcus
Directed by Steven Hilliard Stern

Saved by the Bell's Mario Lopez stars as champion Olympic diver Greg Louganis, who went public with his homosexuality and HIV status. The film, based on Louganis's best-selling autobiography, examines Louganis's extraordinary diving career and his personal struggle to hide his homosexuality.

Played by the amiable Paul Regina, the athletic, masculine Cliff isn't a stereo-typical gay male. But Donald, just like *Will & Grace*'s Jack, is gay enough for both of them. Although some viewers may have found his character objectionable and the humor somewhat base, the series lasted four seasons (1984-1989).

In 1984, a seemingly mainstream situation comedy with this much gay content was considered groundbreaking, especially considering the best known gay series regular was *Dynasty*'s Steven — "I'm gay; no, wait, I'm straight; yup, I'm gay" — Carrington. *Brothers*, rejected by ABC before landing at Showtime, opened new doors by featuring not one, but two gay characters, and tackling some serious gay-themed issues, like AIDS and gay-bashing. The sitcom was also an early indication of the direction Showtime would soon be heading.

In 1994, the network's CEO, Matt Blank, hired Jerry Ofsay, as the new President of Programming. Ofsay was a labor lawyer and a former executive at ABC Productions, where he was involved in the development of such quality TV series as *My So-Called Life*. Blank and Ofsay implemented a new programming strategy that put greater emphasis on original programming.[47] The network increased their programming budget from $150 million in 1994 to $400 million in 2001. The number of made-for-cable films also rose significantly from eight to approximately 35 titles per year. In the process, Showtime gained a reputation with writers and actors as a "creator friendly" network because they gave talent the artistic freedom to produce their "pet projects," often scripts that couldn't get made as feature films. Some films, like *Gods and Monsters*, which earned writer/director Bill Condon an Academy Award for Best Adapted Screenplay, were even released as feature films before airing on Showtime.

Financially, Blank and Ofsay's strategy paid off. Since 1994, the number of Showtime subscribers rose from 8.9 million in 1994 to 12.8 million in the first quarter of 2001. The number of subscribers to the Showtime Network, which includes Showtime, The Movie Channel, and Flix, rose 121 percent from 13.4 to 29.6 million.[48]

An important aspect of Showtime's programming strategy was the inclusion of weekly series that targeted a specific demographic audience. With a subscribership that's roughly 24 percent African-American and more than 12 percent Latino, Showtime started airing two family dramas with specific cultural/ethnic appeal: *Soul Food* (2000-), which examines the lives of three African-American sisters in Chicago; and *Resurrection Blvd.* (2000-), at the time the first and only English language drama about Latinos, focusing on a family in East Los Angeles.[49]

A third demographic Showtime aimed for was gay men and lesbians. Over the years, the network has aired several original films and miniseries that address specific social and historical gay issues (see inset). It was only a matter of time before they developed a drama for their gay audience. Instead of creating an original series, the network decided to produce a weekly series based on the Channel Four British miniseries, *Queer as Folk*. The original was quite contro-versial in Britain due to male nudity and some graphic depiction of gay sex. It also developed a cult following in the States, where it played in gay film festivals across the country. Bootleg copies began circulating until the series was finally released on DVD and video in 2001.

Showtime reportedly spent $10 million promoting the weekly series as part of their "No Limits" campaign, which started back in 1998. According to executive V.P. of original programming Gary Levine, "'No Limits' can mean many things. It may mean going to the edge of the envelope in terms of sexuality, language, nudity, and traditional beliefs, and sometimes it means we will reach into a community the TV world has turned its back on. It also means we are not afraid of politically hot topics."[50]

If anything was limited about Showtime before this, it was the channel's popularity with gay and lesbian viewers. According to *Variety*, Showtime executives were concerned about a recent report that stated 66.8 percent of gays and lesbians subscribe to cable television, but Showtime didn't make the list of the top twelve watched stations.[51] *QAF* was financially risky because it appealed to a niche audience, yet Showtime continued its aggressive marketing campaign for the series, launched in Spring 2000, which included:

•A special toll-free number, 1-800-COMINGOUT to sign up new Showtime subscribers

•Direct mail advertisements to members of the New York, Los Angeles, and San Francisco gay and lesbian communities

•Showtime's sponsorship of gay pride festivals, gay film festivals, and other events

•Ads in gay magazines and websites

•Promotional "V.I.P. Coming Out Parties" at gay clubs around the country

The word indeed got out because *QAF* became Showtime's highest-rated dramatic series. By the end of the its first season in June of 2001, the average rating was double Showtime's overall prime time average. The show also scored high numbers with 18- to 35-year-olds and female viewers.

The series's broad appeal isn't surprising. Male nudity and the occasional graphic sex scene aside, *QAF* is essentially a gay soap opera about the relationship problems — romantic, platonic, and familial — among a group of twenty-somethings. While the American version certainly warrants some comparison with the British series, it is, in all fairness, like comparing apples and oranges (the fruit analogy is purely intentional). The original *QAF* was the vision of a single writer, Russell Davies, who penned all eight episodes of the first series and the two-hour conclusion.[52] The American version was developed by the producing/writing team of Ron Cowen and Daniel Lipman, creators of *Sisters* and the Showtime series *Leap Years*.[53] Cowen and Lipman wrote a total of six episodes, including the first three. Writing credit for the remaining fourteen hours was split among a team of six writers.

In the Americanized version, Cowen and Lipman adhered to Davies's basic premise: Brian (Stuart in the U.K.) is a sexy, smarmy advertising executive who can have any guy he wants. His best friend, the amiable Michael (Vince) is in love with him, as is Brian's (Stuart's) latest trick, 17-year-old Justin (Nathan, who is 15 in the U.K. version). The first few episodes follow the British series closely, including the birth of Brian's son to his lesbian friends, Lindsay and Melanie (Thea Gill and Michelle Clunie).

The American series's plotlines then begin to take a different direction. For example, in the original, Stuart and Vince's friend Ted overdoses when a trick gives him some crystal meth. In the U.S., Ted recovers and later becomes involved with the trick (Blake, played by Dean Armstrong), who has difficulty staying clean. More screen time is also devoted to Michael's relationship with his older and more experienced lover, Dr. David Cameron (Chris Potter), which is taken to the next level when they move in together.

Obviously, a series affords its writers more screen time to develop characters and situations. Unfortunately, neither the writing nor the acting is up to par with the Brits. What made the British *QAF* so terrific was its subtlety, particularly in terms of how it examined the interrelationships among the characters. In building on Davies's premise, an otherwise simple love triangle is inflated to the point of being stripped of emotional resonance. The result is a rather bland and at times uninspired look at gay life. The three lead actors, Hal Sparks (Michael), Gale Harold (Brian), and Randy Harrison (Justin) lack the experience and edge of their British counterparts. Gale Harold's Brian exudes none of the charisma of Stuart Allen Jones, which is problematic for a character who is reputedly the object of everyone's desire.

As the first season progressed, the three lead actors began to grow into their roles. Fortunately, they received some strong support from other cast members, namely Peter Paige, who is terrific as Emmet; Scott Lowell, who has turned Ted into the show's most interesting character; and Sherry Miller, who, as Justin's mom, emerges as the series's most believable character. Then there's the terrific Sharon Gless, who started way, way over-the-top as Michael's supportive, spirited PFLAG mother. There's a difference between "character acting" and "acting like a character." Gless's Debbie is loud, brash, and a tad overbearing — characteristics that unfortunately apply to her acting style as well. (As Debbie herself would say, "Tone it down, honey.")

As for the message *QAF* is "delivering" to Showtime's million plus subscribers about gay life, it's important to remember the year under discussion is 2002, not 1972. These aren't the only gay characters on TV, so to claim anyone who tunes into the series may conclude all gay men are sexually promiscuous, do drugs, and go to bars and discos every night, isn't giving the audience enough credit. The same goes for Showtime and the show's producers, who should have more faith in their viewers and eliminate the disclaimer in the closing credits stating that the characters are intended to represent only a segment of the gay population.

Although *Queer as Folk* is certainly the "gayest" show on Showtime (or any other channel), it's not the only series to include gay characters. *Beggars and Choosers* (1999-2001), which was canceled after only two seasons, took a satirical look at the inner workings of a television network and featured a gay character in its ensemble cast.

Former NBC programming executive Brandon Tartikoff, who died of Hodgkin's Disease in 1997, created this dramedy that takes a satirical, behind-the-scenes look at the television industry. LGT (Luddin Global Television) is a fictional television network owned by E.L. Luddin, a cantankerous old man. Among the top executives is Malcolm Laffley (played by the talented Tuc Watkins), the network's closeted gay vice president of casting. By show business standards, Malcolm is essentially one of the few nice guys, continually faced with moral dilemmas.

Malcolm's first-season central plotline deals with a bogus sexual harassment suit filed against him by a sleazy actress, Sandra Cassandra, which the network wants to settle out of court. But when Malcolm is forced to represent the network on a television talk show to discuss the "Velvet Curtain" (Hollywood's discrimination against gay actors), he gets into a heated exchange with another panelist and ends up outing himself. Sandra's lawyers think it was all done to settle the suit. To complicate matters more, the press publishes a story about a heterosexual fling from Malcolm's past. As a result, LGT ends up settling the case.

The sexual harassment storyline takes a realistic look at the struggle many gay men and lesbians continue to face in their professional lives. Even in the entertainment business, which many people assume to be homophobia-free, there is still a gay stigma. Although the lawsuit was settled in the first season, the show's executive producer/writer Peter Lefcourt continued to address the theme of homophobia. Incidentally, Lefcourt is the author of *The Dreyfuss Affair: A Love Story*, a novel about an affair between a major league short stop and a second basemen. The project has been in development for nine years (first at Disney, then at New Line Cinema). According to Lefcourt, the issue is casting — the film requires "a major star because the hardcore homophobe in America doesn't want to see two men kissing."[54]

Casting is an issue early in *Beggars and Choosers*'s second season when Malcolm must hire an actor for the role of Dodi Fayed in a TV-movie about his love affair with Princess Diana. In one of the series's best episodes ("The Naked Truth"), Malcolm tries to hire a gay actor to play the role. Although he gives a terrific reading, network chief Rob Malone (Brian Kerwin) admits he won't hire him because he is gay. Ironically, Rob receives an award that evening for taking a stand against the Hollywood Blacklist — an award he publicly admits he doesn't deserve.

GAY TV TEENS (AND QUEENS AND WITCHES, OH MY!)

In the early 1970s, network executives considered homosexuality a mature subject matter requiring sensitivity and care. The networks were certainly aware that controversial subjects like homosexuality could generate high ratings. Yet, at the same time, they didn't want to alienate their viewers — and sponsors — and/or be accused of promoting the gay rights agenda. This seemed highly unlikely considering, at the time, the networks were airing some of their most blatantly homophobic episodes, such as *Marcus Welby, M.D.*'s "The Outrage" (1974) and *Police Woman*'s "Flowers of Evil" (1974).

The networks also played it safe my limiting the representation of gay men and lesbians in the early 1970s to adult characters, most of whom remain in the

GAY-THEMED ORIGINAL SHOWTIME FILMS

As Is (1985)
Written by William M. Hoffman
Directed by Michael Lindsay-Hogg

TV adaptation of William Hoffman's powerful play about the AIDS crisis and its effect on a pair of ex-lovers (nicely played by Robert Carradine and Jonathan Hadary), who are reunited when one falls ill. Colleen Dewhurst co-stars as a sympathetic hospice worker.

Bastard Out of Carolina (1996)
Written by Anne Meredith
Based on the novel by Dorothy Allison
Directed by Angelica Huston

Ted Turner refused to air this adaptation of lesbian novelist Dorothy Allison's semi-autobiographical story of a young girl sexually abused by her stepfather. Terrific performances by Jena Malone as the young girl and Diana Scarwid as her sympathetic lesbian aunt. This disturbing account of sexual abuse marked Huston's directing debut.

Blind Faith (1998)
Written by Frank Military
Directed by Ernest R. Dickerson

Exceptional period courtroom drama starring Courtney B. Vance as a small-time attorney who defends his nephew (Garland Whitt, Jr.) when he is accused of murdering a white youth. Charles Dutton co-stars as the defendant's intolerant father, who has trouble accepting the truth about his son.

Common Ground (2000)
Written by Paula Vogel, Terrence McNally, and Harvey Fierstein
Directed by Donna Deitch

This anthology film, written by three leading gay and lesbian playwrights, focuses on three generations of gay men and lesbians living in a small Connecticut town. McNally's story starring Steven Weber as a gay French teacher and Jonathan Taylor-Thomas as his gay student is the best of the vignettes.

Dirty Pictures (2000)
Written by Ilene Chaiken
Directed by Frank Pierson

Docudrama about Cincinnati art museum director Dennis Barrie (James Woods), charged with obscenity for displaying a controversial Robert Mapplethorpe photography exhibit. Woods is terrific, but too much screen time is devoted to Barrie's personal life. Still, the film raises important issues about obscenity, subjectivity, and artistic expression.

Execution of Justice (1999)
Written by Michael Butler
Based on the play by Emily Mann
Directed by Leon Ichaso

Film adaptation of Emily Mann's play about Dan White, the San Francisco city councilman who murdered Mayor George Moscone and gay councilman Harvey Milk in 1978. The film is a conventional

THE PRIME TIME CLOSET

closet until their late twenties/early thirties. To avoid being accused of endorsing the gay lifestyle, prime time television rarely dealt with the topic of teen homosexuality before the mid-1980s. That testy subject was limited to medical dramas, which essentially ducked it by focusing on heterosexual teens undergoing a sexual identity crisis. However, some dramatic series did a little better, albeit in an indirect manner.

MAYBE, MAYBE NOT

The first television drama to address the subject of teen homosexuality is *Channing*, a 1963-1964 drama set on a fictional midwestern college campus. In

biopic that aims to provide insight into what drove White into committing such a heinous act. Tim Daly is a convincing White, but the film lacks the emotional impact of Robert Epstein's 1984 Oscar-winning documentary, *The Times of Harvey Milk*.

A Girl Thing (2001)
Written and directed by Lee Rose

Stockard Channing stars in this four-hour miniseries as a New York therapist treating four female patients, each with a very different problem. The first features Elle McPherson as an insecure lawyer having an affair with another woman, an art designer played by Kate Capshaw. An honest portrayal of a female relationship that for once doesn't skirt around the sexual aspects of their relationship. The remaining stories are equally fine, thanks to a first-rate cast that includes Mia Farrow, Glenne Headly, Allison Janney, and Camryn Manheim.

Holiday Heart (2000)
Written by Cheryl L. West
Based on her play
Directed by Robert Townsend

Ving Rhames is dynamite as drag queen Holiday Heart, who takes care of a crack addicted mother (the always terrific Alfre Woodard) and her daughter. While the story is filled with clichés and a predictable ending, Rhames manages to avoid the obvious and create a complex, three-dimensional character.

Losing Chase (1996)
Written by Anne Meredith
Directed by Kevin Bacon

Helen Mirren gives another first-class performance as a woman recuperating from a nervous breakdown whose intense friendship with her "Mother's Helper" (Kyra Sedgwick) awakens her repressed sexual desires and renews her passion for living. Bacon's directorial debut is impressive. Sedgwick and Beau Bridges as Mirren's husband do some of their best work.

Twilight of the Golds (1997)
Written by Jonathan Tolins
Based on his play
Directed by Ross Kagan Marks

Adaptation of Tolin's stage play poses a hypothetical question: if genetics could reveal the sexual orientation of your unborn child, and you knew he or she would be gay, would you abort? The question is interesting, but this over-wrought family drama is marred by serious overacting via the miscast Faye Dunaway and Garry Marshall as Jewish parents coming to terms with their opera-loving gay son (Brendan Fraser) and their pregnant daughter (Jennifer Beals in a subtle, stand-out performance), who is faced with a "big decision."

"The Last Testament of Buddy Crown," a student named Buddy tragically drowns while trying to swim across a lake. Buddy was intelligent, but he lacked athletic ability and social skills, which made him an easy target for the other guys' put-downs. Even his roommate, a fast-talker named Hal (Russ Tamblyn), taunted Buddy when he wasn't bumming cigarettes or money off him. After Buddy drowns, Hal takes advantage of the situation and tries to win over his late room-mate's wealthy father, Dr. Crown (David Wayne), by playing the part of the grieving best friend. Dr. Crown is impressed with Hal and considers adopting him to insure someone carries on the Crown name.

The plot thickens when Hal finds Buddy's note revealing Buddy knew he'd drown if he tried to swim the lake. The reason why he may have risked his life becomes even clearer when his English professor, Joseph Howe (Jason Evers) reads Buddy's last English assignment. Based on Jonathan Swift's satirical essay, "A Modest Proposal," Buddy's composition describes a world in which men like his father aren't allowed to have children. Prof. Howe confronts Dr. Crown and accuses him of forcing his son to live up to his unreasonable standards:

PROF. HOWE: ...standards which imposed a mandatory either or. Either a man —

DR. CROWN: Or a homosexual, which he was.

PROF. HOWE: You made him think he was.

DR. CROWN: Think? Oh, Professor, his letters were so obvious it was embarrassing . . .

PROF. HOWE: Buddy was different, yes. He paid for that difference every day of his life. He didn't fit. He didn't belong. He lacked the ability to make friends. He could survive their ridicule, their slights. It was your assessment of him, Dr. Crown, that destroyed him. You introduced a poison into his bloodstream just as surely as if you'd used a hypodermic syringe.

DR. CROWN: The poison was there. I merely gave it a name. If he died trying to prove his manhood, it was a pointless sacrifice.[55]

On the surface, "Buddy Crown" is not about homosexuality, but the pressure society exerts on young people to subscribe to traditional, socially acceptable masculine and feminine roles. As Prof. Howe explains, Buddy was ostracized by his peers because he was different, but it was his father's contempt that drove him to knowingly risk his life in the name of manhood. Yet Dr. Crown claims the "poison" (meaning homosexuality) was already there — he just gave it a name. We never find out if Buddy was indeed gay and, moreover, Prof. Howe never

THE PRIME TIME CLOSET

even considers whether it may have been true. If it were, perhaps viewers in the early 1960s may have been less sympathetic and have even felt Dr. Crown's attitude toward his gay son was justified.

Less than ten years later, *Room 222*, a comedy/drama about a racially integrated Los Angeles high school, addressed some of the same issues surrounding gender roles, conformity, and sexual orientation. In "What Is a Man?" a talented student named Howard (Frederick Herrick) performs a female role in a reading of Shakespeare's *Twelfth Night* and gets teased by his classmates. The name-calling escalates and when someone writes "fag" across his locker, Principal Kaufman (Michael Constantine) asks Howard's Social Studies teacher, Mr. Dixon (Lloyd Haynes), if he thinks Howard is a homosexual.

"In my opinion," Dixon admits, "I have no idea."

When his friends start to avoid him, Howard decides he needs to prove he's a man. So he joins the track team, but his asthma makes it difficult for him to compete. He finally gets the chance to prove his manhood when challenged to a fight by one of his detractors, Mark (Ric Carrott). Instead of using his fists, Howard gives Mark and the crowd that gathers around them an answer to the question posed by the episode's title:

> HOWARD: I want to know if by putting me down, it makes you all feel like men? I want to know if writing "fag" on my locker is your standard for real guts....I call it cheap and gutless. And if that's the best way you had to make yourselves look good then you're welcome to it. Do you really think I'd play the girl's part in a play if I was really trying to hide what you say I am? Why don't you think on that? And even if you could make something of it, what about you? I notice you guys on the football field when you win a game — all over each other. Suppose people picked up on that and made something of it...What would you say? "Oh, that's different. That's sports."...I'm not sure what a man is. But I do know what he isn't. And that's you.[56]

Like "Buddy Crown," "What Is a Man?" aims to expose masculinity as a patriarchal construction rooted in ignorance and fear. Once again, the homosexual question is raised, but it is immediately put on the backburner in favor of the more universal message about accepting our differences. Television was still not ready to answer the question "What Is a Homosexual?" — at least as far as teenagers were concerned.

With the exception of a 1976 episode of *Family* (see inset, page 161), television continued to proceed with caution when teenagers were involved. In the 1976 made-for-TV movie *Dawn: Portrait of a Teenage Runaway* and its sequel, *Alexander: the Other Side of Dawn*, Eve Plumb (best known to TV viewers as *The Brady Bunch*'s Jan Brady) plays a runaway-slash-prostitute. She falls in love with a handsome male hustler, Alexander Duncan (Leigh McCloskey), who is adept at servicing both male and female clients.

In the 1977 sequel, Dawn returns home to Tucson to finish high school and Alex, an aspiring artist, remains in Los Angeles to earn some money so the two can settle down together. But nobody will hire Alex because he is underage, so he returns to the streets and immediately gets arrested by a vice cop. Alex is bailed out by Ray Church (Earl Holliman), a psychologist who encourages him to get his head together by attending some of the programs at the Gay and Lesbian Community Center. Alex chooses to take an easier route and becomes a "houseboy" for a closeted gay pro football player, Charles "Snake" Selby (Alan Feinstein). Snake showers Alex with gifts and attention, at least until a blonde-haired, blue-eyed replacement comes along. When Alex is arrested for copping drugs for Snake, he saves himself from a prison sentence by telling the judge he wants to be able to take control of his own life, rather than have others tell him what to do. He makes a convincing case and the charges are dropped. Dawn and Alex are reunited and head north to start a new life.

So is Alex gay? He repeatedly insists he's not. Is he bisexual? Maybe, maybe not. He has sex with men, but only for money and the nature of his relationship with Snake is ambiguous (nor do we really know if Alex is even attracted to him or men in general). Although the question about Alex's sexuality is raised, it is not the real issue.

His "bisexual odyssey" is actually an oedipal search for a surrogate father, who kicked his artistic son out of the house because he was more interested in drawing pictures of the family farm than working on it. In Los Angeles, he seeks the approval his own father denied him from a series of "father figures:" Don Umber (Georg Stanford Brown), the social worker in *Dawn* who reaches out to him; Ray, the gay psychologist and friend of Don's who tries to get Alex to open up emotionally; and Snake, who offers financial security and encourages Alex to pursue his dream of becoming a painter. They all try, in their own way to help Alex, but he resists both Don and Ray's assistance and the attention he receives from Snake. Alex finally ends his oedipal journey to adulthood in a Los Angeles courtroom. Just as the judge is sentencing him to juvenile detention, Alex, speaking on his own behalf, admits it is time for him to take control of his own destiny. "When it comes down to it," he explains, "I haven't done a very good job of growing up. I'd like to do what I want to do for once." His choice is, of course, to live a happy heterosexual life with Dawn.

Although Alex may have slept with men for money or their approval, his confusion doesn't stem from his repressed sexual desire toward the opposite sex, but his father's rejection. The two are thematically linked when Alex reluctantly attends a men's rap session at the Gay Center. When one participant recalls how he desperately wanted his father's approval, his story triggers something in Alex. "I should have at least tried to make him happy," Alex mutters under his breath. When the others try to get him to open up and explain what he meant, he gets defensive and runs out.

Although its treatment of topics like prostitution, teen runaways, and homosexuality are sensationalistic and heavy-handed ("A young male hustler struggles to make a new life!" read NBC's ad), there was at least some attempt made to present a "balanced" image of gay men (Russ, the dedicated, morally upright gay psychologist vs. Snake, the closeted pro football player who likes them young). Yet, we never know for sure where Alex falls on the Kinsey scale. Ultimately, whether or not Alex is gay, bisexual, or just confused, doesn't matter because he has no trouble closing the (closet) door on his gay past and living happily, heterosexually ever after with Dawn.

Eighteen years after *Alexander*, the Fox Network aired *The Price of Love* (1995), an original made-for-TV movie about a 16-year-old, Bret (Peter Facinelli), who is kicked out of his parents' house. He heads to Los Angeles and befriends a male hustler, Bo (Jay R. Ferguson). Unable to get a job, Bret turns to hustling. But unlike Alexander, Bret's sexual orientation is not ambiguous — he is strictly gay for pay. In fact, he's even a little homophobic and makes the mistake of asking the flamboyant Bo to tone it down when his girlfriend comes to stay with them. All Bret wants is a normal, stable life, but unlike Alexander, who wants to do it his own way, he feels his only choice is to give himself over to child authorities and become a ward of the state.

In the 1970s, teenage lesbianism received sensationalistic treatment in two made-for-TV movies set in in a juvenile detention center for young women. *Born Innocent* (1974) and *Cage Without a Key* (1975) are both harsh indictments of a system that fails to rehabilitate our nation's youth and subjects them to the horrors of lesbianism, rape, and violence. However, in their attempt to expose the harsh realities of prison life, *Innocent* and *Cage* are both guilty of exploiting the same conditions they're exposing.

In *Born Innocent*, Linda Blair portrays Chris Parker, a 14-year-old chronic runaway sentenced to a detention center. When she rejects the sexual advances of the center's ringleader, an evil lesbian named Moco (Nora Heflin), she's brutally gang-raped in the shower with a broom handle. The rape sequence became the focus of a 1978 lawsuit filed against NBC that claimed it inspired a copycat crime. Consequently, the scene was deleted from the film.

Cage Without a Key is also set in a women's detention center, the San Marcos School for Girls, where Valerie Smith (Susan Dey) is serving time for her role in a botched liquor store robbery that left one man dead. Valerie was an unwilling participant in the hold-up, which was committed by a casual acquaintance who offered her a ride. She had previously rejected his sexual advances, so he told the police she was involved. Like Chris Parker, Valerie soon finds herself in detention hell, where she ends up in the middle of a violent power struggle between several gangs. Fortunately, she is rescued before one of the inmates, Noreen (*Eight Is Enough*'s Lani O'Grady), sexually molests her. The film's subject matter and violent content were too dicey for some CBS affiliates, which decided not to air the film or run an edited version.

Not all teenagers can resolve their sexual identity so easily (especially in one hour's time, minus commercials). In a 1979 episode of *The White Shadow* ("One of the Boys"), Ray Collins (Peter Horton) transfers to Carver High School from the more upscale Palisades High to escape a rumor he is gay. At Carver, he's recruited for the basketball team, but when the rumor finds it way across town, Coach Reeves (Ken Howard) considers cutting him from the team. The coach's sister Katie (Robin Rose) tries to talk some sense into him. "You know you sound like an Anita Bryant scare brochure..." she scolds. "You don't know if the kid is a homosexual in the first place and if he is he hasn't done anything."

Coach Reeves soon finds himself defending Ray and accusing the team of McCarthyism because they're judging their teammate on the basis of rumors. Finally, Reeves asks Ray if he is gay. Ray says he doesn't know, but explains the rumors started when he admitted to a male friend he was jealous when the guy started spending time with other people. When word got around school, the trouble began, so his father transferred him to Carver to toughen him up.

Ray decides his only option is to drop out of school, yet in the final, emotionally charged scene, Vice Principal Buchanan (Joan Pringle) convinces him to return to Palisades High. She recalls what happened when her family moved to Oregon back in 1952 into a community where her brother was only one of two black students in his grade school. One day he found a racist drawing in his desk. When he went home crying to his mother, she offered some words of wisdom:

> BUCHANAN:...She told him she found the world was broken up into four different types of people. 25 percent that like you for the right reason. 25 percent that like you for the wrong reasons. 25 percent that don't like you for the wrong reasons. And 25 percent that don't like you for the right reasons. And she said that it was only the last group of people that anyone should be concerned about.[57]

Buchanan's moving story, which is eloquently delivered by Pringle, effectively makes an analogy between homophobia and racism. As I said in my introduction, the episode also delivers a more universal message about how we must not allow hatred and intolerance to control our lives.

In the 1980s, made-for-TV movies and dramatic series continued to focus on teenagers coming to terms with their sexuality. While some teens, mostly females, are left feeling confused after engaging in a little same-sex foreplay (like kissing and hugging), others realize their attraction to members of the same sex is not simply a phase they'll outgrow.

Male teenagers were the first to take that giant step out of the closet in a series of made-for-TV movies. The genre, which had been tackling serious social issues since the early 1970s, provided the ideal forum for exploring a teenager's coming out ordeal. TV movies also paved the way for the inclusion of recurring and regular young gay and lesbian characters on teen-oriented dramas and drama hybrids like *Beverly Hills, 90210, My So-Called Life, Dawson's Creek, Buffy the Vampire Slayer*, and *Popular*.

CURIOUS AND CONFUSED

A previously discussed episode of *Medical Center* ("Impasse") portrays a hysterical young patient who almost jumps off the hospital roof because she thinks she's a lesbian. Fortunately, her lesbian psychiatrist stops her in time and explains that having a single sexual experience with a woman does not mean she is a lesbian. Sexual experimentation is a healthy, normal part of an adolescent or young girl's sexual development, but can also be a source of anxiety.

In a controversial episode of the offbeat drama *Picket Fences* (1992-1996), two curious teenage girls decide to see what it would be like to kiss each other ("Sugar and Spice"). But when Sheriff Jimmy Brock (Tom Skerritt) and his doctor-wife Jill (Kathy Baker) learn Jimmy's daughter Kimberly (Holly Marie Combs) kissed her best friend Lisa (Alexandra Lee), they find it difficult to remain calm. Jimmy and Jill consider themselves liberal-minded people who support gay rights. (They refused to vacation in Colorado during the boycott.) However, they both admit it's different when it's your own daughter you want to protect from a cruel, homophobic world. Kimberly admits she's scared because she was aroused by the kiss. She's also afraid she is gay because her free-spirited biological mother, Lydia (Cristina Rose), had a lesbian affair.

Kimberly receives the guidance she needs from Lydia, who explains that her lesbian relationship in college was during the women's movement. At the time, she had a stronger emotional connection with her female friends than with men. She became involved with a woman, but realized she was confusing intimacy with

---

"Rites of Friendship"
Family (ABC-TV)
September 28, 1976
Written by Gerry Day and Bethel Leslie
Directed by Glenn Jordan

One of the best dramatic series of the 1970s, *Family* examines the lives of an upper-middle-class Pasadena, California family. Sada Thompson and James Broderick star as Kate and Doug Lawrence, the understanding and soft-spoken parents of three children: Nancy (Meredith Baxter-Birney), a divorced, single mother; 17-year-old Willie (Gary Frank); and 13-year-old Buddy (Kristy McNichol). The story lines, more character- than plot-driven, tackle such serious topics as cancer, alcoholism, infidelity, and child abuse without resorting to daytime soap opera theatrics.

In "Rites of Friendship," Willie's childhood friend Zeke (Brian Byers) gets arrested during a raid on a gay bar. Kate and Doug, who treat Zeke like their son, are supportive and take him in when his

father throws him out. Even Buddy doesn't care when Zeke, who, paraphrasing her definition of a homosexual, explains he's "one of those boys [who likes boys]." Willie, on the other hand, gives him the cold shoulder and admits he feels betrayed because Zeke waited so long to tell him. Before Zeke returns to college, Willie offers an apology and his friendship.

In its review of the episode, *Variety* noted that among the recent programs dealing with the subject of homosexuality, "no place was it handled more effectively and sensibly."[58] Day and Leslie's intelligent script does indeed offer an honest and sensitive account of a young gay man's struggle to gain his friend's acceptance and love. Homosexuality is presented as a simple fact of life that doesn't need to be qualified by a medical or psychological explanation. It's not about understanding why someone is gay, but why someone needs the love and support of their family and friends when he/she comes out of the closet.

sexuality. She advises Kimberly to explore where her feelings for Lisa are coming from. Lisa admits she's in love with Kimberly, who finally understands her feelings toward Lisa are not sexual. In a final point of irony, Kimberly thanks her three parents for not freaking out, which makes them even more ashamed about their initial homophobic reaction.

Series creator David E. Kelley's terrific script treats a sensitive subject with honesty and intelligence. Jimmy, Jill, and Lydia are well aware their emotional response to Kimberly's confusion is rooted in fear and contradicts their liberal ideals. Even Lydia, who has the most insight into the situation, admits she is relieved Kimberly isn't gay. More importantly, Kelley keeps it "real" by not resorting to the usual eleventh-hour theatrics. No one delivers the standard "it's O.K. to be gay" speech to Kimberly, who admits to Lisa she is relieved to know she's not gay.

Kimberly and Lisa's parents weren't the only ones upset over the kiss. CBS was afraid if the kiss aired as it was originally shot, the network might forfeit advertising revenue. So Kelley and the network compromised and re-shot the scene in the dark — a decision executive producer Michael Pressman told CNN he didn't feel "watered down the power of the episode." One affiliate, KSL-TV in Salt Lake City, didn't air the episode (as well as a previous episode about polygamy). Viewers did actually get a chance to see the "undarkened" kiss on an *Entertainment Tonight* news report, in which anchor Mary Hart invited viewers to judge the scene for themselves.

Despite CBS's interference, *Picket Fences* paved the way for other dramatic series to examine the confusion that teenagers often experience when they find themselves drawn to the same sex. On *Party of Five* (1994-2000), Julia Salinger (Neve Campbell) develops a strong bond with a visiting writing professor, Perry (Olivia D'Abo), who happens to be a lesbian. In appreciation for helping her revise her short story, Perry submits Julia's essay to her publisher. An excited Julia surprises Perry with a kiss on the lips ("I'll Show You Mine"), followed by a slower, more romantic kiss (one we can actually see).

The kiss leaves Julia very confused because she is heterosexual, yet being around Perry makes her feel good about herself. Perry believes Julia's feelings for her have more to do with her bad relationships with men, especially with her last, abusive boyfriend. In "Haunted," the three-episode story arc concludes with Julia understanding, with Perry's help, that her feelings for her have less to do with sexual orientation and more to do with her fear of being alone.

"When does friendship become something more?" The question was posed by the promo for "I'll Show You Mine," which teased the audience with a shot of Julia and Perry about to kiss. The sensationalistic ad (airing during May 1999 sweeps) cheapened a moment that is actually well-integrated into the storyline. More importantly, despite what the promo suggests, homosexuality is ultimately not the issue.

Fans of the show may have been surprised by just how comfortable Julia was around Perry. Three seasons earlier, she was taken off-guard when Allison

(Poppy Montgomery), Justin's (Michael Goorjian) friend from England, made a pass at her ("Poor Substitutes"). Julia flips out and makes a clueless Justin sit between them at the movies. But the situation also freaks out Allison, who tries to prove she is heterosexual by picking up a guy in a club. Julia comes to the rescue and offers Allison some good advice about not moving away from home to escape her problems — something Julia herself can relate to.

Julia isn't the only Salinger with a same-sex admirer. Bailey (Scott Wolf) finds himself in a difficult situation when his ex-girlfriend, Sarah (Jennifer Love Hewitt) has a new boyfriend, Elliot (Christopher Gorham), who'd rather spend time with him. Elliot and Sarah are both virgins, but she decides she's ready to take their relationship to the next level.

In a humorous scene, Bailey tries to find out in a not very subtle way if Elliot's gay or not ("Here and Now"). Did Elliot watch last night's hockey game? Answer: No, he was listening to opera for his music class, but would have preferred to watch the game. Has he seen *Cats*? Answer: No, he hates musicals. The conversation gives Elliot the wrong idea, so when he finally comes out to Bailey, who tells him he's straight, Elliot becomes upset and confused. Bailey doesn't have the heart to tell Sarah the truth, but when Elliot breaks up with her without giving a reason, poor Bailey has no choice to explain that Elliot is gay and there's nothing wrong with her.

Several teen-oriented series, like *Popular* (1999-2001) and the short-lived *Opposite Sex* and *Young Americans* (both 2000), have touched on the issue of sexual confusion. Directed at a younger audience than *Picket Fences* and *Party of Five*, the tone of these and other series is lighter, the characters less complex, and, a sign of the changing times, the gay or lesbian teenager is accepted by his or her peers.

The most original of the teen series, *Popular*, takes a satirical look at life in a Los Angeles high school, where the student population is divided into two distinct groups: the popular crowd and the wannabees. But when the father of the most popular girl in school, Brooke McQueen (Leslie Bibb) marries the mother of the popular crowd's harshest critic, Samantha McPherson (Carly Pope), the rivalry between the two groups heats up.

The popular vs. the unpopular conflict provided series creators Ryan Murphy and Gina Matthews a forum to deal with issues like self-esteem, sexual harassment, and political correctness in a hip, fresh, and honest manner. On the outside, the characters are pure stereotypes (the handsome jock, the attractive homecoming queen, the overweight girl), but through a blend of melodrama and self-referential humor (particularly in terms of popular culture), we get to see the real person hiding underneath the label.

In "Caged," the ongoing feud between the blondes (popular) and brunettes (unpopular) gets out of control, prompting the guys to lock the girls together in the bathroom to iron out their differences. To pass time, Nicole (Tammy Lynn Michaels), the most vicious of the populars, decides they should play a little game. Earlier that day, in their feminist studies class, the women were discussing Nathaniel Hawthorne's *The Scarlet Letter*, a novel their teacher Mr. Bennett

(Mitchell Anderson) explains "is his life" because like Hawthorne's protagonist, Hester Pryne, he once had a secret — he's gay. In order to empathize with Hester, he asks them to write down a big secret about themselves, but not sign their name. Nicole swipes the confessions after class, and suggests trying to match each confession to its author. One of the secrets — "I've questioned my sexuality" — belongs to Lily Esposito (Tamara Mello), the group's resident political activist. When she tries but fails to lose her virginity to her pal and fellow virgin Harrison (Christopher Gorham), she begins to wonder what's wrong with her. Her best friend Carmen (Sara Rue) suggests maybe she's not into guys. Their conversation ends with an innocent kiss, though once again we cut away before their lips meet.

The reaction she receives from the other girls are varied: Brooke admits she's thought about it; Carmen gets angry at Lily for sharing what happened and insists she knows what she wants ("and it ain't women"); and Samantha's angry she was never told what happened. Lily admits meeting a guy ended her confusion. What is refreshing is the fact that no one is horrified over the idea of the two women kissing or that Lily might be a lesbian. The show's real message is: don't let shame or secrets control you.

Popular also addressed the issue of homophobia in two episodes. In "Booty Camp," Nicole is accused of mentally torturing a fellow student, Freddy Gong (Kelvin Yu), by making anti-gay slurs, even though he insists he's not gay. She's sentenced to a consciousness raising camp for the weekend, along with her male and female classmates on both sides of the popularity line who are guilty of making sexist remarks. The camp is run by a drill sergeant named Rock Glass, a relative of the group's science-teacher-from-hell, the mannish Bobbie Glass (Diane Delano, playing both roles), who makes Nicole run laps and watch *Philadelphia* on an endless loop. Although she pretends the weekend had no effect on her, Nicole later apologizes to Freddy.

The high point of this inventive series was an episode about homophobia and intolerance ("Fag"). Lily overhears her male friends making "fag" jokes in front of a new student, Bryan Rose (Joel Michaely), who she assumes by his appearance is gay. She decides to form a chapter of G.L.A.S.S. (Gay and Lesbian Alliance of Supportive Students). When the idea of the group starts to cause problems around school, no one, including her friends, will join. Even Bryan, who gets the word "FAG" painted on his locker, stays away.

But Lily's friends start to see the light when they each become the target of discrimination. While Sam and her boyfriend George (A.T. Montgomery) are out shopping, some girls make disparaging comments about them because they are an interracial couple. Sugar D. (Ron Lester) is turned down for a job at a hotel because he's overweight. Brooke's friend, Jamie (Nick Stabile), reveals he's faced anti-Semitism, while Carmen (Sara Rue) discovers the manager of the clothing store where she works is a bigot.

Consequently, Lily's G.L.A.S.S. meeting turns into a rap group for her friends to talk about prejudice and discrimination. But the group needs a faculty advisor, so it tries to recruit Ms. Glass, who refuses, but later admits she has questions about her sexuality. Lily takes Ms. Glass to the Gay and Lesbian Center to get some pamphlets. While walking back to the car, they're gay-bashed. Lily lands in the hospital and in a touching moment, Miss Glass thanks her for taking her there, but admits she's just not ready to deal with her issues. Lily's friends are all ready now to join the group, but it's disbanded because they don't have a faculty advisor. To show she has made a difference, Bryan, who admits to writing "FAG" on his own locker to get Lily to stop her crusade, comes out to her.

This well-executed episode demonstrates how prejudice comes in all forms, none of which, including homophobia, should be tolerated. Lily's friends learn the necessity of speaking out and of taking action against bigotry. In an amusing montage, each student returns to the place where he or she experienced discrimination to confront the guilty party. "Fag" is a rare example of a teen drama that teaches a valuable lesson without preaching to its young audience.

MADE-FOR-TV TEENS

Before the 1990s, drama series generally avoided gay and lesbian teenagers. With few exceptions, such as the "Rites of Friendship" episode of *Family*, the subject was limited to teens who are not gay, just confused. As we've seen, their anxiety, shame, and/or guilt are alleviated by some "straight talk" from a physician, psychiatrist, psychologist, detective, or high school counselor.

Before drama series were ready to acknowledge the existence of gay teens, several made-for-TV movies made in the mid-1980s/early 1990s examined a gay male's struggle with his homosexuality and its effect on his family. The central conflict typically involved the teen and his father, who always has the most difficulty accepting his son's homosexuality.

The first made-for-TV to address the subject was the 1985 television adaptation of Laura Z. Hobson's 1975 novel, *Consenting Adult*. Hobson's best-known work, *Gentleman's Agreement*, examined anti-Semitism in post-war America. The novel was the basis for the 1949 Academy Award-winning film starring Gregory Peck. *Consenting Adult* looks at another form of prejudice — homophobia — and how an all-American college student's "coming out" affects his family. The novel, inspired by Hobson's relationship with her gay son, Christopher, was set in the late 1960s/early 1970s during the emergence of the gay rights movement. The TV version stripped the novel of its historical/political context by setting the story in the present day. The novel's basic themes remain the same, though the AIDS crisis isn't directly addressed, perhaps because it was considered too complex. (The first network TV movie about AIDS, *An Early Frost*, would air nine months later.)

One afternoon Tess Lynd (Marlo Thomas) meets her son Jeff (Barry Tubb), who gives her some disturbing news.

"I'm a homosexual. I know you didn't want to believe it. I don't want to either," he admits, "but I've been fighting against it for years. But it's true and just gets truer."

Tess puts on a brave front for Jeff and thanks him for confiding in her. But her true feelings are revealed when she rushes to her family doctor to ask why her son is homosexual ("I can't even say the word! I choke on it! It's an ugly, ugly word!") and what she can do about it. Feeling guilty and responsible, Tess enlists the help of a psychiatrist, Dr. Daniels (Thomas Peacock), who also believes homosexuality is an illness and claims that 25 percent of his patients "have turned to heterosexual behavior." Jeff's father, Ken (Martin Sheen), recovering from a stroke, is disgusted by the very thought of his son being gay. Upon hearing the news, he locks himself in the bedroom and bursts into tears. Later, when Jeff comes home for a visit, Ken avoids him. But we find out Ken is having some problems of his own in the bedroom department. He and Tess are no longer intimate, which he blames on his health.

When Jeff enjoys his first homosexual experience (in the back of a van during a rainstorm with a guy he meets in a diner), he realizes all the therapy in the world isn't going to make a difference. "He can't cure me. I'm not sick!" he tells Tess. "I'm a queer, a fag, a fairy, a homosexual!" Although his college roommate (John Terlesky) throws him out when he learns Jeff has been lying about all his sexual conquests with women, his sister (Talia Balsam) and brother-in-law (Matthew Laurance) offer him their support and a place to stay.

Tess isn't ready to accept the truth and Ken clearly never will. So Jeff cuts his parents out of his life, only to return home to attend his father's funeral. Afterwards, Tess gives Jeff a letter Ken wrote to him, but never mailed, in which he attempts to reach out. "I'm not ready to embrace the whole homosexual world," he writes, "but I will not give up on my son."

Consenting Adult is an earnest made-for-TV movie about a gay college student's struggle to gain the acceptance of his controlling mother and homophobic father. The story's primary focus isn't so much Jeff's homosexuality, but his parents' inability to cope. Once a homosexual liaison confirms what he already knew, Jeff simply has to wait for his mom and dad to come around. What little we learn about Jeff's gay life, like the sudden appearance of his live-in lover Stuart (Joseph Adams), is revealed in a series of short scenes that establish he's happy, well-adjusted, and still thinking about mom and dad.

While it's not difficult to believe a parent would reject his/her son or daughter when he/she comes out, the film relies heavily on typical made-for-TV theatrics and plot contrivances to send a warning to heterosexual viewers: don't let this happen to you. In the final scene, Tess makes sure it doesn't by picking up the phone and extending an invitation to Jeff and his friend Stuart to spend the holidays with her.

The following year, CBS aired its own gay teen movie-of-the-week, *Welcome Home, Bobby* (1986). The original story involved a high school senior, Bobby Cavalero (Timothy Williams), who is arrested during a drug raid while in the company of an older gay man. Unlike Jeff, Bobby isn't entirely sure he is gay, though their fathers feel the same way about having a queer son. But while Ken is able to distance himself from Jeff, Bobby's dad, Joe (Tony LoBianco), has to deal with the situation because Bobby is a minor still living at home.

When rumors about the arrest spread around school, Bobby starts getting harassed by a gang of students who nearly drown him in the swimming pool. The only support Bobby receives is from a bohemian couple, Beth and Cleary (Nan Woods and Adam Baldwin), and a gay teacher, Mr. Geffin (John Karlen).

Unfortunately, the film's potential to expose the rejection, hatred, and violence a gay teenager is confronted with at school and at home is compromised by the decision to play it safe and keep Bobby's sexuality ambiguous. Also, by depicting Mark Reed (Stephen James), the older man Bobby becomes involved with, as a letch who preys on teenagers, homosexuality is hardly painted in a positive light. Yet his teacher, Mr. Geffin is obviously introduced to demonstrate that there are healthy, normal, well-adjusted gay men in the world. He opens up to Bobby and tells him he lives a quiet, happy life with his longtime lover. However, his closeted status at school (he clues Bobby by secretly writing "I am gay" on the blackboard) contradicts any positive message he is trying to send. Furthermore, as Keith Howes observes, "there is, as usual, nary a hint that anything approaching a gay community or a small group of understanding individuals could be there for Bobby to help him sort through his muddled feelings."[59] Despite some overly melodramatic moments between father and son, Williams's performance perfectly captures the confusion and angst experienced by many teens coming to terms with their sexual identity.

Far more problematic is the critically acclaimed *Doing Time on Maple Drive* (1992). Directed by *thirtysomething* star Ken Olin, *Maple Drive* is the story of the Carters, an All-American dysfunctional family. The family is under the control of Phil Carter (James B. Sikking), an ex-military man, whose idea of parenting is demanding perfection from his troubled children: Tim (Jim Carrey), an alcoholic who feels like a failure; Karen (Jayne Brook), the insecure daughter hiding her pregnancy and contemplating an abortion because her husband Tom (David Bryon) can't support his family; and Matt (William McNamara), the overachiever who attempts suicide to avoid telling his family he is gay.

The family's secrets begin to surface when Matt's fiancée, Allison (Lori Loughlin), discovers he's gay. Matt confides in his best man, Andy (Phillip Linton), who is surprised but supportive (as long as he doesn't sing show tunes on long car rides).[60] Still afraid to tell his family, a distraught Matt comes close to crashing his car on purpose. When he finally tells his parents the truth, his mother, Lisa (Bibi Besch) becomes hysterical. We find out she's been in denial about her son because she once walked in on Matt and a male friend in the middle of an intimate moment. But she is mostly concerned about what their friends will think when they cancel the wedding. Meanwhile, Phil gets very quiet and tries to understand why his son would think his parents would rather have him dead than disappoint them.

For the first 85 minutes, Phil is an oppressive monster, so it's difficult to accept his transformation into a somewhat rational, calming force in the final ten. Equally problematic is Lisa's near-breakdown when her son admits he is gay. Her reaction is way, way over-the-top, which seems unfair considering Phil is the one demonized up until this point. Of course, it's reasonable to believe Matt's suicide attempt would be enough of a wake-up call for Phil. Though it's made clear he'll need time to come to terms with his son's homosexuality (the fact Alexander the Great was gay and a great general is in Matt's favor), the film ends on a quiet, hopeful note. But after 95 minutes of *sturm und drang*, it's all tied up a little too neatly and far too quickly.

GAY TEENS AND THE TEEN DRAMA

The inclusion of teenage gay and lesbian characters on television dramas such as *Beverly Hills 90210*, *Dawson's Creek*, and *My So-Called Life* has no doubt had a positive impact on young gay men, lesbians, and bisexuals who may be feeling isolated or confused. Most plotlines revolve around a gay teen who has accepted the fact he/she is gay and is now ready to come out to a close friend or family member. It's not only important for teenagers — gay and straight — to see a gay teen getting the support of his/her peers, but to see gay characters like Rickie on *My So-Called Life*, Jack on *Dawson's Creek*, and Willow on *Buffy* as series regulars treated as just "one of the gang."

Of course, right-wing Christian groups fail to see the increased visibility of gay youth on television as progressive. The Christian Action Network made a failed attempt in 1999 to convince the networks to rate programming specifically for HC — "Homosexual Content" — as part of the industry's new self-imposed (and very confusing) rating systems. In an appearance on CNN's *Talkback Live*, CAN President Martin Mawyer accused certain shows of "trying to...change the value systems of Americans, and, in particular, change the value system of children."[61] A more direct attack was launched in March of 1999 against *Dawson's Creek* over the "coming out" of Jack McPhee (Kerr Smith) on a two-part episode that aired on February 10 ("To Be or Not to Be...") and 17 ("...That is the Question"). Mike Gabbard, president of the Hawaii-based Stop Promoting Homosexuality International, led the protest outside the Wilmington, North Carolina studio where the show is filmed. Robert Hales, a 17-year-old who was one of the 30 teens participating in the protest, told an AP reporter, "We're sick and tired of Hollywood trying to force its pro-homosexual values down teenagers' throats...This show is one hundred times worse than *Ellen* because they're targeting high school kids."[62]

It is high school and junior high school students, however — both gay and straight — who need to know that it's "O.K. to be gay" the most. According to Columbia University researcher Joyce Hunter, who has been studying gay youth since the 1970s, teenagers are confronted with the issue at an earlier age. In a poll conducted with U.S. teens, 3 to 10 percent identified themselves as gay, lesbian, bisexual, or "questioning" their sexuality. In San Francisco, it is as high as 18 percent. Hunter believes the percentage is higher than past years because there are more opportunities today to interact through the internet or community support groups.

Increased visibility also creates more problems for gay teens, who have become the target of violence on student campuses and are prone to depression and suicide. The latter assertion, made back in 1994 by the Centers for Disease Control, the National Institutes of Health, and the American Psychological Association (A.P.A.), was refuted by researchers. They claim there is no evidence to support the link between sexual orientation and suicide. But such data is difficult to collect and, as Clinton Anderson of the A.P.A. states, "the lack of 'good science' on the issue should not be an excuse for not helping teens who need it."

The majority of gay teenagers on television are males who are non-stereotypical in appearance and behavior. In an obvious attempt to challenge their audience's pre-conceived ideas of what a homosexual looks and acts like, these guys are usually athletes (which, ironically, makes it tougher for them to come out to their friends, who tend to be more homophobic than most).

Two early examples are HBO's *The Truth About Alex* (1986) and an episode of the CBS Schoolbreak Special, *What If I'm Gay?* (1987). *Alex* is a well-crafted drama about the relationship between two high school football teammates, Brad (Scott Baio), the star quarterback who is headed for West Point, and Alex (Peter Spence), the team's wide receiver and a gifted pianist. The teleplay is an adaptation of *Counterplay*, a young adult novel by Anne Snyder and Louis Pelletier. The novel recounts the background of Brad and Alex's friendship, including a backpacking trip they took together when Alex comes out to Brad, who tells him it doesn't make a difference.

The TV version, however, uses an incident later in the book as the impetus for Alex's coming out to Brad. When Alex stops in a local gas station bathroom during a jog, a trucker makes a pass at Alex. When the teen resists, the trucker accuses Alex of putting the moves on him. A panicked Alex tells Brad what happened and suggests calling the police, but Alex says he can't because he is gay. The scene is problematic because it reinforces a gay male stereotype (the homosexual preying on teenage boys in a restroom). From a narrative standpoint, Alex's "coming out" to Brad, which is so simple and honest in the novel, is overshadowed by the nasty incident.

Once the truth about Alex begins to spread, both guys find themselves up against their homophobic coach and teammates. In addition, Brad's girlfriend, Kay (Jessica Steen) resents how his friendship with Alex is affecting their social status as the school's "coolest couple." Brad's biggest obstacle is his father, Major Stevens (Michael J. Reynolds), who orders him to stay clear of Brad because it could jeopardize his commission to West Point. Fortunately for Alex, his father (Robin Ward) is sympathetic and supportive. The story concludes with the quarterback and the receiver scoring the touchdown that wins the big game.

Brad, who threw the winning pass, defies his father and refuses to end his friendship with Alex.

Although the story contains many familiar elements — the big game finish, the controlling military officer/father — *The Truth About Alex* does offer what was at the time a rare depiction of gay-straight male teen friendship. In an ideal world, every high school students would have a friend as loyal and understanding as Brad.

Unfortunately, this isn't the case in the CBS Schoolbreak Special, *What If I'm Gay?*, which spins a similar story involving a high school soccer player named Todd (Richard Joseph Paul), who tries to come to terms with his homosexuality and loses his best friend in the process.

Todd's secret is uncovered when his friends Alan (Evan Handler) and Kirk (Manfred Melcher) find a "fag mag" in Todd's desk. Todd pretends he bought it for a weight lifting article, but they soon figure out the truth when he starts making derogatory remarks about homosexuals in public. The tension between Todd and Kirk causes a rift in their friendship. Alan, who has always felt somewhat different himself, remains loyal, though concerned about Todd. At one point, he mistakenly thinks Todd may even try to kill himself.

Fortunately, Todd is able to have a heart-to-heart with his understanding coach/school counselor (Ed Marinaro), who encourages him to simply be himself. The issue of AIDS is raised during their conversation, though Todd assures him it's not an issue because he's a virgin. Although their exchange sounds a little didactic, it still carries a gay affirmative message to its young audience.

In the final scene, Todd confronts Kirk about his homophobia, which is tied into his fear he might be gay too. But Todd sets him straight by assuring him their sexual experimentation as kids was healthy, normal, adolescent behavior. Kirk gets the message and suggests they return to being friends.

Although his change in attitude is a little quick and unconvincing, the fact that they engaged in some childhood hanky panky is indeed significant. Same-sex experimentation and masturbation are taboo subjects, even though it's an integral part of the sexual development of both heterosexual and homosexual adolescents.

But Alex and Todd would be glad to know they're not alone. In the 1990s, it seemed every high school on television had their token gay jock. During her summer vacation, *Beverly Hills 90210*'s Kelly Taylor (Jennie Garth) makes a play for a member of the West Beverly High School track team, Kyle Connors (David Lascher). When they go out on a date ("Summer Storm"), she is disappointed he doesn't display any sexual interest in her — until he reveals the reason. "I never slept with a girl before," Kyle admits, "and I don't know if I want to." So Kelly feels better about herself, as does the confused Kyle, who has admitted to someone for the first time he's confused.

Kyle returns in a later episode ("A Competitive Edge") that concerns steroid use by the track team. When Brandon (Jason Priestly) decides to write an exposé for the school paper, he starts sniffing around the weight room to find out where he can score something to get himself bigger faster. Later that night, Kyle meets

Brandon in a dark remote spot to share "his" secret — but not the one you think. "I don't like keeping secrets," Kyle explains. "That's why I'm here...I'm good at reading people, especially when they have secrets to hide." When the story is published, the steroid users gang up on their teammate, Steve Sanders (Ian Ziering), who also recently started to partake himself, because he's tight with Brandon. Fortunately, Kyle steps forward and "comes out" as Brandon's source by admitting "I can't keep living a lie."

"A Competitive Edge" is essentially Kyle's "coming out" episode, except homosexuality is displaced onto the dangers of steroid use. To refresh the audience's memory, there is a flashback to the scene in "Summer Storm" in which Kyle coumes out to Kelly. The pair obviously have remained friends since. Kyle also seems to be less confused about his sexuality and expresses to Kelly how much he enjoys being with her because he can be himself. It's too bad the producers didn't seize the opportunity to explore the gay angle more directly, though the series would make up for it later with several story lines devoted to gay and lesbian characters (see pg. 175).

While Kyle is a sensitive, soft-spoken high school jock, *Buffy the Vampire Slayer*'s Larry Blaisedale (Larry Bagby III) is a loudmouth, sexist bully. Beneath his neanderthal exterior, however, is a gay man screaming to get out. In "Phases," Xander (Nicholas Brendon) is trying to track down the identity of a killer werewolf preying on Sunnydale High. He's convinced it's Larry ("The guy's practically got wolf-boy stamped on his forehead"), so he decides to force a confession out of him. When Xander confronts Larry about what he's been doing at night, he does indeed confess, except not to being a werewolf:

LARRY: What, do you think you have a cure?

XANDER: No, it's just...I know what you've been going through because I've been there. That's why I know you should talk about it.

LARRY : Yeah, that's easy for you to say. I mean, you're nobody. I've got a reputation here.

XANDER: Larry, please, before someone else gets hurt.

LARRY : Look, if this gets out it's over for me. I mean, forget about playing football. They'll run me out of this town. I mean, come on! How are people going to look at me after they find out I'm gay. (Pause.) Oh, wow! I said it. And I felt...okay, I'm gay. I am gay.

XANDER : I heard you the first time.[63]

Larry is eternally grateful to Xander for helping him come out, but Xander never gets a chance to fully explain. So now Larry thinks Xander is also gay. What makes the situation so comical isn't simply the whole mistaken identity situation, which has been done so many times before on situation comedies, but rather Xander's reaction to Larry's revelation. He becomes homophobic and paranoid, causing him to misinterpret his conversations with Buffy, who he fears knows about his conversation with Larry. So when Xander states he'll never be able to look at "him" again, Buffy thinks he means their friend Oz (Seth Green), who turns out to be a werewolf. Buffy replies "He's still a human being most of the time."

The parallel drawn between Larry (the homosexual) and Oz (the werewolf) offers a positive message about the importance of accepting those who are different. Larry also doesn't disappear at the end of the episode, but returns the next season to help Oz and Buffy's watcher, Giles (Anthony Stewart Head) battle vampires ("The Wish"). He is also there on the front line when his graduating class leads the charge against the Mayor and a horde of vampires during the infamous Graduation Day showdown ("Graduation Day, Parts 1 & 2").

College can also be a difficult time for a gay "straight acting guy" who is forced to live a double life or risk losing his friends. On *90210*, the "gay-nervous" Steve Sanders confronts his homophobia when he and Brandon wait in a gay coffee house for a tow truck. Steve is shocked to see the president of his fraternity, Mike Ryan (Jack Armstrong), who mistakenly thinks Steve is gay. Later, back at the Kappa Epsilon Gamma house, some of Steve's frat brothers coincidentally start making anti-gay jokes aimed at Steve, who defends himself by outing Mike. When most of the brothers, led by Artie Devers (Todd Bryant), try to kick Mike out, Steve comes to his defense.

The episode illustrates why we have a moral obligation to speak up when we see injustice being committed, especially if it means confronting our own fears. The fraternity holds a meeting to oust Mike, who, speaking on his own behalf, explains that he imagines how the first African-American, Hispanic, Jewish, and Asian pledges must have felt. Consequently, he understands that being gay isn't really the problem, but rather the fear of not understanding people who are different. Artie doesn't buy the comparison between race and sex, but Steve steps in and convinces the fraternity to keep Mike on as their president by appealing to their sense of brotherhood. In true *90210* fashion, the conflict is resolved a little too quickly. But the change in Steve's attitude from the first scene in the gay coffee house to his final speech is realistic.

Before its April 1994 airing, screenings of *90210*'s "Blind Spot," sponsored by GLAAD/LA, were held in Los Angeles for the Youth Services branch of the Gay and Lesbian Services, the Gay and Lesbian Adolescent Social Services (GLASS) and the Eagle Center. A question-and-answer session was held after each screening with one of the show's executive producers, Chuck Rosin, and Todd Bryant, who plays the homophobic Artie Devers.

The *90210* writers continued to have fun with Steve Sanders, who is still a tad gay-nervous. In a plot reminiscent of Richard Dreyfuss's pursuit of Suzanne Somers in *American Graffiti*, Steve pursues a "goddess in a Cadillac" who turns out to be a transvestite named Elle (Monika Schnare) ("P.S., I Love You," Parts 1 & 2). The idea i snot exactly original, and, more importantly, it's another primary example of how transgender people are too often used for a cheap laugh.

Nor does the joke end there, because the following year Steve and his girl-friend Clare (Kathleen Robertson) run into Elle, who Clare doesn't believe is really a guy. Later, at a college journalism conference ("Nancy's Choice"), Elle meets Clare's father, California University Chancellor Milton Arnold (Nicholas Pryor). When Steve learns they're going out on a date, he asks Elle not to reveal he is a she because the Chancellor is just getting back into the dating scene and might not be able to handle the truth. Elle makes one final appearance in the sixth season's finale at Steve's 21st birthday bash on the *Queen Mary* ("The Say It's Your Birthday"). By this time, the joke has certainly worn out its welcome. A less offensive situation involves Steve's ill-fated attempt to set up a double-date for Brandon and himself ("Crimes and Misdemeanors"). Alas, the women he invites are a lesbian couple, who mistake Steve and Brandon for a gay couple.

Another situation that hits closer to home for Steve involves his actress-mother, Samantha Sanders (Christine Belfrod), who the tabloids report is dating her much younger co-star ("I'm Back Because"). Steve gets belligerent when he sees her alleged boyfriend kissing another woman. Samantha explains what is really going on — the tabloid story isn't true. In fact, she's a lesbian. Steve is ashamed his mother is gay and doesn't exactly hide his feelings when *The National Whisperer* calls for a quote about his mother's love life.

When the network (presumably not Fox) finds out she's gay, Samantha gets fired, which angers Steve, who finally comes around and gives his mother his full support. *90210*'s treatment of Samantha Sander's coming out to her son certainly simplifies what would otherwise be a complex situation. Yet, in their favor, the writers make an effort to keep Steve's character consistent. When Steve gets engaged to a pregnant Janet (Lindsay Price), he tries to hide the fact that his mother is a lesbian and the woman she brought to their engagement party, Karen (Lisa Thornhill), is her lover. Ironically, when Steve asks his father Rush (Jed Allan) to keep Karen's identity a secret, he discovers his dad has no idea his ex-wife is now playing for the other team.

Samantha Sanders was not television's only gay mother. In 1993, a CBS Schoolbreak Special entitled *Other Mothers* examined the effects of homophobia on a high school freshman named Will (Justin Whalin), who has not one but two lesbian mothers (Meredith Baxter and Joanna Cassidy). Will's chances at making new friends and playing basketball (as opposed to sitting on the bench during games) are jeopardized when word gets around that Will has two mommies. After a series of conversations with his mothers and an understanding uncle, Will realizes there's nothing wrong with having two moms who love him so much. The hour drama does an excellent job at introducing the subject of gay parenting to young viewers by exposing how prejudice is rooted in fear and ignorance.

For more advanced teenage viewers, there is a memorable episode of *Popular* ("Wild, Wild Mess"), which received a GLAAD Media Award in 2000 for

Outstanding TV Individual Episode. One storyline has the kids choosing a "Principal-for-a-Day" for Kennedy High. The popular girls want Gwyneth Paltrow, while the unpopular choose George Stephanopoulos. When Harrison reveals his mother, Robin (Alley Mills), once dated George, the popular girls decide to ask her for a favor. But what they discover is that Robin is a lesbian. It's completely cool with them, but not with Harrison, who gets even more upset when they suggest nominating his mom for guest principal.

When his mother confronts him about why he has been keeping the fact she is a lesbian a secret, he admits he's afraid people will think *he's* gay. He eventually

THOSE WHO ARE...TEACH

Gay and lesbian teenagers in TV dramas often receive the support of a teacher or school counselor who may have some personal experience in this area. While most gay teachers are forced to remain closeted for fear of losing their job, television has introduced us to several gay, lesbian, and transgender teachers who have served as positive role models for their students, both gay and straight.

Mr. Geffin (John Karlen): In the made-for-TV film *Welcome Home, Bobby*, sexually confused Bobby Cavalero (Timothy Williams) is told by his gay math teacher Mr. Geffin that he can be gay and still enjoy a happy life.

Miss Jessup (Blair Brown): In this memorable episode of *Family* ("We Love You, Miss Jessup"), Buddy Lawrence's (Kristy McNichol) favorite teacher resigns when she becomes the target of a PTA witch hunt. When Buddy learns Miss Jessup is a lesbian, she is forced to confront her own feelings for a teacher she deeply admires.

Miss Lorraine (Lonette McKee): One of *The Women of Brewster Place*, Lorraine loses her teaching job for being a lesbian. In this 1989 made-for TV movie, set in 1967, she and her lover Tee (Paula Kelly) face their neighbors' bigotry and hatred with tragic results.

Miss Louise (Natalija Noaulich): is a music teacher who causes a stir in Rome, Wisconsin, on *Picket Fences* ("Pageantry") by staging a religious pageant in a public school. She is subsequently fired when it's discovered she is a male-to-female transsexual. Fortunately, her job is protected under Wisconsin law.

Mr. Gil Roberts (Steven Weber): The second part of Showtime's original film, *Common Ground*, set in 1975, focuses on a

closeted French teacher, Mr. Roberts (pronounced "Row-bear"), who comes out of the closet to support his prize pupil (Jonathan Taylor-Thomas) when he's brutally beaten and raped by his homophobic classmates.

Mr. Don Jackson/Miss Debbie (Louis Mustillo): *Popular's* favorite shop teacher, Mr. Jackson, informs his students he's having a sex change and wants to be called Miss Debbie. When she is fired, her students stage a protest, but are unable to get her job back.

Mr. Bennett (Mitchell Anderson): An openly gay teacher who supports Miss Debbie. He teaches feminist studies at *Popular's* Kennedy High School.

Ross Werkman (Mitchell Anderson): On *Party of Five*, Claudia (Lacey Chabert), a music prodigy, takes private lessons from Ross, who is also a close friend of the Salinger family. He often takes care of little Owen and eventually adopts a daughter named Tess.

Ms. Walcott (Kelly Rowan): In *The Truth About Jane*, high school student Jane (Ellen Muth) comes out and receives support from her lesbian teacher, Ms. Walcott. Her favorite teacher even welcomes a distraught Jane into her home after she runs away from her controlling mother (Stockard Channing).

recognizes the error of his ways and, in one of those tender mother-son moments, he apologizes and Robin admits she's not perfect, but will always be honest with him.

As with Harrison and Steve, teenagers often find themselves on both sides of the coming out scenario — as the bearer of "good news" as well as the recipient. Typically, the other person involved is a parent or sibling the teenager identifies with, though some straight teens have had the misfortune of falling for someone who has romantic inclinations toward members of the same sex. No matter the players involved, the message is always the same: gay and lesbian teenagers need your kindness, love, and support, particularly those in the early stages of coming out. We also see how difficult it is for a brother or parents to accept the news and deal with their confusion, anger, and guilt, even though they may have a close friend or relative who's gay or lesbian.

A GAY FRIEND IN NEED: *90210*

During *Beverly Hills 90210*'s ten-season run, the gang befriended their share of gay men and lesbians, most of whom were in a time of crisis. The series regulars played an integral role in resolving the problem, after which the gay character would disappear (or perhaps relocate to another zip code).

David Silver (Brian Austin Green) & Ben Wester (Esteban Powell)

While working at a car wash, David befriends Ben, a gay teenager kicked out of the house by his parents who now lives in the car-wash garage ("Comic Relief"). When David discovers Ben is suicidal, he appeals to Ben's parents (Jennifer Savidge, Christopher Curry). On Christmas Eve ("Santa Knows"), his parents have a change of heart and show up at the Walshes' to bring their son home.

Kelly Taylor (Jennie Garth) & Allison Lash (Sara Melson)

When the abandoned house where the gang throws a rave catches fire, Kelly and another guest, Allison, get trapped in the basement. Allison is severely burned, while a guilty Kelly resumes her modeling career. Kelly and Allison grow closer, which starts to raise eyebrows among Kelly's friends. When Allison professes her love, Kelly lets her down easy. The situation is handled with sensitivity and demonstrates the importance of respecting each other's differences.

Dylan McKay (Luke Perry) & Andrew Emery (Robb Derringer)

Dylan returns to the fold after a three-year absence and befriends Andrew, his co-worker at the Children's Community Center. When Dylan and Andrew are gay-bashed, Andrew is afraid of reporting the incident for fear of losing his job, which is exactly what happens. Fortunately, Dylan comes to the rescue ("Family Tree"). Andrew makes one more appearance in the series in a story about Dylan's temper, which gets him in trouble when he hits a disgruntled neighbor in front of the kids. Although the story lines are uneven, giving Dylan McKay, the King of Cool, a gay friend carries a powerful "Gay is OK" message to teen viewers.

On *Felicity* ("Love and Marriage"), Noel (Scott Foley) receives a visit from his older brother, Ryan (Eddie McClintock), a successful graphic artist. Noel wishes to follow in his brother's artistic footsteps, but is stunned when Ryan reveals he broke up with his longtime girlfriend because he's gay. Noel tries to act cool, but is having a difficult time accepting it. That night, Noel and Felicity (Keri Russell) join Ryan and his boyfriend Alex (Nathan Anderson) for dinner. Ryan drops another bombshell: he and Alex are going to have a commitment ceremony on their first anniversary. The news makes Noel even angrier, but Ryan gets the last word when he admits he was crazy to think his younger brother could support him when he told his parents. ("Imagine that, you actually supporting me for once." Ryan says.)

Noel has a change of heart thanks to Javier (Ian Gomez), Felicity's flamboyant Spanish boss. In the same episode, Felicity agrees to marry Javier to get him the green card he needs to stay in the country with his lover, Samuel (Spencer Beglarian). In the end, Felicity doesn't have to go through with it because Samuel agrees to go to Spain with him so they can be together. Javier comments to Noel that Felicity is so accepting of his relationship. "You know, you'll be surprised — a lot of people disapprove," he explains, "but Felicity, no, she believes in love." Noel realizes he's been selfish and, more importantly, that love is love. So he apologizes to Ryan and assures him he will always be there for him.

The episode, wonderfully written by Jennifer Levin and Andrea Newman, is the perfect example of how a legal issue currently affecting gay people everywhere can be effectively addressed without being preachy. Furthermore, Noel's reaction is believable because he seems more upset that Ryan took so long to come out to him and chose to tell him the news all at once. His reaction is not homophobic — he is just hurt and had a certain image of his brother in his mind.

Both Ryan and Javier would eventually return. Ryan visited his brother when *Felicity* tackled another issue — depression — which Ryan and his father both suffer from. Ryan is concerned about Noel, who recently lost his job for making out with the boss's daughter. When Noel picks up a one-night stand, who robs him and handcuffs him to a motel bed, Noel reconsiders the fact he might be depressed and may possibly need medication.

Javier eventually returns after getting his green card. At the beginning of the show's second season, he once again becomes Felicity's supporter and confidante. His character, played with a mixture of warmth and humor by the talented Ian Gomez, is also given a life of his own when he returns to school to pursue his dream of becoming an actor.

MY SO-CALLED LIFE'S ENRIQUE "RICKIE" VASQUEZ

From the producers of *thirtysomething*, *My So-Called Life* was hailed as one of the best new series of the 1994-1995 season. Yet, in their "infinite wisdom," ABC quickly pulled the plug halfway through the first year because of low ratings. The series, which took an honest look at teenage life through the point-of-view of 15-year-old Angela Chase (Claire Danes), was created by former *thirtysomething* scribe Winnie Holzman. Holzman and her team of writers successfully captured that awkward period when we're trying to find ourselves and life seems like one major emotional crisis after another. Like *thirtysomething*, the storylines are not complex, but simply revolve around Angela's on-again, off-again relationship with Jordan Catalano (Jared Leto) and her friendships with the free-spirited "bad girl" Rayanne (A.J. Langer); former best friend Sharon (Devon Odessa); and the overachiever-next-door, Brian Krakow (Devon Gummersall).

Then there's Enrique "Rickie" Vasquez (Wilson Cruz), American television's first gay teenager. When Angela's overprotective mother (Bess Armstrong) first meets Rickie, she is not sure what to think of her daughter's androgynous friend who wears eyeliner and hangs out in the girls' room. "I find Rickie a little confusing," she tells Angela, who explains *he's* not confused, he's bi. "Do you hear the terms she's throwing around? *Bi?*" Patty asks Angela's dad, Graham (Tom Irwin). Rickie is actually gay, or at least that's what he admits to Delia (Senta Moses) when she develops a crush on him. He considers the possibility of going straight ("In Dreams Begin Responsibilities"), but when Rickie asks Delia out, she asks him if he is gay, and he says yes. "I've actually never said it...out loud," he admits.

Although his family is never shown, we learn more about Rickie's home life over the course of the series. He comes from a mixed background (Black and Hispanic) and lives with an abusive uncle, who kicks him out of the house, then moves away without telling him. A homeless Rickie crashes at Angela's house for a few days, but then lies and says he has some place to go, only to end up back on the street. He finally asks for help from his English teacher, Mr. Katimski (Jeff Perry), who recognizes "Enrique's" (that's what he calls him) potential and takes a personal interest in his welfare. Mr. Katimski, who is gay, tries to get Rickie into a group home, and ends up taking him in, at the risk of losing his job.

My So-Called Life offers one of television's most realistic accounts of a gay teenager rejected by his family. Wilson Cruz is sensational in a role that no doubt hit close to home. In an interview with *The Advocate*, Cruz discussed how his father, who refused to accept his homosexuality, also threw him out of the house.[64] He explained he could relate to his character's status as an "outsider," though he describes Rickie as having it "a little more together" than he did in high school.[65] On occasion, we also see Rickie getting harassed by other students. In one scene, he is slammed up against his locker and called "fag," which Cruz admits happened to him more times than he can remember.[66]

The appeal of Cruz's character is his sensitivity and sense of loyalty to his friends. He is extremely vulnerable, yet at the same time, more insightful than his peers. For example, when Angela and Rayanne are on the "outs" because she fooled around with Jordan, Rickie explains that Rayanne, a perpetual screw-up, has always wanted to be more like sweet, innocent Angela. Rayanne not only makes out with Jordan, but imitates Angela to land the role of Emily Webb in the

Rickie Vasquez
(Wilson Cruz) and the
gang from
My So-Called Life:
Jared Leto,
A.J. Langer, Cruz,
Devon Odessa,
Devon Gummersall
(l-r, rear); Lisa Wilhoit
and Claire Danes
(l-r, front).

school's production of Thorton Wilder's *Our Town*.

Although he is doubly marginalized within his peer group because he is gay and of mixed race, Rickie manages to bond with all the other characters because he is not competing for anyone's friendship, attention, or love. As for the latter, Rickie never gets a chance to get a boyfriend, though he is highly susceptible to crushes. He thinks Jordan is cute and also has his eye on Corey Halfrick (Adam Biesk), who, unfortunately, only has eyes for Angela.

Rickie certainly provided a much-need positive role model for gay teenage viewers, who over the years have been made to feel invisible in the heterosexual world of television. As for Cruz, he moved onto roles in independent features — *Johns* (1996), *All Over Me* (1996) — and guest spots on *Ally McBeal* ("Boy to the World") and *Sister, Sister* ("Double, Double Date"). In 1999, he landed the role of Victor, the Salingers' self-assured nanny, on *Party of Five*. Initially, Victor's sexuality was a bit ambiguous, though toward the end of the season, it's clear he is gay. When Claudia tries to fix him up with Ross, Victor doesn't like the idea because he thinks love should just happen by accident. He finally comes to his senses and the two go on a coffee date ("Isn't It Romantic?"). The series ended in May of 2000 and although we don't really know what happened to Victor and Ross, one can only hope they're living happily ever after together in San Francisco.

DAWSON'S CREEK'S JACK MCPHEE

During *Dawson's Creek's* second season, Jack Mcphee and his sister Andie (Meridith Monroe) arrived in Capeside and soon became part of teenager Dawson Leery's (James Van Der Beek) inner circle. At the time, there were no hints when Jack pulled into town that he was anything but heterosexual. *Dawson's* creator Kevin Williamson, who describes the series as "very personal and autobiographical," decided "to create a character to represent my sexuality, which is my greatest asset in life...[and] to explore the complexities of a young boy coming to terms with his homosexuality, very much the way I did in a small town."[67] The decision to have a series regular come out of the closet also let Williamson and the series's producers follow Jack through the various stages of the coming out process. Over time, we witness Jack coming out to his friends and family, deal with his father's (David Dukes) rejection, experience his first kiss, and fall in love.

When we first meet Jack, he is introverted and socially awkward, particularly in comparison to sister Andie, an overachiever who is a tad on the manic side. It's Jack's interest in art that brings him closer to Joey Potter (Katie Holmes). Their friendship blossoms into a romance, but everything changes in a two-part episode ("To Be or Not to Be...That is the Question"). In the middle of reading a poem (entitled "Today") he wrote for English class that has homoerotic overtones, Jack breaks down and the gay rumors begin to circulate. His friends and family have mixed reactions: Pacey (Joshua Jackson) defends him against their bullying English teacher, Mr. Peterson (Edmund J. Kearney); sister Andie doesn't want it to be true, but eventually offers Jack her love and support; and Jack's disapproving father, who tries to "guilt" his son into admitting he is not gay, makes a hasty exit when both Jack and Andie stand up to him. Interestingly, the most powerful scene involves Jen's (Michelle Williams) current boyfriend, Tyson Hicks (Eddie Mills), a born-again Christian, who, contrary to his Bible quoting demeanor, knows how to have a good time. Tyson calls Jack a "fruit fly" and insists that homosexuality is a choice. He starts to deliver the party line about how homosexuality is wrong because it says so in the Bible, and the gay movement has been "medically and morally" damaging to his country. Fortunately, Jen's Christian grandmother, affectionately called Grams (Mary Beth Peil), steps in and teaches Tyson a much needed lesson in tolerance:

GRAMS: If Jack is gay, he does not need your judgment, young man. The Lord above will be the one to judge him, as he will all of us. What he needs from you, from me, from everyone else in this world is love and tolerance. If anything, that boy must feel scared, and alone, and he will need the understanding of his fellow man to help him through this. Let's save judgment for someone much more experienced than you.[68]

By giving the obligatory tolerance speech to Jen's grandmother, the source becomes as important as the message because it's coming from another Christian (or shall I say a "true Christian"). From a story standpoint, the scene also sets up Jack's future relationship with Jen as well as Grams, who invites the teen to live with them at the end of the second season when Andie is institutionalized and he is left all alone.

Once Jack is out, the series takes its time to explore this aspect of his character. More importantly, Jack is never treated like the token gay character and his homosexuality never limits his involvement in storylines. Since the beginning, he has always had, in Andie's words, "that march to a different drummer thing going." As a gay man, he continues to maintain his individuality.

At the start of season three, Jack joins the Capeside Football team and becomes their star quarterback. At first, he thinks his teammates are being hard on him because he is gay, but he soon discovers it has nothing to do with his sexuality — he's just not mentally and physically ready to be pulverized by the opposition ("None of the Above").

Jack subsequently becomes something of a local celebrity when Dawson shoots a news piece about Jack. He begins corresponding over the internet with a gay guy from a neighboring town, but when they arrange to meet, Jack backs out at the last minute. He has the same reaction when a hunky photographer named Colin (Nick Stabile) takes an interest in him and asks Joey to set them up ("Psychic Friends"). Poor Jack freaks out and later admits he's just not ready to start meeting guys.

When Jack finally is ready for a little romance, he proceeds cautiously. While traveling on a train from Boston back to Capeside ("First Encounters of the Close Kind"), he meets Ethan (Adam Kaufman), who's just ended a two-year relationship. It's obvious to Ethan that Jack is a "newbie," which he explains is "any sweet inexperienced young man destined for broken hearts." Jack is too shy to ask for Ethan's phone number, but fortunately he runs into him again and the two end up sharing a tent at an overnight concert ("Barefoot at Capefest"). Jack's disappointed when nothing happens but, as Ethan explains, he didn't think Jack was ready for a physical relationship, though he does want to remain friends with the possibility of something more.

At the end of the season three, Jack takes Ethan to the "alternative prom" Dawson and the gang organize in protest of the school's refusal to let Jack attend with a male date ("The Anti-Prom"). The more experienced Ethan's intentions, however, still aren't clear, though he does admit to having feelings for Jack. Jack asks him why he hasn't kissed him. Again, Ethan says he doesn't believe Jack is ready, and challenges Jack to initiate the kiss:

ETHAN: O.K., so here we are. Alone in a train station. No one around. No lights, no cameras, no network television to cut to a commercial. It's just you and me. So kiss me Jack. I dare you.

A teary-eyed Jack is simply not able to bring himself to...until the next episode ("True Love"). Realizing he doesn't want to go through life regretting he never

The new kid in town: Kerr Smith as Jack McPhee and the gang from *Dawson's Creek*. From left to right: Michelle Williams, James Van Der Beek, Joshua Jackson, Katie Holmes (front), Meredith Monroe, Kerr Smith.

kissed Ethan, Jack tracks him down and shows him he's not afraid. Unfortunately, Jack impetuously kisses him without knowing Ethan is back together with his boyfriend, Brad (Burgess Jenkins), who just happens to be sitting right there.

Jack has better luck the next season when he meets Tobey (David Monahan) at a Gay-Straight Student Coalition Meeting. At first, the guys take an instant disliking to one another. Jack resents Tobey's judgmental attitude toward him and his implication he's had it easy because he's a football player. But as Tobey later explains, he has a tendency to jump to conclusions based on appearances because, as a child, he was called names by the other kids and his sister had to defend him.

"But you don't know what that's like, do you?" he asks.

"No, I don't, but that doesn't make me any more straight," Jack replies.

The situation is not only consistent with Jack's character, but touches on how even within the gay community, people judge each other by the way they look and act. Jack and Tobey eventually work out their differences and become a bona-fide couple. But as with most high school romances, it doesn't last once Jack goes off to college.

BUFFY'S WILLOW ROSENBERG

Born in Sunnydale, California, Willow (Alyson Hannigan), daughter of Ira and Sheila Rosenberg, is a highly intelligent teenager who has spent most of her high school years battling the forces of evil. Willow's life changes when Buffy Summers (Sarah Michelle Gellar), the Vampire Slayer, a.k.a. the Chosen One, arrives in Sunnydale, not knowing the small suburban town is actually the opening into the demonic underworld. The Slayer possesses superhuman strength and agility, which she uses to kill vampires, demons, and other evil creatures. Buffy receives guidance from her Watcher, school librarian Rupert Giles and a group of teens that refer to themselves as the "Slayerettes" or the "Scooby Gang" (as in the cartoon *Scooby Doo*).

Willow is intelligent and has an extensive knowledge of computers. In fact, while still a student, she is hired as a substitute teacher when science teacher Jenny Calendar (Robia LaMorte) is killed. When she's not at her computer,

REAL LIVE GAY TEENS

An American Family (PBS)
1973
Produced by Craig Gilbert

The first and the best of the reality series introduced us to Bill and Pat Loud and their five children, of Santa Barbara, California. Lance, the eldest son, didn't hide his gayness. Flamboyant, funny, and outrageous, he gave everyone who tuned in to this groundbreaking series something to talk about. Lance later sang in a band, did some acting, and worked as an entertainment journalist in Los Angeles until his death of AIDS-related complications on December 22, 2001 at the age of 50.

American High (Fox Network, PBS)
2000-2001
Directed by R.J. Cutler and Dan Partland

This provocative reality program follows fourteen students at Highland Park High School in Illinois. Among the students is Brad Krefman, an openly gay student who feels isolated, but shares a deep friendship with his gay-friendly pal, Robby Nathan. Robby's completely supportive of his friend when he comes out. Fox made the mistake of canceling this one after a few weeks; luckily, PBS picked it up (and won a much-deserved Emmy for Best Reality Series in 2001).

The Real World (MTV)
1992-
Created by Mary-Ellis Bunim and Jonathan Murray

On MTV's long running reality series, seven strangers are chosen each season to live together in a house for a few months — just to see what'll develop on video-tape. The cast and location change each

season, so the results are mixed (the first season, set in New York, is still the best by far).

Over the years, the series has featured several gay, lesbian, and bisexual cast members, most notably San Francisco's Pedro Zamora (1994), an AIDS activist and educator who showed the MTV audience the reality of living with AIDS. Pedro died at the age of 22 on November 11, 1994, the day after his final episode aired. His friendship with cartoonist and Real World housemate Judd Winick is the subject of Winick's touching cartoon memoir, *Pedro and Me: Friendship, Loss, and What I Learned*.

In addition to Pedro Zemora, the other gay, lesbian, and bisexual cast members have included:

Norm Korpi — New York City, 1992
Beth Anthony — Los Angeles, 1993
Dan Renzi — Miami, 1996
Genesis Moss — Boston, 1997
Ruthie Alcaide — Hawaii, 1999
Justin Daebler — Hawaii, 1999
Jason Daniel Roberts — New Orleans, 2000
Chris Beckman — Chicago, 2002
Aneesa — Chicago, 2002

Senior Year (PBS)
2002
Created, directed, and produced by David Zeiger

Los Angeles's Fairfax High School is the setting for this reality series that follows fifteen students during their senior year. Among them is Jet, a strong-minded gay Asian student who is out to his parents. Produced by PBS in a style similar to *American High*.

College student and recovering witch Willow Rosenberg (Alyson Hannigan), who came out of the closet during season four of *Buffy the Vampire Slayer*.

Willow is usually plowing through Giles's library of ancient books that at times can be quite helpful in tracking down a demon, vampire, or witch. As a result, Willow begins to dabble in witchcraft and starts assisting Giles with spells, which leads to some "experimenting" on her own.

Willow falls in love with Oz, a guitarist for a local band, Dingoes Ate My Baby. Like Willow, Oz also has a high I.Q. and is something of a computer whiz. In fact, he and Willow officially start their relationship on career day when both are being recruited by the same computer company. However, their relationship hits a wall when his cousin Jordy, who turns out to be a werewolf, bites Oz. Oz, who now has to be locked up when there's a full moon, has an affair with a female werewolf, Veruca, who he later must kill to protect Willow.

Oz eventually leaves town, while Willow goes on to college. At her Wicca meeting (a polytheistic Neo-pagan religion that worships the Mother Goddess and whose followers practice benign witchcraft), Willow meets a fellow witch, Tara (Amber Benson). When Sunnydale is invaded by a group of demon-like invaders known as The Gentlemen, who steal everyone's voices, Tara and Amber join forces and magical powers to defend themselves ("Hush").

Over the course of the season, they grow closer and seem more like a couple. At one point, Tara wonders why Willow doesn't introduce her to her friends.

183

Willow assures her she's not ashamed of their relationship; she only wants her all for herself. They eventually declare their love and when Oz pays a surprise visit to Sunnydale, Willow is forced to explain the situation to him ("New Moon Rising").

Buffy creator Joss Whedon has ushered the representation of gay characters on television into the next millennium with the "coming out" of Willow. Both Willow and Tara are prime examples of how gay and lesbian characters, teens as well as adults, can be fully integrated into a series without their homosexuality ever being an issue. Whedon's approach is truly groundbreaking because when Willow comes out, there's no "very special" episode or long speech beginning with the phrase "I've discovered something about myself." Like Willow, we're made to feel her love for Tara is the most natural thing in the world.

In a memorable episode from the 2000-2001 season, Buffy's mother Joyce (Kristine Sutherland) dies unexpectedly ("The Body"). Willow's devastated by the news and becomes somewhat frantic. In an effort to calm her down, Tara kisses her on the lips. It's a simple kiss. A quiet, simple moment.

Two lovers kissing. Just like lovers do.

CHAPTER FOUR

"NOT THAT THERE'S ANYTHING *WRONG* WITH IT"
HOMOSEXUALITY AND TELEVISION COMEDY

Television situation comedies follow a relatively simple format: a conflict or dilemma is introduced, the characters exchange one-liners as they work toward a solution, and, thirty minutes later, all problems are resolved. Of course, the characters do learn a valuable lesson, which, thankfully, by next week is forgotten. Lucy will again wreak havoc trying to get into Ricky's nightclub act. Ralph Kramden will attempt another one of his get-rich-quick schemes. The castaways will once again try (but fail) to get off the uncharted desert island.

There were no gay men or lesbians living next door to the Ricardos and the Kramdens or waiting to be rescued on *Gilligan's Island.* Gay, lesbian, bisexual and transgender characters didn't appear in situation comedies until the early 1970s. Around the same time, sitcoms began to devote single-episode story lines to mature subjects and themes, such as racism, alcoholism, abortion, anti-Semitism, and homosexuality. Before sitcoms like *All in the Family, Barney Miller,* and *Maude* hit the airwaves, gay viewers had to settle for shows exhibiting a certain "gay appeal."

At the top of this list are sitcoms that highlight a female character constantly breaking the rules: *I Love Lucy's* Lucy Ricardo (Lucille Ball), *The Burns and Allen Show's* daffy Gracie Allen, *I Married Joan's* clownish Joan Stevens (Joan Davis), *Our Miss Brooks's* wisecracking Connie Brooks (Eve Arden), and *My Little Margie's* mischievous Margie Albright (Gale Storm). These independent-minded women of the 1950s sitcom world, who were always defying their husbands, fathers, and bosses, made challenging authority fashionable. They also had a special knack for creating chaos in the process. The "rule breakers" spoke to gay and lesbian viewers because they defied the traditional gender roles being reinforced *ad nauseum* by their "family-oriented" competition, i.e., *The Adventures of Ozzie and Harriet, Father Knows Best, The Donna Reed Show,* and *Leave It to Beaver.*

In the early 1960s, a second wave of sitcoms gave that backbone of American patriarchal society — the nuclear family — a much-needed makeover. Although they advocated the same pro-family values, *The Addams Family, Bewitched,* and *The Munsters,* all of which debuted in the 1964-1965 TV season, had definite gay appeal. They represented the "other" kind of American family — the one that didn't live in the white-picket-fenced-in world of the Nelsons and the Cleavers. *The Addams Family* and *The Munsters* were domesticated ghouls and monsters who thought *they* were normal and everyone around them was odd. Like many gay men and lesbians, the Stephens family had a secret — Mom's a witch! But witchcraft sure made their lives more colorful than Ozzie and Harriet's.

The third group of sitcoms features characters in supporting roles that for all purposes *should* be gay or lesbian. There's certainly something different about the way these characters walk, talk, dress, and crack a joke. Many were played by gay, lesbian, and bisexual actors (and if they weren't gay, to quote a friend of mine, "they should be").

Sometimes it was difficult to separate the actor from the role. The gay-straight male characters were typically flamboyant or had "feminine" character-istics: *Bewitched's* practical joker Uncle Arthur (Paul Lynde), shy science teacher *Mr. Peepers* (Wally Cox), *Ghost and Mrs. Muir's* scaredy-cat landlord Claymore Gregg (Charles Nelson Reilly), and *The Odd Couple's* fussy Felix Unger (Tony Randall). On the other hand, a touch of masculinity made female gay-straight characters, such as *The Beverly Hillbillies's* Miss Jane Hathaway (Nancy Kulp) and *The Brady Bunch's* mannish maid, Alice Nelson (Ann B. Davis), the models of efficiency.

The first situation comedy to devote an entire episode to the subject of homo-sexuality was *All in the Family*. In "Judging Books By Covers," Mike (Rob Reiner) and Gloria (Sally Struthers) invite their friend Roger (*General Hospital's* Tony Geary) over for lunch. A sensitive, effeminate intellectual, Roger talks, walks and acts like a stereotypical gay man. Before he arrives, Archie (Carroll O'Connor) goes on a tirade about "Sweetie Pie Roger," whom he claims is as "queer as a four dollar bill."[1] Tired of listening to his father-in-law's homophobic comments, Mike blurts out that it's not Roger who is gay, but Archie's friend Steve (another future soap star, *One Life to Live's* Phillip Carey). Archie refuses to believe it, even

GAY-STRAIGHT SITCOM CHARACTERS

- Mr. Harry Bentley (Paul Benedict) *The Jeffersons*
- Mr. Lynn Belvedere (Christopher Hewett), *Mr. Belvedere*
- Hazel Burke (Shirley Booth), *Hazel*
- Harrison Otis Carter (Gale Gordon), *Here's Lucy*
- Darlene Conner (Sara Gilbert), *Roseanne*
- Mel Cooley (Richard Deacon), *The Dick Van Dyke Show*
- Gunnery Sgt. Alva Bricker (Beverly Archer), *Major Dad*
- Monroe Ficus (JM J. Bullock), *Too Close for Comfort*
- Mr. French (Sebastian Cabot), *Family Affair*

- Zelda Gilroy (Sheila James), *Many Loves of Dobie Gillis*
- Claymore Gregg (Charles Nelson Reilly), *The Ghost & Mrs. Muir*
- Det. Ron Harris (Ron Glass), *Barney Miller*
- Miss Jane Hathaway (Nancy Kulp), *The Beverly Hillbillies*
- Arnold Horshack (Ron Palillo), *Welcome Back, Kotter*
- Jackie (Robin Wilson), *Hot l Baltimore*
- Andrew J. Lansing III (Paul Reubens), *Murphy Brown*
- Larue (Lynette Winter), *Gidget*
- Capt. Doreen Lewis (Eileen Brennan), *Private Benjamin*

when Steve admits it's true during a friendly arm wrestling match. First broadcast in February of 1971, "Judging Books" broke new ground by directly challenging viewers' preconceived ideas of how a homosexual looks and acts. In what seems today like an obvious reversal, heterosexual Roger is fey and flamboyant, while homosexual Steve, an ex-pro football player, is 100 percent all-American male. More importantly, unlike the portrayal of gay men in many dramatic series of the late 1960s/early 1970s (*N.Y.P.D.*, *The Bold Ones*, *Marcus Welby, M.D.*, etc.), Steve isn't ashamed, embarrassed, or troubled about being gay. The real issue here isn't Steve's sexual orientation, but the unreliability of labels and the danger of stereotyping on the basis of appearance.

The humor in *All in the Family* stems from Archie Bunker's ignorance, which continually puts him at odds with his liberal son-in-law. Throughout the episode, Archie spews a seemingly endless stream of derogatory terms, including such anti-gay favorites as "fag," "pansy," "fairy," and "queer." Mike retaliates by arguing how even if Roger was gay, it's acceptable these days in certain places such as England, where homosexuality was legalized in 1967. Archie believes that doesn't prove anything. "England is a fag country," he declares. "Aren't they always picking handkerchiefs out of their sleeves?...The whole society is based on a kind of fagdom."

The studio audience's reaction to Archie's homophobic comments is difficult to read. Is the audience (in the studio, on the laugh track, or at home) laughing *at* Archie or *with* Archie when he makes fun of Roger? Is the episode's message about judging others undermined by Archie's anti-gay jokes and his use of words like "fag" and "pansy" to get laughs?

- Dr. Paul Mercy (Paul Lynde), *Temperatures Rising*
- Ralph Monroe (Mary Grace Canfield), *Green Acres*
- Mr. Mooney (Gale Gordon), *The Lucy Show*
- Alice Nelson (Ann B. Davis), *The Brady Bunch*
- Niles (Daniel Davis), *The Nanny*
- Mr. Robinson Peepers (Wally Cox), *Mr. Peepers*
- Jo Polniaczek (Nancy McKeon), *The Facts of Life*
- Sally Rogers (Rose Marie), *The Dick Van Dyke Show*
- Paul Simms (Paul Lynde), *The Paul Lynde Show*

- Dexter Stuffins (Franklyn Seals), *Silver Spoons*
- Uncle Arthur (Paul Lynde), *Bewitched*
- Felix Unger (Tony Randall), *The Odd Couple*
- Felix Unger (Ron Glass), *The New Odd Couple*
- Henry Warnimont (George Gaynes), *Punky Brewster*
- Nigel Wick (Craig Ferguson), *The Drew Carey Show*
- Major Charles Winchester (David Ogden Stiers), *M*A*S*H*

"Judging Books by Covers:" *All in the Family*'s Archie Bunker (Carroll O'Connor) learns the truth about his drinking buddy Steve (Phillip Carey).

The questions also apply to a 1977 episode of another Norman Lear sitcom, *Maude*. In "The Gay Bar," liberal Maude's (Beatrice Arthur) ultra-conservative neighbor, Dr. Arthur Harmon, is upset a gay bar has opened in Tuckahoe. Arthur (Conrad Bain) thinks homosexuality is sick and that impressionable youth must be protected. He intends to form an organization called "Fathers Against Gay Society" (which, as Maude points out, forms the acronym F.A.G.S.) and launch a campaign to close down the bar because it violates several city ordinances. Maude thinks Arthur's views on gays, like Tuckahoe's ordinances regarding morality, are archaic. Although he's more educated than Archie Bunker, Arthur's opinions about homosexuals and homosexuality are also rooted in ignorance, as revealed in his discussion with Maude's young grandson, Phillip (Kraig Metzlinger):

ARTHUR: The first fact is gay people are sick. They have sort of a disease.

PHILLIP: Is it a contagious disease? Is that why you want to close the bar?

ARTHUR: No, it's not contagious really. You see, gay people shouldn't be out at a bar having a good time. They should be home, alone, being ashamed that they are gay. Trying to get cured.

PHILLIP: What's the cure for being gay?

ARTHUR: Bowling...These gay guys have to start doing something manly. That's what brings them around.

PHILLIP: I thought you didn't want them around.

ARTHUR: Phillip, I seem to be having trouble getting you to understand the dangers of this gay bar. What's wrong? I always used to be able to communicate with you.

PHILLIP: Oh, it's not your fault Dr. Harmon. It's just this year in school
I'm taking a course in logic.[2]

Maude educates Arthur by taking him to the bar in question, The Gay
Caballero. There they talk to a "real-live homosexual person," (Craig Richard
Nelson) who Arthur accuses of indulging "in strange sexual behavior" that "has
no place in this community." ("But you straight people have to live someplace,"
the gay man replies.) Arthur eventually calls off the protest when he discovers the
bar is actually located outside the Tuckahoe city limits and thus not in violation
of any law. Although he may not support the civil rights of gay people, he does
believe in abiding by the law.

Whenever addressing the subject of homosexuality, sitcom "auteurs" like
Norman Lear (*All in the Family, Maude*), Danny Arnold (*Barney Miller*), Susan
Harris (*Soap, The Golden Girls*), and Susan Bloodworth-Thomason (*Designing
Women, Hearts Afire*) are unquestionably liberal in their treatment of gay themes
and characters. The aim is to expose the ignorance and fear generated by the
Archie Bunkers and Arthur Harmons of the world by challenging the following
social myths:

•Homosexuals are identifiable on the basis of their appearance and
behavior.
•All gay men are overtly effeminate.
•All lesbians are overtly masculine.
•Gay people pose a threat to the health, welfare, and safety of our
children.
•Gay men prey on young boys.
•All gay men and lesbians are interested in only one thing: sex.
•All gay men are sexually interested in all straight men.
•All lesbians are sexually interested in all straight women.
•A child's sexual orientation can be influenced or determined by his/her
exposure to a gay people and/or by participating in certain traditionally
gender-specific activities (like playing sports or with dolls).

As a situation comedy works to dispel any or all of the above social myths, it
must also keep its audience entertained. Sitcom writers are continually faced with
the challenge of creating comical situations around the most serious subjects. In
terms of homosexuality, the task is a difficult one because, as in both "Judging
Books" and "The Gay Bar," the writers utilize the very same social myths they're
trying to expose as false as the source of their humor. Whether a character's views
on homosexuality are ignorant (like Archie's) or illogical (like Arthur's), the
danger lies in perpetuating the very same misconceptions simply by
acknowledging them. In other words, is it possible for sitcoms to have it both

ways — be gay friendly but at the same time deliver laughs at the expense of a homosexual character?

The issue is complicated further by the tradition in American film and television of representing gay men as comical stereotypes. As Vito Russo demonstrates in *The Celluloid Closet*, one faction of gay male stereotyping involved the depiction of homosexuals and transgender characters as overtly effeminate men. Lesbians weren't treated in the same manner because they weren't perceived as a threat to the heterosexual male audience. Knowing their audience is familiar with the sissy character, TV comedy writers have to choose between creating gay male characters with stereotypical characteristics or going against type (like Archie's friend Steve).

With the increased visibility of gay men and lesbians in the post-Stonewall era, TV comedy writers have addressed the social myths surrounding homosexuality by concentrating on gay identity. Gay-themed episodes, some with recurring or regular gay and lesbian characters, challenged these preconceived ideas about homosexuality by putting a comical spin on the questions "Who is gay?" and "Who isn't gay?" The answers are intended to surprise the audience. Consequently, the issue of identity plays a central role in the majority of gay-themed sitcom plots, which typically involve someone coming out of the closet ("the coming out episode"), someone being mistaken as gay or straight ("the mistaken identity episode"), or a heterosexual pretending to be gay for fun or profit ("the pretend episode").

While sitcoms get high marks for attempting to expose false social myths, they often fall short when it comes to affirming homosexuality as a healthy lifestyle. In his 1971 work, *Homosexual: Oppression and Liberation*, gay activist/historian Dennis Altman argues that liberals will speak out against the persecution and discrimination of homosexuals "without really accepting homosexuality as a full and satisfying form of sexual and emotional behavior."[3] For Altman, there is also a sharp difference between "tolerance...a gift extended by the superior to the inferior" and "acceptance...which implies not that one pities others...but rather one accepts the validity of their lifestyle."[4]

The difference between "tolerance" and "acceptance" is particularly evident in 1970s sitcoms, when homosexuality was still relatively uncharted territory for television and the issue of gay rights was emerging as a national political movement. When challenging Archie's anti-gay slurs, the closest his liberal son-in-law Mike comes to making a gay-positive statement is pointing out how in countries such as England homosexuality is legal. Yet, Mike never comes "straight" out and states there's nothing wrong with being gay. When he "outs" Archie's friend Steve, he even resorts to using the same type of anti-gay slurs as Archie by suggesting Steve could "prance down the street..."

The writers on *Maude* actually addressed the difference between tolerance and acceptance among liberals in a 1974 episode entitled "Maude's New Friend." Walter (Bill Macy) has become jealous of the time his wife is spending with her new friend Barry (Robert Mandan), a snobby, elitist writer who enjoys putting down Walter because he's a high school dropout. Maude laughs off the suggestion gay Barry might be provoking genuine jealousy in her hubby, causing him to accuse Maude of being "one of those guilt-ridden liberals that can't enjoy anything — not even your own prejudices."

Maude, insulted, fires back: "You call yourself my friend. You've known me all these months. Now you tell me I have a hang-up about your homosexuality. Let me tell you something *Mary* — I mean *Barry*."[5] Barry leaves and a guilty Maude vows never to say anything derogatory about *anyone* again. In her next breath, she suggests going out to dinner for Chinese food, or as she calls it, "Chinks."

Two decades and many gay-themed episodes later, sitcoms continue to rehash these same plots and characters. Homophobia certainly still exists, yet television sitcom characters also seem more aware of it. If anything, the social and political changes since the early 1970s have increased the visibility of gay men and lesbians in not only American society, but on American television. In a memorable episode of *Seinfeld* entitled "The Outing," Jerry Seinfeld and his best friend George Constanza (Jason Alexander) are mistakenly outed as a gay couple by Sharon (Paula Marshall), a student reporter for a New York University newspaper. Throughout the episode, Jerry's forced to explain to his friends and family that he's not gay. George does the same, but then cagily decides to convince his current girlfriend, Allison (Kari Coleman), that he and Jerry *are* lovers as an excuse to break up with her.

Jerry is continually forced to openly declare his heterosexuality, but, to show he's not homophobic, always adds what becomes the episode's disclaimer — "Not that there's anything *wrong* with it!"[6] The catch phrase is repeated by Jerry's mother (Liz Sheridan) and George's mother (Estelle Harris), who both become upset after reading the story. When Kramer (Michael Richards) also runs across it, he scolds Jerry and George for being secretive. Although Jerry and George's lives are turned upside down by the mistake, they continually stop to remind everyone that even though they're denying they're gay, there's *nothing wrong with it.*

The episode, in a way, becomes a wry, self-reflexive commentary on television's uncertain treatment of homosexuality. Yet, the same question raised by the 1970s sitcoms remains — even with the disclaimer, is it okay to derive humor by having characters mistaken for, or pretending to be, gay? The majority of sitcoms, as we see, do try to have it both ways. Through gay plots and gay characters — real, mistaken, and only pretending — homosexuality is treated comically, yet, at the same time, the audience is constantly being assured "there's nothing *wrong* with it."

PLOTLINE #1: THE "COMING OUT" EPISODE

The most common gay-themed sitcom plot is the "coming out" episode, typically concerning a series regular who learns someone in his or her life — best friend, family member, current or ex-boyfriend/girlfriend, co-worker, or roommate — is gay, lesbian, bisexual, or transgender. Although hard to accept at first, the character eventually offers his/her support.

The primary purpose of the coming out episode is to educate the audience, to let them know there's nothing *wrong* with it. Once the message is delivered, the gay character, like Archie's good friend Steve, typically disappears and, in most cases, is never seen, heard, or mentioned again.

There's always an element of surprise in a coming out episode. The discovery that your older brother or 55-year-old father is gay, as opposed to your teenage son, has greater comic potential because it's more unexpected. The individual who comes out is usually the least likely. The men are overtly masculine (i.e., the ex-football player), the women are intensely feminine, and neither displays any stereotypical traits. As for the character who is the recipient of the gay person's "good news," he or she is typically the most intolerant, closed-minded, and unprepared to handle the news, which, of course, makes the situation all the more comical.

On the premiere episode of *Alice* ("Alice Gets a Pass"), waitress Alice Hyatt (Linda Lavin) falls for Mel's (Vic Tayback) friend, a gay ex-pro football player, Jack, played by former UCLA basketball star Denny Miller. Once Jack comes out to Alice, she must decide whether to allow her son Tommy (Phillip McKeon) to go fishing with him. Jack is offended. "If I wasn't gay, would you trust me with your daughter?" he asks. "Don't label me...I respect other people's rights to live their way. I want other people to respect my right to live my way."[7] Alice realizes her fears are unfounded and Tommy goes on the trip.

In its review of the episode, *Variety* noted how the "over-reaction of the 'straights' in the story were carefully limned as silly and short-sighted," yet "the script treated its gay guest...as an exotic object — something rare and different than human."[8] An important aspect of the script *Variety* overlooked is how instead of a third character (i.e., a well-informed, liberal-minded, non-gay person) educating Alice, writer Martin Donovan allows Jack to confront her directly. As we shall see, this is not the usual protocol.

Ex-pro football players Steve and Jack aren't the only professional athletes to emerge out of the sitcom closet. On *Cheers* ("Boys in the Bar"), ex-Red Sox pitcher Sam Malone (Ted Danson) allows his former teammate and drinking buddy Tom Kindeson (Alan Autry) to hold a press conference in the bar to promote his new autobiography, *Catcher's Mask*. Sam doesn't take the time to read Tom's book (or, for that matter, any book), so he has no idea Tom has come out. Upon hearing the news, Sam has difficulty accepting it. "Guys should be guys!" he tells Diane (Shelly Long), who, fulfilling the role of the progressive straight friend, talks some sense into the bartender.

Like Alice, Sam is then faced with a second dilemma. His regular customers, including Cliff (John Ratzenberger) and Norm (George Wendt), threaten to boycott the bar because they believe the publicity from Tom's book is attracting a gay clientele. When Diane confirms there are, in fact, gay men in the bar, the regulars ask Sam to kick them out. At the last second, Sam realizes it's wrong and offers the table of attractive, well-dressed guys a round of drinks. The regulars go into action and trick everyone in the bar into believing it's closing time. Once they're gone, Diane informs them those guys weren't gay (one even hit on her). The gay men are two regulars who've been there the entire time. The men both reveal themselves by giving Norm a kiss on the cheek. Once again, the message is clear: don't judge a book by its cover, whether you read it or not.[9]

On an episode of *Coach* ("A Real Guy's Guy"), Minnesota State University's football coach Hayden Fox (Craig T. Nelson) discovers one of his players, Terry Wilcox (Rob Youngblood), is gay. Hayden finds out when he fixes Terry up with his daughter Kelly (Clare Carey), who picks up a definite "gay vibe" from him. When it becomes clear Hayden can't deal with having a gay player, Terry quits the team.

The episode ends in a hilarious coach-to-player talk. What Hayden doesn't know is they're sitting in a gay bar. So while he's explaining to Terry his discomfort with homosexuality, the male patrons (including two of his former players), unbeknownst to him, are slow dancing behind them. Compared to other episodes, the ending is more realistic because Hayden doesn't undergo some radical eleventh-hour transformation. He simply acknowledges his hang-ups and vows to deal with them.[10]

While some characters, like Alice and Hayden, are forced to confront the issue when someone currently in their lives comes out, most coming out episodes portray a reunion between a series regular and someone from his/her past. The time and distance between the two characters makes it possible for one character to have no idea the other now plays on the other team. No one is prepared for the news, particularly when your friend, like Mel's pal Jack and Sam's buddy Tom, has a reputation as a ladies man.

On *The Love Boat* ("Frat Brothers Forever"), another former stud is reunited with his fraternity brother, the ship's doctor (Bernie Kopell). Doc is happy to see his old college chum Buzz (Roy Thinnes), and introduces him to the ship's crew as "the second biggest ladies man on campus." What Doc doesn't know is Buzz's traveling companion Jim (Michael McGrady) isn't his cousin, but his lover. When Buzz admits the truth, Doc seems completely accepting: "Of course I understand. You found yourself and you're happy." However, as their conversation continues, it seems Doc is not completely content:

BUZZ: Doesn't it make any difference to our friendship?

DOC: Not in the slightest.

BUZZ: Really?

DOC: What am I saying? It does make a difference. But we all have to do what's right for us. So long as it doesn't hurt anyone else. Even though it might make a difference to some people.

BUZZ: How much of a difference does it make to you?

DOC: Well, it changes some things. But most important, we're still friends.

BUZZ: Well, that's what's important to me. Frat brothers forever, huh?

DOC: Frat brothers forever.

[They exchange their secret fraternity handshake.][11]

Why it makes a difference, and what exactly it *does* change are questions that go unanswered. Doc assures Buzz that despite their differences, they will remain friends. Their bond as fraternity brothers serves as a context, albeit a safe one, to continue their friendship. Doc never actually says he disapproves (and it's never exactly clear if he does). There is, however, a slight hint of discomfort not entirely out-of-character for a square like Doc.

Doc is at least more understanding than most straight male characters when a close friend comes out. In *Hearts Afire* ("Birth of a Donation"), everyone keeps telling Billy Bob (Billy Bob Thornton) his long-time friend Jeff Hastings (Charles Frank) is gay, but he won't believe it. Billy is uncomfortable with the subject, so when he finally asks Jeff the big question, he doesn't like the answer and gets angry. When Jeff leaves, Billy admits to his friends he acted like an idiot. In the show's final tag, he phones Jeff and fumbles through an apology by making a peace offering — a cappuccino machine — and then admits he himself "doesn't go in much for those sissy drinks."[12]

Another reunion occurs on the short-lived series *The Fanelli Boys*. In "Pursued," Dominic Fanelli (Joe Pantoliano) is looking forward to seeing his childhood friend, Tommy Esposito (Chazz Palminteri). At first, Dominic is jealous when Tommy, who's a real heartbreaker with the ladies, chooses to spend more time with his other friends than with him. That is, until Tommy drops the pink bombshell. When Dominic's younger brother, Frankie (Chris Meloni), decides to go away for the weekend with Tommy, Dominic panics and heads up to the cabin. Frankie talks some sense into Dominic, who then has the tables turned on him when Tommy misinterprets his hero-worshipping as something more than friendship and forces him to sleep on the other side of the room.[13]

Although the situations, characters, and jokes are broad, the episode makes an important point about male relationships: there is a clear dividing line in our society separating homosocial (platonic) bonding and male homosexual relationships. All his life, Dominic has sought Tommy's approval. But when he finds out his hero is gay, Dominic's homophobia goes into overdrive because he doesn't believe a gay and straight man can be true friends. Interestingly, macho Dominic doesn't share his brother's attitude. He is completely cool about Tommy being gay and has no problem sharing a cabin alone with him.

Sometimes a reunion isn't only unexpected, but unwelcome. On *Too Close for Comfort* ("Shipmates"), cartoonist Henry Rush (Ted Knight) is reunited with the chief petty officer he served under in the navy, Frank Rutger (Gerald S. O'Loughlin). The two men can't stand each other, but somehow Muriel (Nancy Dussault) convinces her husband to invite him over for dinner. Frank accepts Henry's invitation and agrees to bring Carol, who he's been living with for 25 years. Carol turns out to be Carroll (William Prince) — a man — which makes Henry extremely uncomfortable. After they leave, Henry reveals that Frank told him Carroll is dying. When Muriel compares Frank and Carroll's relationship to their marriage, Henry gets annoyed and dismisses the pair as "just a couple of gays living together."

MURIEL: Henry, we are not talking about sexes, we are talking about people. I mean, what makes you think they're incapable of feeling the same love and compassion as we do? That they can't experience the same loneliness, the same emptiness.

HENRY: It's not the same thing, Muriel...I can be just as liberal, just as progressive as you are. But we have a son we're bringing up. And I don't want some day for Andrew to walk in that door and say, "Dad, I want you to meet the person I am going to marry," and for that person to have a mustache.

[Laughter and scattered applause from the audience.][14]

Henry doesn't recognize Frank and Carroll's long-term relationship as a marriage because, by doing so, it would send the wrong message to his son Andrew. Henry believes Andrew needs to know homosexuality is unacceptable to prevent him from becoming one (if that's the case, he may want to consider moving his family out of San Francisco). Ironically, while the Rushes are entertaining their guests, Andrew is in the care of their gay-straight tenant, Monroe (played by openly gay actor, JM J. Bullock).

Henry undergoes a rapid change of heart when he finds Carroll's watch in his house and reads the inscription: "To Carroll, 'Til the End of Time, Frank." Like a magic spell, Henry's homophobia disappears. Two weeks later, he finds Frank, who tells him Carroll has died. Henry comforts his friend and invites him out for a cup of coffee. Although Henry's change in attitude is quick, at least he recognizes his error. But what's truly disturbing is the sound of offstage applause at the end of Henry's speech to Muriel about protecting their son. It signals that some people (in the audience or on the laugh track?) didn't anticipate that Henry's reaction to Frank's homosexuality was the product of ignorance and fear.

Finding out an old navy buddy is gay is nothing compared to the shock of a close friend making some alterations in the gender department. On *In the House* ("Boys II Men II Women"), ex-NFL star Mario Hill (L.L. Cool J.) discovers his old pal (played by RuPaul) works as a drag queen, but is still straight (yeah, right).[15] In an episode of *The John Laroquette Show* ("Dirty Deeds"), John is caught off guard when he runs into his college roommate, now a professional Marlena Dietrich imitator. John doesn't even recognize Artie Fogel (Lane Davies) during the performance. They used to chase women together, so it's an even bigger surprise for John when he learns Artie considered having a sex change operation, but decided against it because "vaginas are very expensive."[16]

Laroquette finds himself in a similar situation on a previous series, *Night Court*. In "Best of Friends," homophobic Dan (Laroquette) discovers his old college friend Chip Collins, who he describes as "old beer blasting, panty-raiding, full-mooning Chiperoo" has had a sex change and is now Charlene (female impersonator Jim Bailey). Dan is shocked to learn the guy he considered his "spiritual twin" is now a woman — and about to get married! "I was just one of the guys on the outside," Charlene explains. "On the inside I was desperately yearning to be one of the girls." But when Dan gets hostile, Charlene socks him in public ("He got bitchy, so I decked him!"), leaving Dan feeling even more emasculated. Dan comes around, but only after hurling more insults and disparaging remarks at Charlene. Although she stands up for herself, it doesn't change the overall tone of the episode. She is still treated like a freak by Dan and his co-workers, except for Bull (Richard Moll), who has trouble grasping the concept of a transsexual.[17]

In "Brandy, You're a Fine Girl," *Just Shoot Me*'s Finch (David Spade) has the opposite reaction when he is reunited with his boyhood pal Burt, now a beautiful blonde named Brandy (Jenny McCarthy). Finch is stunned to find out he is now a she, but once he gets over the initial shock, he has a great time reliving his childhood with her by playing arcade games and having water pistol fights. Finch then becomes distressed when he realizes he has the hots for Brandy. After first peeling him off her, she tells him they're too much like "brother and sister" to be lovers, which Finch can accept (much more easily than we can believe Jenny McCarthy was once named Burt).[18] But it's not only men who are surprised to discover an old friend is donning a dress and high heels. On *Sex and the City* ("Old Dogs, New Dicks"), Samantha (Kim Cattrall) is not exactly flattered to learn her old boyfriend has modeled his drag persona after her.[19]

A character doesn't necessarily have to go back into his/her past. Sometimes there's a homosexual — surprise! — right in front of them all along. On *Gimme a Break*, one of crusty Chief Kanisky's (Dolph Sweet) officers reveals he is gay during a stakeout. "Chief's Gay Evening" is anything but. The Chief doesn't appreciate Officer Jerry's (Eugene Roche) honesty until his friend is gunned down in front of him at the end of the episode (probably because it's much easier to love a dead gay friend than a live one).[20]

Another cop who comes out of the closet (and survives) is Officer Zitelli (Dino Natali), who works at *Barney Miller*'s 12th Precinct. In "Movie, Pt. 1," Zitelli admits to Capt. Barney Miller (Hal Linden) that he wrote the anonymous letter to the squad informing them one of their co-workers is gay. So now everyone knows, except Lieutenant Scanlon (George Murdock), who is determined to find the letter writer. Zitelli's secret is safe until Det. Wojohowicz, a.k.a. Wojo (Maxwell Gail), is accused of sexually harassing a male suspect after reaching into his pants to yank out a stolen wallet. In defending himself, Wojo accidentally outs Zitelli. Scanlon wants his resignation, even though it's against police policy to discriminate against gay people. In the end, Zitelli isn't fired, but gets transferred to an administrative assistant in the Chief Inspector's Office.[21]

Homophobia was addressed in a medical context in three 1970s sitcoms. A 1974 episode of the popular medical comedy *M*A*S*H* ("George") featured a gay soldier named George Weston (Richard Ely), who is admitted into the 4077 with bruises he got from brawling. George confides to Dr. Hawykeye Pierce (Alan Alda) that two guys got beat up in his outfit — "one colored and one homosexual." ("So you're a Negro, who would have guessed?" Pierce replies).[22]

Pierce promises to keep George's secret, but Frank Burns (Larry Linville) finds out and tells Hawkeye and Trapper (Wayne Rogers) there's "one of those types" in the camp "that don't like girls." Burns threatens to report Weston, a decorated soldier, and have him kicked out of the army. But Hawkeye and Trapper manage to get Frank to confess to cheating on his medical exams in order to blackmail him into not filing the report. In today's era of "Don't Ask, Don't Tell," the episode is even more relevant because it exposes the ignorance behind the discrimination of homosexuals in the military. Unlike other gay-themed sitcom episodes of the period, there are no jokes made at the expense of Private Weston — except from Frank Burns, who's the only one in the 4077th homophobic enough to care about getting the gay soldier discharged.

On a 1975 episode of the short-lived *Bob Crane Show*, the former *Hogan's Heroes* star plays Bob Wilcox, an insurance salesman in his 40s who enrolls in medical school. In "The One With the Misdiagnosis," Bob treats an old friend named Charles Lowen (John Astin), a rich architect who checks into the hospital for an ulcer condition. When Bob runs a glucose test, he discovers Charles is hypoglycemic and therefore doesn't need the operation. In a newspaper article with the headline "Renowned Architect Lauds Med Student," Charles publicly thanks his "old and dear friend, Robert Wilcox" for his diagnosis and pledges to raise money for a geriatrics wing for the hospital. The article identifies the "outspoken Lowen" as an active member of the gay liberation movement. Bob worries people might think he's gay too, but finds himself defending his friend when the bigoted Dr. Peterson (Edward Winter) offers his unsolicited opinion about Charles:

> PETERSON: Listen, Wilcox. I know it's fashionable to accept those people as gay, and pretend that we're all the same, but I want to tell you we're not. As far as I'm concerned, the cops should bust every one of them. Just looking at them offends me. The way they talk. They way they gesture. The way they stand....Wilcox, you can say whatever you want, but deep down we both know what he is...a fag![23]

Bob responds by calling Peterson a "miserable, pea-brained bigot." In the final scene, Charles appears at Bob's door with flowers — not for him, but for Bob's wife Ellie (Trisha Hart) — and thanks him again for his friendship. For the first time on a sitcom, homosexuality is recognized as a political issue. The episode aired in May of 1975 and was clearly in sync with the emergence of the national gay rights movement. At the time, gay activists were busy fighting to legalize gay marriage, get a gay civil rights bill (HR 166) passed in the House of Representatives, and overturn state sodomy laws.

The third example from the 1970s is a memorable episode of *The Bob Newhart Show* ("Some of My Best Friends Are"), in which Dr. Hartley invites Mr. Prager (Howard Hessman) to join his therapy group. During his first session, he begins to discuss his relationship problems with his boyfriend Gerald. The group is shocked to find out their new member is gay and one-by-one they leave Bob's office. Dr. Hartley, who had no idea either, shows Mr. Prager his support (but stammers when he tries to say the word "gay"). Later, he begins to understand how Mr. Prager must feel when his wife Emily (Suzanne Pleshette) and neighbor Howard (Bill Daily) make fun of him when he puts on his old glee club tuxedo with the "sissy shirt." Bob explains to Howard why he shouldn't use words like "sissy:"

BOB: Howard, all I'm trying to say is we are going to have to change our attitude a little. It's just that kind of Dark Ages thinking that has kept homosexuals in the closets after all those years.

HOWARD: They're probably looking for shirts like that.[24]

At the next group therapy session, only Mr. Prager shows up. He is clearly upset ("For the first time in my life I feel sad to be gay.") The group eventually arrives and tells Dr. Hartley they want Prager out. Bob chastises them for being narrow minded. They apologize and let him stay, but as soon as he begins to talk about his lover, the two men seated next to him on the couch quickly get up.

For some TV characters, the issue hits even closer to home. In an episode of *Doogie Howser M.D.* ("Spell It M-A-N"), college student Vinnie (Max Casella) is happy to move in with Mark (Gil Cates, Jr.), until he finds out his new roommate is gay and misinterprets Mark's friendly "I love you" as *I love you.* Doogie (Neil Patrick Harris) advises Vinnie to talk it out with Mark, who assures him he's not in love with him. Vinnie confesses he's still a virgin and is afraid he'll remain one if everyone thinks he's gay. But when Mark discloses he's also a virgin looking for a monogamous relationship, Vinnie realizes they have more in common than he knew and decides not to move out (though he still has the need to tell Mark's friends he's a card-carrying heterosexual).[25]

On *Empty Nest* ("Single White Male"), Charley (David Leisure) faces a similar dilemma. He invites a co-worker from the cruise ship, Hank (Douglas Sills), who has just ended a relationship, to move in with him. When Charley spends a night out on the town with Hank and his buddies, he discovers Hank is gay. Like

Vinnie, Charley freaks and decides to ask Hank to move out. But when Charley's date makes a "fag" remark in front of Hank without realizing he's gay, he comes to his defense and asks Hank to stay. While it's certainly admirable for Charley to stick up for Hank, the gay man remains silent during the entire exchange as if he is incapable of defending himself.[26]

Finding out a friend or roommate is gay or lesbian becomes even more complicated when you're the object of the gay friend's affection. On *Blossom* ("Double Date") Joey Russo (Joey Lawrence) gets a love letter from a secret admirer named Leslie. He's stunned to find out Leslie is the full name of the third baseman on his team, Les (Paul Wittenburg). Leslie gives Joey another note apologizing for making him uncomfortable with the first letter. Joey is still freaked out. ("He used to be one of the guys, now he just gives me the creeps.") To make Joey more empathetic and understand what his friend is going through, his African-American sister-in-law Shelley (Samaria Graham) shares an incident from her childhood. When she was a young girl, Shelly was not permitted to go swimming with her friends at a private country club because it was restricted. Joey understands (sort of) how difficult it must be for Leslie. So later, in school, he not only defends his gay friend against a bully, but assures him if his father ever joins a country club, he's invited.[27]

Another high school student with a similar problem is *That 70's Show*'s Eric (Topher Grace). He becomes fast friends with his science lab partner Buddy (*Third Rock From the Sun*'s Joseph Gordon Levitt), a rich kid with a hot car. While riding home one night from the movies, Buddy surprises Eric with a kiss. Buddy admits he's gay, which sends Eric running back to his girlfriend Donna (Laura Prepon).

When Eric sees Buddy in school and asks why he's attracted to him, Buddy explains it's because he's "smart, sensitive, and nice-looking."[28] *That 70's Show* may be set in the era of disco and Watergate, but the kids have a progressive 1990s attitude about homosexuality. All are basically cool about Buddy being gay, including Eric, who accepts the compliment and vows to continue being his friend.

TV adults can find themselves in similar situations. At a bachelor party ("The Guilty Party"), *Dream On*'s Martin Tupper (Brian Benben) finds out his childhood friend from summer camp, Jerry Dorfer (David Hyde Pierce), had a crush on him. On *Dharma and Greg* ("Invasion of the Buddy Snatchers"), Dharma becomes friends with Greg's poker buddies and discovers one of them, Howard (Hamilton Van Watts), is gay and has a huge crush on Greg. And on *Living Single* ("Woman to Woman"), Max (Erika Alexander) is unprepared when her college roommate, Shayla (Karen Malina White), comes to town to get married — to a woman. Max is upset Shayla never came out to her, prompting Shayla to admit she was in love with her in college, but was afraid Max would drop her as a friend if she knew. Max understands and gives Shayla and her bride-to-be, Chris (Tanika Ray) her blessing.

An episode of the summer comedy *M.Y.O.B.* ("Boys in the Band") puts an unusual spin on the crush situation. A high school teacher, Mary Beth (Kellie

Waymire), jeopardizes her job by having an affair with one of her students, Evan (Steve Moreno). They haven't gone all the way yet and Mary Beth thinks it's because he's shy, but sassy teenager Riley (Katharine Towne) figures out the real reason when she catches Evan having sex with another guy. Riley assures him it's all right. ("I don't have a problem with gays. I watch *Frasier* all the time.") To help Mary Beth save her job, Riley gets Evan to come out of the closet.

Not everyone can handle a crush with maturity and grace, particularly when a third person is involved. On *Love and War* ("Bali Hai"), Nadine (Joanna Gleason) develops a serious crush on her literature teacher, Neil (Corbin Bernsen). He seems interested and invites her over to dinner, only to find out he really has his eye on Jack (Jay Thomas). In "Elaine's Strange Triangle," *Taxi*'s Tony (Tony Danza) finds himself in a similar situation. On the rebound from another failed relationship, Elaine (Marilu Henner) meets the sweet and successful Kirk (John David Carson), who tells Tony he has a crush on him. Tony turns to Alex (Judd Hirsch), who has a heart-to-heart with Kirk. Once the air is cleared, the scene erupts into a comical disco dance number featuring a reluctant Alex and a bar full of gay men. Although the scene is gratuitous and played strictly for laughs, it doesn't detract from the series's comical approach to bisexuality, a subject rare to sitcoms.

Another bisexual storyline on *Sex and the City* ("Boy, Girl, Boy, Girl") involves Carrie (Sarah Jessica Parker). She is hesitant about getting involved with her handsome new boyfriend Sean (Donovan Leitch), who admits he once had a boyfriend himself. Carrie is skeptical if bisexuality even exists. "I think it's just a layover on the way to gay town," she tells her friends. So a paranoid Carrie keeps asking Sean about his experiences with men and is convinced he's checking out other guys. One night Sean takes her downtown to a party where everyone — gay, straight, and bi ("a pupu platter of sexual orientation") — seems to have been married to each other. One game of pansexual spin-the-bottle later, during which Carrie is the recipient of a smooch from another woman, Dawn (singer Alanis Morissette), she realizes she really is too old for what she calls Generation XY.

Some heterosexual characters find themselves in even more awkward situations when they are the object of a gay man or lesbian's crush. *Taxi* alumni Judd Hirsch finds himself the object of another man's affection on a memorable episode of *Dear John* ("Stand By Your Man"). Hirsch plays John Lacey, a member of "One-Two-One Club," a singles support group. He befriends the group's new member, Tony Larkin (Cleavon Little), who divorced his wife after fourteen years because "something" stopped working in their marriage. After spending a week together going to dinner and attending basketball and hockey games, Tony tells John what went wrong — he's gay. John encourages him to share this with the group and afterwards he reveals privately to John another little secret: he's in love with him. John doesn't understand why, but Tony tells him he's "wonderful, sensitive, caring, and has a good sense of humor." While John thinks it's an infatuation, Tony becomes persistent and starts sending him flowers and leaving messages on his answering machine.

Taking the advice of one of his support group members, John invites Tony out for dinner so he can tell him in a public place they can no longer be friends. John expects to let Tony go quietly, but he makes a big scene instead and starts shouting and crying in the restaurant. "You think you're some great prize," Tony cries. "I can't believe I ever loved you!" The episode misses the comic mark not only because it perpetuates the myth that gay men prey on straight men. Tony is written and portrayed by the talented Little as a crazed hysteric — obsessive, unstable, and borderline hostile.

Niles (David Hyde Pierce) has his turn at the object of another man's affection in the memorable *Frasier* episode ("The Ski Lodge"). When Roz (Peri Gilpin) wins a raffle, she treats the gang to a ski trip. The prize also includes a handsome French ski instructor named Guy (James Patrick Stewart), who has the hots for an unsuspecting Niles. The night at the ski lodge turns into a door-slamming, bed-swapping farce. Once Guy confirms with Frasier's father Martin (John Mahoney), who's having problems with his hearing, that Niles is gay, a naked Guy waits in Niles's bed to surprise him. Niles is indeed surprised.

A gay crush is even funnier when it's a case of mistaken identity. On *The John Larroquette Show* ("An Odd Cup of Team"), Officer Hampton (Lenny Clarke) is thoroughly confused when he receives flowers from his doctor, Dr. Lewis (Lenny Wolpe). What the policeman doesn't know is the flowers are really from John's assistant, Mahalia (Liz Torres). In a hilarious scene, Hampton goes in to confront the doctor, who has trouble convincing his patient he didn't send him flowers.

Perhaps the funniest example involves fictional talk show host Larry Sanders (Garry Shandling) and real-life actor David Duchovny. In "The Bump," Larry is unnerved by all the attention Duchovny is giving him — the phone calls, an *X-Files* jacket (that says "The Truth Is Out There," which Larry thinks has a gay connotation), and an invitation to stay overnight at his beach house. Larry asks Hank Kingsley's gay assistant, Brian (Scott Thompson), about Duchovny's

---

"The Matchmaker"
Frasier (NBC-TV)
April 10, 1994
Written by Joe Keenan
Directed by David Lee

When it comes to having a "quality," *Friends*'s Chandler is not even in the same league as the Crane brothers — Dr. Frasier (Kelsey Grammer) and Dr. Niles (David Hyde Pierce). They are effete, nicely dressed, well-educated siblings who love *haute cuisine*, fine wine, and the opera. So it's no surprise that the radio station's new manager, Tom Duran (*Caroline in the City*'s Eric Lutes), misinterprets Frasier's dinner invitation as a date. Actually, Frasier was trying to fix him up with Daphne (Jane Leeves). Over the course of the evening, they all discover, one-by-one, a mistake has

occurred, beginning with Niles, who takes delight in breaking the news to Frasier.

Written by openly gay writer Keenan and directed by the series's gay producer Lee, the episode never turns homosexuality or the gay character into "the joke." Tom thinks Frasier is gay and Roz (Peri Gilpin) confirms it to get revenge on her boss, who is always cracking jokes about her active sex life. The dinner party scene is hilarious because every word out of the clueless Frasier's mouth is a gay double entendre that Tom interprets as a come-on.

"The Matchmaker" is a textbook example of what a situation comedy can achieve when all the elements — a great script, solid direction, and a terrific ensemble cast — are in place.

sexuality. Brian tells him a third of his friends think he's gay, a third think he's bi, and the "rest don't care. They just want to kiss him anyways, which would be me." Feeling increasingly uncomfortable, Larry confronts Duchovny to tell him he is straight. David says he's also straight, but makes a startling confession:

> DAVID: Sometimes I do wish I was gay recently because I find you very attractive. I know that it's not a gay thing because the feeling I have with you, it's the kind of feeling I normally have with a woman I like. It's like a warmth or a buzz. It's very confusing for me. Do you understand that?[29]

Duchovny's hilarious confession, which he delivers in a totally sincere, deadpan fashion, leaves Larry even more confused. The talk show host later pretends to be angry when Duchovny gets bumped from the show (Larry actually arranged for him to be rescheduled for the following week, so he'll be on with guest host Jon Stewart). Sensing Larry's upset, Duchovny puts his hand against the talk show host's cheek, quiets him down, and softly says, "You really do care about me." On the series's last episode and Larry's final show ("Flip"), Duchovny returns for another homo-laden encounter. When Larry visits Duchovny in his hotel room to ask him to appear on the final show, the actor is wearing only a bathrobe. During their conversation, he partly exposes himself to Larry.[30]

Not all episodes involving gay crushes are played strictly for laughs, such as a more serious episode of *The Golden Girls*. In "Isn't It Romantic?," Dorothy's (Bea Arthur) old college friend, Jean (Lois Nettleton), whose lover Pat recently died, develops a crush on an unsuspecting Rose (Betty White), who has no idea Jean is a lesbian. When Jean confesses her feelings, Rose lets her down easy. "I don't understand these kinds of feelings," Rose admits, "but if I did understand, if I was, you know, like you, I would be very flattered and proud you thought of me that way."[31] Sweet, naive Rose's response is completely in character because her reaction is so honest and genuine. This episode's obligatory "Gay is OK" speech is delivered by Sophia (Estelle Getty) in response to her daughter Dorothy's question about what she'd do if she had a gay child. "I wouldn't love him one less bit," Sophia says. "I would wish him all the happiness in the world." Besides delivering a very heart-felt, gay positive message, Sophia's speech also balances out the sharp-tongued senior citizen's rapid-fire wisecracks about Jean having a crush on "goody two-shoes" Rose.

Designing Women's Suzanne Sugarbaker (Delta Burke) finds herself in a similar situation in "Suzanne Goes Looking for a Friend." The former beauty queen finds one in her former pageant competitor, Eugenia Weeks (Karen Kopins), who now works as a weather forecaster on a local Atlanta station. When Eugenia tells Suzanne about her recent "coming out," Suzanne mistakenly thinks she means at a cotillion (which Suzanne notes would make her "the oldest living debutante"). When Julia (Dixie Carter), Charlene (Jean Smart), and Mary Jo (Annie Potts) set her straight, Suzanne panics because she thinks Eugenia must be in love with her.

And if they're seen together, men might think she's unavailable. The episode winds down with a humorous heart-to-heart talk between the women in a steam room, where someone directs an anti-gay remark toward Eugenia. Suzanne begins to understand how difficult it must be for her and vows to continue being her friend, perhaps more out of sympathy than anything, which of course is a big step for a character as narcissistic as Suzanne Sugarbaker.[32]

It's also possible to be the object of someone's crush without even knowing it. On an episode of *Wings* ("Honey, We Broke the Kid"), Antonio (Tony Shaloub) is thrilled when his idol, openly gay television actor Deke Hathaway (Clint Carmichael), star of *Austin Houston P.I.*, arrives on Nantucket. Antonio, who has no idea Deke is gay, has the time of his life showing the actor around the island. When it's time to say goodbye, Deke invites Antonio to come for a visit and leaves without his number one fan ever finding out the truth.[33]

The crush scenario has great comic potential when it involves a naive and/or uninformed character like Rose Nyland, Suzanne Sugarbaker, or Antonio Scarpacci. But the joke can be carried too far, as in an episode of *Ned and Stacey* ("Saved By the Belvedere"). The main plot involves Ned (Thomas Haden Church) directing a television commercial starring actor Christopher Hewett. Ned hires Hewett to recreate his role as TV's *Mr. Belvedere* for the commercial, but he runs into trouble when Hewett really thinks he is the famous TV butler. Like his TV character, Hewett begins dispensing advice to everyone, including a member of Ned's crew, Jody (Andrew Craig), who admits he has a crush on another man. In the final tag, Ned returns home and listens to a series of answering machine messages from Jody, beginning with "let's get together" to "let's go to the theatre tonight" to "I'm here at the theatre, where are you?" to "I'm waiting for you in the bedroom right now wearing a thong."[34] At that moment, Ned pulls a gun out of his pocket.

GLAAD criticized Fox Television for "perpetuating the hateful stereotype of gay men as predators, particularly in pursuit of straight men" and for "sending a clear message that it's acceptable for me to respond to unwanted admiration from gay men with violence."[35] In light of the murder of Scott Amedure, who was gunned down by Jonathan Schmitz after revealing his secret crush on him on *The Jenny Jones Show*, GLAAD found the scene in *Ned and Stacey* "...irresponsible, malicious and dangerous."[36] On February 28, 1997, GLAAD posted an apology from Trae D. Williams of Fox Broadcast Standards:

> I would like to apologize on behalf of the network if this scene was interpreted as anything other than what was intended — which was certainly not to depict any particular group of persons in an unfair light. I assure you that such an unfair portrayal would be contrary to all that we as a network strive for each and every day and would never knowingly be approved."[37]

In other words, it never occurred to the producers or the network the scene was offensive. In spite of their apology, the scene aired during its syndication run on the USA Network.

What most straight male characters find just as disquieting as attracting gay admirers is discovering their ex-wife or girlfriend is a lesbian. Most of these narcissistic males assume responsibility for sending their mates into the arms of another woman. In "Kirk's Ex-Wife," *Dear John*'s obnoxious Kirk Morris (Jere Burns) is still suffering from a severely damaged male ego when he runs into his successful ex-wife Carol (Kate McNeil) and her female lover, Donna (Elizabeth Moorehead). "I turned my wife into a womanizer!" he cries.[38] *Hearts Afire*'s John Hartman (John Ritter) doesn't like to be reminded his ex-wife, Diandra (Julie Cobb), left him for their marriage counselor, Dr. Ruth Colquist (Conchata Farrell). In "The Smelly Car," *Seinfeld*'s George Constanza is certain he's responsible for his ex-girlfriend Susan's (Heidi Swedberg) relationship with her current lover, Mona (Viveka Davis).[39]

On *Muscle* ("Episode 5"), bodybuilder Sam (Steve Henneberry) doesn't even get a chance to pursue the love of his life, WNKW newscaster Browyn Jones (Amy Pietz). When she learns she's going to be outed by a New York newspaper, she beats them to it and opens her newscast by telling her viewers, "I'm a lesbian." Her producer Hal (John Putch) is concerned at first, until he realizes the station can capitalize on it to improve ratings. At the top of her next show, Browyn is introduced as a "newscaster lesbian."

Some men handle the situation with a little more style. Although *Friends*'s Ross (David Schwimmer) still carries a torch for his ex-wife Carol (Jane Sibbet), he's man enough to walk her down the aisle when she marries Susan (Jessica Hecht) in "The One With the Lesbian Wedding."[40] Another good sport is *Nine to Five*'s Bud Coleman (Edward Winter), who realizes he has no chance of rekindling an old romance with his girlfriend from college, Liz (Gail Strickland), when *her* ex-girlfriend Chris (Hilarie Thompson) interrupts their date. He had no idea Liz was a lesbian when their evening started, but being a true gentleman, he not only leaves the restaurant quietly, he sends a bottle of Dom Perigon to their table.

Some men have limits when it comes to old girlfriends. On *Herman's Head* ("Spermin' Herman") Herman (William Ragsdale) is delighted to see his ex, Rebecca (Liz Rassey) until she hits him with a double whammy: she's a lesbian and wants him to be the father of her child. Herman considers taking her up on her offer, until he realizes she's only interested in his sperm.

Women are not immune to making a similar discovery about their ex- or current boyfriend. While men find it a reflection on their manhood, women are generally more supportive. On *Phyllis* ("Out of the Closet"), Mary Richards's self-involved former landlady Phyllis Lindstrom (Cloris Leachman), now residing in San Francisco, is relieved when her new beau Scott (Edward Winter) announces he's gay. "Oh, that's wonderful," she tells him. "I was worried you weren't attracted to me." Phyllis is reluctant, however, to let Scott introduce her to his parents as his girlfriend. The situation becomes even more complicated when he announces their engagement. Phyllis convinces Scott to come out to his parents at their engagement party, but he gets carried away and comes out to all of his guests. "I'm gay," he exclaims, "and I have this woman [indicating Phyllis] to thank!"

While Phyllis is reluctant to play the part of Scott's beard, *Seinfeld*'s Elaine (Julia Louis-Dreyfuss) volunteers for the job. She attends the ballet as a friend-of-a-friend's girlfriend and makes the mistake of falling in love with him. She plans to convert Robert (Robert Mailhouse) to her team, but Jerry is skeptical: "You think you can just get him to change teams? When he joins that team it's not a whim. He likes his team. They're only comfortable with *their* equipment."[41] Although Elaine manages to "turn him," she discovers she can't have the same "expertise" with their equipment as someone who has access to it 24 hours a day, so he quickly returns back to his own team.

In "The Turtle and the Hair," *Sex and the City*'s Carrie (Sarah Jessica Parker) becomes fixated on the idea of getting married after attending a wedding. When her current beau, Mr. Big (Chris Noth), a divorcé, announces he has no intention of getting married again, she begins to wonder if it will ever happen for her. Carrie's gay friend Stanford Blanche (Willie Garson) has a great suggestion: Carrie should marry him, so he will get his inheritance from his grandmother (Mimi Wedell), who controls the family purse strings. It sounds like a good plan, but when the grandmother tells Carrie she knows her grandson is a "fruit," she realizes there's no inheritance in Stanford's future and no marriage in hers.

Teenagers can experience the same disappointment about a potential suitor. On *Blossom* ("It Happened One Night"), Nick (Ted Wass) volunteers his daughter (Mayim Balik) to show his friend's son Fred (Charlie Heath) around Los Angeles. The situation becomes awkward when Nick is caught spying on the couple. Later, an even more embarrassed and clueless Nick finds out from Fred's father, Dan (Chris Mulkey), in a rather refreshing, matter-of-fact way, that Fred is gay.

A somber episode of *Moesha* provides an interesting contrast to the breezy, gay-positive tone of *Blossom*. In "Labels," Moesha (Brandy) meets Hakeem's (Lamont Bentley) cousin, Omar. On their first date, she figures out he's gay and makes the mistake of telling her gossipy friends about it, who spread the news all around school. Hakeem doesn't believe it's true and gets angry at Moesha for starting rumors about Omar. In the final scene, Moesha reads the lyrics from an Edie Brickell song "I Know What I Know if You Know What I Mean." While she reads the poem, we see (but don't hear) Omar telling Hakeem he's gay. Hakeem is clearly upset and in the final scene, he visits Moesha on her porch and says hello. As the two sit in silence, we hear Moesha say in voiceover, "Dear Diary, I got my friend back."

While the episode delivers a positive message to youngsters about being true to oneself, the ending skirts the gay issue by making it more about Hakeem and Moesha's friendship. Omar's "coming out" and Hakeem's reaction are never fully played out, which makes the ending all the more confusing. Hakeem and

Moesha's silence in the end is also ambiguous. Although it seems to be more about the tension in the friends' relationship, it can also be read, particularly because of the lack of dialogue between Omar and Hakeem, as if they're mourning his gayness. Moesha got her friend back, but what about poor Omar?

Unlike the *Moesha* episode, most sitcom characters find it easier to accept a friend stepping out of the closet than when the door swings open in their own house. The issue seems to hit closer to home when a father, mother, brother, or sister decides to let the family in on their little secret. Consequently, the situation has greater comic potential because the gay or lesbian parent or sibling is typically someone the rest of the family *really* thought they knew.

For example, *Dream On*'s Martin Tupper has a real shock in "Pop's Secret," when his dad Mickey (Paul Dooley) moves back to New York. Martin is afraid to live in the same city as his father because it will cramp his style, but instead his father spends all his time with his new roommate Roger (Dion Anderson). After Martin observes the two men acting like a married couple, Martin asks his father if he's gay. Mickey admits it's true and a reluctant Martin accepts Roger into the family.

Unfortunately, the relationship doesn't last ("The Courtship of Martin's Father") and Martin's worst nightmare comes true when Dad appears at his door with his suitcase. Although he still feels uncomfortable with his father's homosexuality, Martin encourages his father to meet someone else. He brings his father to a gay bowling alley and even tries to educate him about safe sex. When Mickey begins to interfere in Martin's personal and professional life, Martin gets angry and finally admits he wishes his father wasn't gay. Surprisingly, Mickey admits he feels the same way and wonders if it would be easier for everyone if he went back into the closet. Martin eventually realizes it's not his father's homosexuality that's troubling him — but the fact that he, like his father, is also a single man living in Manhattan looking for love. Father and son come to an understanding and in the final scene, they enjoy a warm and fuzzy father-and-son moment sitting in their bathrobes watching The Weather Channel and drinking beer.

Dream On's humor is derived from the incorporation of old movie and TV clips to illustrate what Martin's thinking. In situations involving his father, the clips are used to punctuate how uncomfortable Martin is about his father's sexuality. Martin isn't homophobic; he's *homo-nervous*. When Martin first suspects Mickey and Roger are more than just roommates, everything he hears and sees has a gay connotation. In discussing their golf game, Roger says "Your dad putts like an old lady." (Cut to Bette Davis saying "What was that word?") While snooping in their medicine cabinet, Martin sees two shavers. (Cut to an image of W.C. Fields and another man shaving each other.) Created by David Crane and Marta Kaufman, who'd later strike gold as the co-creators of *Friends*, *Dream On*'s camp sensibility made it one of the more gay-friendly shows of the 1990s. This is particularly unusual for a sitcom that is essentially about a horny straight divorcé trying to get laid. With its adult language and brief glimpses of female nudity, *Dream On* paved the way for other adult-oriented cable comedies like HBO's *Sex and the City* and Showtime's *Beggars and Choosers* and *Rude Awakening*.

Like Martin Tupper, *Grace Under Fire*'s Grace Kelly (Brett Butler) is shocked when she discovers her father-in-law Emmet (Bryan Clark) is gay. In "Emmett's Secret," Grace and her boyfriend Rick (Alan Autry) mistakenly go into a gay sports bar in St. Louis to watch a game. There they run into Emmet and Danny (Michael Winters), his lover for fifteen years. Unlike Martin, Grace prides herself on being the only gay-friendly member of her family. Her favorite relative is her ex-husband's cousin, DeForest Kelly (Barry Steiger). When Grace's ex-husband's clan invades her house on Thanksgiving ("Cold Turkey"), DeForest (named, like all the others, after a famous Kelly) is the only one she's happy to see.

Grace promises to keep Emmet's secret from his wife Jean (Peggy Rea), who suspects her husband may be having an affair with another woman. Jean finally finds out the truth when Emmet dies suddenly ("Emmet, We Hardly Knew You") and Dan makes an appearance at the funeral. Grace is sympathetic to Dan, but at the same time she tries to protect Jean from finding out the truth. In the middle of the eulogy, a grief-stricken Danny stands up and declares, "He loved me and I loved him!" Jean tries to ignore him, but a few days after the funeral she finally breaks down. Grace is there to lend a shoulder to cry on and reassure her that although Emmet lived a double life, he really did love her.

Both *Dream On* and *Grace Under Fire* explore issues surrounding homosexuality often ignored by television until the 1990s. Mickey and Emmet are two men who were born in an era when choosing an openly gay lifestyle over a more traditional heterosexual existence was never even considered an option. Although he was lying to his wife, Emmet still emerges as a sympthetic character. "I just thought you got married, had kids, and that would make these feelings I had for men go away," he explains to Grace, "but it didn't and then Danny came along, and everything changed."[42] Mickey also suppressed his feelings and came out later in life. "I'm winging this," he explains to Martin. "I don't know what I'm doing. It's all new. I'm living with a guy. He's buying me slippers. And I'm liking it." Both programs demonstrate that there are gay men over the age of 50 capable of falling in love.

The same subject is treated with less sensitivity on an episode of *Seinfeld* involving George's future father-in-law, Henry Ross (Warren Frost). The trouble begins when Susan makes the mistake of inviting George, Jerry, and Elaine up to her parents' cabin for the weekend. Kramer accidentally burns down the cabin, but George manages to recover a metal box ("The Cheever Letters") which, to everyone's surprise, contain love letters to Henry from real-life closeted gay author John Cheever. The revelation makes Cheever and Henry's relationship more like a dirty secret that would have been better left unopened.

Several coming out episodes have dealt with older women revealing their sexual orientation to their children and families. Once again, *All in the Family* broke new ground with an episode ("Cousin Liz") set at a party after the funeral of Edith's cousin Liz. Cousin Liz's roommate Veronica (K. Callan) explains to Edith she and Liz were lovers. Edith agrees to let Veronica keep a family heirloom, a silver tea set, which angers Archie because he knows it's valuable. Edith tries to explain the situation to her husband, who's ready to take her to court. But Veronica would not be able to go to court because she is a teacher and in 1977, it could mean losing her job. As always, Edith emerges as the sympathetic voice of reason:

> EDITH: She's [Veronica] all alone in the world now. And she has no one to take care of her like I have. And she can't help how she feels. She didn't hurt you, so why would you want to hurt her?

In response, Archie tries to play the "God Card:"

> ARCHIE: Who the hell wants people like that teaching our kids? I'm sure God don't. God's sitting in judgment.

> EDITH : Well, sure he is. But he's God. You ain't.[43]

Archie gets the message and reluctantly lets Veronica keep the tea set, but not without getting the last word in. "Can't understand you people at all," he grumbles. "Why don't you all just stop that!" The Bunkers exit and as with the majority of 1970s sitcom characters, Veronica (and the tea set) are never seen or mentioned again.

While Liz never got a chance to come out to her cousin Edith, Mandy D'Arcy is given the opportunity in a funny episode of *Married With Children*, in which openly lesbian actress Amanda Bearse is featured in the dual role of identical cousins Mandy and Marcy. In "Lez Be Friends," the overbearing Marcy reveals she has been jealous of Mandy all her life because she's sweet and has always been more popular. Even Al (Ed O'Neill), who can't stand Marcy, likes Mandy and prefers her company to that of his own wife, Peg (Katey Segal), because she likes going to ball games, plays a mean game of foosball, and enjoys cooking. Peg isn't too fond of Mandy, but she changes her mind when Mandy compliments Peg on her gorgeous looks.

The situation comedy *Roseanne* had its share of lesbian characters during its nine-season run. In the fall of 1991, Nancy, played by sharp-tongued bisexual comedian Sandra Bernhard, married Dan's (John Goodman) old army buddy Arnie (Tom Arnold). Like Roseanne and Tom's marriage, it didn't last too long. When Arnie disappears at the end of the season (Tom Arnold moved on to his own series, *The Jackie Thomas Show*), Nancy announces in "Ladies' Choice" that she has a new love in her life — Marla (Morgan Fairchild).

The following season, Roseanne and a very nervous Jackie (Laurie Metcalf) venture into a gay bar, where Nancy's current girlfriend Sharon (Mariel Hemingway) plants a kiss on Roseanne. The episode ("Don't Ask, Don't Tell") included the now infamous kiss that ABC feared would result in a major loss of advertising revenue. But ABC went ahead with the kiss and the March 1, 1994 episode was the week's highest rated program.

Fortunately, Roseanne didn't stop there. In an episode during the show's final season ("Home Is Where the Afghan Is"), Rosie's mother Bev (Estelle Parson) makes a startling revelation over Thanksgiving dinner — she hates sex with men and had to look at a *Playboy* magazine before she could make love to her late husband. Everyone is shocked — and *Roseanne* makes television history by introducing us to America's first lesbian grandmother. Later in the season ("Rosanne-feld"), Bev gets a girlfriend, a boozy lounge singer named Joyce (Ruta Lee). In the series's final episode ("Into That Good Night Pts. 1 & 2"), Roseanne reveals Dan had died the previous year and the entire season was actually the product of her imagination. She says what really happened that year was her sister Jackie was the one who came out of the closet.

Another recurring character who goes gay in the 1990s is Paul Buchman's (Paul Reiser) sister Debbie (Robin Bartlett) on *Mad About You*. In "Ovulation Day," Debbie tells Jamie the story about a romantic evening she had with another woman, a doctor named Joan (Suzie Plakson). She plans to break the news to her parents, Sylvia (Cynthia Harris) and Burt (Louis Zurch) that evening over dinner. They stop by Paul and Jamie's apartment, where Paul is about to impregnate an ovulating Jamie. Their baby-making is put on hold when Debbie decides to tell her family she's a lesbian. While Burt seems fine with the news and Paul needs more time to process it, Sylvia heads for an open window. "Why do you say these things?" she asks, "To aggravate me?...We should have never named her Debbie. We should never have let her play field hockey." Sylvia is prevented from jumping and when everyone leaves, Paul has trouble getting back in the mood, until Jamie uses Debbie's story to describe a fictional lesbian encounter she once had with her college roommate to get her husband excited.

On *Malcolm and Eddie*, Malcolm (Malcolm-Jamal Warner) is totally cool about his sister Maura (JoNelle Kennedy) being a lesbian, but in "Sibling Rivalry" they both find themselves pursuing Malcolm's new waitress, Brenda (Paulette Braxton). They both make fools of themselves in the process, especially when Brenda picks Eddie (Eddie Griffin) over both of them.

While lesbian characters like Nancy, Bev, Debbie, and Joan have recurring status, gay brothers usually stop in for a brief visit — just long enough to come out. The earliest example is "My Brother's Keeper," a 1972 episode of *The Mary Tyler Moore Show*. Phyllis tries to fix Mary up with her brother Ben (Robert Moore). She's not happy when he hits it off with Rhoda (Valerie Harper). The thought of Ben and Rhoda getting married is Phyllis's worst nightmare. When Rhoda tells her flat out that Ben is not her type, she's offended.

PHYLLIS: What do you mean, not your type? He's attractive, he's witty, he's single —

RHODA: He's gay![44]

Phyllis is of course relieved. The moment is significant because there's nothing negative said or even implied about Ben's gayness. It's handled in a very matter-of-fact fashion, which is unusual considering the dozens of comedy and dramatic television series that would soon be devoting an entire episode to the same subject.

Sixteen years later, *The Golden's Girls*'s Blanche (Rue McClanahan) has a very different reaction when she learns her baby brother is gay ("Scared Straight"). Whenever her handsome brother Clayton (Monte Markham) is in town, Blanche tries to fix him up with eligible women. Clayton confesses to Rose he's gay and she encourages him to tell his sister. At first, Blanche doesn't believe him. "I know you too well," she tells him. "You're my brother." In the end, Blanche says she accepts Clayton for who he is, but proves she still has a long way to go when he returns to Miami the following season ("Sister of the Bride") with his new beau, a policeman named Doug (Michael Ayr). When Clayton announces he and Doug are going to get married, Blanche is horrified. "Hey, I can accept the fact that he's gay," she admits, "but why does he have to slip a ring on this guy's finger so the whole world would know?" She eventually comes around (again) when an older and wiser Sophia explains that Clayton and Doug want to get married for the same reason Blanche married her late husband George: to make a life commitment to each other, to let everyone know, and to have someone to grow older with.

On *Roc*, Andrew (Carl Gordon) has a similar reaction when his successful brother Russell (Richard Roundtree) comes home for a visit ("Can't Help Loving That Man"). Within five minutes, Russell reveals he's gay and getting married this weekend to his boyfriend Chris (Stephen Poletti). And if that isn't enough for the family to handle — Chris is white! As Roc (Charles Dutton) explains, homosexuality is something you see on television talk shows, but it's not something you expect to have in your own family. Russell can't even get past the idea of a black person being gay: "White people I can understand. They are all descended from those sissy European countries. But an educated, proud black man like Russell — gay — why would he choose that?" In the end, Andrew, like Blanche, realizes what's important is not how he feels, but that his brother is happy. Not that this necessarily means he has come to terms with it.

In a later episode ("Brothers"), Russell returns to tell Andrew he and Chris are moving to Paris. Russell takes his brother out to a gay restaurant so Andrew will understand what it's like for him to live in a predominantly straight world. The brothers admit they have grown apart since Russell came out and have avoided the issue by not contacting one another. Andrew admits he's still not totally comfortable with his brother being gay, but in a touching final scene, they agree to stay in closer touch.

Another brother reunion occurs on *Suddenly Susan* when Luis (Nestor Carbonell) is reunited after twelve years with his baby brother Carlos (Bruno Campos), who is no longer the little fat boy he left back in Cuba. Luis is ready to show his brother a good time on the town, until he reveals he's gay. He's upset and confesses to Susan (Brooke Shields) he doesn't know any gay people (in San

Francisco?) except *The Gate's* mail boy Pete (Bill Stevenson). Pete suggests Luis take his brother to a local gay country-western bar (where, in the episode's funniest moment, the statuesque Shields is mistaken for a drag queen). No matter how hard he tries, Luis is unable to accept his brother's sexuality. Thankfully, Susan convinces Luis to stop his brother from leaving town and have a heart-to-heart with him.

Adults — fathers, mothers, and siblings — step out of the closet on situation comedies with more frequency than teenagers. Perhaps some feel it's too serious a subject for comedy and it's better left for made-for-TV movies and dramatic series like *Beverly Hills 90210* and *Dawson's Creek*. In the 1990s, a few sitcoms ventured into this territory, beginning with an early episode of *Wings* ("There's Always Room for Cello"). During his cello lesson, R.J. (Abraham Benrubi), a high school football star, comes out to his teacher, Helen (Crystal Bernard). She's supportive, but discourages him from telling his conservative father, Roy (David Schramm). Roy is less than enthusiastic about the news and decides to challenge his son to a game of one-on-one basketball to determine if his son is gay. Not that it makes any difference, but Roy loses and reluctantly accepts his son's sexuality.

As with *Roc* and *Golden Girls*, *Wings* brought R.J. back for a follow-up episode. Six years later, an adult R.J., now a lawyer, returns to Nantucket as a surprise visit for his father's birthday party. Although they haven't seen each other for six years, Roy's happy to see him, but he's not interested in hearing about his love life, let alone in meeting his lover Luke (Tim Bagley). Roy makes everyone miserable by refusing to acknowledge Luke, but Helen makes him realize he better reconcile with his son before he loses him for good. So before R.J. and Luke leave the island, he gets on the airport microphone and announces: "My son is gay. There is my gay son and his boyfriend. He's gay too. And I love him. Well, not the boyfriend. I just met him..."

Not all television parents are as close-minded as Roy. On the pilot episode of *Good News*, David Randolph (Davis Rasey) assumes the role of acting pastor of the Church of Life in Compton, California. One of his first assignments is to counsel a young member of his congregation, Eldridge Dixon (Dwaine Perry), who wants to come out to his tough-as-nails mother, Hattie (Roz Ryan), the church's volunteer cook. Both Pastor Randolph and Eldridge are expecting Hattie to get hysterical, but her son's announcement is hardly news. "I've known that even before you did. I knew it when you were nine years old," she tells him.

But that's not the whole story. He met someone he wants to invite to mass (that's fine with her) and one more thing — he's white, which sends Hattie through the roof. "What's the matter with you boy, there's not enough black men out there?" she asks. Hattie refuses to acknowledge him, until the Pastor brings her and the boyfriend together during the service.

Another son who fears the worst is Fernando (Gabriel Romero), who lives next door to *Los Beltran* family with his Anglo lover Kevin (James C. Leary). In "The Coming Out of Fernandito," Fernando's macho father, a general in the Spanish army, arrives to visit his doctor son. Nervous about coming out to his macho father, Fernando panics and pretends he's married to his neighbor Letti, who realizes there's no reason for the charade when the General makes a pass at her husband Manny ("You have the body of a gazelle!" he tells him). The first Spanish-language situation comedy to feature regular gay characters, *Los Beltran* received a GLAAD nomination in the Spring of 2000 for best comedy series, a list which also included *Will & Grace*, *Sex and the City*, *Action*, and *Oh Grow Up*.

PLOTLINE #2: THE "MISTAKEN IDENTITY" EPISODE

A person with "gaydar" has the ability to tell if a person is gay or straight. Many people claim to have it. Those who do can determine in a matter of seconds which team an individual is playing on by detecting a "certain quality," which can reveal itself in the person's attitude, style of dress, manner of speaking, or a gesture. Every gay person doesn't necessarily have "gaydar" or even a "quality." In fact, there are plenty of gay men and lesbians who go undetected.

Even before the discovery of gaydar, situation comedies featured plotlines in which a straight character is mistaken for gay. Three 1970s series — *Sanford and Son*, *WKRP in Cincinnati*, and *C.P.O. Sharkey* — played on the alleged homosexuality of its lead characters. Fred Sanford (Redd Foxx) and his son Lamont (Demond Wilson), Chief Petty Officer Otto Sharkey (Don Rickles), and newscaster Les Nessman (Richard Sanders), are all mistaken for being gay courtesy of another character's false assumption.

One of the earliest mistaken identity plots is *Sanford and Son*'s "Lamont...Is That You?" (which borrows its title from comedian Redd Foxx's 1976 gay-themed feature comedy, *Norman...Is That You?*). When Fred's son Lamont and his friend Rollo (Nathaniel Taylor) are seen going into a gay bar, The Gay Blade, Fred suspects his son is gay. He calls Dr. Caldwell (Davis Roberts), who, after examining and questioning an unsuspecting Lamont, tells him to look for changes in his "speech, behavior, and dress." ("Don't tell me he's going to put on a dress?" Fred asks.) When Lamont starts spending too much time combing his hair and puts on a little too much Brut cologne, Fred becomes worried and decides to check out The Gay Blade for himself. Then Rollo sees Fred and his friend Bubba (Don Bexley) go into the bar and tells Lamont, who now suspects his father is gay. But just as they are about to confront each other, they discover that they each have dates with a member of the opposite sex.[45]

Like *All in the Family* and *Maude*, the humor is derived from ignorance. The Gay Blade is referred to as a "sissy bar." The word "gay" is never uttered, but rather indicated with a gesture — an extended hand movement back and forth. Fred also thinks Dr. Caldwell will be able to determine if his son is gay by asking a few questions ("Do you miss your mother?" or "Was your mother the dominant one in your family?"). He's unable to diagnose Lamont, but the warning signs he tells Fred to look for are based on the social myth that one can spot a homosexual from the way he speaks, behaves, and dresses. In comparison to Archie Bunker and Arthur Harmon, Fred Sanford's comments are mild. However, the underlying message is the same: people who are "that way" are not normal. And so, not one, but two characters get to breathe a heterosexual sigh of relief when they discover the other is not gay after all.

When *WKRP in Cincinnati*'s news director Les Nessman is mistakenly labeled a homosexual by a ballplayer and gets barred from the locker room, he heads straight for the window ledge ("Les on the Ledge"). His co-workers try to prevent him from jumping by promising to straighten out the matter, but that's not enough for Les. "There will always be a black mark besides my name," Les says. Herb (Frank Bonner) tries to talk his best friend off the ledge: "If you're gay, you're gay," Herb tells him. "It doesn't matter." But then in the next breath he adds, "If you're not gay, *then people shouldn't go around saying you're gay.*" Of course that's true. Nobody should be going around saying you're something you're not. But the issue here is the implication that being called gay is in itself an insult. Substitute the word "gay" for "Jewish" or "Italian" and the underlying message is clear. And, for Les, being labeled gay is enough to ruin his reputation and end his life. Jennifer (Loni Anderson) proves to be the most enlightened of the WKRP staff members. "So what if he is gay?" she asks Herb. "He comes to work. He does his job. He's a fine person. His sex life is his own business."[46]

A character can be suspected of being a homosexual without even knowing it. In "Sharkey's Big Secret," *C.P.O. Sharkey* (Don Rickles) is suspected of being a — (once again, an extended hand movement back and forth). Mignone (Barry Pearl), who seems to know all the terms ("closet queen," "transvestite"), suggests that it isn't easy to tell if someone is a homosexual anymore. Seaman Pruitt (Peter Isacksen) laughs the idea off, until he spots a man walking into Sharkey's office to retrieve his handbag. The man is actually an effeminate toupee salesman named Sylvester (Jack DeLeon), who is visiting Sharkey for a fitting. Pruitt tells Chief Robinson (Harrison Page) he thinks Sharkey is gay. So when Sharkey describes how tonight he's "going a whole different direction" in terms of his love life (meaning wearing a toupée and dating a younger woman), Robinson assumes Pruitt was telling the truth. Everyone is relieved when they meet Sharkey's date, Frankie, who turns out to be a hot blonde. Yet, Sharkey later realizes he's too old to be acting so young and returns to his old girlfriend.[47]

Once again, a character is guilty by association. The conversation between the men in Sharkey's platoon reflects how in an era of increased visibility of gay men and lesbians, there was some concern that homosexuals were not necessarily identifiable. Ironically, the idea that homosexuals are undetectable is undermined by Pruitt's conclusion that Sharkey is gay because he sees the shoulder-bag carrying Sylvester in his office. Once again there's the obligatory sigh of relief by Robinson, Pruitt, and the platoon when they discover his date is 100 percent female. Interestingly, insult king Rickles, whose character is totally oblivious he's been labeled gay, makes no anti-gay cracks toward Sylvester. In fact, he's unchar-actersitically gracious and polite to the toupee salesman.

These very same plots from the 1970s built around misunderstandings and miscommunication are still widely used today. Case in point is an amusing episode of *Cosby* ("Older and Out") in which Hilton (Bill Cosby) and Griffin (Doug E. Doug) are mistaken for a gay couple. Chuck (Joseph Bologna), an ex-cop who's the member of the "Older and Out" softball team, overhears a conversation between Hilton and Griffin which sounds like an argument between a bickering couple. Chuck invites Hilton to join the team and he accepts because he has no idea "out" means as in "out of the closet." The plot becomes more complicated when Hilton tries to fix Chuck up with his friend Pauline (Madeline Kahn). But when Hilton asks him if he's available, Chuck thinks he's inquiring for himself.

Meanwhile, Ruth (Phylicia Rashad) finds out Chuck is gay. She and Hilton then have one of those conversations people only have on television. When Hilton claims he's had "similar feelings" as Chuck, he is referring to Chuck's conservative politics, but she thinks he's talking about homosexuality. Hilton finally realizes what's going on when he and Griffin, dressed in western garb, attend Chuck's country-western party, where they see "cowboys" dancing with each other. Chuck is disappointed to find out Hilton is straight, but he invites him to continue playing on their team. "What our second baseman does in the

---

"The Censors"
The Associates (ABC-TV)
April 10, 1980
Written by Stan Daniels and Ed Weinberger
Directed by Tony Mordente

This is a terrific episode of a funny series that never found an audience. Created by the producers of *Taxi*, *The Associates* focuses on a group of young lawyers who work for a Wall Street law firm, Bass and Marshall. Among the lawyers is a young, somewhat naive associate named Tucker, played by an unusually restrained Martin Short. Tucker is assigned to accompany a representative from a television network's broadcast standards division, Gerald McMartin (Lee Wallace). to provide legal support in dealing with the obstinate producer, Phil Kramer (Stuart Margolin), of a new sitcom, *Stevie and Me*, about a single father raising a son.

The scene in question involves little Stevie coming home unexpectedly to find his father (played by *Three's Company*'s John Ritter) having sex with a woman he picked up. The dialogue contains the phrase, "queer as a three dollar bill," which Gerald wants to delete because gay activists will be upset. To prove it's not offensive, Phil invites a representative from the Gay Task Force to read the script. Enter Mr. Anderson (Richard Brestoff), who's a walking stereotype of a

gay man — a flamboyant, swishy queen who talks with a lisp. When asked about the line, he says it's not offensive "in context" because they don't find words offensive.

MR. ANDERSON:...We are deeply offended by the fact supposedly sophisticated men like you can so readily accept the fact that a gay person would come in here talking like Sylvester the Cat. That's what really offends us. That people like you who control the media and influence the way millions of people look at the world still have this image of us. Until you change that, these stupid little jokes of yours aren't going to make one damn bit of difference.[48]

The moment is a rarity on television — a TV show actually critiquing its own industry and the way they represent gay and lesbian characters. The studio audience's reaction is equally interesting. They seem to be playing into the show's writers' hands by laughing in all the right places (perhaps with the help of a laugh track) when Mr. Anderson swishes into the room. And when he finishes his speech, they break into applause.

privacy of his own home is his business," Chuck tells him. Although the situations are not terribly original, in a time when the majority of gay male characters on sitcoms are forty and under, it's refreshing to see older, active gay men looking for love and having a little fun.[49]

A misunderstanding can also be created if someone purposely plants the notion in someone else's mind. In "The Homecoming Queen," *Dream On*'s Martin Tupper learns the girl he lusted after in high school, Jeannie (Kim Cattrall), thought he was gay because his best friend Eddie (Jess Josephson) told her. Martin sets her straight, but she still has doubts when his "horse jumps the gate" during sex.[50] On the very short-lived *Holding the Baby* ("The Gay Divorcee"), Kelly (Jennifer Westfeldt) finds out the woman who single-dad Gordon (Jon Patrick Walker) has his eye on isn't interested in starting a family. So Kelly tells Roxanne (Katy Selverstone) Gordon is gay. The misunderstanding creates a hilarious situation in which Gordon tells Roxanne all about his son, Dan, yet all the while she thinks he is talking about his gay male lover. When Gordon invites her home to meet his son, she thinks she's getting an invitation to a *ménage-à-trois*. Fortunately, the misunderstanding is cleared up, but not before Roxanne tries to get things warmed up with Gordon's brother, Jimmy (Eddie McClintock), who she mistakes for Dan.[51]

A similar situation is even more awkward for Matt Peyser (Fred Savage). In an episode of *Working* ("Rumoring"), Matt's co-workers play a little joke on their supervisor, Tim Deale (Maurice Goldin), by telling him Matt is gay. To make a good impression on his boss, Tim, a racist, sexist, ass-kisser, volunteers an unsuspecting Matt to go on a date with his boss's gay son, Crispen (Ric Coy), who just moved to town. Matt finally figures out what's going on as he's sitting with his male "date" in a gay bar. He gets revenge on his boss by telling him he pushed Crispen out of a moving car. To make up for his *faux pas*, Tim is forced to take Crispen on a date. Even in the world of sitcoms, this ending doesn't make sense. Of course it's great to see such a gay-positive father who dreams of walking his son down the aisle one day. But why would Crispen's father make his son go out with such a despicable loser like Tim? Who's punishing whom there?[52]

When someone's gaydar malfunctions, it can mistakenly pick up a signal from a character who has a "quality," but isn't gay. On *Friends* ("The One Where Nana Dies Twice"), Chandler's co-worker Shelly (Nancy Cassaro) mistakenly offers to fix him up with another guy in the office, Lowell (Stuart Fratkin). When Chandler (Matthew Perry) asks his friends if anyone ever thought he was gay, Ross and Joey (Matt LeBlanc) claim it never occurred to them. (Joey apparently has a bad memory because in "The One With the Flashback," we see Joey meeting his future roommate for the first time and telling him he's "totally O.K. with the gay thing.") Phoebe (Lisa Kudrow) explains to Chandler that people think he's gay because he's smart and funny, while Monica (Courtney Cox Arquette) tells him he has a "quality." Chandler starts to feel exceedingly self-conscious about his behavior, yet in the end he's relieved when Lowell, "speaking for his people," assures him that he doesn't have a "quality."[53]

Throughout the series, there have also been questions raised about Chandler's sexual orientation in regards to his relationship with his roommate, Joey. In one episode ("The One With the Baby on the Bus"), the duo are mistaken for a gay couple when they use Ross's baby son Ben to try to pick up women.[54] When Joey decides to finally move out in the middle of the second season (in an episode aptly titled "The One Where Joey Moves Out"), Chandler is heartbroken. "It's not like we agreed to live together forever," Joey explains. "We're not Bert and Ernie."

At the end of the episode, Chandler and Joey are each alone, looking out their respective apartment windows watching the rain as we hear Eric Carmen's "All By Myself." The moment is just another tease — another suggestion by the writers that maybe Joey and Chandler should be more than just friends. The sappy tune turns the otherwise sentimental moment into a joke, thereby assuring us there *really* is nothing going on between the couple. Fortunately, for Chandler and Joey (and us), the separation lasted only a few episodes. Yet even after Chandler marries Monica, questions are raised about his sexuality. In "The One With the Tea Leaves," we learn Chandler owns not one, but two copies of the Broadway musical cast album of *Annie*. And he knows all the words.

Chandler has a "quality," but Joey is constantly finding himself in situations involving close contact with another male. In "The One With Barry and Mindy's Wedding," Joey goes up for a role in Warren Beatty's new film and has to learn how to kiss a guy. He tries to find someone to practice with, but both Chandler and Ross refuse. At the end of the episode, Ross, feeling guilty about not helping out his friend, walks into Joey's apartment and plants one on his lips. Joey compliments him on the kiss, but tells him the audition was this morning (and he didn't get the part). Ross and Joey grow even closer when they fall asleep on top of each while watching a movie ("The One With the Nap Partners"). They wake up at the same time, see what happened, and freak out. Later, Joey admits it was the best nap he's ever had. Ross agrees, but tells him they can't do it again because "it's too weird." But Joey keeps dropping hints to Ross that he should come over to take a nap with him. They eventually "do it again," only to get caught by the gang.[55]

Joey finds himself in an equally odd situation ("The One With the Ballroom Dancing") when he offers to teach the building's super, Mr. Treeger (Michael G. Hagerty), how to ballroom dance. On the night of the big ball, the two men go up on the roof for a final spin around the dance floor to Frank Sinatra's rendition of "Night and Day."[56] Homosexuality is never turned into a joke on *Friends*, but then again, there is also never anything *really* gay going on.

Apparently Chandler and Jerry Seinfeld, who is mistaken for being gay because (in his own words), he's "thin, single, and neat," are not the only heterosexual men in the New York area with a "quality." When his apartment is flooded, *The Single Guy's* Johnny Eliot (Jonathan Silverman) moves in with his gay neighbors, Mike (Michael Winters) and Jeff (Mark Harelik), who assume he is gay ("Neighbors"). But they're not the only ones. Jonathan meets *Friends's* Ross Geller (guest star David Schwimmer) and invites him to see Jeff in a production of *Hamlet* starring Leonard Nimoy. Through a series of misunderstandings, they each think the other is gay. The situation is resolved during an awkward, yet funny conversation in a taxicab. Both men want to say they're not gay without offending the other. After straightening things out with Ross, Jonathan next comes out as a heterosexual to his neighbors, who he thinks are upset by the news. "Why would I be upset?" Mike asks. "Some of my best friends are straight. My parents are straight. Well, at least my mother."[57]

Another New Yorker with a quality, at least as far as his father is concerned, is *Just Shoot Me*'s Dennis Finch. To his friends, Finch is a horny, duplicitous devil whose behavior borders on lecherous. For example, in "Two Girls for Every Boy," Finch tries to fulfill his fantasy by arranging a *ménage a trois* between a lesbian model, Jill (Dara Tomanovich), and his unsuspecting heterosexual co-worker, Maya (Laura San Giacomo).

So it comes as quite a surprise in "Pass the Salt" when Finch's father — Fire Chief Red Finch (guest star Brian Dennehy) — arrives in the Big Apple with Finch's butch fire fighting brothers, Buck (Christopher Michael Moore) and Scottie (Adam Setliff) for a firemen's convention. The Chief takes the opportunity to tell his gay son how much he loves him (and takes him to see the Broadway musical *Showboat*). Nina (Wendie Malick) and Elliot (Enrico Colantoni), Finch's co-workers, don't have to be convinced he's not gay because he's a terrible dancer, is neither tan nor toned, and has an ugly apartment, no sense of space or style, and no women friends. No matter how much Dennis insists he is straight, his father doesn't get the message until the end of the episode, when Chief Finch discovers it's actually his son Scottie who's gay. Red's only response is the conversation stopper — "Pass the salt" — which Finch explains is the most emotional thing his father ever said at the dinner table.[58]

The mistaken identity plot is taken a step further in an episode of *The Secret Lives of Men* ("Dating Is Hell") when Mike (Peter Gallagher) assumes his gay client Brad (Tom Virtue) has the hots for him. When Mike shows his buddy Phil (Brad Whitford) the new leather jacket Brad bought him, Phil puts the idea in his head that he's sending out "gay signals" to Brad by the way he walks and holds a glass. When Brad invites Mike out to the Hamptons for the weekend, Mike, in a comical display of straight male narcissism, tells Brad he's not gay. That's no news to Brad, who's known it all along. Just as Lowell assured Chandler, Brad tells him, "I've been in the gay business a long time. I know who's gay. You're not gay."[59]

Sometimes the character you least expect can have a "quality." On *Everybody Loves Raymond*, a question is raised about Robert's (Brad Garrett) sexuality ("What's With Robert?") when he breaks up with his girlfriend Amy (Monica Horan) once again. Amy has her doubts as well. She tells Ray's wife Debra (Patricia Heaton) she wonders if Robert is gay because "he color coordinates his clothes, he can dance, he's certainly very attached to his mother, and he didn't pressure me to sleep with him when I wasn't ready the first whole year." Debra passes on her suspicions to Raymond (Ray Romano), who mistakenly raises the question to his father Frank (Peter Boyle) and mother Marie (Doris Roberts).

Ray realizes maybe his brother is in the closet because their father is the kind of homophobe who tosses around gay slurs like "Nancy."

RAYMOND: That's not nice to gay people.

FRANK: You're right, I'm sorry, Mary.[60]

Like Archie Bunker and Arthur Harmon's comments, Frank's anti-gay slurs keep the audience laughing. But to show times have indeed changed, Marie reminds her husband about a non-sexual encounter (at least we assume) Frank had in Korea with another soldier who he huddled with to stay warm.

Ray and Robert have a brother-to-brother talk and even though he listens to *Hello, Dolly*, has knickknacks on his mantle, and notices other guys at the gym, Robert insists he's not gay. In one of those touching sitcom moments, Robert tells him it wouldn't matter, "You'd still be my brother. My big homosexual brother."

As all male homosexuals are supposedly cultured creatures, it only makes sense that if a straight man befriends a gay man he too must be gay. On *Doctor, Doctor* ("Torch Song Cardiology"), Dr. Mike's (Matt Frewer) colleague Dr. Grant Linowitz (Beau Gravitte) gets help writing a speech from Mike's gay brother Richard (Tony Carriero). Grant and Mike, who share an interest in fine wine and theatre, hit it off and plan a weekend together in New York, until Grant realizes his colleagues are wondering if he's gay. Convinced Richard has a crush on him, Grant comes down with a bout of homosexual panic and admits to Richard he's afraid people will think he's gay. Richard is hurt: "I look at you and I see a friendship. You look at me and all you see is a fag."[61] After spending a weekend with Mike doing "manly" things (like drinking beer and watching female mud wrestling), Grant realizes he misses Richard. He apologizes and they become friends once again.

What's puzzling in this otherwise hilarious episode is Dr. Mike's reaction to the whole situation. At first he chastises his colleagues Abe (Julius Carry) and Dierdre (Maureen Mueller) for making jokes about Grant being gay. Then Mike does a complete reversal and confronts Grant when he sees him wearing a leather jacket and scarf. He seems to be more worried about Grant, almost as if he's protecting him from his own brother. At the same time, Mike expresses how sorry he feels for his brother because their own father won't talk to him. Mike also has nothing at stake in being concerned about Grant's sexuality. If he's fine with his own brother being gay, why turn it into an issue? (Answer: it's a sitcom.)

In "Toe in the Water," *Designing Women* takes the mistaken identity plot to the extreme. The title refers to Julia stepping back into the dating pool after the death of her husband. When the obnoxious Allison (Julia Duffy) meets Julia's new beau, Mark (Charles Frank), she tells her he's "the gayest human being I've ever met."[62] Allison's gaydar has him pegged immediately: Mark is wearing a Lacoste shirt and makes a passing reference to Ida Lupino. Allison tells her it makes perfect sense for her to be seeing a gay man because he's a safe date. Julia is sure

Allison is wrong, until she walks into his apartment and sees a wall adorned with theatre posters (including *Torch Song Trilogy* and *Follies*) and a record collection featuring gay icons like Judy Garland, Lena Horne, and Ethel Merman. He also complains about his weight ("I'm as big as a house"), lives close to his mother, and vacations in Key West.

When Mark makes a pass at her, a confused Julia asks him if he's gay. He denies it and later proves it by pretending to be a macho, sexist idiot. Wearing a ripped T-shirt, he crushes a beer can on his head, and tells Julia to "get that blouse off, get in the kitchen, and fix me up some vittles so I can watch the big game." Julia gets the message and even though he's not gay, she admits she needs more time to get over her husband's death before getting involved.

Sex in the City's Charlotte (Kristin Davis) finds herself in a similar situation in "Evolution" when she begins dating a gay-straight pastry chef Stephan (Dan Futterman). When she accepts his invitation to the theatre, Charlotte is sure he's gay, until he gives her an intense good night kiss. Carrie explains he may be a gay-straight man, "a new strain of heterosexual males spawned in Manhattan as the result of over-exposure to fashion, exotic cuisine, musical theatre, and antiques." Samantha believes it's better if he is a straight man with a lot of great gay qualities, as opposed to a straight-gay man, who "plays sports and won't fuck you."[63]

Charlotte continues to get mixed signals, such as when he recognizes her dress as "a Cynthia Rowley" and talks about how much he loves Cher ("She's such a survivor!"). Carrie even introduces him to Carrie's gay friend Stanford, whose gaydar is unable to determine where Stephan falls on the Kinsey scale. Finally, during foreplay, Charlotte asks him.

"I'm a 35-year-old pastry chef who lives in Chelsea," he responds. "If I were gay, I would be gay."

Charlotte is relieved until she sees the man of her dreams standing on a chair in his kitchen shrieking because he saw a mouse. She realizes then that perhaps Stephan is a little too in touch with his feminine side for her taste.

If a woman is a little too much in touch with her masculine side, she may also become suspect. On an early episode of *The Facts of Life* ("Rough Housing"), Blair (Lisa Welchel) makes disparaging remarks to her competition for the Queen of the Harvest crown, a tomboy classmate named Cindy (Julie Anne Haddock). When Blair sees Cindy hug her friend, Blair tells her she's "strange." Cindy tells Mrs. Garrett (Charlotte Rae) that maybe Blair's right ("maybe I'm not normal"). The Eastland School's favorite house mother offers Cindy a little "milk and sympathy" and some words of wisdom: "There's nothing wrong with hugging and touching. It shows you're a loving person. And that's good. The only people who will tell you it's wrong are the ones who can't reach out and do it themselves." To teach Blair a lesson, Mrs. G. uses reverse psychology and accuses her of being easy with boys because she wears low cut dresses. Blair realizes it's wrong to jump to conclusions based on appearances and apologizes to Cindy, who dons a dress and enters the Harvest contest (and comes in second to Blair).[64]

While the episode is not really about homosexuality per se, it seems to deliver a contradictory message. On one hand, wise Mrs. Garrett dispenses Cindy some good advice when she explains the value of being yourself. To assure Cindy it's okay to be a female and athletic, she names several famous women athletes (Billie Jean King, Nadia Comenici, etc.). Yet, there is a sense of relief that Cindy is heading down the road to heterosexuality because she's fallen for a guy she met at the dance.

Women who are mistaken for gay may also find themselves being pursued by another woman. On *Titus* ("Sex With Pudding"), Christopher Titus suspects his girlfriend Erin (Cynthia Watros) is having an affair, so he and his buddies ransack her office to find evidence, which they do: some fancy lingerie with a card reading, "Hi, Sexy. Saw these and thought of you" and personal e-mails — signed "Pudding" — inviting her to dinner at "the usual spot." When Erin confesses she's being sexually harassed but has it under control, Titus takes it upon himself to find the culprit. While many men in the office confess to lusting after Erin, the person who's been sending Erin the notes and gifts is her boss — Paula (Lesley Fera) — who was under the mistaken impression Erin was a lesbian and romantically interested in her. Erin, who wanted to be friends, as opposed to *girlfriends*, simply didn't know how to tell her the truth. The fact it may be inappropriate for a boss to be sending her employee panties is never addressed, let alone why an intelligent woman would be in love with an adolescent schmuck like Titus to begin with (even after he and his cohorts invade her workplace, read her private e-mail, and ransack her office).[65]

As in the *Titus* episode, most mistaken identity episodes involving women have less to do with having a "quality" and more to do with misunderstandings and miscommunication between characters. On *Golden Girls* ("Goodbye Mr. Gordon"), Rose and Blanche are mistaken for lesbians when Rose recruits them to participate in a panel discussion on "Women Who Live Together" on a morning television program, *Wake Up Miami*. They don't find out until the live segment begins that the subject is really lesbians who live together. Rose is eventually forgiven for the mistake, even though Blanche keeps getting asked out by women.[66]

On *Two Guys, a Girl, and a Pizza Place* ("Two Guys, a Girl, and a Tattoo"), Sharon (Traylor Howard) tries to find out if Pete's (Richard R. Ruccolo) new girlfriend, Nicole, who used to go out with Berg (Ryan Reynolds), still has Berg's name tattooed on her ass. Sharon, tired of being ogled by men at her gym, joins an all-women's gym, where Nicole also works out. When Berg sends her into the shower to see if Nicole still has the tattoo, she looks in every shower stall. The women on the other side of the curtains scream and give her dirty looks (she also gets an invitation to play golf). The owner warns Sharon that the gym is not a meat market, there's no ogling allowed, and she should stick to the personal ads.[67]

On *The Mommies* ("Mr. Mommie"), new series regular Tom Booker (Jere Burns) moves in next door to Marilyn (Marilyn Kentz), Caryl (Caryl Kellogg) and Barb (Julia Duffy). Tom claims his wife is working out-of-state, which raises everyone's suspicions. Marilyn thinks he's a bigamist because he's from Utah, while Caryl thinks he's a spy. Barb is sure he's gay because he doesn't undress her with his eyes. Tom plays a joke on the women by pretending to be all three, until he finally shines through as just a plain, old 1990s, heterosexual stay-at-home dad.[68]

Sometimes it's the heterosexual male himself who might have a reason to question his sexual orientation. For example, a homoerotic dream may cause some men to wonder if they have been playing on the wrong team. On *Murphy Brown*, Miles (Grant Shaud) panics when he has a gay dream featuring the Washington Monument, dolphins, and the station's new gay publicity director Rick (Brian McNamara). In "Come Out, Come Out, Wherever You Are," Miles talks to several psychiatrists, who offer contradictory interpretations of his dream. After avoiding Rick for several days, Miles goes to lunch with him. Rick thinks Miles has a problem with him being gay, but when Miles tells him about the dream, he is very understanding and assures him one dream doesn't mean he's gay. Miles is relieved. This therapy session also was no doubt cheaper than the earlier ones, in addition to being more accurate.[69]

While Miles is going through his crises, *F.Y.I.* reporter Frank Fontana (Joe Regalbuto) begins to worry he too might be gay because like Miles, he's single, can't maintain a relationship with women, and is more comfortable being around the guys. In fact, Rick is surprised to find out Miles thought he might be gay, but he's even more surprised to find out Frank isn't.

Several seasons later, Frank writes a play ("A Comedy of Eros") — a love story about the romance of his life — which gets produced at a local theatre. Unfortunately, Frank is called away on assignment and entrusts Murphy (Candice Bergen) to oversee the production. She is less than attentive, so at the play's opening, Frank is horrified to discover his play has been transformed into a gay love story. But the audience loves the play and, as Murphy explains, the sex of the couple is irrelevant because he still moved people and that's what's important.[70]

On a memorable episode of *Maude* ("Arthur's Worry"), Walter has a Miles-like experience on the eve of a fishing trip with Arthur. Walter dreams he kisses Arthur, which Maude explains is simply an expression of the love he feels for his best friend. Arthur finds out about the dream and becomes uncomfortable being alone in the cabin with Walter. But when Walter finally convinces Arthur the true meaning of the dream, Arthur even manages to muster up enough courage to tell Walter, in a barely audible tone, he loves him, but not before checking outside to make sure no one's around. He obviously didn't look carefully enough because just as Walter and Arthur are locked in a platonic embrace, the maid walks in.[71]

Spin City's James (Alexander Gaberman) is unnerved by his dream in which he's an astronaut blasting into space. Stuart (Alan Ruck) convinces him it's a gay fantasy. James is naive enough to believe it, especially after having just had three successive daydreams of kissing his male co-workers. The next day he shows up wearing an "I'm Not Gay, But My Boyfriend Is" T-shirt. Stuart takes the joke even further by fixing James up with a gay-co-worker. The next morning, Stuart asks him how it went. "I'm not gay," James quickly responds. In the tag, Stuart gets his comeuppance when he has a similar dream in which he kisses Carter (Michael Boatman). In comparison to Miles, Walter, and Stuart, James's attitude about suddenly being gay is refreshing. He's neither upset nor panicked, but adapts rather easily to his perception of gay culture — the "boyfriend" T-Shirt, shaving his chest, and using words like "girlfriend."[72]

What sounds like a dream could have in fact been reality for John Hemingway (John Larroquette). On *The John Larroquette Show* ("The Past Comes Back"), a fellow member of Alcoholics Anonymous (Ted Schackelford) tracks down John to make amends. He apologizes to John for seducing him, but John has no recollection of it. John breathes a sigh of relief when his friend realizes it was indeed someone else, though a half-asleep John was in the room at the time.[73]

If men are not worrying about themselves, there is always fear their own son could grow up gay, particularly if he develops certain "interests." On *The Hughleys* ("Guess Who's Coming Out for Dinner"), D.L. Hughley is concerned when he hears his son Michael (Dee Jay Daniels) say he doesn't like girls.[74] On *Guys Like Us* ("In and Out"), Jared is not happy his little brother Maestro likes to play with dolls and watch Martha Stewart ("she's making a cobbler!"). His attempt to butch Maestro up by taking him to a hockey game fails, making him finally realize he needs to let Maestro be his own person.[75] Similarly, *Friends*'s Ross is not pleased to discover his son Ben's favorite toy is a Barbie doll ("The One with the Metaphorical Tunnel"). He tries to turn the kid onto dinosaurs, monster trucks, and GI Joe. Monica reminds Ross of his favorite game as a child — dressing up in his mother's clothes ("The big hat, the pearls, the little pink handbag"), calling himself Bea, and singing "I am Bea. I like tea. Won't you dance with me?" A hilarious tag at the end of the episode shows little Ross at play.[76]

The doll issue is also addressed in a hilarious episode of *Coach*. Christine (Shelly Fabares) and Hayden's son Timmy gets a Princess Tiffany doll as a present from his kooky friends ("A Boy and His Doll"). Luther (Jerry Van Dyke) convinces Hayden the boy needs more masculine influences, so he purposely leaves the doll behind in a diner. Only Timmy won't go to sleep without it, leaving poor Hayden to go head-to-head with the bratty little girl who found it. When he manages to get a new one (in exchange for football tickets), Christine commends him for being such a good father, but informs him Timmy fell asleep using his athletic sock as a substitute.[77]

While *Guys Like Us*, *Friends*, and *Coach* treat the situation quite comically, Caryl and Paul (Robin Thomas) on *The Mommies* take the question surrounding their son's sexual orientation a little more seriously. When their son Blake (Ryan Merriman) joins the school band, he opts for the flute ("I Got the Music in Me"). Paul is disappointed his son didn't pick a more masculine instrument. When Blake comes home with a black eye, his parents assume he got it because he was teased for playing the flute. Without saying the word "gay," Paul tells Jack (David Dukes) his fears about Ryan being — you know:

PAUL: Blake might be...Well, what if he were? I mean would it really make any difference because he's still Blake. Blake is a great kid. I still love Blake and that's not going to change. So there's really not a problem.[78]

Paul delivers a gay-affirmative message to parents about unconditional love, but, by some odd coincidence, Ryan's heterosexuality just happens to be affirmed before the credits roll. When the football coach sees how well Blake can throw a ball, he asks him to join the team. Blake says he'd rather be in the band. The coach retorts, "That's the kind of answer I expect from a flutist." Caryl goes off on the coach and defends her son, who later relieves any doubt about his heterosexuality in our minds by admitting he received a black eye because another kid was jealous of the attention he was getting from a girl. So Blake isn't gay (sigh of relief)...not that there's anything *wrong* with it.

The mistaken identity scenario can easily accommodate any sexual orientation. Just as straight characters are continually being mistaken for homosexuals, gays and lesbians are on occasion mistaken for straight. At the place where everyone knows your name, the *Cheers* gang can instantly tell that Rebecca's (Kirstie Alley) old boyfriend Mark (Harvey Fierstein) is gay. In "Rebecca's Lover...Not," she is convinced that even after all these years, he's the one. So she invites him back to her apartment, puts on a sexy negligee, and gets ready to pounce. Of course he's more interested in the fabric she's wearing than what's underneath. The casting of gay actor/playwright Harvey Fierstein as Mark makes Rebecca's obliviousness all the more hilarious.[79]

Another character who finds himself in a similar situation is *The Nanny's* employer Max Sheffield (Charles O'Shaughnessy). In "Oh Vey, You're Gay," Max falls head-over-heels for his new publicist Sydney (Catherine Oxenberg). When Sydney admits to Nanny Fran (Fran Drescher) she's a lesbian, a delighted Fran breaks the bad news to Max, who is once again open game.[80] On *Night Court*, Judge Stone (Harry Anderson) discovers a reporter (Annette McCarthy) has a crush on him ("Passion Plundered").[81] What he doesn't know is she's a lesbian and a closet romance novelist, so the tape he listened to, in which he thinks she's pouring out her feelings for him, is actually notes for her next book. Christine (Markie Post) prevents him from making a total fool of himself, though he still confesses he listened to her tape recorder. Unfortunately, no one stops *Temporarily Yours's* Deb DeAngelo (Debi Mazar) from making a fool out of herself with yet another romance novelist, Dulles Lee (John O'Hurley). In "Temptation," Deb shows her friends the seduction scene Dulles has been dictating to her for his highly erotic new novel. They're convinced he's hitting on her. The next day, Dulles starts talking about how he's having trouble getting "his juices flowing." Deb lashes out at him. "I'm a temp and I deserve to be treated with respect!" she demands. "Do you have that?" When their conversation is interrupted by Dulles's lover Allen (Scott Thomas Baker), Deb realizes she's made a big mistake.[82]

An even bigger gaffe is made by *Third Rock From the Sun's* Dr. Dick Solomon

(John Lithgow) when Frank (Enrico Colatoni), a former student of his girlfriend Mary's (Jane Curtin), comes to visit ("Frankie Goes to Rutherford"). Unaware Frank is gay, Dick grows jealous, until Frank confesses he has a secret. Dick jumps to the conclusion Frank is also an alien, so he starts hanging out at the local gay bar thinking it's actually a bar for aliens. Frank counsels Dick about whether he should "come out" to Mary, who eventually tracks down Dick and clues him in about Frank and the bar.[83]

Mistaken identity can also play off an individual's gender. The most common is not recognizing a female was, or still is, actually male. Inevitably, the one fooled is usually the least equipped to handle the situation. On *Evening Shade* ("The Perfect Woman"), Ponder (Ossie Davis) is fixed up with a beautiful woman who is actually a transsexual (Diahann Carroll). On a trip to Dayton, *WKRP in Cincinnati*'s sales director Herb Tarlek tries to woo the assistant of a potential client ("Hotel Oceanview"). In the middle of necking, Nicki (Linda Carlson) reveals she was once Nick, one of his former high school chums. *Golden Girl* Blanche finds herself in the middle of scandal with a local politician Gil Kessler (John Schuck), who she discovers was once a she ("Strange Bedfellows").

PLOT #3: THE "PRETEND" EPISODE

The third most common "gay" sitcom plot is the character only pretending to be gay. In the "real world," there is rarely a great advantage to being a gay man or a lesbian. But on television, it's an entirely different story. In the world of the situation comedy, posing as a gay man or lesbian can help you keep a roof over your head, get you a cheaper rate on your health benefits, further your career, and improve your relationships with the opposite sex.

Of course, there are *some* drawbacks for these pretenders. Your love life may be impeded because a potential girlfriend would rather be your *girlfriend* (that's *girlfriend* with two snaps and a twist). You may have to be outed publicly, which will confuse your family and friends. And then there is the worst case scenario — every heterosexual male's nightmare — you may have to *kiss* a member of your *own* sex!

Prior to becoming a stock sitcom plot, the pretend story line was the entire premise of one of the 1970s' most successful half hours. In the pilot episode of *Three's Company*, Jack Tripper (John Ritter) wakes up in a stranger's bathtub the morning after a wild party. The bathtub belongs to Janet Wood (Joyce DeWitt) and Chrissy Snow (Suzanne Somers), who decide to ask Jack, who is looking for a place to live, to move in with them. Their landlord, Mr. Roper (Norman Fell), refuses at first because he doesn't want any shenanigans going on in his building. But when Janet lies and tells him Jack is gay, he agrees.[84]

Though there's still something not quite convincing about Mr. Roper's tenant policies, the early episodes of the series played off Jack trying to hide his heterosexuality from Mr. Roper, which made having a social life, or at least a straight

"Strange Bedfellows:" A horrified Mr. Roper (Norman Fell) wakes up in bed with his "gay" neighbor Jack Tripper (John Ritter) on an early episode of *Three's Company*.

social life, difficult. In "Mr. Roper's Niece," Jack is paid $50 by Roper to take out his attractive niece, Karen (Christina Hart). Roper figures gay Jack is a safe date until he walks in on them kissing. He throws Jack out, but later apologizes when Karen admits *she* is the one who tried to seduce him.[85] Another close call occurred in "Strange Bedfellows" when Jack and Mr. Roper wake up in the same bed after an all-night party. Thinking something happened between them, Mr. Roper is horrified, forcing Jack to admit he's not gay. Roper doesn't believe him, but thanks him for lying to save his reputation.[86]

Three's Company is basically a heterosexual male's *ménage-à-trois* fantasy. And although no hanky-panky ever occurred between Jack, Janet, Chrissy and Chrissy's replacements, Cindy (Jenilee Harrison) and Terri (Priscilla Barnes), we were constantly bombarded with the possibility. The humor consists primarily of sexual innuendoes, double entendres, and farcical situations created by miscommunication.

Homosexuality is reduced to a running gag. The hyper-heterosexual Jack is comfortable enough in his own masculinity to feign being gay. We know he's only pretending, so he never poses a real threat to the male heterosexual audience. On the contrary, the sitcom was one of the 1970s' most egregious "jiggle shows." Most important of all, the homophobic Roper, who is clearly portrayed as a fool, is the only one threatened by Jack's homosexuality. Once again, it's difficult to discern if the audience is laughing *with* or *at* Jack when he camps it up, or when Mr. Roper waves his pinkie in the air and calls Jack "Tinkerbelle."

Some characters had to devise an even more radical pretense to keep a roof over their heads. The premise of *Bosom Buddies* involved two young advertising executives, Kip (Tom Hanks) and Henry (Peter Scolari), who in the series pilot need to find an apartment in realty-challenged Manhattan. They decide to dress as women and move into an all-female residence, The Susan B. Anthony Hotel. As their alter-egos, Buffy (Kip) and Hildegard (Henry), the duo enjoy being surrounded by beautiful women, though their lives get complicated when they're forced to change gender at a moment's notice. The show had the potential of bringing a touch of genuine camp to ABC's prime time line-up, except that hidden beneath the dresses, wigs, and make-up was not just a couple of regular guys, but another jiggle-giggle comedy, complete with a blonde sexpot à la *Three's Company* named Sonny (Donna Dixon).

Living in a low-rent apartment is not the only reason a sitcom character will pretend to be gay or lesbian. Many characters discover how posing as a gay man or lesbian can advance their career. On *The Naked Truth* ("Women Gets Plastered, Star Gets Even"), Nick (Jonathan Penner) and David (Mark Roberts) try to develop a friendship (in other words, suck up to) their new boss, Les (George Wendt). Thinking they're a gay couple, Les accepts their invitation to dinner and the guys decide to play along. At dinner, Les becomes suspicious and asks them to kiss each other to prove they're gay. They try, but can't, and their true sexual identity is exposed.[87]

On an episode of *Ned and Stacey* ("The Gay Caballeros"), advertising executive Ned (Thomas Haden Church) pretends to be a friend of Dorothy's to hold onto an important client. When designer/club owner Brent Barrow (Stephen Kearney) discovers Ned's relationship with Stacey (Debra Messing) is a marriage of convenience, he assumes Ned is a closeted gay. So Ned, along with his best pal Eric (Greg Germann), decide to "come out" and end up together on the dance floor. Brent soon figures out they're not gay (their dancing is a dead give-away), but he appreciates the effort and doesn't cancel the account.[88]

A similar situation occurs on the short-lived *Getting Personal* when commercial director Milo (Duane Martin) makes a homophobic joke in front of a new client ("Chasing Sammy"). He apologizes and explains that he is gay (because it's acceptable if you're talking about one of your own.) Milo's lie comes back to haunt him, especially when he falls for one of the client's sexy representatives, Alex (Alexia Robinson). However, his plan to get her in bed backfires to the point where, instead of bedding Alex, he finds himself between the sheets instead with his pal Sammy (Jon Cryer).[89]

The ruse is not confined to men. On *Sex and the City* ("Bay of Married Pigs"), Miranda (Cynthia Nixon) is mistaken for a lesbian by a co-worker, who fixes her up with another woman. Believing she's a lesbian (and therefore less threatening to men), one of the senior partners of her law firm, Chip (David Forsyth) invites her into his power circle. Donning a men's suit, Miranda goes along with it, but eventually admits to Chip she is straight. Just to be absolutely sure, she kisses a woman (which confirms she definitely is).[90]

Richard (Malcolm Getts), Caroline's assistant on *Caroline in the City*, is another character who feigns being gay to get ahead. In "Caroline and the Gay Art Show," Richard gets his first art show at one of New York's top galleries, only to discover it's exclusively for gay artists. Richard decides to go ahead with the plan when he finds out he can get $20,000 for a single painting. At the opening, he decides to come clean, but he's stopped at the last minute by his straight friend, Del (Eric Lutes), who pretends to be his lover. When gallery owner

Kenneth Arabian (played by openly gay actor/playwright Dan Butler) tells Richard how proud he is to support a new gay artist, Richard reveals his true sexual orientation and loses the sale, but maintains his integrity.[91]

The pretend-gay plot relies heavily on the "gay" professions to generate laughs. In the pilot episode of the Lifetime sitcom *Maggie*, Amanda's (Morgan Nagler) boyfriend Reg (Todd Biebenhain), an aspiring cartoonist, pretends he's gay because "all the best artists are gay."[92] On *Cheers* ("Norm...Is That You?"), Norm (George Wendt) discovers he has a natural flair for decorating. Frasier and Lilith (Bebe Newirth) recommend him to their snooty friends, Robert and Kim Cooperman (George Delroy and Jane Sibbet), who simply *must* have a gay decorator. So Norm recruits Sam to pose as his lover. When the Coopermans find out the truth, they still agree to hire Norm, but at a decidedly lower straight rate.[93]

Heteros in sitcom-land can even delude themselves about their orientation. On an episode of *Friends* ("The One With Phoebe's Husband"), Phoebe is reunited with her green card husband, Duncan (Steve Zahn), a gay Canadian ice skater. When Duncan shows up to get a divorce, Phoebe realizes she's still carrying a torch for him. But then Duncan makes a startling revelation — he's straight and getting married to a woman. In a hilarious reversal of the "coming out" episode, Duncan confesses how he can't live a lie anymore. "How can you be straight?" Phoebe asks. "You're so smart, and funny, and throw such great Academy Award parties." Duncan explains how he always knew all his life: "I thought I was supposed to be something. I'm an ice dancer. All my friends are gay. I was just trying to fit in." Phoebe is devastated by the news:

DUNCAN: Well, I've never told you this. There was one or two times back in college when I'd get really drunk, go to a straight bar, and wake up with a woman next to me. But I told myself it was the liquor. And everyone experiments in college. Now I know I don't have a choice about this. I was born this way.

PHOEBE: I don't know what to say. You're married to someone for six years. You think you know him. And then one day he says "I'm not gay."[94]

A similar reversal occurs on an episode of *For Your Love* ("House of Cards") when Tom (Jason Bateman), Sheri's (Dedee Pfeiffer) best friend, visits. Bobbi (Tamala Jones) has her reservations about Tom being gay because he said her shoes were "interesting" and he didn't call her "Miss Bobbi" or "girlfriend" once. Actually, Bobbie knows what she's talking about. Sheri admits to Malena (Holly Robinson Peete) that Tom isn't gay, but only pretending so they can remain close without her husband Dean (D.W. Moffet) getting jealous. When Dean finds out the truth, he gets angry. But the joke is on Sheri — Tom really is gay and he'd always thought Sheri wanted him to pretend as a way of encouraging him to come out. He also thought deep down it would change their relationship.[95] The *Victor/Victoria*-like premise is convoluted (a gay man pretending to be a straight man pretending to be gay), but Bateman makes an appealing gay-straight-gay man, so much so he was subsequently cast in the 2000-2001 midseason replacement, *Some of My Best Friends*.

For some characters, posing as gay can be financially rewarding. *Drew Carey* pretends he's playing on the other team so he can pay for his dog's expensive hip operation ("Man's Best Same Sex Companion"). At the suggestion of Nora (Jane Morris), a fellow animal lover and the benefits manager for Winfred-Louder Department Store, Drew applies for health insurance for his fictional boyfriend Aaron. To show he's not totally dishonest, he plans to pay back the money with interest. When the claim is questioned by his boss, Mr. Wick (Craig Ferguson) and the store's owner, Mrs. Louder (Nan Martin), Drew enlists Oswald (Diedrich Bader) to pose as his lover.

At the inquiry, the "couple" are separated and asked a series of questions to see how much they know about each other. They fail, but when they start to bicker, Mr. Wick and Mrs. Louder agree they sound like a couple. When Wick

"Landlady"
Kate and Allie (CBS-TV)
October 15, 1984
Written by Bob Randall
Directed by Bill Persky

Kate (Susan Saint James) and Allie (Jane Curtin) may lose their Greenwich Village apartment in this funny and touching episode which questions the meaning of the word "family." When they discover their lease is for a one family dwelling, their landlady Janet (Gloria Cromwell) threatens to double their rent. However, the rule would not apply if they were a couple, so Kate and Allie decide to pretend to be lesbians. This little white lie creates major complications when Janet reveals she's also a lesbian and introduces the women to her lover Miriam (Chevi Cotton). And when Janet and Miriam hold a dance at the gay and lesbian center to honor Kate and Allie, the women are forced to tell the truth.

Eight years later, the question — "What constitutes a family?" — would be the focus of a political debate in the 1992 presidential election thanks to Dan Quayle's "family values" speech in which the Vice-President criticized single TV mother Murphy Brown. While other series and made-for-TV movies have tackled the subject, Kate and Allie's approach was refreshing and ahead of its time, because it's the lesbian characters, rather than the heterosexuals, who are asked to revise their definition of family. When Janet discovers the truth, Kate and Allie defend their right to live together as a family: "It's love that defines a family...any kind of love — your kind, our kind, theirs. Who's to say which kind of family is the best? You above all people ought to know that..." The lesbians get the message and they all go out and celebrate at the gay and lesbian center.

suggests using Drew and Oswald in their new ad campaign targeting gay shoppers, Drew retreats to heterodom and his benefits are suspended until he pays back the money.[96]

Several seasons later, Drew enters another phony gay marriage with the nasty Mr. Wick, who is trying to duck the INS so he can stay in the country ("Drew and the Trail Scouts").[97] The Wick situation gets even more out of hand when the Englishman moves into Drew's home and starts getting too chummy with his friends. In the end ("All Work and No Play"), Drew has no choice but to end the charade and throw the bloke out.[98]

Caroline in the City offers a similar plot ("Caroline and the Little White Lies") involving business partners Del (Eric Lutes) and Charlie (Andrew Lauer). They decide to purchase health insurance as a same-sex couple because it's cheaper. When their gay insurance broker Todd (Sean Masterson) invites them to a party, the situation starts to get out of hand. Charlie is totally into it, first because it makes Del so uncomfortable and second, because he likes "the clothes, the camaraderie, the grooming products...I like everything except sleeping with men."[99] (In the episode about Richard's gay art show, Charlie revealed he has a gay brother.) Del is uncomfortable and frustrated when he meets Todd's beautiful business partner Susan (Angie Everhart) and can't tell her he's really straight. When the "couple" find themselves on the stage of a gay rights rally supporting same-sex health benefits, Del realizes it's time to come clean and apologizes to all gays for the sham (he also thanks them for "disco").

You don't always have to set out to cheat the system to get same-sex benefits.

Redefining the nuclear family: Kate McArdle (Susan Saint James, right) and her housemate Allie Lowell (Jane Curtin, left).

On *The Jamie Foxx Show* ("Partners fo' Life"), Jamie takes his friend Andre (Bill Bellamy) to the County Hospital when he hurts his toe playing basketball. Jamie promises to pick up the bill, which runs to an astronomical $1700. He asks the attendant if there's any way he can get a discount because Andre is his partner and friend. Thinking they're a gay couple, she gives him an insurance claim form for a domestic partner, which Jamie thinks means "Home Boy." When he shows Fancy (Garcelle Beauvais) the form he filed, she explains what "domestic partner" means. Worried about going to jail for insurance fraud and, worse, that people will think he's gay, he cancels the claim with his company's human resources manager. Only he still thinks Jamie is gay and invites him to his bachelor party that night. When Jamie and his friends arrive, they're shocked to see a male stripper jump out of the cake.[100]

Pretending to be gay can get you "in" with a member of the opposite sex because on sitcoms, all straight women love gay men. They open up to them and tell them things they'd never tell their boyfriends. In *Guys Like Us*, Sean (Chris Hardwick) has his eye on his new neighbor Kara (Jennifer Grant). She assumes Sean and his roommate Jared (Bumper Robinson) are a couple and Maestro (Maestro Harris), Jared's little brother, is their son. To get Kara interested in him (*and* win a bet with Jared), he pretends she is awakening heterosexual feelings for him. It only takes a few kisses and *voilà* — it worked! Jared gets wind of this and starts playing the part of a jealous lover. When Jared demands a kiss ("like when you were my cowboy"), Sean can't bring himself to do it and, alas, must fess up to Kara. The inanity of the plot aside, the episode becomes problematic when Jared's idea of being gay is sashaying into a room and talking in an affected manner. Once again, it all comes down to a kiss. When presented with a choice — the truth or a kiss — the less than usually candid Sean seems to have no choice but to tell the truth for once.[101]

Just in case anyone *is* offended, the tag at the end of the show concludes the subplot involving Jared's concern about Maestro being more interested in dolls and ballet than hockey. Jared realizes there's nothing wrong if a little boy wants to squeeze some dolls and watch ballet.

Two straight men pretending to be a gay couple can also be found on the first episode of *The Love Boat: The Next Wave* ("Smooth Sailing"). Josh (*Melrose Place*'s gay resident, Doug Savant) is left at the altar by his bride, so he decides to take his best man, Luke (Jason Brooks) on the honeymoon cruise. As the pair are lodging in the Pacific Princess's honeymoon suite, the single women on the ship mistake them for a gay couple. Like many other straight men pretending to be gay, Josh decides to use his honorary gay status to score with the ladies. Luke thinks it's wrong to be dishonest and comes clean himself by telling Josh he *is* gay, which his friend has no trouble accepting.[102]

Besides checking into a honeymoon suite, another way to be mistaken for gay is to wear a T-shirt with a large pink triangle on it. In *Alright Already* ("Again with the Laser Surgery"), Vaughn (Maury Sterling) has no idea he's wearing a gay symbol on his shirt. He gets the attention of an attractive, yet not too bright, model named Kelsey (Michele Maika) who's tired of being harassed by straight men. Striking up a platonic friendship with her, Vaughn confesses to having had sexual thoughts about women and wonders if he could be straight. Kelsey volunteers for the experiment but when the big moment arrives, Vaughn gets what he deserves: he's impotent, leaving Kelsey absolutely sure he's gay.[103]

Pretending is also an effective strategy for keeping a member of the opposite sex away. On *Men Behaving Badly* ("The Odds Couple"), Jamie (Rob Schneider) misbehaves when he begins spying on the nurse living next door, Brenda (Dina Spybey) and her friend Ellen (Heather Page Kent), who is in town on a visit. Convinced Brenda and Ellen are lesbians, Jamie tries to catch some girl-on-girl action. He tries drilling a hole through his closet into their apartment, but the drill accidentally goes through Brenda's aquarium, killing her fish. His next approach is less subtle — standing outside on her window ledge. Figuring it's the best way to get rid of him, the two women pretend to make out, which causes an excited Jamie to topple right off the ledge.[104]

On *Frasier* ("Out With Dad"), Martin (John Mahoney) reluctantly accompanies his son to the opera and catches the eye of Frasier's girlfriend's mother (Mary Louise Wilson). To avoid going out with her, Martin pretends he's gay, so Frasier's girlfriend decides to fix Martin up with her gay uncle Edward (Brian

Bedford). In one of the 1999-2000 season's funniest moments, Martin tells Edward he's involved with Niles (David Hyde Pierce), who has no idea what's going on, but plays along and pretends to be his father's lover. Although Martin's original lie was in his self-interest, his perseverance in sustaining his ruse turns into a gallant gesture because he doesn't want to embarrass Edward or ruin Frasier's chances with his girlfriend.[105]

Tired of being seated next to losers at weddings, *Then Came You*'s Cheryl (Miriam Shor) decides to pretend she's a lesbian ("Then Came a Wedding").[106] What she doesn't count on is the cute guy she finds sitting at her table. Another wedding guest who poses as gay (but not by his own choice), is Steve Rutledge (Tom Amandes). On *Pursuit of Happiness*, Steve agrees to pose as his law partner Alex's (Brad Garrett) date ("Wedding Dates") in order to show an ardent ex-boyfriend he's attached.[107] Steve's extremely uncomfortable, particularly when the groom publicly introduces Steve and Alex as a couple and has them join in the first dance. The scheme doesn't exactly work because when Alex's ex cuts in, it's to dance with Steve.

Posing as gay may take a character down a path he or she never expected to go. On *Talk to Me* ("About Being Gay"), radio host Janey (Kyra Sedgwick) livens up a boring advertisers' dinner by taking her co-workers dare and hitting on another woman. Janey plants a kiss on Teresa (played by model Paulina Porizkova), who turns out to be a lesbian. Feeling guilty, Janey agrees to go on a date with her and starts to like the attention and gifts. But deep down, she knows she prefers what men have. When Teresa learns Janey is straight, she admits she could tell because she kisses like a straight woman![108]

On *Suddenly Susan*, Todd (David Strickland) joins a lesbian computer chatroom under the name Pepper E-Z ("Past Tense"). He strikes up a relationship with "another" lesbian, Coco B 1-2-3, who shares Todd's interest in mountain biking, rainy days, and *Xena Warrior Princess*. Todd decides to come clean and meet Coco face-to-face, only to discover Coco is another guy (Shawn Hoffman) pretending to be a lesbian.[109]

Military school cadet Francis (Christopher Masterson) on *Malcolm in the Middle* is in heaven when he's assigned honor-guard duty at the Miss Alabama beauty pageant. However, the contestants thinks he's gay, so he becomes their confidante, including one young woman who tries to get the poor boy sexually deprogrammed.[110]

The mistaken lesbian plot gets a new twist on a funny episode of *Caroline in the City* ("Caroline and *Victor/Victoria*"). Broadway star-in-the-making Annie (Amy Pietz) dons male garb to prepare for her audition to be Julie Andrews's understudy in the Broadway show, *Victor/Victoria* (which she got by hijacking Andrews's limo). When Annie shows up at Remo's, the gang's hangout, dressed as a man, she proves to Del (Eric Lutes) she can pick up a lone beautiful blonde named Leslie (Andrea Bendewald). Annie gets the date, then owns up she's really a woman. "And?..." asks a bewildered Leslie — a lesbian — who assumed so all along. When Leslie laughs at Annie's attempt to pose as a man, they get into a heated argument. Too bad Annie didn't know Leslie is one of the *Victor/Victoria* casting directors she's about to audition for. Guess who volunteers to tell Annie she didn't get the part?[111]

Wings put its own creative spin on the drag plotline in "Escape From New York." Helen (Crystal Bernard) and Brian (Steven Weber) travel to New York City so she can see the musical *Rent*. They end up losing all their money and Helen is forced to enter a drag queen contest under the name "Hell - in a Handbasket" lip-syncing to "I Will Survive." She loses, but is given two tickets to *Rent* as a consolation prize.[112]

PLOTLINE #4: "A VERY SPECIAL EPISODE . . ."

When a commercial for a sitcom advertises a "very special episode," it signals the series will handle some issue beyond the norm. Typically more dramatic than comic, such episodes may, for example, involve a character facing a crisis (a cancer scare, death of a loved one, etc.) or tackle a social issue like alcoholism, drug abuse, illiteracy, or sexual harassment. Sometimes the issue is controversial, as in the 1973 *Maude* episode in which she struggled over the decision to have an abortion ("Maude's Decision"). It may be tied to an actual event, like the end of the Korean War on the final episode of *M*A*S*H* ("Goodbye, Farewell, and Amen"). Or it may be something truly groundbreaking, such as *Ellen*'s infamous coming out episode.

In terms of homosexuality, what constitutes a "special," let alone controversial, episode has evolved since the early 1970s. The subject of homosexuality was in itself considered a taboo subject when first addressed on episodes of *All in the Family*, *Maude*, *M*A*S*H*, and *The Bob Crane Show*. While homophobia would remain the dominant theme of "coming out," "mistaken identity," and "pretend" episodes, some comedies became a forum to address more timely issues, such as gay and lesbian teachers and AIDS.

THE GAY TEACHER

In "Cousin Liz," a 1977 episode of *All in the Family*, Archie finds out Edith's late cousin Liz and her "roommate" Veronica, both teachers, were lovers. He tells Edith "people like that" shouldn't be teaching kids. At the time, gays in the classroom was a national issue, thanks to homophobic crusaders like Anita Bryant, who successfully led the fight to overturn the anti-gay discrimination ordinance in Dade County, Florida in June of 1977.

"Cousin Liz" first aired on October 9, 1977. A week before (September 29, 1977), an episode of *Carter Country* entitled "Out of the Closet" featured a story line about a local high school teacher who is fired when he comes out of the closet. Sheriff Roy (Victor French) of Clinton Corners, Georgia (located next to

Plains, President Carter's hometown) is shocked to learn his old friend and fishing buddy Bill Peterson (Richard Jaeckel) is gay. Bill explains that when the school board passed a resolution banning gay teachers, he felt it was his duty to come out publicly. Consequently, his honesty got him canned.

Bill plans to sue the school board to get his teaching job back and wants Roy to testify as a character witness. Not only is Roy having a difficult time accepting that his friend for twenty years is gay, he's also torn about the issue itself (and his memory of sharing a sleeping bag on a fishing trip to stay warm isn't helping). Roy, who is single and has no children, is simply not sure if homosexuals are good role models for children and should be allowed to teach.

When the gay liberation movement decides to sponsor a rock concert in Clinton Corners to raise money for Bill's defense, the town is divided. Mayor Burnside (Richard Paul) is afraid the controversy will hurt the town's economy, so he convinces the school board to rehire Bill as an administrator. Bill turns it down because he knows he's a good teacher who belongs in the classroom.

Meanwhile, everyone at the sheriff's station offers their opinion about homosexuals, among them Deputy Jasper DeWitt Jr. (Harvey Vernon) who displays his ignorance in his explanation of the "homosexual conspiracy":

JASPER: Part of their plan is to recruit children. You see, they sneak around the school yard til they spot somebody who is not doing good in sports. Then they dress him up in a lavendar suit. They they take him to one of those fancy French restaurants for dinner. And then they start filling his head with all that lady-like stuff...you know, like poetry, music and art. And before you know it — zap — you have an interior designer.

Chief Roy knows Jasper is talking nonsense. In the end, he agrees to testify on his friend's behalf because he believes the school board was wrong to claim Bill isn't a suitable role model:

ROY: You know I've been thinking about what I said about Bill Peterson not being a good example for children. Now here's a man who's been a perfect teacher for 15 years — and was willing to risk everything to stand up and speak up for what he believed in. Now I think that's a pretty good example...[113]

The Chief testifies, yet we never learn the outcome of the trial. And like Veronica, the Deputy's good friend disappears and is never seen or heard from again.

Before shooting the episode, producer Douglas Arango sent a copy of the script to gay activist Morris Kight along with a letter soliciting support from "influential leaders of the Gay Community, as to the inoffensiveness and appropriateness of the script from the gay view point."[114] *Los Angeles Times* critic Lee Margulies commended the show's producers for coming down "strongly enough in support of the homosexual character," yet felt the episode devoted too much time to Roy's reaction to the situation and not enough on the gay teacher issue itself.[115] What Margulies failed to recognize is the strategy being employed by the episode's writers, Arango and Phil Doran. By having the series's central character simultaneously question his feelings about his gay friend and whether gays should be permitted in the classroom, the issue is personalized and Roy is able to arrive at a more informed decision.

In June of 1978, California voters went to the polls to vote on the Briggs Initiative. Sponsored by conservative State Senator John Briggs, the initiative, also known as Proposition Six, would not only ban gay men and lesbians from the classroom, but prohibit any teacher who presented homosexuality in the classroom in a positive way. The Briggs Initiative received support from Anita Bryant, the American Nazi Party, and the Ku Klux Klan.[116] In a victory for gay rights, Californians defeated the Briggs Initiative by a 58-42 percent vote, a wider margin than activists expected.

The following year, the issue was addressed again on *The Baxters*, an experimental sitcom executive produced by Norman Lear. The first-run syndicated series, which was first televised as a local public affairs show in Boston, opened with a fifteen-minute vignette about the lives of a middle class American family. Fred Baxter (Larry Keith) was an insurance salesman who lived in the suburbs with his wife Nancy (Anita Gillette), and their three children — adopted daughter Naomi (Derin Altay), a college student; 14-year-old Jonah (Chris Peterson); and 10-year-old Rachael (Terri Lynn Wood). Each week the family faces a new moral dilemma around an array of issues such as inflation, child molestation, health care for the aging, etc.

In "Homosexual Teachers," the family discovers Jonah's beloved teacher, Mr. Whitehead, is gay when a story appears in the local paper with the headline "Teacher Speaks Out for Gay Rights." The homophobic father of one of Jonah's classmates, Jerry Johnson (Chuck McCann), who believes homosexuality is not normal, wants Fred to sign a petition to get Mr. Whitehead (or as he calls him, the "fruit") fired. Nancy tells her husband not to sign. "If we have done our jobs right," she explains, "then Jonah and Marty [Jerry's son] should know what roles they should play."[117] Fred agrees with Nancy intellectually but on an emotional level is not comfortable with a homosexual teaching his children. At the end of the segment, a question is posed to the viewer: should Fred sign the petition?[118]

After presenting both sides of the issue, the remainder of the half-hour is devoted to a town hall meeting style discussion with a studio audience, who, immediately after watching the vignette on tape, are invited to share their views. The series was syndicated around the country, so the discussion portion was produced locally within each TV market. The participants for the "Homosexual Teachers" discussion in Los Angeles, hosted by Steve Edwards for KTLA-TV, included some openly gay teachers as well as some people (let's just call them idiots) with a clear anti-gay bias. One of them is allowed to go on a long tirade about how homosexuality is "wrong, sick and immoral." In sharp contrast, many agreed it was a non-issue. Several young people gave high marks to their gay teachers, while the educators in the audience described first-hand the harassment they experienced from students. The idea to combine a sitcom and a talk show was extremely inventive. Unfortunately, the segment was severely edited to fit the time slot, thereby limiting the depth of the discussion.

THE AIDS STORY

In the 1970s, the *issue du jour* was gay teachers. In the 1980s and 1990s, it was AIDS. The disease proved to be an even more challenging subject for sitcoms to tackle because it's difficult to find humor in so devastating a disease. A gay story line involving AIDS also poses an even greater challenge for TV writers because, in addition to the disease itself, they needed to address the homophobia surrounding AIDS and the stigma attached to AIDS as the "gay plague."

With too much ground to cover, many sitcoms focused on an adult hetero-sexual or a child who became infected through a blood transfusion. The story generally involves a series regular who meets someone who has AIDS or is HIV positive. Through their interaction, the series regular witnesses first-hand the injustice PWAs and HIV-positive people experience in such areas as education, employment, and health care. The situation usually gives the main character the opportunity to examine his/her own feelings, while at the same time demon-strating how society should be treating PWAs and people who are HIV positive. Thus the episode's primary goal is to educate its public about the transmission of HIV so they will understand there is no reason to fear someone who's positive or has AIDS. In many instances, the individual who is HIV positive or has AIDS isn't given the opportunity to speak for him or herself. That task is assigned to the show's main character who demonstrates empathy for the outcast by delivering a passionate speech.

Mr. Belvedere featured a sensitive episode ("Wesley's Friend") about 9-year-old Wesley (Brice Beckham), who's afraid to be around his friend Danny (Ian Fried), a hemophiliac who contracted the disease through a blood transfusion. Danny isn't allowed to attend school because his classmates' parents are afraid their children will catch it. During a school pageant, Wesley assures the audience Danny poses no danger and should be allowed to attend school. Through his friendship with Danny, Wesley, along with his family and classmates, learn the straight facts about AIDS.[119]

Adam Arkin, who spent most of the 1990s playing Dr. Aaron Shutt on *Chicago Hope*, guest-starred on the *Golden Girls/Empty Nest* spin-off *Nurses* as an AIDS patient. In "Love, Death, and the Whole Damn Thing," Peter checks into Miami's Community Medical Center, where he's reunited with one of his many old girlfriends, Nurse Julie (Mary Jo Keenan). She's afraid of contracting the disease, but eventually comes to her senses and assures a lonely and angry Peter he won't die alone.[120]

On *Doogie Howser M.D.* ("A Life in Progress"), a street artist with AIDS, Jeff Moore (Robert Clohessy), paints a wall mural in the children's wing of Eastman Hospital. When word gets around Jeff has AIDS, the hospital takes him off the mural. Doogie goes up against the hospital board, which prompts one board member (James McMullan) to admit he contracted AIDS from a blood transfusion. The board reconsiders and the mural is completed.[121] On *Grace Under Fire* ("Positively Hateful"), Grace reluctantly helps the curmudgeonly HIV-positive janitor at her kids' school, Mr. Mullens (Robert Klein), when his job is in jeopardy.[122]

Another strategy for tackling the subject involves a character taking the AIDS test because they risked exposure via contaminated blood or unprotected sex. On *The Golden Girls* ("72 Hours"), Rose fears she may have received infected blood during her gall bladder operation.[123] *Sex and the City*'s sexually active Samantha Jones (Kim Cattrall) takes the test at the request of her new boyfriend ("Running With Scissors").[124] When a woman who contracted AIDS through unprotected sex comes to speak to the students of Hillman College on *A Different World* ("If I Should Die Before I Wake"), Dwayne (Kadeem Hardison) and Ron (Darryl M. Bell) both decide it's time to get tested.[125] On *Titus* ("The Test"), Christopher and girlfriend Erin both get tested because they each had unprotected sex during a brief period apart. To no one's surprise, all of the series regulars test HIV negative.[126]

Ironically, few sitcoms have featured gay male characters with AIDS or who are HIV positive. The first show to approach the subject is an episode of *Designing Women* entitled "Killing All the Right People." Written by series co-creator Linda Bloodworth-Thomason, whose mother contracted the disease from a blood transfusion, the show views the issue from two perspectives. The first involves Mary Jo (Annie Potts), who reluctantly participates in a PTA debate about distributing birth control materials to students. The second involves an interior designer, 24-year-old Kendall Dobbs (Tony Goldwyn), who announces to the women he's dying and asks if they'll decorate a room at the funeral home which can be used for others who die of AIDS. Sweet and soft-spoken, Kendall is chastised by Julia's old "friend" and client, Alma Jean Salinger (Camilla Carr), who overhears the women planning Kendall's funeral. Right in front of Kendall, she tells them "if these boys hadn't been doing what they were doing, they wouldn't be getting what's coming to them now...As far as I'm concerned this disease has one thing going for it...it's killing all the right people." An angry Julia boots Alma Jean out, but not before going on one of her tirades over the suggestion AIDS is God's punishment:

> JULIA: Alma Jean, get serious! Who do you think you're talking to? I've known you for twenty-seven years and all I can say is if God was giving out sexually transmitted diseases to people as punishment for sinning, that you would be at the free clinic all the time. And so would the rest of us![127]

This prompts Mary Jo to express her position — it's not just about preventing births anymore, it's about preventing deaths:

> MARY JO: More important than what any civic leader, or PTA or Board of Education thinks about teenagers having sex or any immoral act that my daughter or your son might engage in, it's the bottom line that I don't think they should have to die for it.

A touching episode of *Dream On* ("For Peter's Sake") approaches AIDS from a more personal perspective when book editor Martin Tupper is assigned to edit the memoirs of AIDS-afflicted western writer, Peter Brewer (David Clennon). Martin's sleazy boss Gibby (Michael McKeon) decides Whitestone Publishing needs a bestseller for Christmas. He decides it should be the memoir of someone dying of AIDS because "it's hot, it's now, it's got sex, it's got drugs, everyone is getting it."[128] Martin is reluctant, but agrees to work with Peter. At first Martin is uncomfortable — he can't bring himself to say the word AIDS in front of Peter, let alone drink from his glass when he offers him water. He eventually loosens up and even plays along when he's introduced to Peter's mother, Kitty (Gwen Verdon) as his lover. When Kitty has a minute alone with Martin, she tells him "I'm so glad he's found someone. Take good care of him." He assures her he will.

Gibby throws a wrench into Peter's book when he decides to cancel it and replace it with the memoirs of a famous male heterosexual athlete with AIDS. Martin can't find it in his heart to tell Peter when he visits him in the hospital. Instead, he helps his friend get comfortable. ("You make me feel like Ali McGraw," Peter quips.) In the final scene, it's revealed Peter has died. Martin returns to the apartment which Kitty has just finished packing up. He gives her a copy of Peter's manuscript, which will be published at Christmas by Random House. Kitty gives him something to remember Peter by — a silver yo-yo given to Peter by his father.

RECURRING AND REGULAR GAY CHARACTERS

The first television sitcom to regularly feature an identifiably gay character was the 1972 limited-run comedy, *The Corner Bar*. Produced by comedian Alan King, the series was set in a New York City tavern, Grant's Toomb, owned and operated by Harry Grant (Gabriel Dell, one of the original Bowery Boys). One of the six regular customers who frequented the bar was a gay theatre set designer named Peter Panama (Vincent Schiavelli). Rich Wandel, president of the Gay Activists Alliance, noted the historical significance of having a regular gay character. Still, he called Peter's character a "ludicrous stereotype," which the GAA could not accept "no more than the black community would accept a watermelon-eating, tap-dancing stereotype of a black man."[129] According to *Variety*, the series included a scene featuring a male character with exaggerated femme gestures and intonation complaining to a group at the table in the bar about the said trend in New York parties. He attended one recently, he says, that was loaded with weirdos — all married couples.[130]

In their review, *Variety* noted how Schiavelli's interpretation of Peter "could raise beefs from some quarters...but he was treated no better or no worse in the rapid fire repartee exchanges — and belongs on the show."[131] In response to the criticism, actor Schiavelli observed

It's a little curious playing a fag especially if you're not...Peter isn't feminine and doesn't do drag numbers. He is as sexual as everyone else in the place...He isn't stupid. He's a warm funny human being. He's as real as everyone else in the bar, and his emotional range is the same — he's not toned down.[132]

Nevertheless, in response to the GAA's criticism, King agreed to tone down Peter's character if the show returned. When it did the following year, Gabriel Dell and most of the original cast, including Schiavelli, were gone.

As with the majority of regular and recurring gay characters, Peter served a dual purpose: he was the source as well as the target of humor. While the gay male characters who appear on single episode of shows like *All in the Family* and *Alice* are overtly masculine, regular and recurring characters are typically more feminine than masculine — a strategy by producers to insure they pose no "threat." Smart, quick-witted, and at times a little bitchy, they often serve as the "entertainment" for the other characters, particularly the series's protagonist, who usually considers the gay character an ally.

But these stereotypical characters also serve as the target for jokes by the other characters. Of course, sitcoms consist mostly of characters, often close friends, slinging insults at each other. While insults directed toward straight characters are usually about a specific character flaw (he's cheap or sloppy or dumb), jokes aimed directly at gay characters are usually about their sexuality. So when Harry's preparing for a congressman's visit to the bar, he tells Peter, "maybe you could put a splint on your wrist."

There's a definite pattern in the roles assigned to gay and lesbian characters, from the premiere of *The Corner Bar* to the present day. Before shows like *Ellen*, *Will & Grace*, and *Normal, Ohio*, gay characters were there primarily to assist, support and advise the main character. The roles they regularly assume — personal assistant, co-worker, and/or close friend/confidante — have been limited, yet there has been definite progress made since the early 1970s in regards to their depth and function.

THE GAY ASSISTANT

Dedicated, loyal, and a model of efficiency, the gay assistant makes the professional and personal lives of many television characters run smoothly. The first gay assistant introduced on a situation comedy was also one of the earliest regular gay sitcom characters. On *The Nancy Walker Show*, Terry Olfson (Scott Folson) is a struggling actor who pays the bills by working as a live-in secretary for Hollywood talent agent Nancy Kitteridge (Nancy Walker) . Terry keeps Nancy's chaotic life in order, which in the show's pilot becomes even more chaotic when her husband Kenneth (William Daniels), retires from the navy and returns home. Kenneth wants Nancy to shut down her business and doesn't understand why she needs Terry, who he thinks is strange.[133]

Equally gay and efficient assistants include the suave and very sexy Stefano (Luigi Amodeo), who helps *High Society*'s Dorothy Emerson (Mary McDonnell) keep her publishing firm running smoothly; Brice (Drew McVety), who also worked for a New York publishing house with *Molly Dodd* (Blair Brown); *N.Y.P.D. Blue*'s John Irvin (Bill Brochtrup), who transferred to a vice squad unit for a single episode of *Public Morals*; and Jules "Julie" Bennett, Catherine Hughes's (Ann Magnuson) assistant at *Chicago Weekly* magazine on *Anything But Love*.

And then there's *The Simpsons*'s Waylon Smithers (voice of Harry Shearer), assistant to Homer's boss, Mr. Burns. Smithers's sexuality has never been explicitly stated, though it has been made clear repeatedly through innuendoes (seeing him in "Trouble With Trillions" warbling "Everything's Coming Up Roses" while ironing in his pink dressing gown seems like all the reason you really need).[134] In another episode ("Lisa the Skeptic"), in which everyone thinks the world is coming to an end, Smithers says "What the hell!" and plants a kiss on Burns's lips. Afterwards, he assures Smithers the kiss was "merely a sign of respect."[135]

There have never been any kisses exchanged between Brian (Scott Thompson) and *Larry Sanders*'s sidekick Hank Kingsley (Jeffrey Tambor), though that doesn't mean gay Brian is any less devoted. When Hank's assistant quits ("Hank's New Assistant), he hires Brian without knowing he's *a gay*. Hank tries to find an excuse to fire him, but when he overhears Brian talking about Larry's feelings being hurt over comedian Dana Carvey's imitation of him, Hank realizes he's worth having around — gay or not.[136] Brian gets closer to his boss, who takes him to a gay bar when he's upset over a recent break-up ("The Matchmaker") and ends up in *Variety* the next day in Army Arched's column.[137]

When Brian experiences harassment on the job, it's not from his boss, but the show's sexist head writer, Phil (Wallace Langham). Brian decides he's had enough of Phil's cracks and sues him ("Putting the Gay Back in Litigation"). He puts him to the test by showing up in a pair of pink hot pants, a tight black shirt, and a leather hat. Phil cracks in a few seconds. ("Where did you get that? The Freddy Mercury estate sale?") In a heart-to-heart discussion, the boys open up: Brian admits he went too far and Phil admits to having a big mouth. Ironically, their talk turns into an intense make-out session.[138]

At the same time he appeared on *The Larry Sanders Show*, actor Wallace Langham became an assistant himself on *Veronica's Closet*. As lingerie queen Ronnie Clark's (Kirstie Alley) right-hand man Josh, Langham became television's first officially closeted gay male character. Everyone knew Josh was gay except Josh, even though all the signs were there. His idol is Tara Lipinski and he loves Broadway shows. When his co-worker Leo (Daryl Mitchell) temporarily crashes at Josh's apartment ("Veronica's Got a Secret"), Josh enjoys the pampering and gourmet food so much, he doesn't want Leo to leave.[139] Josh almost comes out of the closet when his friend Scotty (played by Langham's *Larry Sanders*'s co-star Scott Thompson) announces he's getting married ("Veronica's Great Model Search"). Josh convinces him to out himself, but unfortunately Scotty can't get Josh to do the same.[140] In fact, Josh soon heads in the opposite direction and becomes engaged to Chloe (Mary Lynn-Rajskub), though he manages to put off having sex with her. Then when she's forced to push the wedding date up because her father's going into the witness protection program, he suffers anxiety attacks.

Everything starts to change when Josh meets his neighbor Brian (Alan Smith), who, like Josh, is engaged and gay as a goose. Although he knows him for only a short period of time, he asks him to be his best man at his wedding. At Josh's bachelor party, Leo catches Josh and Brian smooching. Ronnie finds out and has a heart-to-heart with him on his wedding day. Instead of saying "I do," Josh says "I'm gay." ("That's my boy," Ronnie wails.) As Josh deals with coming out, Brian soon follows him out of the closet and in the close of the series, the couple look like they'll be living happily ever after.[141]

CRYSTAL DOES DALLAS

Jodie Dallas is certainly the most memorable gay character of the pre-Ellen era. Smart, funny, and a tad insecure, Jodie is fairly well-adjusted in comparison to the collection of off-the-wall characters inhabiting this hilarious send-up of soap operas. He was also more three-dimensional than most gay men on sitcoms of the time, thanks to his creators, comedian Billy Crystal and writer/producer Susan Harris, whose credits include *Benson*, *The Golden Girls*, and *Empty Nest*. Crystal's work on *Soap* made him a household name, which is ironic considering that in 1977, actors stayed clear of gay roles for fear of being typecast or, even worse, mistaken for the real thing.

As the announcer states in the opening of each episode, *Soap* is the story of two sisters, Jessica Tate (Katherine Helmond) and Mary Campbell (Mary Damon). Mary, who always appears to be on the brink of a nervous breakdown, has her hands full with her hyperactive, yet impotent, husband Burt (Richard Mulligan); her two sons, Jodie and Danny (Ted Wass), who works for the mob; and two step-sons, Chuck (Jay Johnson), a ventriloquist who travels everywhere with his dummy, Bob; and Peter (Robert Urich), a handsome tennis pro who is bedding every woman in Dunn's River, Connecticut, including his (step) Aunt Jessica.

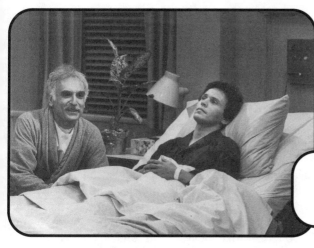

Barney Gerber (Harold Gould, left) comforts his suicidal hospital roommate, *Soap*'s Jodie Dallas (Billy Crystal).

When she's not cheating on her philandering husband Chester (Robert Mandan), the naïve, ditzy Jessica takes care of her shell-shocked father, "The Major" (Arthur Peterson), who is still fighting World War II; and her three children: daughters Eunice (Jennifer Salt) and Corrine (Diana Canova), who both have a tendency to get involved with the wrong guy (a married congressman, an escaped convict, a priest, and so on); and young Billy (Jimmy Baio), who is seduced by his teacher and later joins a cult.

Then there's Benson DuBois (Robert Guillaume), the family's wisecracking black butler. After two seasons, Benson got his own series when he went to work for Jessica's widowed cousin, Governor James Gatling (James Noble). Like his predecessor, the Tate's new butler, Saunders (Roscoe Lee Browne), never hesitated to comment on all the lunacy going on around him.

Soap debuted in September of 1977, a few months before the premiere of *Dallas*, the first of the nighttime serials that dominated the prime time schedule throughout most of the 1980's. Plotlines involving adultery, murder, homosexuality, and fallen priests would soon become commonplace on prime time soaps like *Dynasty* and *Falcon Crest*. Yet, in 1977, several religious groups did not deem these subjects appropriate for prime time and launched a letter writing campaign pressuring ABC to pull the sitcom from its 1977 fall schedule before it even aired. They also pressured advertisers, some of which pulled their commercials.

The controversy was sparked by a June 1977 *Newsweek* article describing the negative reaction the pilot received from network affiliates when it was screened at the annual affiliate's meeting.[142] The description of the series's characters and plots that subsequently appeared in the national press caught the attention of the leaders of such influential religious groups as the National Council of Churches, the United States Catholic Conference, the United Church of Christ, and the United Methodist Church. ABC reportedly received 20,000 letters, mostly negative, prior to the show's debut. In all, a total of twelve affiliates chose not to air the first two episodes.[143]

Religious groups were not the only ones to voice their objections. After previewing the first two episodes, Newt Deiter, head of the Gay Media Task Force, wrote a letter to Tom Kersey, the head of the west coast division of ABC's Broadcast Standards and Practices. While Deiter understood the tone of the show's humor, he felt Jodie was too much of a wimp because he was subjected to homophobic remarks and never stood up for himself. Deiter suggested making the character stronger by turning Jodie into a militant gay activist.[144]

Deiter specifically objected to a storyline introduced in the first few episodes in which Jodie decides to have a sex change so he and his lover Dennis Phillips, a closeted, bisexual professional football player (Olympic Gold medal pole vaulter Bob Seagren), can be together. The idea of a gay man having a sex change so he can be together with another gay man not only conflates homosexuality and transsexualism, but also plays into the myth that, deep down, all gay men really want to be women. In one of Jodie's early scenes, Mary catches her son trying on one of her dresses. ("Oh, you wear that belted!" she exclaims.) While she's supportive of his decision, brother Danny is in denial that Jodie is gay and Burt is clearly uncomfortable and disgusted.

The staff of the National Gay Task Force had a stronger reaction to what they regarded as a stereotypical representation of a gay man. Although they never officially launched an organized campaign against the series (as they had done with *Marcus Welby, M.D.*), they did take out an ad in the September 7, 1977 issue of *Variety* stating they were

> angered by a gay character on *Soap*, who is portrayed as a limp-wristed, simpering boy who wears his mother's clothes, wants a sex-change operation and allows everyone to insult him without a word of response. You know, a "faggot." We are angry that a national network could be so insensitive to 20 million people in their struggle for rights. We are angry that a gay "Stepin Fetchit" is being trotted out for a cheap shot at easy humor. And, we are sickened ABC finds the notion "hilarious."[145]

The ad goes on to demand that Jodie's scenes be reshot, as well as call for some reassurance that the character was not going to meet a girl and go straight, as President of ABC Entertainment Fred Silverman implied in his address at the affiliates meeting.

The Task Force's instincts were not entirely wrong. Dennis, concerned about his pro football career, marries a woman. A despondent Jodie decides not to have a sex change, but instead attempts suicide by taking an overdose of sleeping pills. He recovers and although Dennis reenters his life briefly (his marriage didn't work out), there's no romance in Jodie's life for the remainder of the series's run.

Instead, Jodie falls victim to a mantrap named Carol David (Rebecca Balding), who seduces him and gets pregnant. When Dennis returns, Jodie finds himself in the middle of a love triangle. He does the right thing and offers to marry Carol, but she leaves him at the altar. While a despondent Jodie is sitting on top of the Triborough Bridge contemplating suicide, he meets a lesbian named Alice (Randee Heller), who is also thinking about jumping. In one of the rare instances on TV in which a gay man and a lesbian develop a deep friendship, Jodie and Alice become confidantes and roommates. They come close to having a physical relationship, but their friendship is cut short when Carol's mother, Lorelene (Peggy Pope), arrives from Texas with Jodie's daughter, Wendy. "So you're not a *ho-mo* anymore?" asks Lorelene. When Jodie explains Alice is a lesbian, Lorelene decides she doesn't want her granddaughter living with two homos and forces Jodie to choose between his daughter and his best friend. Little Wendy wins.

When Carol decides she wants Wendy back, Jodie spends the remainder of the series trying to hold on to her. After a judge grants him custody, Carol kidnaps Wendy, so Jodie hires a female detective named Maggie Chandler (Barbara Rhoades). Once again, Jodie begins to question his sexuality when he finds himself attracted to Maggie. He goes to a psychiatrist and through hypnosis, discovers his true identity — a 90-year-old Jewish man from New York. (In other words, Crystal was at last given the chance to play a character he had perfected in his stand-up routine.)

In all, there are basically two ways to look at Crystal's character. On the one hand, *Soap*'s treatment of homosexuality was similar to the way *Dynasty* approached the issue in terms of Steven Carrington: instead of having a gay character find love and happiness with another man, he's in a perpetual state of sexual confusion. Focusing on his relationships with women prevents the viewer from having to deal with "the gay thing" (thus keeping the network and advertisers happy), yet his homosexuality is still an issue (i.e. Jodie trying to gain custody of Wendy).

But the difference between the two series is that while *Soap* was a satire, *Dynasty* was supposedly (at least in the beginning) the real thing. Although Jodie may have never become a card-carrying member of the National Gay Task Force, at the very least he was a thoughtful, caring and decent guy — a gay man we actually wanted playing on our team. Too bad he never had the chance to make up his mind and pick a side.

THE GAY CO-WORKER

Nothing makes going to work every morning easier than knowing there's a gay co-worker waiting to greet you with a "good morning" and a wisecrack. In the real world, gay men work in a wide range of professions, but on television, their choices are more limited. To begin, there are the designing men: *The Corner Bar*'s set designer Peter Panama (Vincent Schiavelli), the first regular gay character on a sitcom; *Diana*'s (Diana Rigg) window dresser for Butley's Department Store, Marshall Tyler (Robert Moore); fashion designers, such as *Daddy's Girls*'s Dennis

Dumont (Harvey Fierstein), and *Style and Substance*'s interior designer, Mr. John (Joseph Maher). Next come the hairdressers: *Cutters*'s Troy (Julius Carry), the first regular African-American gay character, and *Hope and Gloria*'s Isaac (Eric Allan Kramer). TV's gay men also hold customer service-related jobs, including *Check It Out*'s supermarket checker Leslie Rappaport (Aaron Schwartz); the very campy, but not necessarily gay (uh-huh), Mr. Humphreys (John Inman) on the Britcom *Are You Being Served?*; *Archie Bunker Place*'s Fred the Waiter (Dino Scofield); the wisecracking generic gay waiter (Tim Macaulan) on *Cybil*; and *Lush Life*'s bartender Nelson Marquez (John Ortiz), who calls himself Margarita because "everyone needs a nickname to hang their purse on." To tell us the best place to dine in Seattle is *Frasier*'s resident food critic, Gil Chesterton (Edward Hibbert).

Gay characters continue to occupy these professions on television because homosexuals are naturally adept at cutting hair, designing a ball gown, or waiting on a party of six.

Beginning in the 1980s, gay male characters were being assigned more "hetero professions." On *Sara*, Geena Davis works in a storefront law office which actually includes a gay lawyer (imagine — in San Francisco of all places!) named Dennis Kemper (Bronson Pinchot). Dennis is a lawyer with a conscience, which makes him a target of the firm's other male lawyer, the very politically incorrect Marty (Bill Mahar). *Hail to the Chief*, a short-lived Susan Harris sitcom, stars Patty Duke Astin as the first female president of the United States who was protected by a gay secret service agent named Randy (Joel Brooks).

The most intelligent and respectable gay professional on television is *Spin City*'s Carter Heywood (Michael Boatman), director of minority affairs for New York City Mayor Randall Winston (Barry Bostwick). In the pilot episode, Deputy Mayor Michael Flaherty (Michael J. Fox) hired Carter, working at the time as a gay activist, after the Mayor made a disparaging remark about gay people. (When asked on camera if he's marching in the gay pride parade, the Mayor responds, "What are you, drunk?")

Carter is a rarity on television because he's gay, African-American, and political. He's never afraid of speaking his mind and in the first season alone challenges the mayor on such issues as needle exchange programs ("Pride and Prejudice"), gay marriage ("Grand Illusion"), and police discrimination ("In the Heat of the Day"). The latter episode involved Carter being picked up by the police as a suspected mugger while jogging in the park. Mike bails Carter out of jail and tries to calm him down, but Carter is too angry and defies Mike's orders by going on *Good Morning America* and discussing the incident. Instead of firing Carter, Mike rethinks his position and apologizes for being insensitive.

Carter became one half of an odd couple when paired with the insensitive, homophobic Stuart (Alan Ruck). In "Starting Over," the two get drunk and up sleeping in the same bed. Stuart freaks out and feels ashamed, but Carter assures him nothing happened. They're constantly getting on each other's nerves and even in those rare moments when one opens up and offers the other his support, there is usually a zinger attached. Stuart is sympathetic when Carter over the jogging incident: "When I look at you, I see a friend. I see a co-worker. But most importantly, I see a big fruit." At one point ("Carter & Stuart & Bennett & Deirdre") they purposely annoy each other by becoming friends with each other's ex-lovers, Deidre (Beth Littleford) and Bennett (Clayton Prince). Carter also tries to take advantage of his friend by joining his gay gym so he can meet women ("These Shoes Were Made for Cheatin'").

Their relationship takes an interesting turn when they decide to go into business together and open a gay bar. The bar is immediately closed because they're lacking a permit. Both are flat broke, so when Stuart gets evicted and Carter's apartment is robbed, Carter has no other choice but to to take Stuart in as his roommate ("Single White Male"). Although there's nothing remotely sexual going on, they start to feel like an old married couple. When they meet an actual older male couple in their building ("Monkey Business"), Alfred (Richard Hamilton) and Lloyd (Mike Hodge), they wonder if they'll still be together in thirty years.

THE GAYCOM BREAKS OUT

GAYCOM (g ā-käm)
n. 1. a situation comedy featuring one or more gay or lesbian character involved in humorous and embarrassing situations
2. a situation comedy that doesn't reduce gays and lesbians to second-class citizens

ELLEN

On Wednesday, April 30, 1997, comedian Ellen DeGeneres and her sitcom alter ego, Ellen Morgan, made television history by coming out of the closet. For the very first time, a television series 1) featured a lesbian character in the lead role; and 2) the character was played by a real-live, bona fide lesbian.

Prior to starring in her own series, DeGeneres played supporting roles on two sitcoms: a man-hungry receptionist on *Open House* (1989-1990); and a nurse who worked for a female doctor on the short-lived *Laurie Hill* (1992). Two years later, ABC signed DeGeneres to headline her own series, a 1994 mid-season replacement called *These Friends of Mine*. Conceived as ABC's answer to *Seinfeld* (in other words, a show about nothing), *These Friends* starred DeGeneres as Ellen Morgan, a bookstore manager who spends most of her time sitting around gabbing with her three best friends. At the start of its first full season in Fall of 1994, the series was given a new title (*Ellen*) and two of Ellen's friends disappeared. (The original title was no longer appropriate considering Ellen exchanges her two best friends for new ones.)

Ellen was a mediocre sitcom, no better but no worse than most of the comedy series on the air. The show was at its best when the plot lines dealt with Ellen's insecurities, like trying to figure out which member of her book group wrote a note stating they didn't like her ("The Note"); or when she unintentionally causes problems, like toasting her brother and his fiancée at their rehearsal dinner and almost causing them to break up ("The Toast"). Some attempts were made to give Ellen a love life. There was Dan, the pizza delivery guy (William Ragsdale), who would continue to come in and out of her life throughout the run of the series. Another potential suitor was her best friend, Adam (Arye Gross), a photographer who moved away to London after season two.

At the start of season three, Adam's "slot" was filled by her cousin Spence (Jeremy Piven), who became her new roommate. Piven is a fine actor, but like his co-stars Joely Fisher (Paige), David Anthony Higgins (Joe), and Clea Lewis (Audrey), he was given little to do. Unlike *Seinfeld*, which positioned Jerry at the center of the show, but gave Kramer, Elaine, and George their own storylines, the supporting characters were defined strictly in terms of their relationship to Ellen. While the show's team of writers was adept at writing for Ellen, no one seemed to figure out what to do with her friends.

The first sign that change was in the air was in September of 1996, when word leaked out Ellen Morgan would be coming out during the show's upcoming season. A cover story of the September 13-15 issue of *The Hollywood Reporter* stated that Disney, the series's producers, had not arrived at a decision.[146] The following March, the official word was handed down that the "coming out" episode was going into production on March 7, 1997 and would air on April 30, the first day of May sweeps.[147] "The Puppy Episode" was the subject of a major media campaign that included an appearance on *The Oprah Winfrey Show* (Oprah plays Ellen's therapist on the episode); an interview with Diane Sawyer; and a *Time* magazine cover story (April 14, 1997) with a picture of DeGeneres and the headline, "Yep, I'm gay."

The coming out of both Ellens, DeGeneres and Morgan, opened a new chapter in the history of gays and lesbians on television. *The New York Times* reported that "Ellen Coming Out Parties" were going to be held around the country. GLAAD, along with Absolut Vodka, was sponsoring benefit parties in New York, Los Angeles, Washington, San Francisco, San Diego, and Kansas City, Missouri. The Human Rights Campaign even distributed a party kit that included invitations, posters and an Ellen trivia game.[148]

Not everyone got swept away by *Ellen*-mania. Right-wing organizations spurned the trivia game in favor of a ferocious anti-*Ellen* campaign. The Media Research put a full-page ad on the back page of the April 17, 1997 issue of *Variety*. The headline read "America's Families Deserve Better," followed by accusations that ABC and Disney, as well as DeGeneres and the series's producing staff, were "promoting homosexuality to America's families." The ad continued with what are presumably intended as a series of rhetorical questions:

> Could it be Disney and ABC just don't care what American families think? Could it be ABC didn't mean it when it told many of our

nation's leaders it would air more family-friendly programming? What else could account for this insult, this slap in the face to America's families?[149]

The letter is signed by a Who's Who of Homophobia, including Pat Robertson (Christian Broadcast Network), Gary Bauer (Family Research Council), Phyllis Schafly (Eagle Forum), Rev. Donald Wildmon (American Family Association), Oliver North (Freedom Alliance), and, of course, the Reverend Jerry Falwell.

None of this, however, diverted the high ratings, the critical acclaim, and an Emmy Award for Outstanding Writing in a Comedy Series that came *Ellen*'s way. The "event" also gave *Ellen* a much need boost as it entered its fifth season. But now that Ellen was out, what direction should the series take? At the end of season four, Ellen came out to her parents in a touching episode ("Hello Muddah, Hello Father"), in which Lois (Alice Hirson) and Harold (Steve Gilborn) attend a child-parent rap session at the Gay and Lesbian Center. In the season finale, she came out to her boss, Ed (Bruce Campbell), who turns out to be homophobic ("Moving On"). So Ellen quits managing the bookstore and embarks on a new career.

Season five episodes focused primarily on *Ellen* exploring her new gay life, which takes off when she begins dating her mortgage broker, Laurie (Lisa Darr), mother of a 12-year-old, Holly (Kayla Murphy). Her first rlationship offered the comedian a chance to showcase her talents stumbling and bumbling her way through the courtship, while Laurie, of course, is totally together.

The season's highlight is a terrific episode ("Emma") in which Ellen works as a personal assistant for guest star Emma Thompson, playing herself. When Ellen comes out to the Academy Award-winner after accidentally discovering her secret (Emma's gay!), Thompson is inspired by Ellen's honesty and decides to come out publicly during an acceptance speech at an awards ceremony. But Thompson is more concerned about another secret she's hiding — she's not really British. She's from Ohio!

The episode's final punch line is delivered by Sean Penn. He appears via satellite to present Thompson her award. During his speech, he describes how knowing Emma has had such a profound effect on his life, he's decided to come out of the closet. The timely episode takes a self-reflexive look at the pressures of being famous and closeted in Hollywood. Both Penn and Thompson (who won an Emmy) are certainly good sports for playing along.

Like any situation comedy in its fifth season, Ellen had its share of hits and misses. The weakest episodes were those in which Ellen is forced into comic situations, such as participating in a Civil War reenactment ("G.I. Ellen") or getting a job as a talk show radio host ("All Ellen, All the Time"). But the same can be said when the show started heading too far in the other direction, like a fantasy episode when Spence passes out and imagines a world in which being gay is the norm ("It's a Gay, Gay, Gay, Gay World"). It's a funny idea, but better suited for a comedy sketch. In addition to the "Emma" episode, the strongest were those involving Ellen and Laurie's relationship, which was developed just at the right pace over the course of the season.

But not slow enough for some, including ABC, which slapped on a parental advisory similar to the one that appears in the opening of *N.Y.P.D. Blue*. DeGeneres was not pleased and according to an *Entertainment Weekly* cover story, she confronted ABC President Bob Iger and told him she was personally offended by the advisory (she reportedly found out about it while watching her show).[150] The network also started interfering in the show's writing and production and stopped promoting the series. There was even talk within the gay community, including a comment made by GLAAD spokesperson, Chastity Bono, that the show was "too gay." Bono claimed the quote was taken out of context.[151]

Coincidentally, ABC and Disney were experiencing similar misgivings. In the *Entertainment Weekly* story, Stuart Bloomberg, chairman of ABC Entertainment, stated that "as the show became more politicized and issue-oriented, it became less funny and audiences noticed." Instead of simply stating that the show was

"The Puppy Episode"
Ellen (ABC-TV)
April 30, 1997
Written by Mark Driscoll,
Tracy Newman, Dava Savel and
Jonathan Stark
Story by Ellen DeGeneres
Directed by Gil Junger

The most celebrated coming-out of a television character is this historic episode of Ellen, in which the series's title character, Ellen Morgan, admits to herself, her therapist, her six closest friends, and 36.2 million viewers she is a lesbian.

The episode begins with Ellen's reunion with an old friend Richard (Steven Eckholdt), who's in Los Angeles on business with a co-worker, Susan (Laura Dern). Ellen finds herself more drawn to Susan than Richard, but she freaks out when Susan admits she's a lesbian and was getting the same vibe from Ellen. After a session with her therapist (played by Oprah Winfrey), Ellen tracks Susan down at the airport and finally admits to her (and the passengers on a departing flight to Pittsburgh) she's gay. The scene in which Ellen inadvertently tells Susan over an airport loudspeaker she's gay will no doubt go down in history as a classic television comedy moment.

Equally hilarious is the scene in which a nervous Ellen comes out to her cousin Spence (Jeremy Piven) and friends Paige (Joely Fisher), Audrey (Clea Lewis), Joe (David Anthony Higgins), Peter (Patrick Bristow) and Barrett (Jack Plotnick). The real twist at the end is Ellen's discovery that her friends had a betting pool going on whether or not she's a lesbian.

In addition to the Emmy Award-winning teleplay by Mark Driscoll, Dava Savel, Tracy Newman, and Jonathan Stark (from a story by DeGeneres), the episode showcases the talented DeGeneres's skill as both a comedian and an actress. As for the odd title — "The Puppy Episode" — ABC was concerned about Ellen lack of a love interest on the show and at one point suggested DeGeneres get a puppy. I think she was happier coming out as a lesbian.

canceled due to low ratings, he claims that because the material was more *politicized* (translation: gay) and *issue-oriented* (translation: gay), it became *less funny* (translation: too gay). Actually, the fifth season of *Ellen* was as funny, if not funnier, than the pre-"Puppy Dog" episodes.

The concept of something being "too gay" is a troubling one, implying that a show about a gay character can focus *too much* on same-sex relationships. It is especially troubling when one considers that no show has ever been accused of being "too straight" for obsessing on opposite-sex relationships (which describes 99 percent of everything on television). How could Ellen have been "less gay?" Be gay every other week? Every fourth episode? The very aspect of the character that was celebrated in April 1997 had suddenly become a liability. It's almost as if ABC was hoping that after reaping the ratings boost of the coming out episode, both Ellens (DeGeneres and Morgan) could simply slip back into the closet.

WILL & GRACE

Ellen DeGeneres makes television history when her alter ego Ellen Morgan discovers she has the hots for guest star Laura Dern.

Troubles aside, *Ellen* paved the way for *Will & Grace*, an NBC gaycom about the longtime friendship between Will (Eric McCormack), a gay attorney; Grace (Debra Messing), an interior designer; Jack (Sean Hayes), a no-talent wannabe entertainer; and Karen (Megan Mullaley), a boozy socialite. Series creators Max Mutchnick (gay) and David Kohan (straight) originally pitched an ensemble comedy about three couples — two heterosexual and another based on Mutchnick's relationship with his "female soulmate, a New York casting director."[152] NBC President Warren Littlefield reportedly suggested dropping the two straight couples altogether to concentrate on the third. He apparently had pitched a similar idea about a gay-straight couple back in 1983. When he pitched it to then NBC President Brandon Tartikoff, he was laughed out of the room.[153] Not the kind of laughs you want when pitching a sitcom.

When NBC announced *Will & Grace* was on their Fall 1998 schedule, there was speculation whether the series would be, like *Ellen*, too gay. Littlefield explained the two shows were different because *Ellen* was about "one woman's odyssey. We have a different concept, a unique relationship between two people."[154] But as Richard Natale writes in *The Advocate*, the other big difference is that Will is a well-adjusted gay man, while "Ellen Morgan and DeGeneres herself seemed to struggle with the political and emotional ramification of coming out to a worldwide audience."[155] Of course that's exactly what made *Ellen* so groundbreaking for some and too gay for others.

What Mutchnick and Kohan were going for was something completely different — a situation comedy that would have a much broader appeal than *Ellen*. In creating the series, the writing team were smart to have their "well-

The fabulous foursome (counter-clockwise from top): Grace (Debra Messing), Will (Eric McCormack), Jack (Sean Hayes), and Karen (Megan Mullaley).

adjusted gay man" share the spotlight with a heterosexual woman. An October 1998 *Entertainment Weekly* cover story featured a photo of McCormick and Messing with the headline "Gay Men and Straight Women: Why Hollywood Loves Them." Using the gay man-straight woman couples that appear in recent films such as *My Best Friend's Wedding*, *As Good As It Gets*, and *The Object of My Affection*, the article positions *Will & Grace* as part of the trend:

> Gay men and straight women are to the 1990s what Oscar and Felix were to the 1970s. They're certainly the dream odd couple for nervous networks. On one hand, there's enough gayness to grab some hipster cred and lots of Oscar Wilde-ish repartee. On the other, the straight gal keeps the scripts from drifting into Joe Six-pack alienating territory.[156]

Unlike most of his prime time counterparts, Will possesses none of the usual stereotypical traits that signal to an audience he's gay. He tends to dress conservatively because he's a lawyer. He's also a bit uptight, particularly in the early episodes. In fact, according to Mutchnik, focus groups that viewed the pilot for NBC researchers had no idea Will was gay.[157]

However, the same could not be said for Jack McFarland (Sean Hayes), who isn't exactly gay either; he's hyper-gay. Jack does essentially everything Will won't: act effeminate, extroverted, irresponsible, self-involved, narcissistic, and materialistic. Yet, despite his *tres gay* exterior, Hayes and the writers have created a three-dimensional character who, beneath his somewhat shallow exterior, is a strong, confident person. As a gay man, he's also completely comfortable with his sexuality. Although smart and successful, Will is the one who usually needs guidance, particularly about love. Jack frequently goes into his "serious mode" to offer Will his insights and, on occasion, even teaches him a lesson.

Through Will and Jack's relationship, Mutchnick and Kohan have managed to address some relevant issues, particularly in the lives of gay people. For example, one of the more serious episodes ("Will Works Out") involves Will's

R.I.P. GAYCOMS

Normal, Ohio (Fox Network)
2000

John Goodman starred in this short-lived gaycom as Butch Gamble, who came out to his wife (Mo Gaffney) and son Charlie (Greg Pitts) and moved to California. Four years later, Butch returns home to attend a going away party for his son, who's leaving for medical school. When Charlie decides at the last minute not to go to school, Butch decides to stay in Ohio and live with his sister Pamela (Jolie Fisher), a single mother with two kids. The episodes follow Butch trying to make amends to his family and contend with his parents, Joan and Bill (Anita Gillette and Orson Bean), who wish he stayed in California. The series was a run-of-the-mill domestic situation comedy that scored points for Goodman's very un-stereotypical portrayal of a gay man. Unfortunately, his character was never completely fleshed out and the humor, particularly Bill's wisecracks directed at his gay son, were too mean-spirited.

Some of my Best Friends (CBS-TV)
2001

Loosely based on the 1997 independent feature *Kiss Me, Guido*, this modern day odd couple pairs a gay writer, Warren Fairbanks (Jason Bateman) and a straight Italian guy from the Bronx, Frankie Zito (Danny Nucci), who wants to be an actor. Bateman and Nucci are both appealing in their roles and have on-screen chemistry, while Alec Mappa as their gay neighbor,

Vern, steals the show. The series definitely had potential, except the story-lines were either variations on the pretend/mistaken identity plots (Frankie wants Warren to pretend he's straight in front of his friends, Warren and Vern think Frankie might be gay; Frankie thinks Warren has the hots for him) or conventional sitcom plots (Warren is upset when Frankie gets a dog). CBS only aired four episodes before pulling the plug on this mid-season replacement. It deserved a longer plug.

The Ellen Show (CBS-TV)
2000-2001

Ellen DeGeneres returned in this squeaky clean gaycom that never found an audience. Ellen plays Ellen Richmond, a dotcom executive who, in the series pilot, returns to her hometown to receive an award from her high school in recognition of her success in the business world. When her LA-based company tanks while she's at home, she decides to stay indefinitely and move back in with her eccentric mother (Cloris Leachman) and younger sister Catherine (Emily Rutherford). She's then hired by her former high school teacher, Mr. Munn (Martin Mull) as a guidance counselor. Some may consider it a sign of progress that CBS might schedule a prime-time series about a lesbian before 9 p.m., even if the lead character's sexual orientation is a "non-issue." Too bad the show failed to make better use of the comedian's talent.

internalized homophobia and its effect on his relationship with Jack. Will hesitates to take Jack with him to his gym because he often runs into his clients there. But reluctantly, he agrees. When Jack embarrasses him in front of one of them, Will gets upset and tells Grace that "sometimes he's just such a...fag."[158] Jack overhears their conversation and confronts Will, who explains he just wishes Jack could "tone it down." Later, when Will tries to apologize, Jack snidely suggests that he "scoot away" from him because "if the other kids see us playing together, they might think you're a sissy." So Will decides to prove him wrong by introducing him to his straight friend. Jack appreciates the gesture and the result is for once not a disaster for Will.

The success of *Will & Grace* really comes down to one thing — it's funny. What separates *Will & Grace* from the gaycoms that only last a few months has little to do with its politics and more to do with the talent of the performers and

THREE GAYCOMS YOU'VE NEVER SEEN

Adam and Yves
c. 1979-80

Inspired by the French comedy *La Cage Aux Folles*, *Barney Miller* creator Danny Arnold pitched this idea for a situation comedy about a gay couple. When the network announced the series was in development, conservative Christian groups started a letter writing campaign. Pre-addressed postcards to ABC President Elton Rule and FCC Chairman Charles D. Ferris depicted a photograph of two children watching TV on the front with the slogan "ABC Presents: Perverted Filth: Don't Let This Happen." On the flipside, the postcard addressed to Mr. Rule reads: "I hearby request that you refuse to carry ABC's proposed homo-sexual comedy series, *Adam and Yves*, or any similar program. Please place this request in your public file for FCC inspection." The network received over 100,000 postcards by January 1982, but it was all in vain because the series never made it past the development stage.[159]

Don't Ask
2000

The original concept for the short-lived *Normal, Ohio* was a variation on the *Odd Couple*. John Goodman starred as Rex, a gay, single father who shares a house in West Hollywood with his college chum, David (Anthony LaPaglia), also a single dad. According to Terry Turner, who

wrote the pilot with wife/partner Bonnie Turner, *Don't Ask* "made a great pilot, but we realized we didn't have a series. We weren't breaking enough stories."[160] So the concept and LaPaglia's character were scrapped and Goodman's character, renamed Butch, was sent packing to *Normal, Ohio*.

Say Uncle
2001

In this updated version of *Family Affair*, *thirtysomething*'s Ken Olin stars as a gay man who reluctantly agrees to raise his late sister's two children. Jeffrey Richman (*Frasier, Wings*) penned a hilarious pilot, directed by Emmy winner David Lee, but unfortunately CBS decided to go with another gay pilot, *The Ellen Show*. Olin was an interesting casting choice to play the vain, fortysomething host of an *Entertainment Tonight*-type news show (David Hasselhoff, French Stewart, and Gregory Harrison were also reportedly considered for the role). While not known as a comic actor, Olin's "nice guy" persona helps us warm up to a character who is a tad on the shallow side. Teri Hatcher is perfect as his equally self-involved co-host and young Michael Angarano is terrific as Olin's nephew. When *Say Uncle* was passed over, Angarano landed the role of Jack McFarland's biological son on that other gaycom, *Will & Grace*.[161]

the quality of the writing and direction (mainly, James Burrows, one of the best in the business).

A LITTLE VARIETY: COMEDY-VARIETY AND SKETCH COMEDY SHOWS

In his study of human sexuality, Dr. Alfred Kinsey concluded that most people do not identify themselves as exclusively heterosexual or homosexual, but rather occupy a space somewhere in between. To illustrate, Dr. Kinsey devised a scale ranging from 0 to 6, with 0 equalling "exclusively hetereosexual" and 6 equalling "exclusively homosexual."

Although it's not exactly what Dr. Kinsey had in mind, his 0-6 scale can also serve as a valuable instrument to measure the gay appeal of comedy-variety and sketch comedy shows. By "gay appeal," I mean the level at which a show, if it does at all, speaks to a gay, lesbian, bisexual, and transgender audience.

On the basis of the following scale, here is the Kinsey rating of ten of the most memorable sketch comedy and variety shows, in chronological order, from the 1950s to today:

0 = *"As straight as it gets:"* Straight entertainment for heterosexuals and gay Republicans.

1 = *"A touch of pink:"* May contain an occasional, subtle gay moment that the majority of viewers are likely to miss.

2 = *"Don't Ask, Don't Tell:"* It's gay. But don't talk about it.

3 = *"AC-DC:"* It can go either way. You decide.

4 = *"Look, Mary, a show for us:"* The producers know there's a gay audience out there, but the show is still mainstream enough for a general audience.

5 = *"Yep, it's gay:"* That's right, gay.

6 = *"As gay as it gets.:"* Produced specifically for a gay audience.

The Judy Garland Show (CBS-TV), 1963-1964

America's number one gay icon starred in this short-lived Sunday night variety show that went through several producers and format changes before CBS axed it after 26 episodes. But a certain segment of the male population (and their mothers) who were not watching *Bonanza* on NBC did tune in for one reason only — to hear Ms. Garland sing. And sing she did. Some of the show's most memorable moments were Judy singing "Battle Hymn of the Republic" in honor of the late John F. Kennedy; and her duets with fellow gay icon Ethel Merman and icon-in-training, Barbra Streisand, who teamed with Ethel and Judy for a rousing rendition of "There's No Business Like Show Business."
KINSEY RATING = 6

The Carol Burnett Show (CBS-TV), 1967-1979

We were so glad to have this time each week together with Carol and company. Her parodies of daytime soap operas (*As the Stomach Turns*), and classic films (like *Mildred Fierce* and *Went With the Wind*, in which Burnett's Scarlett O'Hara enters wearing a dress made out of drapes, complete with the curtain rod still attached), are classics. Over the years, the show boasted an incredible roster of guest stars, including such Hollywood and Broadway legends as Gloria Swanson, Rita Hayworth, Ethel Merman, and Martha Raye. But the talented Ms. Burnett was reason enough to tune in each week. **KINSEY RATING = 5**

Rowan & Martin's Laugh-In (NBC-TV), 1968-1973

Sock-it-to-me! is one of several catch phrases (along with "You bet your bippy" and "Here come de judge!") coined on this comedy-variety series which combined topical satire, camp, silly jokes, and physical comedy. *Laugh-In* had a high gay appeal because everything about the show was over the top: the bright-colored sets, the outrageous costumes, and its loud and very funny ensemble of players, which included Joanne Worley, Ruth Buzzi, Judy Carne, Barbara Sharma, Goldie Hawn, Lily Tomlin, and Alan Sues. Sues, in particular, brought his brand of sissy humor to gay-coded characters like "Uncle Al — The Kiddie's Pal" and "Big Al" the sportscaster (who twinkled his bell after every item). At the time, Sues and his characters were unique because rather than being the butt of jokes, they were the ones cracking them. **KINSEY RATING = 4**

Saturday Night Live (NBC-TV), 1975-

This long-running comedy-variety series resurrected live television and gave us all an acceptable reason to be home (or in front of a television) at 11:30 p.m. on a Saturday night. When the series premiered in October 1975, it was irreverent, fresh, and funny. Over the years, the quality has been inconsistent due to many changes in the show's writing staff (who seemed to have trouble completing a sketch) and performers. The characters and sketches with explicitly gay content (see list below) are never as strong as those infused with a gay sensibility, such as the hyperactive Judy Miller (Gilda Radner), the singing Sweeny sisters (Nora Dunn and Jan Hooks), Nancy Reagan (Terry Sweeny), and the Church Lady (Dana Carvey), to name a few. Although the sketches continue to be hit-and-miss, the overall quality of the show has definitely improved over the past few years. **KINSEY RATING = 3**

Donny and Marie (ABC-TV), 1976-1979

Marie is a little bit country. Donny is a little bit rock 'n roll. But there was something a little bit gay about this one hour comedy-variety series starring TV's best known brother and sister team. Perhaps it had something to do with the show's writing team, which included the *Hollywood Squares*'s funny man Bruce Vilanch, or the regular appearances by center *Square* alumni, Paul Lynde. The sketches often involved elaborate costumes (Donny dressed as Humphrey Bogart played to Milton Berle's Katharine Hepburn in a parody of *The African Queen*). One of the most lavish and memorable production numbers was a *Star Wars* musical parody featuring guest stars R2D2, CP30, and Chewbacca; Donny and Marie as a singing Luke and Leia; comedian Redd Foxx as Okey Ben Pinocchio; and Lynde as an Imperial Officer, who, with the Ice Vanities dressed as Stormtroopers standing behind him, warbles *"What's your course? Where the force can you be? Come back to me."* **KINSEY RATING = 4**

"LIVE FROM NEW YORK, IT'S SATURDAY NIGHT!" GAYWORTHY SKETCHES

"SoHo Lesbians:" Liz (Gail Matthius) and Susan (guest host Deborah Harry) are lesbians living in Soho who receive a surprise visit from Susan's clueless Aunt Pinky (Denny Dillon) and Uncle Leo (Gilbert Gottfried). February 14, 1981

"Signs of Homosexuality:" Mary Gross convinces Christine Ebersole that guest star James Coburn is gay. February 6, 1982

"Ménage-à-Trois:" Two couples fight over Carl (Eddie Murphy) because both pairs want him for a ménage. April 14, 1984

"Pink Listing:" Satire on paranoia in Hollywood generated by the AIDS crisis with guest star Madonna as actress Melinda Zoomont, a closeted intra-venous drug user, who must perform a love scene with Clint Weston, a closeted gay actor played by openly-gay cast member Terry Sweeny. November 9, 1985

"Gay Communist Gun Club:" Phil Hartman and guest host John Larroquette as Bob and John, who are gay, communists, and love guns. October 22, 1988

"It's Pat:" The androgynous Pat gets a haircut from barber George Wendt. (Remember the opening theme song: "A lot of people ask, Who's he? Or she?...Here comes Pat!"?) May 18, 1991

"Schmitt's Gay:" House sitters Chris Farley and Adam Sandler's gay fantasies come true in this beer commercial parody. September 28, 1991

"Lyle, the Effeminate Homosexual:" Dana Carvey as the effeminate Lyle, who's constantly being mistaken for being gay, and can't understand why. April 4, 1992

"Dracula's Not Gay:" Bizarre sketch with guest host John Travolta as Dracula, who tries to convince his two dinner guests (Janeane Garofalo, Kevin Nealon) that he's not gay. October 15, 1994

"The Ambiguously Gay Duo:" In "It Takes Two to Tango," Big Head tries to take over Metroville by putting his secret formula in the town's water supply. But Ace and Gary are on his trail ("when they're not on each other"). September 28, 1996

"Mango:" Gangleader Lucius Monroe a.k.a. Hard Core (Samuel Jackson) finds himself addicted to Mango (Chris Kattan). January 10, 1998

"Homicil:" Commercial parody for med-ication that relieves anxiety caused by the realization your son is gay. (Tagline: "Because it's your problem, not theirs.") February 17, 2001

Second City Television (HBO/CBS-TV), 1977-1981

This Canadian sketch comedy series, set in the studios of a fictional local television station, Channel 109, is a hilarious send-up of TV programs and commercials. The first rate cast — consisting of Joe Flaherty, Harold Ramis, John Candy, Eugene Levy, Andrea Martin, Rick Moranis, Catherine O'Hara, and David Thomas — were in a league all of their own. Some of the highlights of Channel 109's programming schedule included the cheesy *Monster Horror Chiller Theatre*, with news anchor Floyd Robertson, who doubles as host Count Floyd; the *Great White North* starring Bob and Doug MacKenzie (Thomas and Moranis); and *The Sammy Maudlin Show*, which featured guests like Lola Heatherton (O'Hara) and Lorna Minnelli (Martin). **KINSEY RATING = 4**

The Tracy Ullman Show (Fox Network), 1987-1990
Tracy Takes On (HBO), 1996-

Actress, singer, and comedian Tracey Ullman is the most talented and underrated performer on television. Her first series, perhaps best remembered for introducing America to *The Simpsons*, was a mixture of songs and sketches that capitalized on Ullman's ability to transform herself into a wide-range of characters. One of the most memorable is Francesca, the spirited teenage daughter of a loving gay couple, David and William (Dan Castellaneta and Sam McMurray). Each episode of *Tracy Takes On* is devoted to a different topic ("Sex," "Romance," "Fantasy," etc.). She portrays a series of rotating characters, which includes Trevor, a gay flight attendant, and Chris, the female lover of professional golfer Midge, played by co-star Julie Kavner. The writing is inventive, fresh, hip, and very funny. **KINSEY RATING (*TRACY ULLMAN SHOW*) = 5**
KINSEY RATING (*TRACEY TAKES ON*) = 5

In Living Color (Fox Network), 1990-1994

Television's first black sketch comedy series, which boasted a talented, young cast (Jim Carrey, Tommy Davidson, David Alan Grier, T'Keyah "Crystal" Keymah, Damon Wayans, and series creator/producer/host, Keenan Ivory Wayans), took satirical pot shots at movies, TV shows, celebrities, and all imaginable stereotypes. At its best, the satire was hip, edgy, and right on target, though many felt the humor overstepped its boundaries. As is often the case with satire, it's not always clear if we're laughing *with* or *at* certain ethnic stereotypes, like the hardworking West Indian family who starred in the sitcom parody, "Hey Mon."

Another controversial sketch was "Men On..." which featured Damon Wayans and Grier as Blaine and Antoine, a pair of swishy cultural critics who offered their opinions on such subjects as film, art, books, and football "from a male point of view." If women were involved, the pair chanted "hated it" in unison. When a film, painting, or book involved or even alluded to hot, hunky men, it received a "two snaps up!" The saying caught on and became part of the vernacular, especially in gay circles. But not everyone was a fan of the flamboyant duo, particularly GLAAD, who tried to meet with the series producers in order to, in the words of executive director David Smith, "sensitize them to the defamation that these two characters represent."[162] GLAAD was also outraged over a December 1992 sketch about the Pink Brigade, the army's first gay unit. Smith claimed the sketch reinforced "misconceptions about gay men" and "drew from every false stereotype imaginable."[163] In response, Fox explained "the series is a satire and part of the satire is making stereotypes look silly."[164] **KINSEY RATING = 3**

Kids In The Hall (HBO/CBS-TV), 1992-1995

Five talented comics from Canada (Dave Foley, Bruce McCulloch, Kevin McDonald, Mark McKinney, and Scott Thompson) starred in this irreverent sketch comedy series. The name is derived from a line Jack Benny used ("This one is from one of the kids in the hall") before telling a joke he heard from one of the young writers who stood in the hallway outside the studio. The Canadian kids had an off-the-wall sense of humor and relished in playing both male and female parts. Some of the most memorable characters are office workers Cathy Strupp (Thompson) and Kathie Lassiter (McCulloch); and gay bar patrons Smitty (McDonald), Butch (Thompson), and Riley (Foley); and gay bar owner Buddy Cole (Thompson), whose insightful monologues touched on such issues as racism, outing, love, gay marriage, and virtual sex. A truly hilarious and very gay-friendly series. **KINSEY RATING = 5**

KEEPING THE
CLOSET DOOR OPEN

On January 10, 2002, MTV and Showtime announced a joint plan to kick off America's first cable station for gay and lesbian viewers. The still unnamed channel, which could be up and running as early as 2003, will reportedly be available to subscribers for a fee (about $5–$6 per month). Subscribers will receive around-the-clock gay programming, consisting of "acquired films, original series, imported series, news and travel programs, talk shows, comedy shows, and travel shows."[1]

MTV has tossed around the idea of a gay cable channel since the early 1990s. Showtime, a division of MTV's parent company, Viacom, simultaneously explored the possibility of a 24-hour premium gay channel. The two joined forces "when it was decided the best way to market the channel was a combination of a pay channel, the Showtime model, and a channel with a niche audience supported by advertising, the speciality of MTV networks."[2] Most likely this new media baby will be commercial free, though perhaps with ads briefly bookending programs à la PBS.

The channel may actually face stiff competition for netting gay viewers, a bloc that MTV-Showtime estimates accounts for 6.5 percent of all television households. Pride Vision, Canada's 24-hour gay cabler that debuted in September of 2001, is contemplating a border crossing. Four days after Showtime and MTV made their announcement, MDC Entertainment Group, a Washington D.C.-based company, announced *their* plans to launch ALT1-TV, a commercial cable channel targeting "gay and lesbian viewers with strong audience cross-over appeal."[3]

The impact that one, and possibly three (be still my beating heart!), gay cable channels could have on the future of gay television remains to be seen, but good, bad, or ugly they hold great potential for changing the way America views the lives of gays and lesbians:

- A gay channel free from the constraints of advertisers and the networks censors *could* offer more honest, and accurate portrayals of gay men, lesbians, bisexuals, and transgender people.
- A gay channel *could* tackle those current issues affecting gay people considered not important enough for the general audience.

- A gay channel *could* showcase programming, such as gay-themed documentaries and experimental work; independent and foreign features and shorts; and television series produced outside the United States that heretofore could only be caught on the film festival circuit.
- A gay channel *could* insure the prime time closet door will not only remain open, but permanently removed, hinges and all.

GAY/LESBIAN/BISEXUAL/TRANSGENDER TV EPISODE GUIDE

This guide is an alphabetical listing of TV series broadcast in the United States that feature gay, lesbian, bisexual, or transgender series regulars (**Reg**) and/or recurring characters (**Rec**). Titles and airdates of gay-themed episodes are also included. For series with regular gay characters, I have included the titles of episodes referred to in the book.

A-TEAM, THE (NBC, Action Drama, 1983-1987)	"Cowboy George," Boy George guest stars (2/11/86)
ABSOLUTELY FABULOUS (Comedy Central, Comedy, 1994-)	**Rec:** Justin (Christopher Malcolm), Edina's ex-husband; Oliver (Gary Beadle), Justin's lover
ACTION (Fox, Comedy, 1999; F/X, 2000)	**Reg:** Robert "Bobby G." Gianopolis (Lee Arenberg), studio head; Stuart Glazer (Jack Plotnick), assistant; Cole Ricardi (Richard Burgi), actor "Blowhard," Action star Cole Ricardi comes out (9/30/99)
ADAM AND YVES	Proposed gay sitcom from writer/producer Danny Arnold (1979-1980)
ADVENTURES OF BRISCO COUNTY, JR. (Fox, Western, 1993-1994)	"No Man's Land," All-female western town (9/10/93)
ALFRED HITCHCOCK PRESENTS (CBS, Anthology, 1960-1965; NBC, 1964-1965, 1985-1986)	"An Unlocked Window," Nurse killer on the loose (2/15/65) "An Unlocked Window," Remake of 1965 episode (5/5/85)
ALICE (CBS, Comedy, 1976-1985)	"Alice Gets a Pass," Alice falls for gay ex-pro football player (9/29/76)
ALL IN THE FAMILY (CBS, Comedy, 1971-1979)	**Rec:** Beverly La Salle (Lori Shannon) (1975-1977), female impersonator "Judging Books by Covers," Archie discovers friend is gay (2/9/71) "Archie, the Hero," Archie saves Beverly's life (9/29/75) "Beverly Rides Again," Beverly helps Archie play joke (11/6/76)

GAY/LESBIAN/BISEXUAL/TRANSGENDER
TV EPISODE GUIDE (cont.)

ALL IN THE FAMILY (cont.)	"Cousin Liz," Edith learns cousin Liz was gay (10/9/77) "Edith's Crisis of Faith" Pt. 1, Beverly is murdered (12/18/77) "Edith's Crisis of Faith" Pt. 2, Edith questions her faith in God (12/25/77)
ALL MY CHILDREN (ABC, Soap Opera, 1970-)	**Reg:** Dr. Lynn Carson (Donna Pescow) (1983); Michael Delaney (Chris Bruno) (1995-1998), high school teacher; Kevin Sheffield (Ben Jorgensen) (1995-1998), student; Dr. Bradford Phillips (Daniel McDonald) (1996-1997); Rudy (Lance Baldwin) (1995-1998), assistant at TV station; Bianca Montgomery (Eden Riegel) (2000-), Erica's daughter; Sarah Livingston (Elizabeth Harnois) (2000-2001); Mary Francis "Frankie" Stone (Elizabeth Hendrickson) (2001)
ALL THAT GLITTERS (First-run syn., Soap Opera, 1977)	**Reg:** Linda Murkland (Linda Grey), male-to-female transsexual
ALLY MCBEAL (Fox, Legal Comedy/Drama, 1997-)	**Rec:** Cindy McCauliff (Lisa Edelstein) "Boy to the World," Ally befriends young transvestite (12/1/97) "The Inmates," Hetero waiter fired for not being gay (4/27/98) "Buried Pleasures," Ally "dates" Ling (11/1/99) "Pursuit of Loneliness," Ally falls for bisexual judge (2/21/00) "The Oddball Parade," Discrimination lawsuit (2/28/00) "Prime Suspect," Ally plays detective (3/20/00) "Girls' Night Out," Transgender Cindy is fired (10/30/00) "Two's A Crowd," Mark learns truth about Cindy (11/6/00) "Without A Net," Mark breaks up with Cindy (11/13/00) "Love on a Holiday," Men bid on Fish in charity auction (12/4/00) "Hats Off to Larry," Cindy sues to legally marry (2/5/01) "Judge Ling," Dame Edna Everage guest stars (11/5/01) "Neutral Corners," Dame Edna, Part II (11/12/01) "I Want Love," Elton John guest stars (11/26/01)
ALRIGHT ALREADY (WB, Comedy, 1997-1998)	"Again with the Laser Surgery," Vaughn pretends he's gay (10/5/97)
AMERICAN FAMILY, AN (PBS, Reality, 1973)	Reality series about the Loud family includes gay son, Lance (1/11-3/29/73)

GAY / LESBIAN / BISEXUAL / TRANSGENDER
TV EPISODE GUIDE (cont.)

AMERICAN HIGH (Fox, Reality, 2000/PBS 2001)	**Reg:** Brad Krefman, high school student "Who Am I?" Robby recalls when Brad came out to him (8/2/00) "Boogie Nights," Brad choreographs dance show (8/9/00)
AMERICAN JUSTICE (A&E, Reality, 1992-)	"The Life and Death of Teena Brandon" (9/29/00)
AMERICAN PARADE (CBS, Anthology, 1976)	Rip Torn and Brad Davis as Walt Whitman and Peter Doyle (3/9/76)
ANY DAY NOW (Lifetime, Drama, 1998-2002)	"It's Who You Sleep With," Lesbian couple can't marry in public park (11/3/98) "Family is Family," Renee's gay bro visits with son and lover (10/17/99) "Who Abandoned Who?" RuPaul guest stars (3/12/00)
ANYTHING BUT LOVE (ABC, Comedy, 1989-1992)	**Reg:** Jules "Julie" Kramer/Bennett (Richard Frank), magazine editor's assistant
ARCHIE BUNKER'S PLACE (CBS, Comedy, 1979-1982)	"The Cook," Archie discovers his waiter Fred is gay (11/4/79) "Archie Fixes Up Fred," Archie tries straighten out Fred (2/10/80)
ARE YOU BEING SERVED? (Syndicated, Comedy, 1972-1984)	**Reg:** Mr. Humphries (John Inman), department store salesman
ARGUMENT (KTTV-TV/Los Angeles, Talk, 1962)	"Society and the Homosexual," Los Angeles talk show (5/13/62)
ARLI$$ (HBO, Comedy, 1996-)	"Man of Our Times," Ice skater plans same-sex wedding (8/10/96) "Athletes ARE Role Models," Player mistakenly has sex with drag queen (8/28/96) "My Job is to Get Jobs," Football player rumored to be gay (6/14/98)
ASK HARRIET (Fox, Comedy, 1998)	"Pilot," Sexist hetero sportswriter dons drag as female columnist (1/4/98)
ASPHALT JUNGLE, THE (ABC, Police Drama, 1961)	"The Sniper," Lesbian sniper guns down young girls (4/30/61)
ASSOCIATES, THE (ABC, Comedy, 1979-1980)	"The Censors," Writer vs. network censor over sitcom dialogue (4/10/80)

GAY/LESBIAN/BISEXUAL/TRANSGENDER
TV EPISODE GUIDE (cont.)

AS THE WORLD TURNS (CBS, Soap Opera, 1956-)	**Reg:** Hank Elliot (Brian Stracher) (1988-1989), designer
BABYLON 5 (First-run syn., Sci-Fi, 1992-1998)	**Reg:** Lt. Cmdr. Susan Ivanova (Claudia Christian) (1994-1997); Talia Winters (Andrea Thompson) (1994-1995) "Divided Loyalties," Ivanova's strong attraction to Thalia (10/12/95) "Racing Mars," Frank and Cole pose as newlyweds (4/24/97)
BARE ESSENCE (NBC, Drama, 1983)	**Rec:** Robert Spencer (Ted LePlat); Tim (Jim Negele), pro-football player
BARETTA (ABC, Police Drama, 1975-1978)	"The Sky is Falling," Baretta helps teen hustler (10/26/77)
BARNEY MILLER (ABC, Comedy, 1975-1982)	**Rec:** Marty (Jack DeLeon), shoplifter; Daryl Driscoll (Ray Stewart), marty's lover; Officer Zitelli (Dino Natali) "Experience," Marty is arrested (1/30/75) "Vigilante," Wojo arrests transvestite teamster (3/20/75) "Discovery," Man posing as cop harrassing gays (10/30/75) "Quarantine 1 & 2," Precinct is quarantined (9/30/76, 10/7/76) "Asylum," Marty is caught with marijuana (2/24/77) "Inquisition," Lt. Scanlon hunts down precinct's gay cop (9/13/79) "The Child Stealers," Daryl tries to get his son back (1/24/80) "Movie Pt.1," Wojo outs Officer Zitelli, (1/29/81)
BAXTERS, THE (First-run syn., Drama, 1979-1981)	"Homosexual Teachers," Family discovers son's teacher is gay (10/31/79)
BEANES OF BOSTON (Pilot, Comedy, 1979)	**Reg:** Mr. Humphries (Alan Sues), salesman "Pilot," American version of Are You Being Served? (5/5/79)
BECKER (CBS, Comedy, 1998-)	"The Princess Cruise," Becker is booked on gay cruise (2/5/01) "You Say Gay Son, I Saw Godson," Becker's gay godson asks for help (4/8/01)
BEDTIME (Showtime, Comedy-Drama, 1996)	**Reg:** Donna (Felicity Hoffman) and Liz (Susan Gibney)
BEGGARS AND CHOOSERS (Showtime, Comedy, 1999-2001)	**Reg:** Malcolm Laffley (Tuc Watkins), TV network casting director "The Velvet Curtain," Malcolm outs himself on TV (8/7/99)

GAY/LESBIAN/BISEXUAL/TRANSGENDER
TV EPISODE GUIDE (Cont.)

BEGGARS AND CHOOSERS (cont.)	"The Naked Truth," Malcolm wants gay actor to play Dodi Fayed (7/25/00)
BELTRAN, LOS (Telemundo, Comedy, 1999-2000)	**Reg:** Dr. Fernando Salazar (Gabriel Romero) and Kevin Lynch (James C. Leary) "The Coming Out of Fernandito," Fernando's father comes for a visit (2000)
BERNIE MAC SHOW, THE (Fox, Comedy, 2001-)	"Stop Having Sex," Bernie discovers Jordan's friend's dad is gay (4/17/02)
BETTE (CBS, Comedy, 2000-2001)	**Reg:** Oscar (James Dreyfus), Bette Midler's accompanist
BEVERLY HILLS, 90210 (Fox, Teen Drama, 1990-2000)	**Rec:** Kyle Connors (David Lascher) (1991-1992); Allison Lash (Sara Melson) (1994-1995); Jimmy Gold (Michael Stoyanov) (1996); Andrew Emery (Robb Derringer) (1999) "Summer Story," Kyle comes out to Kelly (7/25/91) "A Competitive Edge," Brandon investigates steroids at school (1/23/92) "Blind Spot," Steve discovers frat brother is gay (4/6/94) "Up in Flames," Kelly and Allison trapped in fire (11/30/94) "Girls on the Side," Kelly discovers Allison loves her (5/3/95) "P.S. I Love You Pt. 1," Allison admits feelings for Kelly (5/24/95) "P.S. I Love You Pt 2," Rumors spread about Kelly and Allison (5/24/95) "A Mate for Life," Kelly befriends Jimmy, gay man with AIDS (9/4/95) "Disappearing Act," Kelly takes HIV test (9/11/96) "Pledging My Love," Jimmy dies (9/18/96) "Santa Knows," David befriends homeless gay teen Ben (12/17/97) "Crimes and Misdemeanors," Steve and Brandon "date" lesbian couple (2/4/98) "The Nature of Nuture" Mother vs. gay couple over custody suit (3/18/98) "I'm Back Because," Samantha comes out to son Steve (12/2/98) "The Following Options," Samantha is fired because she's gay (12/9/98) "The Loo-Ouch," Samantha brings lover to Steve's party (10/20/99) "Baby, You Can Drive My Car," Dylan and Andrew are gay bashed (11/10/99) "Family Tree," Dylan helps Andrew get his job back, (11/17/99)

GAY/LESBIAN/BISEXUAL/TRANSGENDER
TV EPISODE GUIDE (cont.)

BIG BROTHER II (CBS, Reality, 2001)	**Reg:** Bill "Bunky" Miller, 7th contestant evicted from house
BIG EASY, THE (USA, Police Drama, 1996-1997)	"Cinderfella," Murder victim involved with a drag queen (8/25/96)
BLOSSOM (NBC, Comedy, 1991-1995)	"Double Date," Joey's teammate is his secret admirer (1/31/94) "It Happened One Night," Nick is matchmaker with Blossom and friend's son (3/13/95)
BOB CRANE SHOW, THE (NBC, Comedy, 1975)	"A Case of Misdiagnosis," Bob treats old pal, a rich gay activist (5/8/75)
BOB NEWHART SHOW, THE (CBS, Comedy, 1972-1978)	"Some of My Best Friends," Gay man joins Bob's therapy group (10/9/76)
BOLD ONES, THE: THE LAWYERS (NBC, Legal Drama, 1969-1973)	"Shriek of Silence," Politician framed for murder (11/30/69)
BOLD ONES, THE: THE NEW DOCTORS (NBC, Medical Drama, 1969-1973)	"Discovery at 14," Teenager fears homosexuality is genetic (3/5/72) "A Very Strange Triangle," Male doctor falls for lesbian (10/31/72)
BOSOM BUDDIES (ABC, Comedy, 1980-1984)	**Reg:** Kip Wilson/Buffy (Tom Hanks), hetero in drag living in women's hotel; Henry Desmond/ Hildegarde (Peter Scolari), Kip's hetero roommate
BOSTON COMMON (NBC, Comedy, 1996-1997)	"Streetcar Named Denial," Wyleen falls for acting partner (9/15/96)
BOSTON PUBLIC (Fox, Drama, 2000-)	**Rec:** Jeremy Peters (Kaj-Erik Eriksen) (2001-), high school student "Chapter 3," A high school jock is the target of gay rumors (11/16/00) "Chapter 29," Guber discovers Jeremy Peters is gay (12/10/01) "Chapter 30," Jeremy's mother finds out he's gay (12/17/01) "Chapter 31," Guber, Jeremy, and his mom go to therapy (1/14/02) "Chapter 36," Jeremy dates Brooke Harper (2/11/02)
BRIAN BENBEN SHOW, THE (CBS, Comedy, 1998)	**Reg:** Billy Hernandez (Luis Antonio Ramos), weatherman
BRONK (CBS, Detective Drama, 1975-1976)	"The Deadlier Sex," Female cop accused of molestation (1/18/76)

GAY/LESBIAN/BISEXUAL/TRANSGENDER
TV EPISODE GUIDE (cont.)

BRONX ZOO, THE (NBC, Drama, 1987-1988)	"Crossroads," Closeted gay student decides to get married (6/16/88)
BROOKLYN SOUTH (CBS, Police Drama, 1997-1998)	"Doggoneit," Bickering gay couple lose their dog (4/13/98)
BROTHERS (Showtime, Comedy, 1984-1989)	**Reg:** Cliff Waters (Paul Regina); Donald Maulpey (Phillip Charles Mackenzie)
BUFFY THE VAMPIRE SLAYER (WB, Teen Drama/Horror, 1997-2001; UPN 2001-)	**Reg:** Larry Blaisdell (Larry Bagby III) (1997-1999), high school jock; Willow Rosenberg (Alyson Hannigan), witch; Tara (Amber Benson) (1999-), witch/Willow's girlfriend "Phases," Larry comes out to Xander (1/27/98) "New Moon Rising," Oz discovers Willow is in love with Tara (5/2/00) "The Body," Buffy's mother dies (2/27/01) "Forever," Willow and Tara attend Buffy's mom's funeral (4/21/01) "Tabula Rasa," Tara breaks up with Willow for abusing magic (11/13/01)
CBS EVENING NEWS with WALTER CRONKITE (December 7, 1973)	Posing as a college newspaper reporter, Gay Raider Mark Segal interrupts news broadcast by standing in front of a camera with a sign reading "Gays Protest CBS Prejudice" and shouting "Gay people are protesting CBS's policies."
C.P.O SHARKEY (NBC, Comedy, 1976-1978)	"Sharkey's Secret Life," Sharkey's men suspect he's gay (3/16/77)
CAGNEY AND LACEY (CBS, Police Drama, 1982-1988)	**Rec:** Tony Stantinopolis (Barry Sattels) (1986-1987), Cagney's gay neighbor "Conduct Unbecoming," Detective's photo in gay magazine (12/13/82) "Rights of Passage," Tony moves in next door to Cagney (12/1/86)
CAN'T HURRY LOVE (CBS, Comedy, 1995-1996)	"Valentine's Day Massacred," Roger and Didi spend Valentine's Day in gay bar (2/12/96)
CAROL BURNETT SHOW, THE (CBS, Variety, 1967-1979)	
CAROLINE IN THE CITY (NBC, Comedy, 1995-1999)	"Caroline & the Gay Art Show," Richard's show at gay gallery (10/5/95) "Caroline & *Victor/Victoria*," Annie dons male drag (11/19/96)

GAY/LESBIAN/BISEXUAL/TRANSGENDER TV EPISODE GUIDE (cont.)

CAROLINE IN THE CITY (cont.)	"Caroline & the Dearly Departed," Richard fakes his death (2/18/97) "Caroline & the Little White Lies," Charlie and Del pose as gay couple (4/6/98)
CARTER COUNTRY (ABC, Comedy, 1977-1979)	"Out of the Closet," Chief's gay friend, a teacher, is fired (9/29/77)
CHANNING (ABC, Drama, 1963-1964)	"The Last Testament of Buddy Crown," Gay(?) student drowns himself (12/18/63)
CHARLIE'S ANGELS (ABC, Detective Drama, 1976-1981)	"Angels in Chains," Angels go undercover in women's prison-farm (10/20/76) "Angel on the Line," Angels terrorized by a cross-dressing killer (2/14/81)
CHECK IT OUT (USA, Comedy, 1985-1988)	**Reg:** Leslie Rappaport (Aaron Schwartz), gay cashier
CHEERS (NBC, Comedy, 1982-1993)	"Boys in the Bar," Sam's baseball teammate comes out (1/27/83) "Norm, is that You?" Norm pretends he's a gay decorator (12/8/88) "Rebecca's Lover...Not," Rebecca mistakes gay pal for straight (4/23/92)
CHICAGO HOPE (CBS, Medical Drama, 1994-2000)	**Reg:** Dr. Dennis Hancock (Vondie Curtis-Hall) (1995-1999) "Food Chains," Doctors battle over baboon's heart (9/29/94) "Freeze Outs," Grad rejects Hancock's patient for AIDS study (2/20/95) "Informed Consent," Kronk dates a transsexual (3/13/95) "Full Moon," Grad and Hancock operate on AIDS patient (5/15/95) "The Ethics of Hope," Grad is bitten by HIV infected ape (11/27/95) "Right to Life," Kronk treats drag queen with AIDS (1/22/96) "Women on the Verge," Kronk helps transsexual ex-girlfriend (2/12/96) "Sexual Perversity in Chicago," Shutt is mistaken for gay (3/11/96) "The Parent Rap," Intersexual baby (4/29/96) "Ex Marks the Spot," Sutton's ex-wives are lovers (5/13/96) "Liver Let Die," Shutt works with gay researcher (10/7/96) "Sympathy for the Devil," HIV+ teen won't take her meds (10/22/97)

GAY/LESBIAN/BISEXUAL/TRANSGENDER
TV EPISODE GUIDE (Cont.)

CHICAGO HOPE (cont.)	"The Lung and the Restless," Hancock comes out to Shutt (11/5/97) "The Ties That Bind," Grad helps HIV+ woman have baby (2/4/98) "Objects Are Closer Than They Appear," Lesbian fights for dying lover (3/25/98) "Risky Business," Teen boy believes he's a girl (4/29/98) "Austin Space," Gay Orthodox Jewish teen with OCD (10/7/98) "Playing Through," HIV+ patient kills man who molested him (2/3/99) "Teacher's Pet," Grad discovers she's HIV negative (3/24/99) "Boys Will Be Girls," Teen discovers she was born male (2/3/00)
CHINA BEACH (ABC, War Drama, 1988-1991)	"China Men," Boonie falls for transvestite (11/22/89)
CITY, THE (ABC, Soap Opera, 1995-1997)	**Reg:** Azure C. Lee/Chen (Carlotta Chang) (1995-1996)
CIVIL WARS (ABC, Legal Drama, 1991-1993)	"Oceans White with Phone," Gay man in palimony suit (1/15/92) "A Bus Named Desire," Lesbian sues for visitation rights (12/2/92)
CLERKS (ABC, Comedy, 2000)	"Episode 2," Dante's daydreams about marrying a man (6/7/00)
COACH (ABC, Comedy, 1989-1997)	"A Real Guy's Guy," Coach has gay player on team (10/25/91) "A Boy and His Doll," Timmy gets a doll (1/22/97)
COMMISH, THE (ABC, Police Drama, 1991-1995)	"Do You See What I See?" Gay officer witnesses gay bashing (9/2/95)
CONFESSION (WFAA-TV/Dallas, Talk Show, 1957)	Interview with transvestite on local Dallas talk show (12/57)
CONFIDENTIAL FILE (KTTV-TV/Los Angeles, Talk Show, 1955)	"Homosexuals & the Problem They Present," Early tabloid talk show (4/25/54)
COP ROCK (ABC, Police Drama/Musical, 1990)	**Reg:** Ray Rodbart (Jeffrey Allan Chandler), mayor's assistant (1990)

GAY/LESBIAN/BISEXUAL/TRANSGENDER
TV EPISODE GUIDE (cont.)

CORNER BAR (ABC, Comedy, Summer 1972/Summer 1973)	**Reg:** Peter Panama (Vincent Schiavelli) (1972), designer
COSBY (CBS, Comedy, 1996-2000)	"Older and Out," Hilton joins a gay softball team (10/13/97)
COURTHOUSE (CBS, Legal Drama, 1995)	**Reg:** Judge Rosetta Reide (Jenifer Lewis) and Danny Gates (Cree Summer) "Order on the Court," Judge Reed is in the closet at work (10/10/95) "Fair-weathered Friends," Judge Reed's parents visit (11/8/95)
CRACKER (ABC, Detective Drama, 1997-1998; A&E, 1999)	"Best Boys," Troubled teen seeks revenge on foster family (3/5/99)
CREW, THE (Fox, Comedy, 1995-1996)	**Reg:** Paul Steadman (David Burke), airline attendant
CUTTERS (CBS, Comedy, 1993)	**Reg:** Troy King (Julius Carry), hair stylist
CSI: CRIME SCENE INVESTIGATION (CBS, Police Drama, 2000-)	"Identity Crisis," Serial killer is male-to-female transsexual (1/17/02)
CYBILL (CBS, Comedy, 1995-1998)	**Rec:** Nameless restaurant waiter (Tim Macaulan) "Three Women and a Dummy," Cybill and waiter go to his ex's party (5/13/96) "Whose Wife Am I Anyway?" Cybill poses as waiter's fiancée (4/7/98)
DADDY'S GIRLS (CBS, Comedy, 1994)	**Reg:** Dennis Sinclair (Harvey Fierstein), clothing designer
DALLAS (CBS, Drama, 1978-1991)	"Call Girl," J.R. tries to blackmail Pam with lesbian photos (2/23/79) "Royal Marriage," Lucy gets engaged to Kit Mainwaring (3/9/79) "The Outsiders," Kit comes out to Lucy and Bobby (3/16/79)
DAMON (Fox, Comedy, 1998)	"The Designer," Damon goes undercover as a fashion designer (5/18/98)
DAN AUGUST (ABC, Detective Drama, 1970-1971)	"Dead Witness to a Killing," Assist. DA's wife is murdered (1/28/71)

GAY/LESBIAN/BISEXUAL/TRANSGENDER
TV EPISODE GUIDE (cont.)

DARK ANGEL (Fox, Action Drama, 2000-)	**Reg:** Original Cindy (Valarie Rae Miller), Max's sidekick
DATELINE NBC (NBC, News, 1992-)	"Talk on Trial," Report on murder of *Jenny Jones Show* guest (10/29/96) "Gender Limbo," A report on intersexuality (6/17/97) Katie Couric interviews Matthew Shepard's parents (2/11/99)
DAWSON'S CREEK (WB, Teen Drama, 1998-)	**Reg:** Jack Mcphee (Kerr Smith) **Rec:** Ethan (Adam Kaufman) (2000); Tobey (David Monahan) (2000-2001) "To Be or Not to Be..." Rumors circulate about Jack's sexuality (2/10/99) "...That is the Question," Jack comes out to his family and Joey (2/17/99) "Psychic Friends," Photographer takes interest in Jack (3/10/99) "None of the Above," Jack joins football team (10/13/99) "First Encounters of the Close Kind," Jack explores Boston's gay life (12/15/99) "Barefoot at Capefest," Jack hits on Ethan (1/12/00) "Self Reliance," Jack joins a "Gay-Straight Alliance" (2/20/00) "The Anti-Prom," Jack takes Ethan to alternative prom (5/17/00) "True Love," Jack plants kiss on Ethan (5/24/00)
DAYS AND NIGHTS MOLLY DODD (NBC, Comedy, 1987-1988; Lifetime, 1989-1991)	**Rec:** Brice (Drew McVety) (1989-1991)
DAYS OF OUR LIVES (NBC, Soap Opera, 1965-)	**Reg:** Sharon Duval (Sally Stark) (1976-1977); Harold (Ryan Scott) (2001)
DEAN MARTIN SHOW, THE (NBC, Variety, 1965-1974)	Comedy sketch in which wife can't resist a sale — even on sex changes (10/5/72)
DEAR JOHN (NBC, Comedy, 1988-1992)	"Stand By Your Man," Man has a crush on John (2/16/89) "Kirk's Ex-Wife," Kirk runs into his ex, who is now a lesbian (9/20/91)
DEGRASSI HIGH (PBS, Teen Drama, 1990-1991)	"Bad Blood Pt. 1," Dwayne learns girl he slept with is HIV+ (1991) "Bad Blood Pt. 2," Dwayne tests HIV+ (1991) "One Last Dance," Dwayne reveals to his classmates he's HIV+ (1991)

271

GAY/LESBIAN/BISEXUAL/TRANSGENDER TV EPISODE GUIDE (cont.)

DEGRASSI JUNIOR HIGH (PBS, Teen Drama, 1987-1989)	"Rumor Has It," Rumor is Ms. Avery is a lesbian (1987) "He Ain't Heavy," Snake learns his brother Glen is gay (1989)
DESIGNING WOMEN (CBS, Comedy, 1986-1993)	"Killing All the Right People," Designer with AIDS prepares funeral (10/5/87) "Suzanne Goes Looking for a Friend," Suzanne's friend is a lesbian (4/9/90) "A Toe in the Water," Ladies wonder if Julia's beau is gay (9/23/91)
DHARMA AND GREG (ABC, Comedy, 1997-)	"Invasion of the Buddy Snatchers," Greg's buddy has crush on him (5/20/98)
DIAGNOSIS MURDER (CBS, Detective Drama, 1992-2001)	"All American Murder," Transsexual is murdered (12/22/95)
DIANA (NBC, Comedy, 1973-1974)	**Reg:** Marshall Tyler (Robert Moore), window dresser
DIVISION, THE (Lifetime, Police Drama, 2001-)	**Rec:** Casey Exstead (Allen Cutler) (2001-), police officer "Don't Ask," Exstead's brother comes out, gay frat brother is murdered (2/25/01)
DOCTOR, DOCTOR (CBS, Comedy, 1989-1991)	**Reg:** Richard Strattford (Tony Carriero), college professor **Rec:** Hugh Persons (Brian George), host of *Wake Up Providence* "Torch Song Cardiology," Richard helps Grant write speech (12/18/89) "Accentuate the Positive," Hugh discovers he's HIV positive (1/8/90) "The Terminator," Richard dates office's gay assistant (10/25/90) "Providence," Richard is snubbed by his dad (11/1/90) "Sleeping Sickness," Richard gets hooked on pills (1/3/91)
DONNY AND MARIE (ABC, Variety, 1976-1979)	
DON'T ASK (Original Pilot for NORMAL, OHIO (2000), never aired)	**Reg:** Rex (John Goodman)
DR. KATZ, PROFESSIONAL THERAPIST (COMEDY CENTRAL, Animation, 1995-2000)	"Alderman," Patient C.K. Louis describes gay dream (9/21/98)

GAY/LESBIAN/BISEXUAL/TRANSGENDER
TV EPISODE GUIDE (Cont.)

DR. QUINN, MEDICINE WOMAN (CBS, Western Drama, 1993-1998)	"The Body Electric," Walt Whitman visits Colorado Springs (4/5/97)
DOCTORS' HOSPITAL (NBC, Medical Drama, 1975-1976)	"Watchman, Who Will Guard Thy Sleep?" Gay orderly cares for homophobic patient (10/29/75)
DOOGIE HOWSER (ABC, Comedy-Drama, 1989-1993)	"Vinnie, Video, Vici," Artists with AIDS paints a mural in hospital (10/25/89) "Spell it M-A-N," Vinnie's new college roommate is gay (1/6/93)
DREAM ON (HBO, Comedy, 1990-1996)	**Rec:** Mickey Tupper (Paul Dooley) (1992-1994), Martin's father; Roger (Dion Anderson) (1993-1994), Mickey's lover "For Peter's Sake," Martin helps gay author withAIDS write his memoirs (6/20/92) "What Women Want," Martin's girlfriend's ex is a woman (8/15/92) "The Guilty Party," Martin's old friend has a crush on him (9/26/92) "Pop's Secret," Martin discovers his father is gay (6/23/93) "The Homecoming Queen," Girl from past thinks Martin's gay (7/27/94) "Courtship of Martin's Father," Mickey breaks up with Roger (8/14/94)
DREW CAREY SHOW, THE (ABC, Comedy, 1995-)	**Reg:** Steve Carey (John Carroll Lynch), Drew's transvestite brother "Drew's the Other Guy," Gay co-worker has eye on Oswald (11/20/96) "Man's Best Same Sex Companion," Drew pretends he's gay for insurance (3/5/97) "Drew's Brother," Drew's bro is a transvestite (11/19/97) "Drew and the Trail Scout," Drew's phony gay marriage to Wick (11/22/00) "All Work and No Play I," Drew ends gay marriage to Wick (1/24/01) "Hotel Drew," Drew rents room to gay couple (12/12/01) "The Curse of the Mummy," Richard Chamberlain as Wick's mum (1/6/02)
DYNASTY (ABC, Drama, 1981-1989)	**Reg:** Steven Carrington (Al Corley, 1981-1982; Jack Coleman, 1982-1988) **Rec:** Ted Dinard (Mark Withers) (1981); Chris Deegan (Grant Goodeve) (1983); Luke Fuller (William Campbell) (1984-1985); Bart Fallmont (Kevin Conroy) (1985-1986)

GAY/LESBIAN/BISEXUAL/TRANSGENDER
TV EPISODE GUIDE (cont.)

DYNASTY (cont.)	"Episode One" (Premiere), Blake tells Steven to "straighten out" (1/12/81)

ER (NBC, Medical Drama, 1994-)	**Reg:** Dr. Margaret "Maggie" Doyle (Jorja Fox) (1996-1999), third-year resident; Dr. Kerry Weaver (Laura Innes) (1995-), ER Chief; Dr. Kim Legaspi (Elizabeth Mitchell) (2000-2001), psychiatrist
	Rec: Raul Melendez (Carlos Gomez) (1995-1996), paramedic/EMT; Yosh Takata (Gedde Watanabe) (1997-), junior nurse; Sandy Lopez (Lisa Vidal) (2001-), firefighter
	"Long Day's Journey," Ross helps a homeless teenager with AIDS (1/19/95)
	"Make of Two Hearts," Lewis cares for HIV+ little girl (2/9/95)
	"Full Moon Saturday," Man and his fiancée discover he's HIV+ (3/30/95)
	"Everything Old is New Again," Benton treats gay man with AIDS (5/18/95)
	"Dead of Winter," Shep's medic partner Raul is gay (1/4/96)
	"It's Not Easy Being Greene," Gay teen seeks help from Ross (2/1/96)
	"Baby Shower," Gay and lesbian couple have child (2/15/96)
	"Whose Appy Now?" Doyle comes out to Carter (2/6/97)
	"The Healers," Raul is badly burned and dies (2/22/96)
	"Take These Broken Wings," Jeanie's husband is HIV+ (5/9/96)
	"Don't Ask, Don't Tell," Jeanie reveals she's HIV+ (10/10/96)
	"When the Bough Breaks," Weaver reprimands Jeanie (10/16/97)
	"Obstruction of Justice," HIV+ Jeannie sues for her job back (12/11/97)
	"Split Second," Yosh is called "Chinese fag" (10/1/98)
	"Masquerade," Little girl is intersexual (10/29/98)
	"Stuck on You," Greene helps teen hustler (11/5/98)
	"Hazed and Confused," Yosh is called "cookie fairy" (11/12/98)
	"Greene with Envy," Jeanie marries and adopts baby (10/14/99)
	"The Domino Heart," Greene helps gay spouse abuse victim (1/13/00)
	"Sand and Water," Woman denied control of lover's care (10/19/00)
	"Flight of Fancy," Teen discovers he was born HIV+ (11/9/00)
	"Rescue Me," Weaver dines with Dr. Legaspi (11/23/00)

GAY / LESBIAN / BISEXUAL / TRANSGENDER
TV EPISODE GUIDE (cont.)

ER (cont.)	"Surrender," Weaver and Legaspi spend night together (2/1/01) "Thy Will Be Done," Gay man wants to be HIV+ (2/8/01) "Witch Hunt," Legaspi accused of sexual misconduct (3/1/01) "Where the Heart Is," Weaver meets Legaspi's new girlfriend (5/10/01) "Rampage," Weaver comes out to Romano (5/17/01) "Blood Sugar Sex Magic," Malucci calls Weaver a "Nazi dyke" (10/11/01) "Never Say Never," Weaver visits a gay bar (10/18/01) "Quo Vadis?" Weaver asks out Lopez (11/22/01) "I'll Be Home for Christmas," Weaver and Lopez go on a date (12/13/01) "A River in Egypt," Lopez outs Weaver with a kiss (1/17/02)
ED (NBC, Comedy-Drama, 2000-)	"The Whole Truth," Ed prepares closeted gay grandpa's will (12/6/01)
EDUCATION OF MAX BICKFORD, THE (CBS, Drama, 2001-2002)	**Reg:** Erica Bettis (Helen Shaver), Male-to-female transsexual
ELEVENTH HOUR, THE (NBC, Medical Drama, 1962-1964)	"What Did She Mean By Good Luck?" Actress with lesbian tendencies (11/13/63)
ELLEN (a.k.a THESE FRIENDS OF MINE) (ABC, Comedy, 1994-1998)	**Reg:** Ellen Morgan (Ellen DeGeneres); Laurie (Lisa Darr) (1997-1998); Peter (Patrick Bristow) **Rec:** Barrett (Jack Plotnick) (1995-1998), Paige's assistant "Two Ring Circus," Peter and Barrett tie the knot (2/28/96) "The Puppy Episode," Ellen comes out to friends (4/30/97) "Hello Muddah, Hello Faddah," Ellen comes out to her folks (5/7/97) "Moving On," Ellen comes out to her boss (5/14/97) "G.I. Ellen," Ellen in a Civil War reenactment (11/5/97) "Emma," Ellen discovers Emma Thompson is gay (11/19/97) "All Ellen, All the Time," Ellen works as radio talk show host (12/3/97) "It's a Gay, Gay, Gay, Gay, World," Spence dreams gay is the norm (2/25/98)
ELLEN SHOW, THE (CBS, Comedy, 2001-2002)	**Reg:** Ellen Richmond (Ellen DeGeneres), guidance counselor **Rec:** Bunny Hopstetter (Diane Delano), gym teacher

GAY/LESBIAN/BISEXUAL/TRANSGENDER
TV EPISODE GUIDE (cont.)

EMPTY NEST (NBC, Comedy, 1988-1995)	"Single White Male," Charlie discovers new roommate is gay (1/7/95)
EQUALIZER, THE (CBS, Detective Drama, 1985-1989)	"Christmas Presence," Equalizer protects child with AIDS (12/16/87)
EVENING SHADE (CBS, Comedy, 1990-1994)	"The Perfect Woman," Ponder dates a transsexual (1/31/94)
EVERYBODY LOVES RAYMOND (CBS, Comedy, 1996-)	"What's with Robert?" Family wonders if Robert is gay (1/10/00) "Fairies," Ray's sons are fairies in school play (2/19/01)
EXECUTIVE SUITE (CBS, Drama, 1976-1977)	**Rec:** Leona (Patricia Smith); Julie Solkin (Geraldine Smith) "Re: The Sounds of Silence," Julie comes out to Leona (12/6/76) "Re: What are Patterns For?" Leona admits feelings for Julie (12/13/76) "Re: The Identity Crisis," Julie's funeral (12/20/76)
FACTS OF LIFE (NBC, Comedy, 1979-1988)	"Rough Housing," Blair teases tomboy Cindy (8/24/79)
FAME (NBC, Teen Drama, 1982-1983; First-run syn., 1983-1987)	"Best Buddies," Danny's old friend comes out (1987)
FAME L.A. (First-run syn., Drama, 1997-1998)	"Duet," Ryan's girlfriend is bi (1/31/98)
FAMILY (ABC, Drama, 1976-1980)	"Rites of Friendship," Willie's childhood friend is gay (9/28/76)
FAMILY LAW (CBS, Legal Drama, 1999-)	"We Love You, Miss Jessup," Buddy's favorite teacher is outed (11/1/77) "Are You My Father?" Transsexual fights for child custody (2/21/00) "The Gay Divorcee," Gay man fights for custody of adopted kids (4/9/01)
FANELLI BOYS, THE (NBC, Comedy, 1990-1991)	"Pursued," Dominic discovers childhood friend is gay (9/19/90)
FANTASY ISLAND (ABC, Drama, 1998-1999)	**Reg:** Harry (Edward Hibbert), Mr. Roarke's assistant
FELICITY (WB, Drama, 1998-2002)	**Reg:** Javier Clemente Quantata (Ian Gomez) "Love and Marriage," Noel's brother comes out; Javier moves to Spain (1/23/99)

GAY/LESBIAN/BISEXUAL/TRANSGENDER
TV EPISODE GUIDE (cont.)

FELICITY (cont.)	"Ancient History," Noel has his eye on lesbian classmate (10/10/99) "The Biggest Deal There Is," Javier and Samuel get married (5/24/00) "One Ball, Two Strikes," Richard reveals he's not gay, but a virgin (10/8/00) "A Good Egg," Javier and Samuel decide to have a child (11/22/00) "Blackout," Meghan's lesbian friend visits (4/25/01) "Moving On," Female student her eye on Javier (11/28/01)
FIRED UP (NBC, Comedy, 1997-1998)	**Rec:** Ashley (Mark Davis), female impersonator "Truth or Consequences," Ashley quits show biz after bad review (9/29/97)
413 HOPE STREET (Fox, Drama, 1997-1998)	**Reg:** Melvin Todd (Karim Prince)
FIRST YEAR (NBC, Legal Drama, 2001)	**Reg:** Warren Harrison (Mackenzie Astin), lawyer "There's No Place Like Homo," Warren is honored by gay organization (4/2/01)
FOR YOUR LOVE (NBC, Comedy, 1998; WB, 1998-)	"The House of Cards," Sheri's gay friend Tom comes to visit (11/19/98)
FRASIER (NBC, Comedy, 1993-)	**Rec:** Gil Chesterton (Edward Hibbert), restaurant critic "The Matchmaker," New station manager thinks Frasier is gay (4/10/94) "The Impossible Dream," Frasier has a dream he's in bed with Gil (10/15/96) "The Ski Lodge," Ski instructor falls for Niles (2/4/98) "IQ," Lesbian falls for Roz (4/8/99) "Out with Dad," Martin pretends he's gay (2/10/00)
FREAKS AND GEEKS (NBC, Teen Drama, 1999-2000; Fox Family Channel, 2000)	"The Little Things," Ben learns Amy was born intersexual (7/8/00)
FRIENDS (NBC, Comedy, 1994-)	**Rec:** Carol Willig (Anita Barone, 1994, Jane Sibbet, 1995-); Susan Bunch (Jessica Hecht) (1994-) "The One with the Sonogram at the End," Ross and Susan and Carol are pregnant (9/29/94) "The One where Nana Dies Twice," Chandler is mistaken for gay (11/20/94) "The One with the Candy Hearts," Ross and Susan and Carol on Valentines Day (2/9/95) "The One with the Birth," Ross and Susan and Carol are parents (5/11/95)

GAY/LESBIAN/BISEXUAL/TRANSGENDER
TV EPISODE GUIDE (cont.)

FRIENDS (cont.)	"The One with Phoebe's Husband," Phoebe's husband is straight (10/12/95) "The One with the Baby on the Bus," Chandler and Joey mistaken for gay couple (11/2/95) "The One with the Lesbian Wedding," Carol and Susan tie the knot (1/18/96) "The One when Joey Moves Out," Joey and Chandler "break up" (2/15/96) "The One with Barry and Mindy's Wedding," Joey practices kissing guys (5/16/96) "The One with the Metaphorical Tunnel," Ross is upset Ben plays with a doll (10/10/96) "The One with the Ballroom Dancing," Joey teaches janitor to dance (10/16/96) "The One with the Nap Partners," Joey and Ross enjoy taking a nap together (11/9/00) "The One with Chandler's Dad," Chandler's dad is drag performer (5/10/01) "The One with the Secret Closet," Monica really enjoys Phoebe's massage (1/31/02)
GENERAL HOSPITAL (ABC, Soap Opera, 1963-)	**Rec:** John Hanley (Lee Mathis) (1994-1996); Ted Murty (Patrick Fabian) (1997-1998), high school teacher; Elton Freeman (Loren Herbert) (2001-), Laura Spencer's assistant
GETTING PERSONAL (Fox, Comedy, 1998)	"Chasing Sammy," Milo pretends he's gay (5/18/98)
GIDEON'S CROSSING (ABC, Medical Drama, 2000-2001)	"Freak Show," Woman with cancer tells husband she's transsexual (11/15/00)
GIMME A BREAK (NBC, Comedy, 1981-1987)	"Chief's Gay Evening," Chief finds out an old friend is gay (11/13/82)
GO FISH (NBC, Comedy, 2001)	"Go PDA," Hazard thinks Fish's brother is gay (6/19/01)
GOLDEN GIRLS, THE (NBC, Comedy, 1985-1992)	"Pilot," Girls' gay houseboy, Coco (9/14/85) "Isn't it Romantic," Dorothy's lesbian friend has crush on Rose (10/11/86) "Strange Bedfellows," Blanche is involved in a sex scandal (11/7/87) "Scared Straight," Blanche's brother Clayton comes out (12/10/88) "Ebbtide's Revenge," Dorothy's cross-dressing brother dies (12/15/90) "Sister of the Bride," Clayton gets married (1/12/91) "Goodbye Mr. Gordon," Blanche and Dorothy appear on TV as lesbians (1/11/92)

GAY/LESBIAN/BISEXUAL/TRANSGENDER
TV EPISODE GUIDE (cont.)

GOOD NEWS (UPN, Comedy, 1997-1998)	"Pilot," Mrs. Dixon's gay son comes out (8/25/97)
GRACE UNDER FIRE (ABC, Comedy, 1993-1998)	"Cold Turkey," Grace's ex's gay cousin, DeForest Kelly, visits (11/22/94) "Emmett's Secret," Grace discovers father-in-law, Emmett, is gay (12/5/95) "Emmett, We Hardly Knew You," Emmett's lover comes to his funeral (12/18/95)
GROSSE POINTE (WB, Comedy, 2000-2001)	**Rec:** Richard Towers/Michael Johnson (Michael Hitchcock) "Boys on the Side," Johnny's #1 fan is a gay kid (11/19/00) "Passion Fish," Marcy thinks Sarah Michelle Gellar has hots for her (2/16/01)
GROUNDED FOR LIFE (Fox, Comedy, 2001-)	"Relax," Walt accidentally outs a co-worker (3/27/01)
GROWN-UPS (UPN, Comedy, 1999-2000)	"Pilot," J's new roommate thinks he's gay (8/23/99)
GUARDIAN, THE (CBS, Legal Drama, 2001-)	"The Men From the Boys," Nick helps gay teen find a home (10/23/01)
GUYS LIKE US (UPN, Comedy, 1998-1999)	"In and Out," Sean pretends he's gay; Jared worries Maestro is gay (10/12/98)
HAIL TO THE CHIEF (ABC, Comedy, 1985)	**Reg:** Randy (Joel Brooks), Chief Secret Service Agent
HARRY-O (ABC, Detective Drama, 1974-1976)	"Coinage of the Realm," A pair of gay hit men (10/10/74)
HEAD OVER HEELS (UPN, Comedy, 1997)	**Reg:** Ian (Patrick Bristow), celibate bisexual romance counselor
HEARTBEATS (ABC, Medical Drama, 1988-1989)	**Reg:** Marilyn McGrath (Gail Strickland), nurse practitioner **Rec:** Patti (Gina Hecht), Marilyn's lover "To Heal a Doctor," Marilyn reconciles with her daughter (4/20/88) "The Wedding," Marilyn's daughter is married (4/21/88)
HEARTS AFIRE (CBS, Comedy, 1992-1995)	**Rec:** Diandra (Julie Cobb), John's ex-wife; Ruth (Conchata Ferrell), Diandra's lover/marriage counselor "Bees Can Sting You, Watch Out," John finds out about Diandra and Ruth (8/14/92)

279

GAY/LESBIAN/BISEXUAL/TRANSGENDER
TV EPISODE GUIDE (cont.)

HEARTS AFIRE (cont.)	"Significant Others," Diandra and Ruth come to dinner (10/26/92) "Conversations with My Shrink," Georgie seeks help from Ruth (11/16/92) "Birth of a Donation," Billy Bob's old friend is gay (10/22/94) "Mrs. Hartman, Mrs. Hartman," Diandra pays a visit (1/18/95)
HERE'S LUCY (CBS, Comedy, 1968-1974)	"Lucy and Jim Bailey," Female impersonator Jim Bailey guest stars (11/6/72)
HERMAN'S HEAD (Fox, Comedy, 1991-1994)	"Spermin' Herman," Herman's ex, a lesbian, wants his sperm (9/20/92)
HIGH SOCIETY (CBS, Comedy, 1995-1996)	**Reg:** Stefano (Luigi Amodeo), Dott's assistant.
HILL STREET BLUES (NBC, Police Drama, 1981-1987)	**Rec:** Eddie Gregg (Charles Levin) (1982, 1986); Officer Kate McBride (Lindsay Crouse) (1986-1987) "Trial by Fury," Belker befriends male prostitute, Eddie (9/30/82) "Requiem for a Hairbag," Eddie gets arrested (11/18/82) "A Hair of the Dog," Eddie becomes Belker's snitch (11/25/82) "Phantom of the Hill," Eddie's lover is involved in drug murder (12/2/82) "No Body's Perfect," Eddie the informant cracks under pressure (12/9/82) "Here's Adventure, Here's Romance," Closeted cop witnesses murder (10/13/83) "Queen for a Day," Coffey's school coach arrested in gay raid (4/11/85) "Look Homeward, Ninja," Officer McBride accused of molestation (3/13/86) "Slum Enchanted Evening," Belker helps a dying Eddie (3/27/86)
HITCHHIKER, THE (HBO, Anthology, 1983-1987, USA, 1989-1991)	"Man at the Window," Woman hides lesbian affair from husband (3/12/85)
HOLDING THE BABY (Fox, Comedy, 1998)	"The Gay Divorcee," Gordon's date thinks he's gay (12/8/98)
HOLLYWOOD BEAT (ABC, Police Drama, 1985)	**Reg:** George Grinsky (John Matuszak), cocktail lounge owner

GAY / LESBIAN / BISEXUAL / TRANSGENDER
TV EPISODE GUIDE (Cont.)

HOMICIDE: LIFE ON THE STREET (NBC, Police Drama, 1993-1999)	**Reg:** Det. Tim Bayliss (1993-1999), bisexual detective; Det. Rene Sheppard (1998-1999) bi-curious detective "From Cradle to Grave," Congressman tries to conceal his homosexuality (1/13/95) "Hate Crimes," Young man mistaken for gay is gay-bashed (11/17/95) "Betrayal," Bayliss reveals he was sexually abused (1/10/97) "Closet Cases," Det. Bayliss investigates gay murder (1/2/98) "Sins of the Father," Pembleton is confused about Bayliss's sexuality (1/9/98) "Homicide.com," Bayliss's website is linked to internet killer (2/5/99) "Just an Old Fashioned Love Song," Bayliss and Sheppard are bi-curious (10/23/98) "Truth Will Out," Word is out Bayliss is bisexual (3/26/99) "Forgive Us Our Trespasses," Bayliss murders internet killer (5/21/99)
HOOPERMAN (ABC, Police Comedy-Drama, 1987-1989)	**Reg:** Officer Rick Silardi (Joseph Gian); Rudy (Ron Gist) (1988-1989), Hooperman's tenant "Don We Now Our Gay Apparel," Silardi attracts a movie star (10/7/87) "Surprise Party," Silardi's homophobic twin visits (5/18/88)
HOPE & GLORIA (NBC, Comedy, 1995-1996)	**Rec:** Isaac (Eric Allan Kramer) (1995), hairstylist
HOTEL (ABC, Drama, 1983-1988)	"Faith, Hope, and Charity," Woman discovers old friend is lesbian (11/23/83) "Mistaken Identities," Father fears son is gay (2/1/84) "Transitions," Woman discovers husband is bisexual (11/14/84) "Scapegoats," Hetero bartender with AIDS (1/22/86) "Undercurrents," Army officer discovers friend is gay (11/19/86) "Rallying Cry," Gay men fight for child custody (10/2/85) "Contest of Wills," Dad discovers late daughter was lesbian (3/17/88)
HOT L BALTIMORE (ABC, Comedy, 1975)	**Reg:** George (Lee Bergere); Gordon (Henry Calvert) "George and Gordon," The couple have a lover's spat (2/21/75)
HOUSE CALLS (CBS, Comedy, 1979-1982)	"The Magnificent Weatherbees," Dr. Weatherbee has gay alter ego (3/9/81)

GAY/LESBIAN/BISEXUAL/TRANSGENDER TV EPISODE GUIDE (cont.)

HUDSON STREET (ABC, Comedy, 1995-1996)	"The Man's Man," Melanie's ex, a former pro athlete, is gay (10/24/95)
THE HUGHLEYS (ABC, Comedy, 1998-2000; UPN, 2000-)	**Rec:** Joanie Park (Amy Hill) "Guess Who's Coming to Dinner?" Darryl is afraid son Michael is gay (9/18/00)
HUNTER (NBC, Police Drama, 1984-1991)	"The Fifth Victim," Gay serial killer (12/9/89) "From San Francisco with Love," Hunter beds a killer lesbian (11/15/96)
INK (CBS, Comedy, Comedy, 1996-1997)	"Paper Cuts," Mike and Kate lay off lesbian employee (10/28/96)
IN LIVING COLOR (Fox, Comedy/Variety, 1990-1994)	**Rec:** Blaine Edwards (Damon Wayans) (1990-1992), critic, "Men on ..."; Antoine Merriweather (David Allen Grier), critic, "Men on..." "Men on Film," (4/15/90) "Men on Art," (5/5/90) "Men on Books," (5/26/90) "Men on Vacation," (4/7/91) "Men on Television," (5/12/91) "Men on Football," (1/26/92)
IN THE HOUSE (NBC, Comedy, 1995-1996; UPN, 1996-1998)	"Boys II Men II Women," RuPaul as a hetero drag queen (2/4/95)
IN THE LIFE (PBS, News, 1992-)	Gay and lesbian news magazine
INVESTIGATIVE REPORTS (A&E, News, 1991-)	"Transgender Revolution," Report on transgender rights movement (10/5/98) "Anti-Gay Hate Crime," Report on hate crimes in America (7/6/99)
JACKIE THOMAS SHOW, THE (ABC, Comedy, 1992-1993)	"Forces of Nature," Jackie is "outed" by the tabloids (2/2/93)
JAG (JUDGE ADVOCATE GENERAL) (NBC, Military Drama, 1995-1996; CBS, 1997-)	"The People vs. Gunny," Gunny is charged with gay-bashing (2/22/00)
JAMIE FOXX SHOW, THE (WB, Comedy, 1996-2001)	"Partners fo' Life," Andre and Jamie are mistaken for a gay couple (2/18/00)
JEFFERSONS, THE (CBS, Comedy, 1975-1985)	"Once a Friend," George's old navy buddy is now a woman (10/1/77)

GAY / LESBIAN / BISEXUAL / TRANSGENDER
TV EPISODE GUIDE (cont.)

JOB, THE (ABC, Comedy-Drama, 2001, 2002-)	"Gay," Frank is suspected of being a closeted homosexual (2/27/02)
JOHN LARROQUETE SHOW, THE (NBC, Comedy, 1993-1996)	**Rec:** Teddi (David Shawn Michaels) (1993); Drag Queen (Jazzmun) (1994); Officer Hampton (Lenny Clarke) (1993-1996) "The Past Comes Back," AA member makes amends to John for past (10/26/93) "Dirty Deeds," John's college roommate is a female impersonator (2/1/94) "An Odd Cup of Tea," Hampton mistakenly gets flowers (12/19/95) "Happy Endings," Officer Hampton comes out (5/21/96)
JUDD, FOR THE DEFENSE (ABC, Legal Drama, 1967-1969)	"Weep the Hunter Home," Father suspects son is a homosexual (11/8/68)
JUDGING AMY (CBS, Legal Drama, 1999-)	"8 1/2 Narrow," Principal discontinues school's gay pride club (2/6/01) "Between the Wanting and the Getting," Boy wants to dress as girl (5/1/01) "The Extinction of Dinosaurs," Maxine helps gay teen find a home (1/22/02)
JUDY GARLAND SHOW, THE (CBS, Variety, 1963-1964)	
JUST SHOOT ME (NBC, Comedy, 1997-)	"Pass the Salt," Finch's father thinks he's gay (1/29/98) "The Emperor," Maya insults flamboyant designer (4/23/98) "Two Girls for Every Boy," Finch arranges ménage with Maya and model (11/10/98) "Brandi You're a Fine Girl," Finch's childhood friend is transsexual (11/16/00) "Mayas and Tigers and Deans, Oh My," Nina wonders if her new beau is gay (2/15/01)
KATE AND ALLIE (CBS, Comedy, 1984-1989)	"Landlady," The duo pretend to be lesbians to avoid a rent increase (10/15/84)
KATE LOVES A MYSTERY a.k.a KATE COLUMBO (NBC, Detective Drama, 1979)	"Feelings Can Be Murder," Ms. Columbo investigates bi woman's death (12/6/79)

GAY/LESBIAN/BISEXUAL/TRANSGENDER
TV EPISODE GUIDE (cont.)

KEY WEST (Fox, Comedy-Drama, 1993)	**Reg:** Mayor Pembroke (Nicolas Surovy), ex-marine (Pilot only) "Pilot," Gay mayor loses election to conservative, anti-gay opponent (1/19/93) "A Second Day in Heaven," New mayor meets sexually diverse staff (1/26/93)
KIDS IN THE HALL (HBO, Sketch Comedy, 1989-1994; CBS, 1992-1995)	**Reg:** Scott Thompson
KOJAK (CBS, Police Drama, 1973-1978; ABC, 1989-1990)	"A Need to Know," Controversial child molestation episode (10/24/76)
L.A. DOCTORS (CBS, Medical Drama, 1998-1999)	"Under the Radar," Lonner treats friend with AIDS (9/28/98) "Been There, Done That," Female-to-male transsexual (1/11/99)
L.A. LAW (NBC, Legal Drama, 1986-1994)	**Reg:** Cara Jean "C.J." Lamb (Amanda Donohoe) (1990-1992), lawyer **Rec:** Mark Gilliam (Stanley Kamel), lawyer "Pilot," Lawyers discover late senior partner was gay (9/15/86) "The Venus Butterfly," Mercy killing involving AIDS patient (11/21/86) "Fry Me to the Moon," Grace helps gay man convicted of mercy killing (12/4/86) "The Accidental Jurist," Gay judge hears gay athlete case (2/23/89) "Blood, Sweat and Fears," Doctor refuses to operate on AIDS patient (3/15/90) "Outward Bound," Gay cop is outed by journalist (5/10/90) "Smoke Gets in Your Thighs," Gay man refused visitation rights (11/15/90) "He's a Crowd," C.J. kisses Abby (2/7/91) "Speak, Lawyers for Me," Transsexual model sues cosmetics company (4/25/91) "Since I Fell for You," AIDS-stricken Gilliam sues insurance co. (5/16/91) "Do the Spike Thing," Douglas is gay bashed (10/31/91) "The Nut Before Christmas," C.J. defends ex-lover in custody suit (12/19/91) "Cold Shower," Gay man charged with art theft (4/8/93) "Tunnel of Love," AIDS rumors hurt dentist's practice (4/28/94)

GAY/LESBIAN/BISEXUAL/TRANSGENDER
TV EPISODE GUIDE (Cont.)

LARRY SANDERS SHOW, THE (HBO, Comedy, 1992-1998)	**Reg:** Brian (Scott Thompson), Hank's assistant "Hank's New Assistant," Hank hires, then tries to fire Brian (7/26/95) "I Was a Teenage Lesbian," Paula reveals lesbian affair with Brett (10/11/95) "Everybody Loves Larry," David Duchovny has a crush on Larry (11/13/96) "Ellen, or Isn't She," Larry wants Ellen to come out on his show (12/11/96) "The Matchmaker," Hank and Brian go to a gay bar (1/8/97) "Putting the Gay Back in Litigation," Brian files harassment suit (5/17/98) "Flip," David Duchovny returns (5/31/98)
LAW AND ORDER (NBC, Police/Legal Drama, 1990-)	"The Reaper's Helper," Man helps AIDS patients to commit suicide (10/4/90) "Silence," Murder of closeted gay city councilman (4/28/92) "Manhood," Gay cop's cry for help ignored by officers (5/12/93) "Pride," Gay councilman is murdered (5/24/95) "Deceit," Gay lawyer is murdered (3/27/96) "Phobia," Gay male is murdered by child stealer (2/14/01)
LAW AND ORDER: CRIMINAL INTENT (NBC, Police Drama, 2001-)	"One," Bisexual master thief manipulates both men and women (9/30/01)
LAW AND ORDER: SPECIAL VICTIMS UNIT (NBC, Police Drama, 1999-)	"Russian Love Poem," Russians, money, bisexuals, and murder (1/21/00) "Bad Blood," Closeted cop is guest at party near murder site (1/14/00) "Nocturne," Piano teacher accused of child molestation (5/12/00) "Sacrifice," Father works in gay porn to help daughter (11/9/01)
LEAP YEARS (Showtime, Drama, 2001-2002)	**Reg:** Gregory Paget (Garrett Dillahunt), Critic and therapist
LIFE GOES ON (ABC, Drama, 1989-1993)	"Incident on Main," HIV+ Jesse is gay-bashed outside hospice (1/10/93)
LINC'S (Showtime, Comedy, 1998-2000)	**Reg:** Rosalee Lincoln (Tisha Campbell), Army Lieutenant
LIFESTORIES (NBC, Anthology Drama, 1990)	"Steve Burdick," Newscaster with AIDS goes public (12/18/90)

GAY/LESBIAN/BISEXUAL/TRANSGENDER TV EPISODE GUIDE (cont.)

LIVESHOT (NBC, Drama, 1995)	**Reg:** Lou Waller (Tom Byrd), sportscaster "T.G.I.F.," A pro athlete wants to come out on the air (8/5/95)
LIVING SINGLE (Fox, Comedy, 1993-1998)	"Woman to Woman," The gang throws a lesbian shower (3/21/96)
LOT, THE (AMC, Drama, 1999-2001)	"Danny Mathews Takes A Wife," Gay movie star must marry to save career (3/18/01) "Oscar's Wilde," Studio sanitizes Oscar Wilde bio by making him hetero (4/1/01)
LOU GRANT (CBS, Drama, 1977-1982)	"Cop," Reporter Joe Rossi befriends a closeted gay cop (9/17/79)
LOVE & WAR (CBS, Comedy, 1992-1995)	"Bali Hai," Jack has a male admirer (3/14/91)
LOVE BOAT (ABC, Comedy, 1977-1986)	"Strange Honeymoon," Groom and best man mistaken for gay couple (11/8/80) "Frat Brothers Forever," Doc's old frat brother comes out (10/6/84)
LOVE BOAT: THE NEXT WAVE (UPN, Comedy, 1998-1999)	"Smooth Sailing," Two guys are mistaken for a gay couple (4/13/98)
LOVE, SIDNEY (NBC, Comedy, 1981-1983)	**Reg:** Sidney Shorr (Tony Randall)
LUSH LIFE (Fox, Comedy, 1996)	**Reg:** Nelson "Margarita" Marquez (John Ortiz) bartender
M*A*S*H (CBS, Comedy, 1972-1983)	**Reg:** Corporal Max Klinger (Jamie Farr), cross-dresser "George," Frank tries to "out" a gay soldier (2/16/76)
M.Y.O.B. (NBC, Comedy, 2001)	"Boys in the Band," Gay student has affair with female teacher (6/6/00)
MAD ABOUT YOU (NBC, Comedy, 1992-1999)	**Rec:** Debbie Buchanan (Robin Bartlett) (1995-1999); Dr. Joan Herman (1996-1999), Debbie's lover "Ovulation Day," Debbie comes out to Paul, Jamie and her parents (1/7/96) "Dr. Wonderful," Debbie's parents meet Joan (9/17/96) "Tragedy Plus Time," Debbie is not sure if she should marry Joan (10/27/98)
MAGGIE (Lifetime, Comedy, 1998)	"Pilot," Artistic teen pretends to be gay (8/18/98)

GAY/LESBIAN/BISEXUAL/TRANSGENDER
TV EPISODE GUIDE (Cont.)

MALCOLM & EDDIE (UPN, Comedy, 1996-2000)	"The Commercial," TV commercial turns sports bar into gay bar (2/24/97) "Sibling Rivalry," Malcolm, his lesbian friend and Eddie vie for waitress (8/4/97)
MALCOLM IN THE MIDDLE (Fox, Comedy, 2000-)	"Lois vs. Evil," Beauty pageant contestants think Francis is gay (3/19/00)
MARCUS WELBY, M.D. (ABC, Medical Drama, 1969-1976)	"The Other Martin Loring," Confused gay, married, alcoholic diabetic (2/20/73) "The Outrage," Welby treats male teen raped by his teacher (10/8/74)
MARRIED WITH CHILDREN (Fox, Comedy, 1987-1997)	"Dance Show," Peg steps out with two gay men, (10/21/90) "Lez Be Friends," Marcy is jealous of her lesbian cousin (4/10/97)
MARY HARTMAN, MARY HARTMAN (First-run syn., Comedy/Soap Opera, 1976-1977)	**Rec:** Howard McCullough (Beeson Carroll) (1976); Ed McCullough (Lawrence Haddon) (1976); Annie "Tippytoes" Wylie (Gloria DeHaven) (1976)
MARTIN (Fox, Comedy, 1992-1997)	"You've Got a Friend," Martin is jealous of Gina's new male friend (10/10/93)
MARY TYLER MOORE SHOW (CBS, Comedy, 1970-1977)	"My Brother's Keeper," Rhoda and Phyllis's gay brother hit it off (1/13/72)
MATT WATERS (CBS, Drama, 1996)	**Reg:** Russ Achoa (Felix A. Pire), high school student "Who?" Russ explores his family's roots (2/7/96)
MAUDE (CBS, Comedy, 1972-1978)	"Maude's New Friend," Maude befriends a gay author (12/2/74) "Arthur's Worry," Walter dreams he kissed Arthur (11/5/76) "The Gay Bar," Maude vs. Arthur when new gay bar opens (12/3/77)
MAX LIEBMAN PRESENTS (NBC, Musical Variety, 1954-1955)	"Lady in the Dark," Carleton Carpenter as Russell (9/25/54)
MEDICAL CENTER (CBS, Medical Drama, 1969-1976)	"Undercurrent," Gay medical researcher faces homophobia (9/23/70) "Impasse," Lesbian psychiatrist helps sexually confused patient (10/1/73) "The Fourth Sex" (Parts I & II), Surgeon undergoes sex change (9/8/75, 9/15/75)

GAY/LESBIAN/BISEXUAL/TRANSGENDER TV EPISODE GUIDE (cont.)

MELROSE PLACE (Fox, Drama, 1992-1999)	**Reg:** Matt Fielding (Doug Savant) (1992-1997), social worker/doctor **Rec:** Jeffrey Lindley (Jason Beghe) (1994-1995); Dr. Paul Graham (David Beecroft) (1995); Alan Ross (Lonnie Schuyler) (1995-1996); David Johansen (Rob Youngblood) (1996); Dr. Dan Hathaway (1996-1997); Connie Rexroth (Megan Ward) (1997-1998) "Till Death Do us Part," Billy's best man is gay (5/18/94) "Farewell Mike's Concubine," Matt and Dan take it slow (11/18/96) "Brand New Day," Matt moves to San Francisco (9/8/97) "World According to Matt," Amanda reads Matt's diary (8/14/98)
MEN BEHAVING BADLY (NBC, Comedy, 1996-1997)	"The Odds Couple," Jamie tries to prove his neighbor is a lesbian (1/15/97) "Spoils of War," Brenda makes Jamie feel like a gay pal (11/2/97)
MEN, WOMEN, AND DOGS (WB, Comedy, 2001)	"A Fetching New Lawyer," Royce pretends he's gay to get a woman (12/30/01)
MIDNIGHT CALLER (NBC, Drama, 1988-1991)	"After It Happened," Jack learns ex-girlfriend got AIDS from bi man (12/13/88) "Someone to Love," Jack says goodbye to dying Tina (11/7/89)
MILLENNIUM (Fox, Police Drama, 1996-1999)	"Pilot," Serial killer attempts to cleanse city of the "plague" (10/25/96)
MISSION HILL (WB, Animation, 1999)	**Reg:** Gus (voice of Nick Jameson), gay man in his late 60's; Wally (voice of Tom Kenny), Gus's lover for 40 years
MR. BELVEDERE (ABC, Comedy, 1984-1989)	"Wesley's Friend," Wesley's friend has AIDS (1/31/86)
MOESHA (UPN, Comedy, 1996-2001)	"Labels," Hakeem's cousin Omar is gay (10/1/96)
MOMMIES, THE (NBC, Comedy, 1993-1995)	"I Got the Music in Me," Paul is worried his son Blake could be gay (11/6/93) "Mr. Mommies," Is stay-at-home dad next door gay? (3/19/94)
MONTY PYTHON'S FLYING CIRCUS (PBS, Sketch Comedy, 1974-)	**Reg:** Graham Chapman

GAY / LESBIAN / BISEXUAL / TRANSGENDER
TV EPISODE GUIDE (cont.)

MOVIE STARS (WB, Comedy, 1999-2000)	"He's Reese, He's Here, Get Used to It," Reese is a gay icon (6/18/00)
MURDER ONE (ABC, Legal Drama, 1995-1997)	**Rec:** Louis Heinsbergen (John Fleck) (1995-1996), office manager
MURPHY BROWN (CBS, Comedy, 1988-1998)	"Come Out, Come Out, Wherever You Are," Miles has a homoerotic dream (3/4/92) "The Anchorman," Jim's pub is a gay bar (2/24/94) "A Comedy of Eros," Frank's play turns into gay love story (9/30/96)
MUSCLE (WB, Comedy, 1995)	**Reg:** Bronwyn Jones (Amy Pietz), newscaster
MY SO-CALLED LIFE (ABC, Teen Drama, 1994-1995)	**Reg:** Enrique "Rickie" Vasquez (Wilson Cruz), high school student **Rec:** Mr. Kamitski (Jeff Perry), Rickie's teacher "Pilot," Angela's family meet her new friends (8/25/94) "In Dreams Begin Responsibilities," A girl has a crush on Rickie (1/26/95)
N.Y.P.D. (ABC, Police Drama, 1967-1969)	"Shakedown," Detectives uncover a homo blackmail ring (9/5/67) "Everybody Loved Him," Gay theatre producer is murdered (3/18/69)
NYPD BLUE (ABC, Police Drama, 1993-)	**Reg:** PAA John Irvin (Bill Brochtrup) (1995-1996, 1998-); Det. Adrianne Lesniak (Justine Miceli) (1994-1996); Officer Abby Sullivan (Paige Turco) (1996-1997) "Oscar, Meyer, Weiner," Gay screenwriter's Oscar statue is stolen (12/7/93) "Jumpin Jack Fleishman," Murder case involves a cross-dresser (1/18/94) "Simone Says," Lesniak's ex-boyfriend pulls gun in the squad room (11/15/94) "Don We Know Our Gay Apparel," Murder in a gay bar (1/3/95) "Dirty Socks," John Irvin is introduced (3/21/95) "The Bank Dick," John and his cop boyfriend are gay-bashed (5/16/95) "One Big Happy Family," Lesniak tells Medavoy she's a lesbian (11/7/95) "Heavin' Can Wait," Rumors spread about Lesniak (11/14/95) "Dirty Laundry," John cuts Sipowicz's hair (11/21/95) "Curt Russell," Lesniak discusses her sexuality with Russell (11/28/95) "The Nutty Confessor," Lesniak and Martinez become involved (2/20/96)

GAY/LESBIAN/BISEXUAL/TRANSGENDER
TV EPISODE GUIDE (cont.)

NYPD BLUE (cont.)	"Head Case," Gay professor murdered by disturbed student (2/27/96)
	"Auntie Maimed," Martinez breaks up with Lesniak (4/30/96)
	"Unembraceable You," Abby comes out to Medavoy (12/10/96)
	"A Wrenching Experience," Medavoy meets Abby's lover Kathy (4/15/97)
	"I Love Lucy," Transvestite Angela is murdered (4/22/97)
	"Bad Rap," Greg agrees to father Abby and Kathy's child (4/29/97)
	"Three Girls and a Baby," Kathy is shot by Abby's jealous ex-lover (10/14/97)
	"Remembrance of Humps," Transsexual is murdered (12/16/97)
	"What's Up Chuck?" John's friend, PAA Dolores, is murdered (2/16/99)
	"Raphael's Inferno," Man embezzled by transsexual girlfriend (3/2/99)
	"Voir Dire This," John is shot; Sylvia is murdered (5/18/99)
	"A Hole In Juan," Baby dies under care of transsexual (1/18/00)
	"The Man With Two Right Shoes," Gay man is castrated by a hustler (1/25/00)
	"Welcome to New York," John assists with gay love triangle case (3/21/00)
	"Writing Wrongs," John babysits for Sipowicz's son (2/13/01)
	"Thumb Enchanted Evening," Lesbian Lt. Dalto, the squad's new chief (3/27/01)
	"Flight of Fancy," Lt. Fancy gets Lt. Dalto replaced (4/3/01)
	"A Little Dad'll Do Ya," John visits dying father who rejected him (3/19/02)
NAKED TRUTH, THE (NBC, Comedy, 1995-1998)	"Women Get Plastered, Star Gets Even," Nicky and TJ pretend they're gay (1/23/97)
NANCY WALKER SHOW, THE (ABC, Comedy, 1976)	**Reg:** Terry Folson (Ken Olfson), Nancy's assistant
	"The Homecoming," Nancy's husband returns from sea, (9/30/76)
NANNY, THE (CBS, Comedy, 1993-1999)	"A Fine Friendship," Fran thinks attractive male nanny is gay (2/6/95)
	"Oh Vey, You're Gay," Mr. Sheffield's new publicist is a lesbian (10/23/95)
	"The Chatterbox," Pilot spin-off with gay hairdresser, Claude (5/15/95)

GAY/LESBIAN/BISEXUAL/TRANSGENDER
TV EPISODE GUIDE (cont.)

NASH BRIDGES (CBS, Police Drama, 1996-2001)	**Reg:** Stacy Bridges (Angela Dorhmann), Nash's sister; Pepe (Patrick Fischler) (1996-1998), office manager "Javelin-Catcher," Nash is on trail of a transvestite basher (4/19/96) "The Counterfeiters," Nash and Joe pose as gay couple (1/10/97) "Knockout," Nash discovers Stacy is dating his Nash's ex (2/7/97) "Crossfire," Nash thinks his daughter's beau is gay (1/9/98) "Cude Grace," Det. undercover at transgender beauty pageant (4/3/98) "Imposters," Nash and Joe retrieve Cher impersonator's stolen wig (10/2/98) "Girl Trouble," Joe discovers Pepe is his "cybergal" (10/17/99)
NED AND STACEY (Fox, Comedy, 1995-1997)	"The Gay Cabelleros," Ned pretends he's gay to please a client (2/19/96) "Saved By the Belvedere," Ned has secret male admirer (1/20/97)
NED BLESSING (CBS, Western, 1993)	"Oscar," Ned meets Oscar Wilde during his U.S. tour (9/8/93)
NEW YORK UNDER-COVER (Fox, Police Drama, 1994-1998)	"Without Mercy," Mercy killer on the loose at an AIDS clinic (11/21/96)
NIGHT COURT (NBC, Police Drama, 1984-1992)	"The Blizzard," Dan is trapped in an elevator with a gay man (12/6/84) "Best of Friends," Dan discovers old buddy had a sex change (11/7/85) "Passion Plundered," Dan and Harry unknowingly fall for a lesbian (12/20/89)
9 TO 5 (ABC, Comedy, 1982-1983; first-run syn. 1986-1988)	[Title Unknown] Bud discovers old girlfriend is a lesbian (5/87)
NORM (ABC, Comedy, 1999-2001)	"Norm Dates Danny's Dad," Norm thinks Danny's father is gay (4/7/99) "Norm and the Hopeless Case," Norm falls for a lesbian (11/3/00)
NORMAL, OHIO (Fox, Comedy, 2000) (original pilot title: DON'T ASK)	**Reg:** Butch Gamble (John Goodman)

GAY/LESBIAN/BISEXUAL/TRANSGENDER TV EPISODE GUIDE (cont.)

NORTHERN EXPOSURE (CBS, Comedy-Drama, 1990-1995)	**Rec:** Ron (Doug Ballard), inn owner; Erick (Ron R. Mcmanus), inn owner "Slow Dance," Ron and Erick arrive in Cicely (5/20/91) "Cicely," Story of Cicely and Roslyn, the town's founders (5/18/92) "I Feel the Earth Move," Ron and Erick tie the knot (5/2/94)
NURSES, THE (a.k.a THE DOCTORS AND THE NURSES) (CBS, Medical Drama, 1962-1965)	"Nurse is a Feminine Noun," Male nurse teased by co-workers (2/13/64)
OH GROW UP (ABC, Comedy, 1999)	**Reg:** Ford Lowell (John Ducey) **Rec:** Sal (Ed Marinaro), Hunter's boss
100 CENTRE STREET (A&E, Legal Drama, 2001-2002)	**Reg:** Judge Atallah Sims (LaTanya Richardson) (2001-) "The Bug," Judge Sims is outed by the press (3/19/01) "It's About Love," Ramon defends a young man accused of gay bashing (3/5/02)
ONCE AND AGAIN (ABC, Drama, 1999-2002)	**Reg:** Jesse Samler (Evan Rachel Wood) **Rec:** Katie (Mischa Barton) "Gay Straight-Alliance," Jessie and Katie develop crush on each other (3/11/02)
ONE LIFE TO LIVE (ABC, Soap Opera, 1968-)	**Reg:** Billy Douglas (Ryan Phillipe) (1992-1993); Jonathan Michaelson (Bruce McCarty) (1992-1993); Rick Mitchel (Joe Fiske) (1992-1993)
OPEN END [DAVID SUSSKIND SHOW] (Syn., Talk Show, 1958-1987)	"Homosexuality," Discussion on normalcy of homosexuality (2/12/67)
OPEN MIND (c. 1956-1957, Talk Show, WRCA-TV/New York)	"Introduction to the Problem of Homosexuality" (8/4/56) "Homosexuality, A Psychological Approach" (9/29/56) "Male and Female in American Culture" (1/12/57)
OWEN MARSHALL, COUNSELOR AT LAW (ABC, Legal Drama, 1971-1974)	"Words of Summer," Female athlete accused of molestation (9/14/72)
OZ (HBO, Prison Drama, 1997-)	**Reg:** Tobias Beecher (Lee Tergesen), prisoner; Chris Keller (Chris Meloni), prisoner "The Routine," Beecher arrives at Oz (7/12/97) "Strange Bedfellows," Beecher tells Sister Pete he loves Keller (8/17/98) "Escape from Oz," Schillinger and Keller beat up Beecher (8/31/98)

GAY/LESBIAN/BISEXUAL/TRANSGENDER
TV EPISODE GUIDE (Cont.)

OZ (cont.)	"A Word to the Wise," Beecher tells Father Ray he's killed gay men (8/16/01)
PAPER DOLLS (ABC, Drama, 1984)	Conrad (Jeff Richman), Hairdresser
PARTY GIRL (Fox, Comedy, 1996)	**Reg:** Derrick (John Cameron Mitchell), fashion stylist
PARTY OF FIVE (Fox, Drama, 1994-2000)	**Rec:** Ross Werkman (Mitchell Anderson) (1994-1997, 1999-2000); Victor (Wilson Cruz) (1999-2000) "Something Out of Nothing," Ross comes out to Claudia (11/7/94) "Who Cares?" Julia learns friend Danny is HIV+ (2/15/95) "Ides of March," Ross adopts a baby (3/15/95) "Poor Substitutes," Allison makes a pass at Julia (1/17/96) "I Declare," Ross dates Claudia's gay teacher (1/22/97) "What a Drag," Owen dresses up in girl's clothes (9/17/97) "Here and Now," Sarah's new boyfriend is gay (1/28/98) "I'll Show You Mine," Julia kisses her female friend Perry (5/5/99) "Haunted," Julia deals with feelings for Perry (5/12/99) "Isn't it Romantic," Ross and Victor go on a coffee date (4/11/00)
PEARL (CBS, Comedy, 1996-1997)	"The Two Mrs. Rizzos," Annie's ex-boyfriend falls for Prof. Pynchon (6/4/97)
PHYLLIS (CBS, Comedy, 1975-1977)	"Out of the Closet," Phyllis's boyfriend reveals he's gay (1/1/76)
PICKET FENCES (CBS, Drama, 1992-1996)	"Pageantry," Transsexual teacher directs Christmas pageant (12/11/92) "Sugar and Spice," Kimberly and best friend Lisa kiss (4/29/93) "Witness for the Prosecution," Pope witnesses a gay man's suicide (12/8/95) "Bye, Bye Bey Bey," Laurie's baby goes to her gay brother and his lover (4/24/96) "Three Weddings & a Meltdown," Laurie's mom sues for custody of baby (4/24/96)
P.O.V. (PBS, Documentary, 1988-)	Documentary series
POLICE STORY (NBC, Police Drama, 1973-1980)	"The Ripper," Serial killer on the loose (2/12/74)

GAY/LESBIAN/BISEXUAL/TRANSGENDER TV EPISODE GUIDE (cont.)

POLICE STORY (cont.)	"Headhunter," Police Sgt. accused of indecent acts (1/14/75) "The Malfores," Chicano gang wreaks havoc in the barrio (1/25/77)
POLICE WOMAN (NBC, Drama, 1974-1978)	"Flowers of Evil," Lesbian nursing home owners kill their patients (11/8/74) "Trial by Prejudice," Pepper is accused of molesting female prisoner (10/12/76) "Night of the Full Moon," Pepper on trail of a transvestite killer (12/28/76)
POPULAR (WB, Comedy, 1999-2001)	**Reg:** Miss Bobbi Glass (Diane Delano), science teacher; Robin John (Alley Mills), Harrison's mother; Mr. Bennett (Mitchell Anderson), teacher (2000) "Wild, Wild Mess," Harrison hides the fact that his mom is a lesbian (12/2/99) "Caged," Lily reveals she's questioned her sexuality (2/3/00) "Booty Camp," Students attend consciousness-raising boot camp (2/10/00) "C-C-Changes," Pre-op transsexual teacher is fired (4/20/00) "Fag," Lily starts a gay-straight student group (3/9/01)
PRACTICE, THE (NBC, Comedy, 1976-1977)	"Helen's Beau," Helen discovers her boyfriend is gay (10/22/76)
PRACTICE, THE (ABC, Legal Drama, 1997-)	"Betrayal," Joey Heric gets off for murder his ex-lover (9/23/97) "The Civil Right," Jimmy's Mom wants to marry her lover (12/20/97) "Another Day," Heric gets off again for murdering his lover (3/9/98) "Honorable Man," Man fires employee with AIDS (5/14/00) "We Hold These Truths," Married officer is outed during trial (11/5/00) "The Candidate Pt. 1 & 2," Senator is accused of murder (9/23/01) "The Return of Joe Heric," Now he's a lawyer (4/14/02)
PRISONER: CELL BLOCK H (Syn., Prison Drama, 1979-1986)	**Reg:** Freida "Franky" Doyle (Carol Burns) (1979), prisoner; Doreen Anderson/Burns (Colette Mann) (1979), prisoner and Franky's lover; Sharon Gilmour (Margot Knight) (1979), prisoner; Judy Bryant (Betty Bobbit) (1979-1984) Sharon's lover; Angela Jeffries (Jeanie Drynan), lawyer; Vera "Vinegar Tits" Bennett (Fiona Spence) (1979-1981), guard; Joan "The Freak" Ferguson (Maggie Kirkpatrick) (1982-1986), guard

GAY/LESBIAN/BISEXUAL/TRANSGENDER
TV EPISODE GUIDE (Cont.)

PROFILER (NBC, 1996-2000)	**Rec:** George Fraley (Peter Frechette), computer hacker
PUBLIC MORALS (CBS, Comedy, 1996)	**Reg:** John Irvin (Bill Brochtrup), administrative assistant
PURSUIT OF HAPPINESS (NBC, Comedy, 1995)	**Reg:** Alex Chosek (Brad Garrett), lawyer "Celebrations in Hell," Alex comes out to his partner Steve (9/19/95) "Wedding Dates," Steve agrees to be Alex's date (10/10/95)
QUANTUM LEAP (NBC, Science Fiction, 1989-1993)	"Good Night, Dear Heart—11/9/57," Sam investigates lesbian's murder (3/7/90) "Running for Honor—6/11/64," Homophobia in a military academy (1/15/92)
QUEER AS FOLK (Showtime, Drama, 2000-)	**Reg:** Brian Kinney (Gale Harold); Ted Schmitt (Scott Lowell); Michael Novotny (Hal Sparks); Melanie Marcus (Michelle Clunie); Justin Taylor (Randy Harrison); Lindsay Peterson (Thea Gill); Emmett Honeycutt (Peter Paige); Vic Grassi (Jack Weatherall); Dr. David Cameron (Chris Potter) (2000-2001)
QUEER DUCK (Showtime, Animation, 2000-)	
REAL WORLD (MTV, Reality, 1992-)	**Reg:** Norman Korpi (New York, 1992); Beth Anthony (Los Angeles, 1993); Pedro Zamora (San Francisco, 1994); Dan Renzi (Miami, 1996); Genesis Moss (Boston, 1997); Ruthie Alcaide (Hawaii, 1999); Justin Deabler (Hawaii, 1999); Jason Daniel "Danny" Roberts (New Orleans, 2000); Aneesa (Chicago, 2002); Chris Beckmann III (Chicago, 2002) **Rec:** Sean Sasser, Pedro's lover (San Francisco, 1994); Arnie, Dan's boyfriend (Miami, 1996); Johnny, Dan's boyfriend (Miami, 1996); Paul, Danny's boyfriend (New Orleans, 2000); Veronica, Aneesa's girlfriend (Chicago, 2002); Kurt, Chris' boyfriend (Chicago, 2002)
RELATIVITY (ABC, Drama, 1996-1997)	**Reg:** Rhonda Roth (Lisa Edelstein) **Rec:** Suzanne (Kristin Dattilo) "Just One More Thing," Rhonda and her girlfriend break up (9/28/96) "The Day the Earth Move," Rhonda meets Suzanne (1/11/97)
RESURRECTION BLVD (Showtime, Drama, 2000-)	"Saliendo," Tommy arrives home with lover and comes out to family (10/9/01)

295

GAY/LESBIAN/BISEXUAL/TRANSGENDER
TV EPISODE GUIDE (cont.)

ROAD RULES (MTV, Reality, 1994-)	**Reg:** Sophia Pasquis ("The Quest, Season 10)
ROC (Fox, Comdy, 1991-1994)	"Can't Help Lovin That Man," Russell marries a white man (10/19/91) "Brothers," Russell moves to Paris (4/5/94)
ROCKFORD FILES, THE (NBC, Detective Drama, 1974-1980)	"The Empty Frame," Gay art collector is betrayed by lover (11/17/98)
ROOM 222 (ABC, Drama, 1969-1974)	"What is a Man?" Creative student's masculinity is questioned (3/14/71)
ROSEANNE (ABC, Comedy, 1988-1997)	**Rec:** Beverly Harris (Estelle Harris) (1989-1997), Roseanne's mother; Nancy Bartlett (Sandra Bernhard) (1991-1997), Roseanne's bisexual friend; Leon Carp (Martin Mull) (1991-1997), Roseanne's boss; Scott (Fred Willard) (1995-1997), Leon's lover; Joyce Levine (1997), Bev's lover "Trick or Treat," Roseanne is mistaken for a man on Halloween (10/30/90) "Ladies' Choice," Nancy comes out (11/10/92) "Don't Ask, Don't Tell," Roseanne gets a kiss from Mariel Hemingway (3/1/94) "Skeleton in the Closet," Roseanne is made to believe Fred is gay (10/26/94) "December Bride," Leon and Scott wed (12/12/95) "Home is Where the Afghan Is," Bev comes out (11/26/96)
ROSIE O'DONNELL SHOW, THE (Syndicated, Talk, 1996-2002)	**Reg:** Rosie O'Donnell, host
ROWAN & MARTIN'S LAUGH-IN (NBC, Comedy/Variety, 1968-1973)	
RUDE AWAKENING (Showtime, Comedy-Drama, 1998-2000)	**Rec:** Jackie (Rain Pryor) (1998-1999), Billie's AA friend; Clark (Jack Plotnick) (1999-2000), Billie's AA sponsor
RuPAUL SHOW, THE (VH-1, Talk, 1996-1998)	**Reg:** RuPaul
SANFORD AND SON (NBC, Comedy, 1972-1977)	"The Piano Movers," Fred and Lamont move a piano from a gay man's apartment (4/14/72) "Lamont...is that You?" Fred and Lamont mistake each other for gay (10/19/73)

GAY/LESBIAN/BISEXUAL/TRANSGENDER
TV EPISODE GUIDE (cont.)

SANFORD ARMS (NBC, Comedy, 1977)	"Phil's Assertion School," White man befriends gay black attorney (9/22/77)
SANTA BARBARA (NBC, Soap Opera, 1984-1993)	**Rec:** Channing Capwell, Jr. (Robert Wilson) (1984-1985)
SARA (NBC, Comedy, 1985)	**Reg:** Dennis Kemper (Bronson Pinchot), lawyer
SATURDAY NIGHT LIVE (NBC, Variety, 1975-)	**Reg:** Terry Sweeny (1985-1986) **Rec:** Ace and Gary, the Ambiguously Gay Duo
SAY UNCLE (CBS, unaired sitcom pilot, 2001)	Ken Olin as gay man who adopts his late sister's two children
SECOND CITY TELEVISION (HBO/CBS, 1977-1981)	
SECRET LIVES OF MEN, THE (ABC, Comedy, 1998)	"Dating is Hell," Michael wonders if a gay client has a crush on him (10/21/98)
SEINFELD (NBC, Comedy, 1990-1998)	"The Subway," "Best man" Elaine en route to lesbian wedding (1/8/92) "The Cheever Letters," George finds love letters to Susan's dad (10/28/92) "The Outing," Jerry and George are outed by college reporter (2/11/93) "The Smelly Car," George discovers Susan is dating a woman (4/15/93) "The Beard," Elaine falls for a gay man (2/9/95) "The Sponge," Kramer refuses to wear red ribbon at AIDS Walk (12/7/95) "The Wig Master," Wig master for touring musical stays with George (4/4/96)
SEX AND THE CITY (HBO, Comedy, 1998-)	**Rec:** Stanford Blatch (Willie Garson) "Bay of Married Pigs," Miranda is mistaken for a lesbian (6/21/98) "Three's a Crowd," Samantha and Charlotte gets *ménage* offers (6/26/98) "The Turtle and the Hare," Carrie poses as Stanford's beard (8/2/98) "Old Dogs, New Dicks," Samantha's ex models drag persona after her (8/1/99) "Evolution," Charlotte wonders if new beau is gay (8/15/99) "Cock-a-doodle-do," Tranny prostitutes keep Samantha awake (10/15/00)

GAY / LESBIAN / BISEXUAL / TRANSGENDER TV EPISODE GUIDE (cont.)

SEX AND THE CITY (cont.)	"The Real Me," Carrie models in a fashion show (6/3/01) "Defining Moments," Samantha's fling with a lesbian artist (6/10/01) "All That Glitters," Carrie befriends gay man; Miranda outs co-worker (1/13/02)
SHOWCASE (1958-1959?)	(No title) Fannie Hurst hosts discussion on male homosexuality (3/10/58) (No title) Hurst is forced to cancel lesbian discussion (3/11/58) (No title) Introductory discussion of homosexuality (4/21/59) "Problems of the Teenager Who Doesn't Fit," Homosexuality in the home (4/28/59) (No title) Psychological and sociological factors related to homosexuality (5/1/59)
SIGNIFICANT OTHERS (Fox, Drama, 1998)	**Rec:** (?) Josh (Dan Bucatinsky) "The Next Big Thing," Nell, Henry and Campbell attend Josh's birthday party (3/18/88)
SILK STALKINGS (CBS/USA, Detective, CBS/1991-1992, USA/1991-1999)	"The Scarlet Shadow," Rita is accused of being a lesbian (2/13/94) "Compulsion," Wealthy gay couple are murdered (9/22/96) "Pumped Up," Bisexual health club owner is murdered (2/2/97)
THE SIMPSONS (Fox, Animation, 1989-)	**Rec:** Waylon Smithers (voice of Harry Shearer), Mr. Burns' assistant "Simpson and Delilah," Harvey Fierstein as Homer's male secretary (2/16/97) "Homer's Phobia," Homer worries Bart is gay
THE SINGLE GUY (NBC, Comedy, 1995-1997)	"Neighbors," Johnny's gay neighbors thinks he's gay (11/1/95)
SIROTA'S COURT (NBC, Comedy, 1976-1977)	"Court Fear," Sirota marries a male couple (c.1976-1977)
SISTERS (NBC, Drama, 1991-1996)	**Rec:** Norma Lear (Nora Dunn) (1993-1996) "Something in Common," Alex finds out Norma is a lesbian (11/6/93) "Life Upside Down," Norma comes out to her parents (5/7/94) "Deceit," Norma gives birth (10/28/95) "A Sudden Change of Heart," Reed befriends dying drag queen with AIDS (1/6/96)

GAY/LESBIAN/BISEXUAL/TRANSGENDER
TV EPISODE GUIDE (cont.)

SIX FEET UNDER (HBO, Drama, 2001-)	**Reg:** David (Michael C. Hall), funeral director; Keith Charles (Mathew St. Patrick), LAPD Officer **Rec:** Robbie (Joel Brooks), flower arranger "Familia," Dead Latino helps David confront his fears (6/24/01) "A Private Life," David confronts his self-hatred about being gay (8/19/01)
SNOOPS (ABC, Detective Drama, 1999)	"Constitution," Man suspected of being gay is a gay basher (11/21/99)
SOAP (ABC, Comedy, 1977-1981)	**Reg:** Jodie Dallas (Billy Crystal); Dennis Phillips (Bob Seagren) (1978); Alice (Randee Heller) (1979)
SOME OF MY BEST FRIENDS (ABC, Comedy, 2001)	**Reg:** Warren Fairbanks (Jason Bateman); Vern Limoso (Alec Mappa)
SON OF A BEACH (FX, Comedy, 2000-)	**Rec:** Kody C. Massengil (Jason Hopkins), the mayor's gay son "B.J. Blue Hawaii," Mayor comes on to Chip, who pretends he's gay (3/13/01) "Grand Prix," B.J. and Jamaica prevent a lesbian bar from closing (7/3/01)
SOUL FOOD (Showtime, Drama, 2000-)	"Little Girl Blue," Kenny objects to son's friendship with gay man (1/17/01)
SOUTH PARK (COMEDY CENTRAL, Animation, 1997-)	**Reg:** Mr. Garrison (voice of Trey Parker), ambiguously gay teacher; Big Gay Al (voice of Matthew Stone) "Big Gay Al's Big Gay Boat Ride," Stan wants his dog to go straight (9/3/97) "Tom's Rhinoplasty," Mr. Garrison gets a nose job; Chef thinks the substitute teacher is a lesbian, (2/11/98) "Two Guys Naked in a Hot Tub," Kyle and Stan's dads masturbate together (7/21/99) "Cartman Joins NAMBLA," NAMBLA recruits Eric as their poster child (6/21/00)
SPIN CITY (ABC, Comedy, 1996-)	**Reg:** Carter (Michael Boatman), Director of Minority Affairs "Pilot," Mayor makes offensive remark about gay people (9/17/96) "Pride and Prejudice," Carter pushes a needle exchange program (10/8/96) "Grand Illusion," Carter challenges Mayor on same-sex marriage issue (10/29/96) "Starting Over" Carter and Stuart wake up in bed together (1/14/97) "In the Heat of the Day," Police mistake Carter for a mugger (10/22/97)

GAY/LESBIAN/BISEXUAL/TRANSGENDER
TV EPISODE GUIDE (cont.)

SPIN CITY (cont.)	"The Thirty Year Itch," Mayor's nephew pretends he's gay (11/5/97) "My Life is a Soap Opera," Stuart pretends he's gay to date women (11/12/97) "Single White Male," Stuart moves in with Carter (5/6/98) "Carter & Stuart & Bennett & Deidre," Guys befriend the other's exes (4/13/99) "These Shoes Were Made for Cheatin'," Stuart joins gay gym (10/12/99) "The Marry Caitlin Moore Show," Stuart convinces James he's gay (2/9/00)
ST. ELSEWHERE (NBC, Medical Drama, 1982-1988)	**Rec:** Brett Johnston (Kyle Secor); Kevin O'Casey (John Scott Clough) "Release," Dr. Craig's friend checks in for a sex change (2/1/83) "AIDS and Comfort," Closeted married city councilman with AIDS (12/21/83) "Girls Just Wanna Have Fun," Lesbian doctor visits hospital (11/28/84) "Family Feud," Dr. Caldwell is diagnosed with AIDS (1/29/86) "Cheek to Cheek," Dr. Morrison is raped in prison (3/12/86) "A Moon for the Misbegotten," Westphal proposes AIDS clinic (9/30/87) "Night of the Living Bed," Dr. Greenwood is exposed it AIDS (10/28/87) "Heart On," Brett and Kevin are gay-bashed (11/18/87) "Heaven's Skate," Dr. Caldwell's memorial service (1/13/88) "Requiem for a Heavyweight," Greenwood offers Brett spiritual advice (5/4/88) "Split Decision," Brett dies (5/11/88)
STARSKY AND HUTCH (ABC, Police Drama, 1975-1979)	"Tap Dancing Her Way Right Back Into Your Hearts," Duo are dancers (11/20/76) "Death in a Different Place," Closeted gay detective is murdered (10/15/77) "Dandruff," Duo go undercover as hairdressers (11/14/78)
STAR TREK: DEEP SPACE NINE (First Run, Syn., Science Fiction, 1992-1999)	"Rejoined," Forbidden love between Dax and a Trill (10/28/95)

GAY/LESBIAN/BISEXUAL/TRANSGENDER
TV EPISODE GUIDE (cont.)

STAR TREK: THE NEXT GENERATION (First Run Syn., Science Fiction, 1987-1994)	"The Host," Dr. Crusher's forbidden love with a Trill (4/13/91) "The Outcast," Androgynous Soren has female tendencies (3/16/92)
STEAMBATH (Showtime, Comedy, 1984-1985)	
STREET JUSTICE (First Run Syn., Police Drama, 1991-1993)	"Bashing," Malloy's gay brother dies from gay-bashing (11/30/91)
STREETS OF SAN FRANCISCO, THE (ABC, Police Drama, 1972-1977)	"Mask of Death," Psychotic female impersonator (10/3/74) "A Good Cop, But..." Gay detective is forced to come out (1/20/77) "Once a Con..." Lesbian kills lover's best friend (3/3/77)
STRIP MALL (Comedy Central, Comedy, 2000-2001)	**Reg:** Fanny Sue Chang (Amy Hill), Chinese restaurant owner; Althea (Loretta Fox), Fanny's lover; Blair (Bob Koherr), Gay triplet
STRONG MEDICINE (Lifetime, Medical Drama, 2000-)	"Misconceptions," Closeted lesbian TV host wants to get pregnant (8/6/00) "Second Look," Transvestite is menopausal (8/13/00) "Donors," Peter's mother thinks he's gay (8/15/01)
STYLE AND SUB-STANCE (ABC, Comedy, 1998)	**Reg:** Mr. John (Joseph Maher), gay interior designer
SUDDENLY SUSAN (NBC, Comedy, 1996-2000)	**Rec:** Pete Mulligan Fontaine (Bill Stevenson) (1996-1999) Hank (Fred Stoller) (1997-1999) "A Boy Like That," Luis' brother Carlos comes out (4/24/97) "Past Tense," Todd cyberchats in a lesbian chat room (9/29/97) "Oh How They Danced," Vicki & Ben and Hank & Pete's double wedding (5/18/98)
SURVIVOR (CBS, Reality, 2000-)	**Reg:** Richard Hatch (2000-2001); Brandon Quinton (2001); John Carroll (2002)
TALK TO ME (ABC, Comedy, 2000)	"About Being Gay," Janey pretends she's a lesbian (4/11/00)
TAXI (ABC, Comedy, 1978-1983)	"Elaine's Strange Triangle," Elaine's boyfriend likes Tony (12/10/80) "The Unkindest Cut," Hairstylist gives Elaine bad haircut (2/25/82)

GAY/LESBIAN/BISEXUAL/TRANSGENDER
TV EPISODE GUIDE (cont.)

TELETUBBIES (PBS, Children's, 1997-)	**Reg:** Tinky-Winky
TEMPORARILY YOURS (ABC, Comedy, 1997)	"Temp-tation," Deb thinks a romance novelist is coming on to her (3/12/97)
THAT 70's SHOW (Fox, Comedy, 1998)	"Eric's Buddy," Eric's new friend makes a pass at him (12/6/98)
THAT 80's SHOW (Fox, Comedy, 2002-)	**Reg:** Sophia (Brittany Daniel), Corey's bisexual ex-girlfriend "That 80's Pilot" Sophia comes on to Corey's sister Katie (3/20/02)
THEN CAME YOU (ABC, Comedy, 2000)	"Then Came a Wedding," Cheryl pretends she's gay (4/5/00)
THIRD ROCK FROM THE SUN (NBC, comedy, 1996-2001)	"World's Greatest Dick," Sally is mistaken for a drag queen (11/10/96) "The Loud Solomon Family: A Dickumentary," Sally pretends she's gay (1/11/00) "Frankie Goes to Rutherford," Dick thinks Mary's gay friend is an alien (5/9/00)
THIRD WATCH, THE (NBC, 1999-)	"32 Bullets and a Broken Heart," Gun man opens fire at gay wedding (2/14/00)
thirtysomething (ABC, Drama, 1987-1991)	**Rec:** Russell (David Marshall Grant); Peter Montefiore (Peter Frechette) "Trust Me," Melissa meets Russell (1/3/89) "Strangers," Russell and Peter go on a date (11/7/89) "Closing the Circle," Peter discovers he's HIV positive (4/16/91)
THIS IS THE LIFE (Syn., Anthology, 1974)	"The Secret," Teacher at a boy's school comes out (c. 1974)
THREE'S COMPANY (ABC, Comedy, 1977-1984)	"A Man About the House," Jack moves in with Janet and Chrissy (3/15/77) "Roper's Niece," Roper fixes "gay" Jack up with his niece (3/31/77) "Strange Bedfellows," Roper and Jack wake up in bed together, (10/4/77)
TITUS (Fox, Comedy, 2000-)	**Rec:** Amy (Rachel Roth) (2000-) "Sex with Pudding," Erin's female boss has a crush on her (3/20/00) "The Test," Titus and Erin both take an HIV test, (10/10/00) "Tommy's Not Gay," Tommy's dad comes out, (11/28/01)

GAY/LESBIAN/BISEXUAL/TRANSGENDER
TV EPISODE GUIDE (Cont.)

TITUS (cont.)	"Err," Erin's niece Amy is a lesbian (1/16/02)
TOO CLOSE FOR COMFORT (ABC, Comedy,	"Shipmates," Henry's old navy commander is gay (6/2/84)
TOTAL SECURITY (ABC, Detective Drama, 1997)	**Reg:** George LaSalle (Bill Brochtrup), office manager
TOUCHED BY AN ANGEL (CBS, Drama, 1994-)	"The Violin Lesson," Angels help a gay man with AIDS (12/22/96)
TRACEY TAKES ON (HBO, Comedy, 1996-)	**Rec:** Trevor Aryliss (Tracey Ullman), flight attendant; Midge Dexter (Julie Kavner), professional golfer; Chris Warner (Tracey Ullman), Midge's life companion
TRACEY ULLMAN SHOW, THE (HBO, Comedy/Variety, 1987-1990)	**Rec:** David (Dan Castellaneta), 14-year-old Francesca's gay dad; William (Sam McMurray), David's partner and Francesca's gay dad
TRAPPER JOHN, M.D. (CBS, Medical Drama, 1979-1986)	"Straight and Narrow," San Francisco's first openly gay cop is shot (1/11/81) "Friends and Lovers," Nurse Libby's ex-beau is diagnosed with AIDS (12/22/96)
TRINITY (NBC, Drama, 1998-1999)	"Pilot," A married friend of Father Kevin's comes out (10/16/98)
TURNING POINT (ABC, News, 1994-1997)	Report on same-sex marriages (11/7/96)
20/20 (ABC, News, 1978-)	Profile of lesbian teen who was institutionalized in Utah hospital (9/27/96) Profile of expectant parents Melissa Etheridge and Julie Cypher (11/1/96) Profile of lesbian writer in committed relationship with man (4/24/98) Segment on surrogacy and parenting for same-sex couples (3/5/99) Segment on the brutal murder of Billy Jack Gaither (3/9/99) "True, Blue, and Unwanted," Segment on gay and lesbian police officers (4/20/99) "Throwaway Teens," Story of homeless gay and lesbian teenagers (9/99) "Desperate to Change" Controversy surrounding reparative therapy (4/31/00) "Act I: Her Secret Life," Profile of Brandon Teena (2/00)

GAY/LESBIAN/BISEXUAL/TRANSGENDER TV EPISODE GUIDE (cont.)

21 JUMP STREET (Fox, Police drama, 1987-1990; first-run syn. 1990-1991)	"Honor Bound," Homophobia in military school (11/8/87) "A Big Disease with a Little Name," High school student with AIDS (2/7/88) "Change of Heart," Lesbian teacher is murdered (1/15/90)
THE TWILIGHT ZONE (1985-1986, 1987, 1987-1988)	"Dead Run," Gay man is among the undesirables transported to hell (2/21/86)
TWIN PEAKS (1990-1991)	**Reg:** D.E.A. Agent Dennis/Denise Bryson (David Duchovny)
2GETHER (MTV, Comedy, 2000-2001)	**Rec:** Tom Lawless (Dave R. McGowan) "Waxed" Jerry is jealous Mickey has gay fan base (10/30/00)
UNDRESSED (MTV, Comedy, 1999-2001)	"The Porn that Went Bump in the Night," Andy (Nicholas Gonzalez) finds Joe's (Eyal Podell) straight porn and has an intervention with friends Paul (Brandon Karrar) and Jonathan (Phillip Rhys). (1999-2000) "He Ain't Gay, He's My Brother," Andy and Joe pretend their straight when Joe's brother and navy pal come to visit (1999-2000) "Bi-gones," Jonathan and lesbian friend take their green card marriage seriously (1999-2000)
UNHAPPILY EVER AFTER (UPN, Comedy, 1995-1999)	**Rec:** Barry Wallenstein (Ant) (1995-1999)
UNION SQUARE (NBC, Comedy, 1997-1998)	"Michael's First Stand," Gabriella makes date with crossdresser (10/30/97)
UPSTAIRS, DOWN-STAIRS (PBS, Drama, 1974)	"A Suitable Marriage," Richard discovers Baron von Rimmer is gay (U.K. 1971) "Rose's Pigeon," Bellamy's ex-footman murders his ex-lover (12/1/74)
VEGA$ (ABC, Detective, 1978-1981)	"The Man Who Was Twice," Female impersonator is being stalked (3/12/80)
VERONICA'S CLOSET (NBC, Comedy, 1997-2000)	**Reg:** Josh (Wallace Langham), Veronica's assistant **Rec:** Brian (Alan F. Smith) (2000), Josh's lover "Veronica's Christmas Song," Bryce befriends Josh (12/18/97) "Veronica's Got a Secret," Leo crashes at Josh's apartment (1/8/98) "Veronica's Great Model Search," Josh's friend comes out (10/8/98)

GAY/LESBIAN/BISEXUAL/TRANSGENDER
TV EPISODE GUIDE (cont.)

VERONICA'S CLOSET (cont.)	"Veronica's Girls' Night Out," Josh makes out with his best man (6/13/00) "Veronica Helps Josh Out," On his wedding day, Josh comes out (6/20/00)
WASTELAND (ABC, Drama, 1999/Showtime, 2001)	**Reg:** Russell Baskind (Dan Montgomery, Jr.) **Rec:** Steve (Michael Diet); Cliff (Frank Grillo)
WATCH YOUR MOUTH (PBS/WNET-TV (NY), Drama, 1978)	[Title Unknown] Episode involving a gay teacher (9/10/78)
WEBER SHOW, THE (a.k.a. CURSED) (Comedy, NBC, 2000-2001)	"And then Larry brought Charlton Heston Home," Jack meets Katie (12/14/00) "...Wendell Wore Candy Stripes," "Lesbian" Katie tails guys to gay bar (1/4/01) "And Then Jack Found Out," Jack discovers Katie is pretending to be gay (1/18/01)
WELCOME TO PARA-DOX (Sci-Fi Channel, Science Fiction, 1998)	"Options," Procedure allows men and women to change gender at will (10/26/98)
WESTSIDE HOSPITAL (Medical, ABC, 1977)	"The Mermaid," East German teen swimmer is a transsexual (7/7/77)
WEST WING, THE (Drama, NBC, 1999-)	"In Excelsis Deo," Gay high school student is beaten to death (12/15/99) "Take Out the Trash Day," Father of gay victim is embarrassed by President's lack of action on hate crime bill (1/26/00) "The Portland Trip," Gay congressman opposes same-sex marriage (11/15/00) "24 Hours in LA," Studio head discusses ban on gays in military (2/23/00)
WHITE SHADOW, THE (Drama, CBS, 1978-1981)	"One of the Boys," Transfer student can't escape gay rumors (1/27/99)
WILD, WILD WEST (Western, CBS, 1965-1969)	"Night of the Running Death," Female impersonator killer (12/15/67)
WILL & GRACE (Comedy, NBC, 1998-)	**Reg:** Will Truman (Eric McCormack); John "Jack" Phillip McFarland (Sean Hayes) **Rec:** Larry (Tim Bagley) (2000-), Will and Grace's friend; Joe (Jerry Levine) (2000-), Larry's lover "Will Works Out," Will is embarrassed by Jack (4/22/99)

GAY / LESBIAN / BISEXUAL / TRANSGENDER
TV EPISODE GUIDE (cont.)

WINGS (NBC, Comedy, 1990-1997)	"There's Always Room for Cello," Roy's son A.J. comes out (2/14/90) "Honey, We Broke the Kid," Antonio's TV idol visits the island (1/2/96) "Sons and Lovers," A.J. returns home with his lover (1/16/96) "Escape From New York," Helen enters drag contest (2/19/97)
WKRP IN CINCINNATI (CBS, Comedy, 1978-1982)	"Les on the Ledge," Les panics when he's mistaken for gay (10/2/78) "Hotel Oceanview," Herb unknowingly romances a transsexual (11/29/80)
WORKING (NBC, Comedy, 1997-1999)	"Rumoring," Matt's co-workers tell his boss he's gay (10/29/97)
YOUNG AMERICANS (WB, Teen Drama, 2000)	**Reg:** Jacqueline/Jake Pratt (Katherine Moenning) "Pilot," Hamilton questions if he's gay after kissing "Jake" (7/12/00) "Our Town," Hamilton finds himself attracted to "Jake" (7/19/00) "Cinderbella," Jake reveals her true identity to Hamilton (8/2/00)
YOUNG AND THE RESTLESS (CBS, Soap Opera, 1973-)	**Reg:** Kay Chancellor (Jeanne Cooper) (1973-); Joann Curtis (Key Heberle) (1975-1978)

MADE-FOR-TV MOVIES, MINI-SERIES, AND SPECIALS

ALEXANDER: THE OTHER SIDE OF DAWN (NBC, 5/16/77)
Bi hustler straightens out his life

ANATOMY OF A HATE CRIME (MTV, 1/20/01)
TV film about Matthew Shepherd murder and trial

ANDRE'S MOTHER (PBS, 3/7/90)*
Gay man and his late lover's mother reconcile

AND THE BAND PLAYED ON (HBO, 9/11/93)*
AIDS crisis and search for HIV virus

ANY MOTHER'S SON (Lifetime, 8/11/97)
TV-movie of sailor Allen Schindler's murder

APPLAUSE (CBS, 3/15/73)
TV version of Broadway musical, includes gay nightclub scene

AS IS (Showtime, 7/27/86)*
TV adaptation of William Hoffman's AIDS play

BARE ESSENCE (NBC, 10/4-10/5/1982)
Mini-series set in perfume industry

* available on video and/or DVD

GAY/LESBIAN/BISEXUAL/TRANSGENDER
TV EPISODE GUIDE (cont.)

BASTARD OUT OF CAROLINA
(Showtime, 12/15/96)*
Young girl abused by her stepfather

BLIND FAITH (Showtime, 1998)*
Gay black man accused of murder

BORN INNOCENT (NBC, 9/10/74)
Teenage Linda Blair in juvenile detention

BREAKING THE CODE (PBS, 2/2/97)*
Derek Jacobi as Nazi Code breaker Alan
Turing

BREAKING THE SURFACE (USA,
3/19/97)*
TV-movie about Olympic diver Greg
Louganis

BRIDESHEAD REVISITED (PBS, 1/18-
3/29/82)*
British TV version of Evelyn Waugh's
novel

BUMP IN THE NIGHT, A (CBS, 1/6/91)
Christopher Reeve as a gay pedophile

CAGE WITHOUT A KEY (CBS, 3/14/75)
Lesbian predator in girl's detention center

CELEBRITY (NBC, 2/12-2/14/84)*
Mini-series includes murder of closeted
movie star

CHANGE OF HEART (Lifetime, 7/20/98)
TV-movie about man who dumps wife
for a man

CHASING THE DRAGON (Lifetime,
6/19/96)
Housewife heroin addict has a gay pal

CITIZEN COHN (HBO, 8/22/92)*
Biopic of infamous closeted lawyer

COMMON GROUND (Showtime,
1/29/00)*
Three stories about gays and lesbians in
small town

CONSENTING ADULT (ABC, 2/4/85)*
College student comes out to
homophobic parents

DAWN: PORTRAIT OF A TEEN
RUNAWAY (NBC, 8/27/76)
Dawn loves bisexual hustler Alex

DIRTY PICTURES (Showtime, 5/27/00)*
Cincinnati museum director charged
with obscenity

DOING TIME ON MAPLE DRIVE (Fox,
3/16/92)*
Gay man comes out to dysfunctional
family

DYNASTY: THE REUNION (ABC,
10/20-22/91)
Finale to long-running series

EARLY FROST, AN (NBC, 11/11/85)*
Family copes with gay son with AIDS

ELLIS ISLAND (CBS, 11/11,13,14/83)
A teenage girl and a lesbian art dealer in
love

ENGLISHMAN ABROAD, AN (PBS,
1988)
Coral Brown and Guy Burgess in
Moscow

EXECUTION OF JUSTICE (Showtime,
11/28/99)*
Bio of Dan White, who killed Harvey
Milk

FAMILY BUSINESS (PBS, 2/1/83)
Wealthy dying man makes amends to
his sons

FIFTH OF JULY (Showtime, 10/14/82)*
TV version of Lanford Wilson play

FURTHER TALES OF THE CITY
(Showtime, 5/6/01)
Maupin's San Francisco chronicles
continue

GAY/LESBIAN/BISEXUAL/TRANSGENDER TV EPISODE GUIDE (cont.)

FINAL JUSTICE (Lifetime, 6/1/98)
Woman kidnaps attorney who defends gay bro's killer

GIA (HBO, 1/31/98)*
Biopic of super model Gia Maria Carangi

GIRL THING, A (Showtime, 1/30/01)*
N.Y. therapist's patients includes lesbian lawyer

GLASS HOUSE, THE (CBS, 2/4/72)
Truman Capote co-wrote story of male prison life

GLIMPSE OF HELL, A (F/X, 3/18/01)
Navy tries to blame navy tragedy on gay couple

GLITTER DOME, THE (HBO, 1/18/84)
Mystery with Colleen Dewhurst as lesbian film editor

HOLIDAY HEART (Showtime, 12/10/00)
Drag queen cares for drug addict and her daughter

IF THESE WALLS COULD TALK 2 (HBO, 3/5/00)*
Trilogy looks at lesbian life in three decades

INMATES: A LOVE STORY (ABC, 2/13/81)
Prison drama with lesbian inmate couple

IN THE GLITTER PLACE (NBC, 2/27/77)
TV movies about lesbians, blackmail, and murder

IN THE GLOAMING (HBO, 4/3/97)*
Young man with AIDS comes home to die

IS IT FALL YET? (MTV. 8/27/00)*
Animated Daria TV-movie set at camp

JACQUELINE SUSANN'S VALLEY OF THE DOLLS (CBS, 10/19-10/21/1981)
Mini-series remake

JAMES DEAN (NBC, 2/19/76)
Dean's friendship with William Bast

JAMES DEAN (TNT, 8/4/01)*
Dean's career and relationship with father

JUDGMENT (HBO, 10/13/90)*
Cable film about altar boy molested by priest

LABOR OF LOVE (Lifetime, 5/4/98)
Gay man fathers single mom's child

LARAMIE PROJECT, THE (HBO, 3/9/02)
Effects of Matthew Shephard's murder on town

LIBERACE (ABC, 10/2/88)
Biopic starring Andrew Robinson as Liberace

LIBERACE: BEHIND THE MUSIC (CBS, 10/9/88)
Biopic starring Victor Garber

LOSING CHASE (Showtime, 11/29/96)*
Troubled woman forms bond with mother's helper

LOST LANGUAGE OF THE CRANES (PBS, 6/24/92)*
Young man's coming out

MARILYN: THE UNTOLD STORY (ABC, 9/28/80)
Star's bond with Natasha Lytess

MATTHEW SHEPHARD STORY, THE (NBC, 3/16/01)
TV-film chronicles Shephard's life

MORE TALES OF THE CITY (Showtime, 6/7/98)*
Maupin's look at San Francisco life continues

MORE THAN FRIENDS: COMING OUT OF HEIDI LEITER (HBO, 1/24/94)
Lesbian teenager

GAY/LESBIAN/BISEXUAL/TRANSGENDER
TV EPISODE GUIDE (cont.)

MY TWO LOVES (ABC, 4/7/86)
Bisexual widow falls in love with a woman

NAKED CIVIL SERVANT (PBS, 6/15/79)*
The life story of Quentin Crisp

NIGHT SINS (CBS, 2/23,25/97)
Small town mystery includes closeted gay couple

NO EXIT (PBS, 2/27/61)
TV version of Jean-Paul Sartre's play

ORANGES ARE NOT THE ONLY FRUIT (A&E, 1990)*
Lesbian teen raised in religious town

OTHER MOTHERS (CBS, 10/12/93)
Afterschool special about teen with two moms

OVERKILL: THE AILEEN WUOURNOS STORY (CBS, 11/17/92)
Jean Smart as lesbian killer

OUR SONS (ABC, 5/19/91)
Gay man with AIDS is reunited with his mother

PAPER DOLLS (ABC, 5/24/82)
TV-movie set in fashion model industry

PORTRAIT OF A MARRIAGE (PBS, 7/19-26/92, 8/2/92)
British drama, gay content cut for U.S.

PRICE OF LOVE (Fox, 1997)
Homeless teenager turns to hustling for survival

PRIME SUSPECT 3: INNER CIRCLES (PBS, 1994)
Male prostitute is murdered

QUESTION OF ATTRIBUTION (PBS, 10/4/92)*
Sir Anthony Blunt and Burgess spy scandal

QUESTION OF LOVE, A (ABC, 11/26/78)*
Lesbian fights to gain custody of her children

ROCK HUDSON (ABC, 1/8/80)
Biopic of closeted movie star's life

ROOMMATES (NBC, 5/30/94)
Gay and straight male roommates with AIDS

RYAN WHITE STORY, THE (ABC, 1/16/89)
Inspiring telefilm of youth with AIDS

SCREAM, PRETTY PEGGY (ABC, 11/24/73)
Ted Besell as transvestite-killer

SCRUPLES (CBS, 2/25, 26, 28/80)*
Judith Krantz bestseller

SECOND SERVE (5/13/86)
Bio of transsexual Dr. Renee Richards

SECRETS (CBS, 5/15/68)*
Woman kills her son, a gay drug addict

SERGEANT MATLOVICH vs. U.S. AIR FORCE (NBC, 8/21/78)
Gay man sues Air Force

SERVING IN SILENCE: MARGARETHE CAMMERMEYER VS. U.S. ARMY (2/6/95)

SHADOW BOX, THE (ABC, 12/28/80)*
Dying gay man reunited with ex-wife

SIDNEY SHORR: A GIRL'S BEST FRIEND (NBC, 10/5/81)
Gay man befriends single mom

SINS (CBS, 2/2-2/4/86)*
Mini-series with Joan Collins as publishing empire mogul

SISSY DUCKLING, THE (HBO, 9/21/99)
Harvey Fierstein updates children's story

GAY/LESBIAN/BISEXUAL/TRANSGENDER
TV EPISODE GUIDE (cont.)

SOMETHING TO LIVE FOR (ABC, 3/29/92)
Teen Alison Gertz's battle with AIDS

STRANGER INSIDE (HBO, 7/23/01)
Mother and daughter are reunited in prison

STEAMBATH (PBS, 4/30/73)
God is a steambath attendant

TALES OF THE CITY (PBS, 1/10-1/12/94)*
Mini-series of Maupin's novel

THAT CERTAIN SUMMER (ABC, 11/1/72)
Teenager discovers his dad is gay

TIDY ENDINGS (HBO, 1988)
Gay man reconciles with late lover's wife

TRACKDOWN: FINDING THE GOODBAR KILLER (CBS, 10/15/83)
Gay man who killed females

TRU (PBS, 11/23/92)
Robert Morse as gay writer Truman Capote

TRUTH ABOUT ALEX, THE (HBO, 1986)
Gay high school student athlete comes out

TRUTH ABOUT JANE, THE (Lifetime, 8/7/00)*
High school lesbian comes out

TWILIGHT OF THE GOLDS (Showtime, 3/7/97)
Woman learns her unborn child is gay

WAR WIDOW, THE (PBS, 10/28/76)
Woman falls in love with female photographer

WELCOME HOME, BOBBY (CBS, 2/22/86)
TV movie about sexually confused teen

WHAT IF I'M GAY? (CBS, 3/31/87)
Afterschool special about coming out of gay jock

WOMEN OF BREWSTER PLACE (ABC, 3/19/89)*
Mini-series includes black lesbian couple

WOMEN'S ROOM, THE (ABC, 9/14/80)
Marilyn French's bestseller features lesbian couple

NON-FICTION PROGRAMMING
(DOCUMENTARIES & NEWS SPECIALS)

ABSOLUTELY POSITIVE (PBS, 6/18/91)
Documentary profiles 11 who are HIV positive

AFTER STONEWALL (PBS, 1999)*
U.S. gay rights movement after Stonewall

A.I.D.S. SHOW, THE (PBS, 11/86)
Documentary about AIDS theatre piece

AMERICAN FAMILY REVISITED (HBO, 8/9/83)
Follow-up to the 1973 reality series

BEFORE STONEWALL (PBS, 1984)*
Documentary about early U.S. gay rights movement

CBS REPORTS: THE HOMOSEXUALS (CBS, 3/7/67)
Documentary about homosexuality in U.S.

CELLULOID CLOSET, THE (HBO, 1/30/96)*
History of homosexuality in the cinema

GAY/LESBIAN/BISEXUAL/TRANSGENDER
TV EPISODE GUIDE (cont.)

COMMON THREADS: STORIES FROM
THE QUILT (HBO, 1999)*
Profiles of 5 who died

FYI: THE HOMOSEXUAL (WTVJ-TV,
1966)
Miami news doc about "homosexual
child molesters"

GAY POWER, GAY POLITICS (CBS,
4/26/80)
News report on gay politics in San
Francisco

GOLDEN THREADS (PBS, 6/8/99)
Documentary about organization for
older lesbians

HOMOSEXUALITY IN MEN AND
WOMEN(WNDT-TV 5/10/66)
Early British doc on homosexuality

IS IT A BOY OR A GIRL? (Discovery,
3/26/00)
Documentary on intersexuality

IT'S ELEMENTARY: TALKING ABOUT
GAY ISSUES IN SCHOOL (PBS, 6/99)

LICENSE TO KILL (PBS, 6/23/98)
Documentary probes violence against
gays

LITANY FOR SURVIVAL, A: LIFE &
WORK OF AUDRE LORDE
(PBS, 6/18/96)

NEIGHBORHOODS: THE HIDDEN
CITIES OF SAN FRANCISCO—THE
CASTRO (PBS, 3/12/97)

OFF THE CUFF: HOMOSEXUALITY
AND LESBIANISM (WBKB-
TV/Chicago, 3/6/63)

ONE NATION UNDER GOD
(PBS, 6/15/94)*
Documentary about curing homosexual-
ity

OUR HOUSE (PBS, 6/00)
Documentary about children of gays
and lesbians

OUT OF THE SHADOWS (KNBC-TV,
6/26/70)
Documentary on gay life in Los Angeles

PAUL MONETTE: A BRINK OF
SUMMER'S END (Cinemax, 8/14/97)
Profile of writer

THE REAL ELLEN STORY (Bravo,
9/30/98)
Documentary about Ellen DeGeneres

THE REJECTED (KQED-TV, 9/11/61)
San Francisco PBS-produced
documentary

SCOUT'S HONOR (PBS, 6/19/01)*
Young scout fights to overturn anti-gay
policy

SILVERLAKE LIFE: THE VIEW FROM
HERE (PBS, 1993)*
Diary of couple dying of AIDS

SOUTHERN COMFORT (HBO,
4/14/02)
Portrait of female-to-male transsexual

TANTRUMS AND TIARAS (Cinemax,
8/3/97)
Documentary profile of singer Elton
John

TONGUES UNTIED (PBS, 7/16/91)
Marlon Riggs' work on being black and
gay

TRANSFORMATION, THE (PBS,
7/9/96)
HIV+ transvestite converts to
Christianity

WHEN YOU SEE THIS, REMEMBER
ME (PBS, 1970)*
Profile of writer Gertrude Stein

BIBLIOGRAPHY

INTERNET

www.epguides.com (Episode Guides.com)
www.glaad.org (GLAAD website)
www.imdb.com (Internet Movie Database)
www.tvtome.com (TV Tome)
www.library.ucla.edu (UCLA Library, Film & TV Archive)
home.cc.umanitoba.ca/~wyatt/tv-characters.html (Gay, Lesbian, Bisexual Television Characters)

BOOKS

Brooks, Tim and Earle Marsh. *The Complete Directory to Prime Time Network and Cable Shows, 1946-Present* (7th Edition) (New York: Ballantine Books, 1999).
Capsuto, Steve. *Alternate Channels: The Uncensored Story of Gay and Lesbian Images on Radio and Television, 1930s to the Present* (New York: Ballantine Books, 2000).
Eisner, Joel & David Krinsky. *Television Comedy Series* (Jefferson, North Carolina: McFarland Co., Inc., Publishers, 1984).
Frank, Sam. *Buyer's Guide to Fifty Years of TV on Video* (Amherst, NY: Prometheus Books, 1999).
Gianakos, Larry James. *Television Drama Series Programming; A Comprehensive Chronicle* (1947-1986, 6 Volumes). (Metuchen, N.J.: The Scarecrow Press, 1980-1987).
Howes, Keith. *Broadcasting It: An Encyclopedia of Homosexuality on Film, Radio, and TV in the U.K.* (1923-1993) (New York: Cassell, 1993).
McNeil, Alex. *Total Television* (4th Edition) (New York: Penguin Books, 1996).
Marill, Alvin H. *Movies Made for Television; The Telefeature and the Mini-Series (1964-1986)* (New York: Zoetrope Books, 1987).
Morris, Bruce B. *Prime Time Network Serials* (Jefferson, North Carolina: McFarland Co., Inc., Publishers, 1997).
Russo, Vito. *The Celluloid Closet: Homosexuality in the Movies* (Revised Edition) (New York: Harper & Row, 1987.)
Terrace, Vincent. *Encyclopedia of Television: Series, Pilots and Specials, Vol I (1937-1973), Vol. II (1974-1984)* (New York: Zoetrope, 1985 (Vol. 1), 1987 (Vol. II.)).

THE BEST OF THE PRIME TIME CLOSET

W=Writer D=Director
S=Story *=Emmy Winner

Unless otherwise noted, titles are listed in chronological order.

A. THE BEST OF THE BEST

1. *The Naked Civil Servant* (PBS, 1979)
2. *P.O.V.* (PBS, 1988-)
3. "Cicely," *Northern Exposure* (CBS-TV, 5/18/92)
4. *Silverlake Life: The View from Here* (PBS, 1993)
5. *Tales of the City* (PBS, 1994)
6. *Ellen* (ABC-TV, 1994-1998)
7. *The Celluloid Closet* (HBO, 1996)
8. *Will & Grace* (NBC-TV, 1998-)
9. *Queer as Folk* (Showtime, 2000-)
10. *The Laramie Project* (HBO, 2002)

B. THE FUNNIEST SITCOM EPISODES

1. "Judging Books by Covers," *All in the Family* (CBS-TV, 2/9/71)
   W: Burt Styler D: Norman Lear
2. "Cousin Liz," *All in the Family* (CBS-TV, 10/9/77) *W: Bob Schiller,
   Bob Weiskopf *S: Barry Harmon, Harve Brosten D: Paul Bogart
3 "The Gay Bar," *Maude* (CBS-TV, 12/3/77) W: Thad Mumford,
   Michael Endler, William Davenport and Arthur Julian
   S: Thad Mumford and Michael Endler D: Hal Cooper
4. "Isn't it Romantic?" *The Golden Girls* (NBC-TV, 11/8/86)
   W: Jeffrey Duteil D: Terry Hughes
5. "Can't Help Loving That Man," *Roc* (Fox Network, 10/19/91)
   W: Jeffrey Duteil D: Stan Lathan
6. "The Outing," *Seinfeld* (NBC-TV, 2/11/93) D: Larry Charles D: Tom Cherones
7. "The Matchmaker," *Frasier* (NBC-TV, 10/4/94) W: Joe Keenan *D: David Lee
8. "The One With the Lesbian Wedding," *Friends* (NBC-TV, 1/18/96)
   W: Doty Abrams D: Thomas Schlamme
9. "Everybody Loves Larry," *The Larry Sanders Show* (HBO, 11/13/96)
   W: Peter Tolan D: Todd Holland
10. "Homer's Phobia," *The Simpsons* (Fox Network, 2/16/97)
    W: Ron Hauge D: Mike B. Anderson
11. "The Puppy Episode," *Ellen* (ABC-TV, 4/30/97) *W: Mark Driscoll,
    Tracy Newman, Dava Savel, Jonathan Stark
    *S: Ellen DeGeneres *D: Gil Junger
12. "Lows in the Mid-80's," *Will and Grace* (NBC-TV, 11/23/00) W. Jeff
    Greenstein D: James Burrows

THE BEST OF THE PRIME TIME CLOSET

C. THE BEST DRAMATIC/DRAMEDY EPISODES

1. "Rites of Friendship," *Family* (ABC-TV, 12/28/76)
   W: Gerry Day and Beth Leslie D: Glenn Jordan
2. "Cop," *Lou Grant* (CBS-TV, 9/1/79) *W: Seth Freeman *D: Roger Young
3. "Strangers," *thirtysomething* (ABC-TV, 11/7/89)
   W: Richard Kramer D: Peter O'Fallon
4. "Cicely," *Northern Exposure* (CBS-TV, 5/18/92)
   W: Diane Frolov and Andrew Schneider D: Rob Thompson
5. "Sugar and Spice," *Picket Fences* (CBS-TV, 4/23/93)
   W: David E. Kelley D: Alan Myerson
6. "Manhood," *Law and Order* (NBC-TV, 5/12/93)
   W: Robert Nathan S: Walon Green and Robert Nathan D: Ed Sherin
7. "Resolutions," *My So-Called Life* (ABC-TV, 1/5/95)
   W: Ellen Herman D: Patrick R. Norris
8. "Just One More Thing," *Relativity* (WB Network, 9/28/96)
   W: Jason Katims D: Michael Watkins
9. "...That is the Question," *Dawson's Creek* (WB Network, 2/17/99)
   W: Kevin Williamson and Greg Berlanti D: Greg Prange
10. "In Excelsis Deo," *The West Wing* (NBC-TV, 12/15/99)
    *W: Aaron Sorkin and Rick Cleveland D: Alex Graves
11. "New Moon Rising," *Buffy, the Vampire Slayer* (WB Network, 5/2/00)
    W: Marti Noxon D: James A. Contner
12. "Fag," *Popular* (WB Network, 3/9/01) W: Deidre Strohm D: Elodie Keene
13. "Familia," *Six Feet Under* (HBO, 6/24/01) W: Laurence Andries D: Lisa Cholodenko

D. THE BEST MADE-FOR-TV MOVIES, MINI-SERIES, AND SPECIALS

1. *That Certain Summer* (ABC-TV, 1972) W: Lamont Johnson
   D: Richard Levinson and William Link
2. *The Naked Civil Servant* (PBS, 1975) W: Philip Mackie D: Jack Gold
3. *A Question of Love* (ABC-TV, 1978) W: William Blinn D: Jerry Thorpe
4. *Brideshead Revisited* (PBS, 1982) W: John Mortimer
   D: Michael Lindsay-Hogg/Charles Sturridge
5. *Citizen Cohn* (HBO, 1992) W: Nicolas von Hoffman D: Frank Pierson
6. *Tales of the City* (PBS, 1993) W: Richard Kramer D: Alastair Reid
7. *And the Band Played* (HBO,1993) W: Arnold Schulman D: Roger Spottiswoode
8. *Any Mother's Son* (Lifetime, 1997) W: David Burton Morris D: Bruce Harmon
9. *If These Walls Could Talk II* (HBO, 2000) W: Jane Anderson ("1961"), Anne Heche ("2000"), Alex and Sylvia Sichel ("1972") D: Jane Anderson ("1961"), Martha Coolidge ("1972"), Anne Heche ("2000")
10. *The Laramie Project* (HBO, 2002) W: Moises Kaufman, Stephen Belber, Leigh Fondakowski, Amanda Gronich, Jeffrey LaHoste, John McAdams, Andy Paris, Greg Pierotti, Barbara Pitts, Kelli Simpkins, Stephen Wangh D: Moises Kaufman

THE BEST OF THE PRIME TIME CLOSET

E. THE 10 BEST NON-FICTION AND DOCUMENTARY PROGRAMS/SERIES

1. *Before Stonewall* (PBS, 1984) Produced by Robert Rosenberg, John Scagliotti, and Greta Schiller
2. *P.O.V.* (PBS, 1988-)
3. *Common Threads: Stories from the Quilt* (HBO, 1989) D: Robert Epstein and Jeffrey Friedman
4. *Absolutely Positive* (PBS, 1991) D: Peter Adair
5. *Tongues Untied* (PBS, 1991) D: Marlon Riggs
6. *The Real World: San Francisco* (MTV, 1994) Created by Mary Ellis-Bunim and Jonathan Murray
7. *Coming Out Under Fire* (PBS, 1994) D: Arthur Dong
8. *The Celluloid Closet* (HBO, 1995) D: Robert Epstein and Jeffrey Friedman
9. *Paragraph 175* (HBO, 1999) Produced and Directed by Robert Epstein and Jeffrey Friedman)
10. *Southern Comfort* (HBO, 2001) D: Kate Davis

F. THE 10 BEST PROGRAMS FOR AND ABOUT GAY AND LESBIAN YOUTH AND TEENS

1. *The Truth About Alex* (HBO, 1986)
2. "What If I'm Gay?" *CBS Schoolbreak Special* (CBS-TV, 1987)
3. *De Grassi Junior High* (PBS, 1987-1989); *De Grassi High* (PBS, 1990-1991)
4. "Other Mothers," *CBS Schoolbreak Special* (CBS-TV, 1993)
5. *More Than Friends: The Coming Out of Heidi Leiter* (HBO, 1994)
6. *My So-Called Life* (ABC-TV, 1994)
7. *Dawson's Creek* (WB Network, 1998-)
8. *The Sissy Duckling* (HBO, 1999)
9. *American High* (Fox Network/PBS, 2000-2001)
10. *The Truth About Jane* (Lifetime, 2000)

G. THE 10 BEST TV EPISODES, MOVIES, AND SPECIALS ABOUT AIDS

1. *And the Band Played On* (HBO, 1993)
2. *Andre's Mother* (PBS, 1990)
3. *As Is* (Showtime, 1986)
4. *Common Threads: Stories from the Quilt* (HBO, 1999)
5. "Killing All the Right People," *Designing Women* (CBS-TV, 10/5/87)
6. "For Peter's Sake," *Dream On* (HBO, 6/20/92)
7. *An Early Frost* (NBC-TV, 1985)
8. *Life Goes On* (Season 4) (ABC-TV, 1992-1993)
9. "Steve Burdick," *Lifestories* (NBC-TV, 12/18/90)
10. *Silverlake Life: The View From Here* (PBS, 1993)

The Best of the Prime Time Closet

H. The Best U.S. TV Commercials

(The following commercials can be viewed at **www.commercialcloset.com**)
1. IKEA (1994): A gay male couple pick out a dining room table.
2. Nike (1995): Features HIV+ gay runner, Ric Munoz.
3. Volkswagen (1997): A VW, a smelly chair, and 2 guys we assume to be gay..." Da, Da, Da."
4. Olivia Cruises (1997): "Vacations for Women" ad withtwo women on a ship.
5. Virgin Cola (1998): Ad depicting two men getting married on the beach features an affectionate kiss.
6. GLSEN (1999): Powerful public service announcement show on MTV for the Gay, Lesbian, Straight Education Network featuring kids shouting out "fag," "queer," etc. Matthew Shepard's mother, Judy Shepard, who states "The next time you use words like these, think about what they really mean."
7. John Hancock Financial Services (2000): A lesbian couple in an immigration with their adopted Asian infant child.
8. Miller Lite (2001): Woman sends drink over to cute guy in bar. Too bad he's gay.

I. 10 Writers, Producers, and Creative Teams Who Have Made a Difference

1. Norman Lear (*All in the Family, Maude*)
2. David E. Kelly (*L.A. Law, The Practice*)
3. Linda Bloodworth Thomason and Harry Thomason (*Designing Women, Hearts Afire*)
4. Robert Epstein and Jeffrey Friedman (*The Celluloid Closet, Common Threads, Paragraph 175*)
5. Susan Harris (*Soap, The Golden Girls*)
6. Ed Zwick and Marshall Herskovitz (*thirtysomething, My So-Called Life, Relativity*)
7. Ron Cowen and Dan Lipman (*Sisters, An Early Frost, Queer as Folk*)
8. Max Mutchnick and David Kohan (*Will & Grace*)
9. Aaron Spelling (*Dynasty, Beverly Hills, 90210; Melrose Place*)
10. Kevin Bright, David Crane, Marta Kaufman (*Dream On, Friends, Veronica's Closet*)

THE BEST OF THE PRIME TIME CLOSET

J. 12 ACTORS WHO RECEIVED AN
EMMY FOR PLAYING A GAY MAN OR LESBIAN

1. Robert Morse as Truman Capote, *Tru* (PBS, 1982)
2. Cleavon Little as Tony Larkin, "Stand By Your Man," *Dear John* (NBC-TV, 1989)
3. David Clennon as Peter Brewer, "For Peter's Sake," *Dream On* (HBO, 6/20/92)
4. Glen Close as Margarethe Cammermeyer, *Serving in Silence* (NBC-TV, 1995)
5. Tom Hulce as Peter Patrone, *The Heidi Chronicles* (TNT, 1995)
6. Judy Davis as Diane, *Serving in Silence* (NBC-TV, 1995)
7. Diana Rigg as Mrs. Danvers, *Rebecca* (PBS, 1995)
8. John Larroquette as Joey Herric, "Betrayal," *The Practice* (ABC-TV, 9/23/97)
9. Emma Thompson as herself, "Emma," *Ellen* (ABC-TV, 11/19/97)
10. Sean Hayes as Jack McFarland, *Will & Grace* (NBC-TV, 1998-1999 season)
11. Eric McCormack as Will Truman, *Will & Grace* (NBC-TV, 1999-2000 season)
12. Vanessa Redgrave as Edith Tree, "1962," *If These Walls Could Talk 2* (HBO, 2000)

K. 12 ADDITIONAL OUTSTANDING
(AND UNDERRATED) PERFORMERS

1. Mitchell Anderson as Ross Werkman, *Party of Five* (Fox Network, 1994-1997, 1999-2000)
2. Michael Boatman as Carter Heywood, *Spin City* (ABC-TV, 1996-)
3. Patrick Bristow as Peter Barnes, *Ellen* (ABC-TV, 1994-)
4. Wilson Cruz as Rickie Vasquez, *My So-Called Life* (ABC-TV, 1994)
5. Alyson Hanigan as Willow Rosenberg, *Buffy the Vampire Slayer* (WB Network, 1997-)
6. Laura Innes as Dr. Kerry Weaver, *ER* (NBC-TV, 1995-)
7. Ellen Muth as Jane, *The Truth About Jane* (Lifetime, 2000)
8. Lois Nettleton, "Isn't it Romantic?" *The Golden Girls* (NBC-TV, 11/8/86)
9. Peter Paige as Emmet Honeycutt, *Queer as Folk* (Showtime, 2000-)
10. Kerr Smith as Jack McPhee, *Dawson's Creek* (WB Network, 1998-)
11. Gail Strickland as Marilyn McGrath, *Heartbeat* (ABC-TV, 1988-1989)
12. Tuc Watkins as Malcolm Laffley, *Beggars and Choosers* (Showtime, 1999-2000)

ENDNOTES

CHAPTER ONE — DIAGNOSIS: HOMOSEXUAL

[1] In a 1957 policy statement adopted by the American Civil Liberties Union's Board of Directors, the ACLU acknowledged that homosexuals, "like members of other socially heretical or deviant groups, are more vulnerable than others to official persecution, denial of due process in prosecution, and entrapment." Although the ACLU was committed to defend any individual when due process was denied, the ACLU viewed homosexuality as a moral rather than a legal issue and agreed with the federal government's position that homosexuals are a serious "security risk." "Homosexuality and Civil Liberties," *We Are Everywhere: A Historical Sourcebook of Gay and Lesbian Politics*, eds. Mark Blasius and Shane Phelan (New York: Routledge, 1997), pp. 274-275.

[2] "Employment of Homosexuals and Other Sex Perverts in the U.S. Government," Blasius and Phelan, pp. 241-251.

[3] For a detailed account of the oppression of homosexuality in the Cold War era, see John D'Emilio, "The Homosexual Menace: The Politics of Sexuality in Cold War America," *Making Trouble: Essays on Gay History, Politics, and the University* (New York: Routledge, 1992), pp. 57-73.

[4] The philosophical basis for homophile organizations' mission to improve the "plight" of homosexuals in America is Donald Webster Cory's 1951 work, *The Homosexual in America: A Subjective Approach* (New York: Arno Press, 1975).

[5] For a history of The Mattachine Society, see John D'Emilio, "Dreams Deferred: The Birth and Betrayal of America's First Gay Liberation Movement," *Making Trouble*, pp. 17-56. For an account of One, Inc., see *Homophile Studies in Theory and Practice*, ed. W. Dorr Legg (San Francisco: GLB, 1994).

[6] Alfred Kinsey et al., *Sexual Behavior in the Human Male* (Philadelphia: Saunders, 1948), p. 651; Alfred Kinsey, et al., *Sexual Behavior in the Human Female* (Philadelphia: Saunders, 1953), p. 473.

[7] Kinsey, *Human Male*, p. 650; Kinsey, *Human Female*, p. 454.

[8] For a history of the American Psychiatric Association's position on homosexuality, see Ronald Bayer, *Homosexuality and American Psychiatry: The Politics of Diagnosis* (Princeton, N.J.: Princeton University Press, 1981).

[9] Edward Alwood, *Straight News* (New York: Columbia University Press, 1996), p. 31.

[10] *Confidential File* review, *Variety*, May 4, 1954, p. 9.

[11] Ibid.

[12] My discussion of the three *Open Mind* episodes is based on summaries published in *The Ladder*. See Sten Russell, "*Open Mind*: A Review of Three Programs," *The Ladder*, November 1957, Vol. 2, No. 2, pp. 4-7, 22, 23.

[13] David L. Freeman, "For Courage: *One* Salutes Curtis White," *One*, May 1954, p. 27. According to Alwood, White still chooses not to identify himself, but he did go on to a successful career in public relations. For more about his appearance, see Alwood, p. 332, 35n.

[14] Alwood, pp. 34-35.

[15] Phillip Jason, "Mattachine Official Participates on New York Television Program on Homosexuality Subject," *Mattachine Review*, April 1958, Vol. IV, No. 4, p. 25. The Mattachine article does not refer to Segura by name.

[16] John W. Reavis, proposal for "The Gay Ones," January 10, 1961, Mattachine Society, Inc. of New York. Records, 1956-1976. International Gay Information Center Archives, Manuscripts and Archives Division, The New York Public

Library, Astor, Lenox, and Tilden Foundations.

17 As quoted in "Calling Shots," *Mattachine Review,* October 1961, Vol. VII, No. 10, p. 16.

18 *The Rejected* review, *Daily Variety,* September 13, 1961. KQED-TV has been unable to obtain a copy of *The Rejected.*

19 Terrence O'Flaherty, *San Francisco Chronicle,* as quoted in "TV Critics Praise Rejected," *The Ladder,* October 1961, Vol. 6, No. 1, p. 17.

20 "Television Breakthrough Brings Favorable Comment," *Mattachine Review,* October 1961, Vol. VII, No. 10, p. 16.

21 See "Television Columnists Score Program Values," *Mattachine Review,* October 1961, Vol. VII, No. 10, pp. 18-20.

22 Sten Russell, "KTTV Presents *Argument*: Society and the Homosexual," *The Ladder,* June 1962, Vol. 6, No. 9, pp. 9-10. There is also certainly a greater stigma attached to male homosexuality in a patriarchal society because the emotional and physical bonds that characterize female relationships, both gay and straight, are considered taboo in heterosexual male friendships. For a discussion of the differences between homosexual and homosocial bonding between men and women, see Eve Sedgwick, *Between Men: English Literature and Male Homosocial Desire* (New York: Columbia University Press, 1985), pp. 1-5.

23 Reavis, p. 3.

24 *Off the Cuff: Homosexuality and Lesbianism* review, *Variety,* March 6, 1963.

25 "What Did She Mean By Good Luck?" *The Eleventh Hour,* NBC-TV, November 13, 1962, written by Ellis Marcus.

26 For example, in the early 1960s, psychoanalyst Dr. Richard Robertiello argued that various traumatic family patterns, in the form of different scenarios, are present in the background of all lesbians: a competitive, restrictive or cold mother or father, a poor relationship between the parents, a seductive brother, a sexually competitive older sister, and a rivalry between siblings. Furthermore, Dr. Robertiello concludes that homosexual seduction in childhood differentiates the homosexual from the non-homosexual with the same backgrounds. Robertiello expressed his views in a talk to the American Association for the Advancement of Science entitled "A Psychoanalytic Approach to the Female," a taped broadcast of which aired over a Berkeley radio station. For a summary of the broadcast, see Florence Conrad, "A Psychoanalytic Approach to the Female Homosexual," *The Ladder,* April 1961, Vol. 4, No. 7, pp. 10-11.

27 Robin Richards, "Dramatic Arts," *The Ladder,* January 1964, p. 22.

28 *CBS: The Homosexuals* aired almost two years after executive producer Fred Friendly first assigned the project to producer William Peters. Before its scheduled premiere, Friendly was promoted to news president, a position he abruptly left after a dispute with the network brass about CBS's coverage of the Vietnam War. Meanwhile, the network had concerns about the "taste" of the program's content, so Friendly's replacement, Dick Salant, hired producer Morgan to reconceive the documentary. Consequently, only ten minutes of Peters' film, which has never been publicly screened, remain in the version broadcast in March of 1967. Reportedly, the difference between the two films in their approach and content is considerable. According to *Daily Variety,* the original version was largely from society's point-of-view with the homosexual's perspective in the background, while Morgan's version "investigates the where and how of society's impinge-ment of this particular minority." See "Tale of Two CBS Homo Shows," *Daily Variety,* February 22, 1967.

29 *CBS Reports: The Homosexuals,* CBS-TV, March 7, 1967.

30 Charles Socarides, *The Overt Homosexual* (New York: Grune and Straton, 1968).

31 "TV Key Previews," *Washington Star,* March 7, 1967, p. A-16; George Gent, "TV: C.B.S. Reports on Homosexuals," *The New York Times,* March 8, 1967, p. 91; Dean

Gysel, "A Frank Look at Homosexuality," *Chicago Daily News*, March 8, 1967, p. 67. For further background information on the production and critical response to the documentary, see Alwood, pp. 69-74.

32 Clay Gowran, "Repeat: TV No Spot to Unload Garbage," *Chicago Tribune*, March 8, 1967, Sec. 2-A, p. 4.

33 Gent, p. 91. Many years later, Wallace admitted that he should have known better because he had two gay friends who had been living together for years, but at the time he considered them the exception to the rule. See Alwood, p.74. When the program was screened in a Greenwich Village movie theatre in the summer of 1995, Wallace attended the screening and afterwards led an impromptu question-and-answer session with the audience.

34 "Discovery at Fourteen," *The Bold Ones*, NBC-TV, March 5, 1972, written by Robert Malcolm Young, based on a character created by Burt Nodella.

35 "The Other Martin Loring," *Marcus Welby, M.D.*, ABC-TV, February 20, 1973, written by Dick Nelson.

36 Ibid.

37 Kathryn C. Montgomery, *Target: Prime Time* (New York: Oxford University Press, 1989), p. 77.

38 Albin Krebs, "*Welby* is Scored by Gay Activists," *The New York Times*, February 17, 1973, p. 63.

39 Randy Wicker and Martin St. John, "TV Show Sets Off Storm," *The Advocate*, March 14, 1973, n.p.

40 Alwood, p. 142.

41 "Judge Drops ABC Zap Charges," *The Advocate*, April 11, 1973.

42 Krebs, p. 63.

43 "Gay Activists Win ABC Concession," *The New York Times*, February 21, 1973, p. 87.

44 "The Outrage," *Marcus Welby, M.D.*, ABC-TV, October 8, 1974, written by Eugene Price.

45 Alwood, pp. 147-151.

46 As reprinted in David Aiken, "Boy raped on TV show stirs protest," *The Advocate*, September 11, 1974, p. 10.

47 "The Outrage" (revised script), June 27, 1974, *Marcus Welby, M.D.* file, International Gay and Lesbian Archives, Los Angeles, California.

48 Letter to William Page from Richard Gitter, August 13, 1974, *Marcus Welby, M.D.* file, International Gay and Lesbian Archives, Los Angeles, California.

49 Ibid.

50 Letter to legislators from Dr. Bruce Voeller, September 30, 1974, *Marcus Welby, M.D.* file, International Gay and Lesbian Archives, Los Angeles, California. "Went to all key legislators" is hand-written on the top of the letter.

51 Letter to ABC affiliate station manager from Dr. Bruce Voeller, September 30, 1974, *Marcus Welby, M.D.* file, International Gay and Lesbian Archives, Los Angeles, California. "This is going to *home* addresses of all ABC-TV affiliates' station managers. 170 of them." is handwritten on top of the letter.

52 Terrence O'Flaherty, "Science Versus Medicine," *San Francisco Chronicle*, October 9, 1974, n.p.

53 Press release from Rev. Fr. H. Francis Hines, Director of Advertising and Public Affairs for television station WPVI-TV Channel 6, Philadelphia, September 24, 1974, p. 1.

54 Press release from Rev. Fr. H. Francis Hines, p. 2.

55 "Undercurrent," *Medical Center*, CBS-TV, September, 23, 1970, written by Robert Malcolm Young.

56 "Impasse," *Medical Center*, CBS-TV, October 1, 1973, written by Barry Oringer.

[57] Ibid.

[58] "A Very Strange Triangle," *The Bold Ones: The Doctors*, NBC-TV, October 31, 1972, written by Peggy O'Shea.

[59] John J. O'Connor, "TV: Homosexuality Is Subject of Two Programs," *The New York Times*, November 3, 1972, p. 79. The other program referred to in the title of O'Connor's review is *That Certain Summer*, which premiered on November 1, 1972, the night after "A Very Strange Triangle" aired.

[60] An early example of a television talk show addressing the issue of "gender switching" was a December 1957 broadcast of the Dallas talk show *Confession*, which featured an interview with a 22-year-old transvestite named Darrell Wayne Kahler. According to a *Time* magazine article, Kahler was the latest subject "in a line of drug addicts, prostitutes, murderers and alcoholics to answer the unrehearsed questions of Interrogator Jack Wyatt." *Time* praises *Confession* for managing "to keep a responsible grip on its sensational material." The article then goes on to describe the interview, which included a filmed reenactment of Kahler, drunk and in drag, being arrested when three men tried to molest her. "Confession," *Time*, December 30, 1957, p. 37.

[61] "The Fourth Sex, Pt. I," *Medical Center*, CBS-TV, September 8, 1975, written by Rita Lakin.

[62] "The Fourth Sex, Pt. II," *Medical Center*, CBS-TV, September 15, 1975, written by Rita Lakin.

[63] Ibid.

[64] "The Mermaid," *Westside Medical*, ABC-TV, July 7, 1977. My discussion of "The Mermaid" is based on an archival script entitled "The Freak" (though the title is crossed out). The author's name does not appear on the script. Gay Media Task Force Records, 1972-1988, Collection #7315, Division of Rare and Manuscript Collections, Cornell University Library, Ithaca, NY.

[65] "Aids and Comfort," *St. Elsewhere*, NBC-TV, December 21, 1983, written by Steve Lawson, story by John Masius and Tom Fontana.

[66] "Night of the Living Bed," *St. Elsewhere*, NBC-TV, October 28, 1987, written by John PiRoman, story by Channing Gibson and John Tinker.

[67] "Split Decision," *St. Elsewhere*, NBC-TV, May 11, 1988, written by Aram Saroyan, story by John Tinker and Channing Gibson.

[68] "Girls Just Wanna Have Fun," *St. Elsewhere*, NBC-TV, November 28, 1984, written by Channing Gibson and John Tinker.

[69] Anne Lewis, "Prime time's first Lesbian up in the air," *Washington Blade*, February 10, 1989, p. 19.

[70] "The Wedding," *Heartbeat*, ABC-TV, April 21, 1989, written by Dan Wakefield.

[71] Marguerite J. Moritz, "Old Strategies for New Texts: How American Television is Creating and Treating Lesbian Characters," *Queer Words, Queer Images*, ed. R. Jeffrey Ringer (New York: New York University Press, 1994), p. 132.

[72] Moritz, p. 133.

[73] Darlene M. Hantzis and Valerie Lehr, "Whose Desire? Lesbian (Non) sexuality and Television's Perpetuation of Hetero/Sexism," in Ringer, p. 118.

[74] As quoted in "*ER* Comes Out of the Operating Room — and the Closet," GLAAD Alert, February 7, 1997.

[75] My primary source of information pertaining to intersexuality is the Intersex Society of North America website (www.isna.org).

[76] Alice Domurat Dreger, "'Ambiguous Sex' – Ambivalent Medicine?" (www.isna.org/library/dreger-ambivalent.html). This article originally appeared in *The Hastings Center Reporter*, May/June 1998, Volume 28, Issue 3, pp. 24-35.

[77] Cheryl Chase, "Making Media: An Intersex Perspective," *GLAAD Images*, Fall 1997 (www.glaad.org/org/projects/cultural/trans_visibility/index.html?record=2599).

78 "ISNA Recommendations for Treatment," 1994 (www.isna.org/library/recommendations.html).
79 "ISNA Recommendations for Treatment," 1994.
80 Some examples include Geoffrey Cowley, "Gender Limbo," *Newsweek*, May 16, 1997; David Tuller, "'Intersexuals Begin to Speak Out on Infant Genital Operations," *San Francisco Chronicle*, June 21, 1997; Natalie Angier, "New Debate Over Surgery on Genitals," *The New York Times*, May 13, 1997.
81 GLAAD is an excellent source for information on this topic. See GLAAD'S Cultural Interest Media Project (www.glaad.org/org/projects/cultural/trans_visibility/index.html).
82 "ISNA Recommendations for Treatment," 1994.
83 "Exploring Gender Identity on *Chicago Hope*," GLAAD Alert, February 3, 2000 (www.glaad.org/org/publications/alerts/index.html?record=84). During the same season (1999-2000), *Freaks and Geeks* introduced the first intersexual recurring character on television. In "The Little Things," Ken's (Seth Rogan) girlfriend Amy (Jessica Campbell) tells him a secret—she was born with "both male and female parts" and her parents decided she should be a girl. Although he promises not to freak out, it's only a matter of time before he's telling his buddies that Amy is "packing both a gun and a holster." Thinking he must be gay because he's attracted to Amy, he goes to speak to the school's guidance counselor, Mr. Russo (David (Gruber) Allen), who Ken mistakenly assumes is gay ("You kind of have this way about you," Ken explains). Later, Amy finds out that Ken shared her secret with his friends. She becomes angry, but accepts his apology.

CHAPTER TWO: "JUST THE FACTS, MA'AM"

1 For a discussion of the representation of homosexuals as killers in American cinema, see Vito Russo, *The Celluloid Closet* (Revised Edition) (New York: Harper & Row, 1987).
2 When gay, lesbian, and transvestite killers first appeared on television in the late 1960s/early 1970s, they were also wreaking havoc on the big screen in films like *The Detective* (1968), *They Only Kill Their Masters* (1972), *Freebie and the Bean* (1974), and *The Eiger Sanction* (1975).
3 "The Sniper," *The Asphalt Jungle*, ABC-TV, April 30, 1961, written by George Bellak. Virginia Christine, who portrays Miss Brant, is best known as Mrs. Olson on the Folger Coffee commercials. Leo Penn is the late father of actors Sean and Chris Penn.
4 "Shakedown," *N.Y.P.D.*, ABC-TV, September 5, 1967, written by Albert Ruben.
5 *N.Y.P.D* review, *Variety*, September 6, 1967.
6 Jack Gould, "'N.Y.P.D.' Opens on ABC," *The New York Times*, September 6, 1967, p. 95.
7 Ruben, "Shakedown."
8 *N.Y.P.D.* review, *Variety*.
9 "Weep the Hunter Home," *Judd, for the Defense*, ABC-TV, November 8, 1968, written by Mel Goldberg and Arthur Singer.
10 "Dead Witness to a Killing," *Dan August*, ABC-TV, January 28, 1971, written by Arthur Weingarten.
11 Harold Fairbanks, "Pro-gay drivel is still drivel," *The Advocate*, February 13, 1974.
12 "The Ripper," *Police Story*, NBC-TV, February 12, 1974, written by Don Ingalls.
13 Fairbanks, "Pro-gay drivel is still drivel."
14 Wayne Jefferson, "Does Rewritten TV Show Signal Change?" *Gay People's Union News*, February-March 1974, p. 13.
15 Ibid.
16 Lou Romano, "*Kojak* Disclaimer," *The Blade*, December 1975, p. 2.

[17] Ibid.

[18] As quoted in Romano, p. 2.

[19] Letter from Richard L. Kirschner, Vice President, Program Practices, CBS Television Network to Mr. Paul Duncan, November 10, 1976, letter in International Gay and Lesbian Archives, Los Angeles, California.

[20] Les Brown, "'Police Woman' Episode Withdrawn by NBC," *The New York Times*, October 11, 1974, p. 75.

[21] Cecil Smith, "An Emasculated 'Flowers of Evil,'" *Los Angeles Times*, November 8, 1974, p. 27.

[22] John J. O'Connor, "TV View," *The New York Times*, November 24, 1974, p. 23.

[23] Smith, p. 27.

[24] "Flowers of Evil," *Police Woman*, NBC-TV, November 8, 1974, written by John W. Bloch, story by Joshua Hanke.

[25] Les Brown, "NBC-TV Yields to Homosexuals Over Episode of 'Police Woman,'" *The New York Times*, November 30, 1974, p. 61.

[26] Smith, p. 27.

[27] Bloch, "Flowers of Evil."

[28] *Owen Marshall, Counselor at Law* review, *Variety*, September 20, 1972.

[29] Ibid.

[30] "Media Alert," *The Advocate*, January 31, 1976.

[31] As quoted in "Media Alert," January 31, 1976. The list of episode sponsors includes Chrysler Corporation, Johnson and Johnson, General Motors, Armour-Dial, Inc., General Mills, Inc., and Sterling Drugs.

[32] "TV Update: CBS Alters 'Cagney,' Calling It 'Too Women's Lib,'" *TV Guide*, June 12, 1982, p. A-1. For an extensive historical overview and analysis of the series, see Julie D'Acci, *Defining Women: Television and the Case of Cagney & Lacey* (Chapel Hill, NC: University of North Carolina Press, 1994), and Steve Capsuto, "The Cops," *Alternate Channels: The Uncensored Story of Gay and Lesbian Image on Radio and Television* (New York: Ballantine Books, 2000), pp. 192-195.

[33] As quoted in "TV Update: CBS Alters 'Cagney,' Calling It 'Too Women's Lib.'"

[34] Ibid.

[35] As quoted in "NGTF Hits CBS-TV," *Bay Area Reporter*, July 8, 1982.

[36] Ibid.

[37] As quoted in Tim Brooks and Earl Marsh, *The Complete Directory of Prime Time Network and Cable TV Shows (1946–Present)* (New York: Ballantine Books, 1999), p. 472.

[38] "Death in a Different Place," *Starsky and Hutch*, ABC-TV, March 15, 1978, written by Tom Bagen.

[39] Douglass K. Daniel, *Lou Grant: The Making of TV's Top Newspaper Drama* (Syracuse, New York: Syracuse University Press, 1996), p. 107.

[40] Brochtrup departed the series for a short time to play the same role in Bochco's police sitcom, *Public Morals*, which was canceled after one episode. Before returning to *N.Y.P.D. Blue*, he played the office manager on the short-lived 1997 crime drama, *Total Security*.

[41] "Welcome to New York," *N.Y.P.D. Blue*, ABC-TV, January 25, 2000, written by Meredith Stiehm, story by David Milch and Bill Clark.

[42] "*NYPD Blue* Goes to a Fairy Bar," GLAAD Alert, February 3, 2000, p. 1.

[43] In season nine, John Irvin's sister Delia (Cheryl White) and his estranged father (Peter White) are introduced. His father, who is dying, disapproves of his son's lifestyle. Irvin also gets asked out on a date by Ray Maxwell (Brian McNamara), a man whose puppies are stolen, and finally gets a vacation.

[44] "Gay Rights Groups Laud NBC for Showing 'Law' Lesbian Kiss," *The Hollywood Reporter*, February 11, 1991, p. 38.

[45] Ibid.

[46] The source of this summary of the policy is taken from *The Survival Guide: An Overview of "Don't Ask, Don't Tell, Don't Pursue, Don't Harass,"* Servicemembers Legal Defense Network, October 31, 2000. See the Network's website (www.sldn.org).

[47] "Pentagon Fires Record Number of Gays" (Press Release) Servicemembers Legal Defense Network, January 22, 1999, p. 1.

[48] Ibid.

[49] "Report on the Military Environment With Respect to the Homosexual Conduct Policy," Summary of Report No. D-2000-101, Office of the Inspector General, Department of Defense, March 16, 2000, p. 1.

[50] Ibid.

[51] Thomas S. Mulligan, "Gay Group Backs NBC in Episode Flap," *Los Angeles Times,* October 2, 1991, p. D3.

[52] Donald F. Bellisario, "Straight Talk on *Quantum Leap* Dispute," *Los Angeles Times,* January 27, 1992, p. F3.

[53] "GLAAD Set Record 'Straight' on *Quantum Leap* Gay Episode," GLAAD Media Release, October 1, 1991, p. 1.

[54] "The People vs. Gunny," *JAG,* CBS-TV, February 22, 2000.

[55] Dennis Shepard's statement to the court is available online (www.wiredstrategies.com/mrshep.htm).

[56] To learn more about Matthew Shepard's life, go to the website for The Matthew Shepard Foundation (www.matthewshepard.org).

[57] Another version of my analysis of *The Matthew Shepard Story* and *The Laramie Project* was posted on the website, www.popmatters.com. Special thanks to my editor, Cynthia Fuchs, for her assistance and support.

[58] Lorimar Productions, producers of *Midnight Caller,* were also the producers of the controversial 1980 film *Cruising,* in which Al Pacino plays a cop who goes undercover in the New York City gay leather-bar scene to catch a serial killer. The primary suspect in the film is played by Richard Cox, who plays the bisexual Mike Barnes in "After It Happened."

[59] "Malicious *Millennium,*" GLAAD Alert, November 1, 1996.

[60] "*New York Undercover* Bashes Bisexuals," GLAAD Alert, November 27, 1996.

[61] As quoted in Bill Roundy, "On the Air," *Washington Blade,* February 2, 2001.

[62] Ibid.

CHAPTER THREE: DRAMA QUEENS

[1] *That Certain Summer,* ABC-TV, November 1, 1972, written by Richard Levinson and William Link.

[2] As quoted in Vito Russo, *The Celluloid Closet* (Revised Edition) (New York: Harper & Row, 1987), p. 22

[3] John J. O'Connor, "TV: Homosexuality Is Subject of Two Programs," *The New York Times,* November 3, 1972.

[4] Ibid.

[5] In a 1999 interview for ultimateDallas.com, Gray described transsexual Linda Murkland as "one of the best roles" she's ever done and recounts how she researched for the role by talking to a transsexual named Rusty, who shared details about her childhood and sex change operation (see www.dallas.ndirect.co.uk/lindagray.htm).

[6] "Episode One," *Dynasty,* ABC-TV, January 12, 1981, written by Richard and Esther Shapiro.

[7] Keith Howes, *Broadcasting It* (New York: Cassell, 1993), p. 748.

[8] Ibid.
[9] David Galligan, "All That *Glitters* Is Murder, Blackmail, Fraud, and Deceit," *The Advocate*, January 26, 1977, p. 26.
[10] Kevin Thomas, "Plight of the Gay in *Glitter Palace*," *Los Angeles Times*, February 26, 1977.
[11] Terry deCrescenzo, *NewsWest*, March 3-17, 1977.
[12] Howes, p. 839.
[13] "Another Censored Kiss," GLAAD Media Release, May 16, 1994.
[14] "GLAAD/LA Urges Fox Network to Air Season Finale of *Melrose Place* in its Entirety," GLAAD Media Release, April 28, 1994.
[15] "*Melrose* Matt Willing to Go All the Way, But No Kissing," GLAAD Alert, November 22, 1996.
[16] "Psycho Lesbian on *Melrose Place*," GLAAD Alert, January 9, 1998.
[17] Robert J. Thompson, *Television's Second Golden Age: From Hill Street Blues to ER* (Syracuse, New York: Syracuse University Press, 1997), pp. 13-16.
[18] "Special Online GLAAD Alert — Keep *Relativity* on the Air," GLAAD Alert, November 7, 1996.
[19] As quoted in *Sunday Telegraph*, June 15, 1997.
[20] Thompson, pp. 149-50.
[21] Charles Isherwood, "Northern Exposé," *The Advocate*, April 19, 1994, p. 54.
[22] "*Exposure* pulled by 2 CBS affils," *Variety*, May 2, 1994, p. 9.
[23] "*Northern Exposure* Is Target of Protest," *The New York Times*, April 28, 1994, Section D, p. 9.
[24] Ibid.
[25] "*Northern Exposure* to Air a Wedding Without a Kiss," GLAAD Media Release, April 29, 1994.
[26] Isherwood, p. 55.
[27] Thompson, p. 135.
[28] Robin Roberts, *Sexual Generations: Star Trek: The Next Generation and Gender* (Chicago: University of Illinois Press, 1999.), p. 120.
[29] Ibid.
[30] Marlon Riggs, "*Tongues* re-tied?" *Current*, August 12, 1991.
[31] Dick Williams, "*Tongues* isn't art, but a skirmish in the culture wars paid for by tax dollars," *Atlanta Constitution*, July 20, 1991, p. A:19.
[32] Don Kowet, "PBS turns TV rooms into gay-strip film houses," *Washington Times*, July 16, 1991.
[33] "Idaho Public TV to Air *It's Elementary* an Hour Later," *The Advocate*, July 31, 1999.
[34] Steve Greenberg, "No more *Tales*," *The Advocate*, May 31, 1994.
[35] "American Playhouse's *Tales of the City*," Culture Shock, PBS Online (www.pbs.org/wgbh/cultureshock/flashpoints/theater/tales.html).
[36] Steve Greenberg, "No More *Tales*," *The Advocate*, May 31, 1994.
[37] John Carman, as quoted in Greenberg, "No More *Tales*."
[38] Frank Rich, as quoted in Greenberg, "No More *Tales*."
[39] On January 6, 2002, *Queer as Folk* started its second season and *Sex and the City* resumed its fourth. *The New York Times* featured a piece by Alan James Frutkin in which he compares the gay content of the two series. Frutkin credits *Sex* for "portraying gay life with a wit and depth that the more overly gay *Queer as Folk* hasn't achieved." Alan James Frutkin, "The Return of the Gay Show that Gets Gay Life Right," *The New York Times*, January 6, 2002, p. 2:33.
[40] Raymond Murray, *Images in the Dark: An Encyclopedia of Gay and Lesbian Film and Video*, (New York: Penguin Books, 1996), p. 308.
[41] Ibid.
[42] "Strange Bedfellows," *Oz*, HBO, August 17, 1998, written by Tom Fontana.

[43] "Familia," *Six Feet Under*, HBO, June 24, 2001, written by Laurence Andries.

[44] "A Private Life," *Six Feet Under*, August 19, 2001, written by Kate Robin.

[45] Ibid.

[46] Ibid.

[47] Alan Waldman, "Out Front and On the Edge," *Multichannel News*, July 23, 2001.

[48] Ibid.

[49] "Leading in Diversity," *Multichannel News*, July 23, 2001, p. 1.

[50] Waldman, p. 3.

[51] John Dempsey, "Queer is here as Showtime invades HBO's racy turf," *Variety*, December 11, 2000.

[52] The first four episodes of the British *Queer as Folk* were directed by Sarah Harding. The remaining four were directed by Charles McDougall. *Queer as Folk 2* was directed by Menhag Huda.

[53] *Leap Years* (2001) is the story of five friends that switch back and forth through three time periods (1993, 2001, 2008). One of the friends, Gregory Paget (Garrett Dillahunt) is an aspiring filmmaker (1993), turned full-time critic and gay man (2001), turned therapist who lives happily with a police officer (2008). Showtime axed the show after one season.

[54] As quoted in Michael Goodridge, "TV Imitates TV," *The Advocate*, August 29, 2000.

[55] "The Last Testament of Buddy Crown," *Channing*, ABC-TV, December 18, 1963, written by Stanford Whitmore, story by David Shaber.

[56] "What Is a Man?" *Room 222*, ABC-TV, March 14, 1971, written by Dan Balluck.

[57] "One of the Boys," *The White Shadow*, CBS-TV, January 27, 1979, written by John Falsey

[58] *"Family"* (review of "Rites of Friendship"), *Variety*, October 6, 1976.

[59] Howes, p. 910.

[60] Phillip Linton, who portrays Andy, died in February of 1992. The film is dedicated to his memory.

[61] Jeffrey Epstein, "Prime Time for Gay Youth," *The Advocate*, April 27, 1999.

[62] Ibid.

[63] *"Phases" Buffy the Vampire Slayer*, WB Network, January 27, 1998 written by Rob Des Hotel and Dean Batali..

[64] Charles Isherwood, "His So-Called Life," *The Advocate*, November 1, 1994.

[65] Ibid.

[66] Ibid.

[67] Jeffrey Epstein, "Outings on the Creek," *The Advocate*, March 16, 1999.

[68] "...That Is the Question," *Dawson's Creek*, WB Network, February 17, 1999, written by Kevin Williamson and Greg Berlanti.

CHAPTER FOUR: "NOT THAT THERE'S ANYTHING *WRONG* WITH IT"

[1] "Judging Books by Covers," *All in the Family*, CBS-TV, February 9, 1971, written by Burt Styler and Norman Lear.

[2] "The Gay Bar," *Maude*, CBS-TV, December 3, 1977, written by Thad Mumford, Michael Endler, William Davenport, and Arthur Julian, story by Thad Mumford and Michael Endler.

[3] Dennis Altman, *Homosexual: Oppression and Liberation* (New York: New York University, 1993), p. 58.

[4] Ibid.

[5] "Maude's New Friend," *Maude*, CBS-TV, December 2, 1974, written by Rod Parker.

[6] "The Outing," *Seinfeld*, NBC-TV, February 11, 1993, written by Larry Charles.

[7] "Alice Gets a Pass," *Alice*, CBS-TV, September 29, 1976, written by Martin Donovan.

8 *"Alice"* (review), *Variety*, September 29, 1976.

9 "The Boys in the Bar," *Cheers*, NBC-TV, January 27, 1983, written by Ken Levine and David Isaacs.

10 "A Real Guy's Guy," *Coach*, ABC-TV, October 25, 1991, written by Judd Pillot and John Peaslee, story by Richard Raskind.

11 "Frat Brothers Forever," *The Love Boat*, ABC-TV, October 6, 1984, written by Barry O'Brien and Jeffrey Duteil.

12 "Birth of a Donation," *Hearts Afire*, CBS-TV, October 22, 1994, written by Rebecca Parr Cioffi.

13 "Pursued," *The Fanelli Boys*, NBC-TV, September 19, 1990, written by Martin Weiss and Robert Bruce.

14 "Shipmates," *Too Close for Comfort*, ABC-TV, June 2, 1984, written by Arne Sultan and Earl Barret.

15 "Boys II Men II Women," *In the House*, NBC-TV, December 4, 1995, written by Ted Duteil.

16 "Dirty Deeds," *The John Larroquette Show*, NBC-TV, February 1, 1994, written by Don Reo and Judith D. Allison.

17 "Best of Friends," *Night Court*, NBC-TV, November 7, 1985, written by Howard Ostroff.

18 "Brandy, You're a Fine Girl," *Just Shoot Me*, NBC-TV, November 16, 2000, written by Susan Dickes and David Hemingsen.

19 "Old Dogs, New Dicks," *Sex and the City*, HBO, August 1, 1999, written by Jenny Bicks.

20 "The Chief's Gay Evening," *Gimme a Break*, NBC-TV, November 13, 1982.

21 "Movie, Pt. 1" and "Movie, Pt. 2," *Barney Miller*, ABC-TV, January 22 & 29, 1981, written by Frank Dungan and Jeff Stein.

22 "George," *M*A*S*H*, CBS-TV, February 16, 1974, written by Jeff Reiger and Gary Markowitz.

23 "A Case of Misdiagnosis," *The Bob Crane Show*, NBC-TV, May 8, 1975, written by Jim Allen. This quote is from the first draft of the teleplay dated December 9, 1974. Gay Media Task Force Records, 1972-1988, Collection #7315, Division of Rare amd Manuscript Collections, Cornell University Library, Ithaca, NY.

24 "Some of My Best Friends Are," *The Bob Newhart Show*, CBS-TV, October 9, 1976, written by Hugh Wilson.

25 "Spell It M-A-N," *Doogie Howser*, ABC-TV, January 6, 1993, written by Nick Harding.

26 "Single White Male," *Empty Nest*, NBC-TV, January 7, 1995, written by Andy Guerdat.

27 "Double Date," *Blossom*, NBC-TV, January 31, 1994, written by Glenn Merzer.

28 "Eric's Buddy," *That 70's Show*, Fox Network, December 6, 1998, written by Phillip Stark.

29 "The Bump," *The Larry Sanders Show*, HBO, August 9, 1995, written by Judd Apatow and Garry Shandling.

30 "Flip," *The Larry Sanders Show*, HBO, May 31, 1998, written by Peter Tolan and Garry Shandling.

31 "Isn't It Romantic?" *The Golden Girls*, NBC-TV, November 8, 1986, written by Jeffrey Duteil.

32 "Suzanne Goes Looking for a Friend," *Designing Women*, CBS-TV, April 9, 1990, written by Lee LaDuke and Mark Alton Brown.

33 "Honey, We Broke the Kid," *Wings*, NBC-TV, January 2, 1996, written by Lori Kirkland.

34 "Saved by the Belvedere," *Ned and Stacey*, Fox Network, January 20, 1997, written by Bryan Behar and Steve Baldikoski.

[35] "Ned Pulls Gun on Gay Admirer," GLAAD Alert, January 24, 1997.

[36] Ibid.

[37] "Fox Says Sorry For Ned Pulling Gun on Gay Man," GLAAD Alert, February 28, 1997.

[38] "Kirk's Ex-Wife," *Dear John*, NBC-TV, September 20, 1991, written by Marco Pennette.

[39] "The Smelly Car," *Seinfeld*, NBC-TV, April 15, 1993, written by Larry David and Peter Mehlman.

[40] "The One With the Lesbian Wedding," *Friends*, NBC-TV, January 18, 1996, written by Doty Abrams.

[41] "The Beard," *Seinfeld*, NBC-TV, February 9, 1995, written by Carol Leifer.

[42] "Emmet's Secret," *Grace Under Fire*, ABC-TV, December 6, 1995, written by Donald Beck.

[43] "Cousin Liz," *All in the Family*, CBS-TV, October 9, 1977, written by Bob Schiller and Bob Weiskopf, story by Barry Harmon and Harve Brosten.

[44] "My Brother's Keeper," *The Mary Tyler Moore Show*, CBS-TV, January 13, 1972, written by Dick Clair and Jenna McMahon.

[45] "Lamont, Is That You?" *Sanford and Son*, NBC-TV, October 19, 1973, written by James R. Stein and Robert Ilies.

[46] "Les on the Ledge," *WKRP in Cincinnati*, CBS-TV, October 2, 1978, written by Hugh Wilson.

[47] "Sharkey's Secret Life," *C.P.O. Sharkey*, NBC-TV, March 16, 1977, written by Aaron Ruben, story by Bill Richmond and Gene Perret.

[48] "The Censors," *The Associates*, ABC-TV, April 10, 1980, written by Stan Daniels and Ed Weinberger.

[49] "Older and Out," *Cosby*, CBS-TV, October 27, 1997.

[50] "The Homecoming Queen," *Dream On*, HBO, July 13, 1997, written by Adam Belanoff.

[51] "The Gay Divorcee," *Holding the Baby*, Fox Network, December 8, 1998, written by Howard J. Morris and Rosalind Moore.

[52] "Rumoring," *Working*, NBC-TV, October 29, 1997, written by Steve Tompkins.

[53] "The One When Nana Dies Twice," *Friends*, NBC-TV, November 10, 1994, written by Marta Kaufman and David Crane.

[54] "The One With the Baby on the Bus," *Friends*, NBC-TV, November 2, 1995, written by Betsy Bornes.

[55] "The One with the Nap Partners," *Friends*, NBC-TV, November 9, 2000, written by Brian Buckner and Sebastian Jones.

[56] "The One With the Ballroom Dancing," *Friends*, NBC-TV, October 16, 1997, written by Andrew Reich and Ted Cohen.

[57] "Neighbors," *The Single Guy*, NBC-TV, November 2, 1995, NBC-TV, written by David Kohan and Max Mutchnick.

[58] "Pass the Salt," *Just Shoot Me*, NBC-TV, January 28, 1998, NBC-TV, written by Jack Burditt.

[59] "Dating Is Hell," *The Secret Lives of Men*, ABC-TV, October 21, 1998, written by Susan Harris.

[60] "What's With Robert?" *Everybody Loves Raymond*, CBS-TV, January 10, 2000, written by Cindy Chupack.

[61] "Torch Song Cardiology," *Doctor, Doctor*, CBS-TV, December 18, 1989, written by Bill Diamond, Michael Saltzman, Terri Minsky and David Blum.

[62] "Toe in the Water," *Designing Woman*, CBS-TV, September 23, 1991, written by Pam Norris.

[63] "Evolution," *Sex and the City*, HBO, August 15, 1999, written by Cindy Chupack.

[64] "Rough Housing," *The Facts of Live*, NBC-TV, August 24, 1979, written by Dick

Clair and Jenna McMahon.

[65] "Sex With Pudding," *Titus*, Fox Network, March 20, 2000, written by Jack Kenny and Brian Hargrove.

[66] "Goodbye, Mr. Gordon," *The Golden Girls*, NBC-TV, January 11, 1992, written by Gail Parent and Jim Vallely.

[67] "Two Guys, a Girl, and a Tattoo," *Two Guys, a Girl, and a Pizza Place*, ABC-TV, October 7, 1998, written by Mark Ganzel.

[68] "Mr. Mommie," *The Mommies*, NBC-TV, March 19, 1994, written by Nick LeRose

[69] "Come Out, Come Out, Wherever You Are," *Murphy Brown*, CBS-TV March 4, 1992, written by Gary Dontzig and Steven Peterman.

[70] "A Comedy of Eros," *Murphy Brown*, CBS-TV, September 30, 1996, written by Joshua Sternin and Jeffrey Ventimilia.

[71] "Arthur's Worry," *Maude*, CBS-TV, November 15, 1976, written by Arthur Julian, story by Michael Smollin and Kathy Gori.

[72] "The Marry Caitlin Moore Show," *Spin City*, ABC-TV, February 9, 2000, written by Tad Quill.

[73] "The Past Comes Back," *The John Larroquette Show*, NBC-TV, October 23, 1993, written by Don Reo and Judith D. Allison.

[74] "Guess Who's Coming Out for Dinner," *The Hughleys*, UPN Network, September 18, 2000, written by Kim Friese.

[75] "In and Out," *Guys Like Us*, UPN Network, October 28, 1998, written by Barry O'Brien.

[76] "The One with the Metaphorical Tunnel," *Friends*, NBC-TV, October 10, 1996.

[77] "A Boy and His Doll," *Coach*, ABC-TV, January 22, 1997, written by Ellen Sandler and Cindy Chupack.

[78] "I Got the Music In Me," *The Mommies*, NBC-TV, November 6, 1993, written by Lisa A. Bannick.

[79] "Rebecca's Lover...Not," *Cheers*, NBC-TV, April 23, 1992, written by Tracy Newman and Jonathan Stark.

[80] "Oh Vey, You're Gay," *The Nanny*, CBS-TV, October 23, 1995, written by Eileen O'Hare.

[81] "Passion Plundered," *Night Court*, NBC-TV, December 20, 1989, written by Gail Rock.

[82] "Temp-tation," *Temporarily Yours*, ABC-TV, March 12, 1997, written by Mark Solomon.

[83] "Frankie Goes to Rutherford," *Third Rock from the Sun*, NBC-TV, May 9, 2000, written by Gregg Mettler and Will Forte.

[84] "A Man About the House," *Three's Company*, ABC-TV, March 15, 1977, written by Don Nicholl and Michael Ross.

[85] "Mr. Roper's Niece," *Three's Company*, ABC-TV, March 31, 1977, written by Paul Wayne and George Burditt.

[86] "Strange Bedfellows," *Three's Company*, ABC-TV, October 4, 1977, written by Paul Wayne and George Burditt.

[87] "Woman Gets Plastered, Star Gets Even," *The Naked Truth*, NBC-TV, January 23, 1997, written by Ed Yeager and Phillip Vaughn.

[88] "The Gay Caballeros," *Ned and Stacey*, Fox Network, February 19, 1996, written by Del Shores.

[89] "Chasing Sammy," *Getting Personal*, Fox Network, May 18, 1998, written by Gregory Thomas Garcia and Kriss Turner.

[90] "Bay of Married Pigs," *Sex and the City*, HBO, June 21, 1998, written by Michael Patrick King.

[91] "Caroline and the Gay Art Show," *Caroline in the City*, NBC-TV, October 5, 1995, written by Ian Praiser.

[92] "Pilot," *Maggie*, Lifetime Television, August 18, 1998, written by Dan O'Shannon.

93 "Norm...Is That You?" *Cheers*, NBC-TV, December 8, 1988, written by Cheri Eichen and Bill Steinkellner.

94 "The One With Phoebe's Husband," *Friends*, NBC-TV, October 12, 1995, written by Alexa Junge.

95 "The House of Cards," *For Your Love*, WB Network, November 19, 1998, written by David M. Matthews.

96 "Man's Best Same Sex Companion," *The Drew Carey Show*, ABC-TV, May 5, 1997, written by Diane Burroughs and Joey Gutierrez.

97 "Drew and the Trail Scouts," *The Drew Carey Show*, ABC-TV, November 22, 2000, written by Daniel O'Keefe.

98 "All Work and No Play," *The Drew Carey Show*, ABC-TV, January 24, 2001, written by Spiro Skentzos.

99 "Caroline and the Little White Lies," *Caroline and the City*, NBC-TV, April 6, 1998, written by Nancy Steen.

100 "Partners fo' Life,' *The Jamie Foxx Show*, WB Network, February 18, 2000, written by Michael Carrington.

101 "In and Out," *Guys Like Us*.

102 "Smooth Sailing," *The Love Boat: The Next Wave*, UPN Network, April 13, 1998, written by Kay Camden and Elizabeth Orange.

103 "Again With the Laser Surgery," *Alright Already*, WB Network, October 5, 1997, written by Bill Kunstler.

104 "The Odds Couple," *Men Behaving Badly*, NBC-TV, January 15, 1997, written by Tom Brady.

105 "Out With Dad," *Frasier*, NBC-TV, February 10 , 2000, written by Joe Keenan.

106 "Then Came a Wedding," *Then Came You*, ABC-TV, April 5, 2000, written by Jen Levin.

107 "Wedding Dates," *Pursuit of Happiness*, NBC-TV, October 10, 1995, written by Suzanne Martin.

108 "About Being Gay," *Talk to Me*, ABC-TV, April 18, 2000, written by Jonathan Stark and Tracy Newman.

109 "Past Tense," *Suddenly Susan*, NBC-TV, September 29, 1997, written by Mimi Friedman and Jeanette Collins.

110 "Lois vs. Evil," *Malcolm in the Middle*, Fox Network, March 19, 2000, written by Jack Amiel and Michael Begler.

111 "Caroline and *Victor/Victoria*," *Caroline in the City*, NBC-TV, November 19, 1996, written by Bill Masters.

112 "Escape From New York," *Wings*, NBC-TV, February 19, 1997, written by Jeffrey Richmond.

113 "Out of the Closet," *Carter Country*, ABC-TV, September 27, 1977, written by Phil Doran and Douglas Arango.

114 Letter From Douglas Arango to Morris Kight, August 18, 1977, International Gay and Lesbian Archives, Los Angeles, California.

115 Lee Margulies, "Gay Topic for *Carter Country*," *Los Angeles Times*, September 29, 1977.

116 Barry D. Adam, *The Rise of the Gay and Lesbian Movement* (Boston: Twayne, 1987), pp. 105-106.

117 "Homosexual Teachers," *The Baxters*, Syndicated, October 31, 1979, written by John Steven Owen, story by Joel Paley.

118 Ibid.

119 "Wesley's Friend," *Mr. Belvedere*, ABC-TV, January 31, 1986, written by Frank Dungan, Jeff Stein, and Tony Sheehan.

120 "Love, Death, and the Whole Damn Thing," *Nurses*, NBC-TV, December 14, 1991, written by Susan Harris.

121 "A Life in Progress," *Doogie Howser*, ABC-TV, January 30, 1991, written by Hollis Rich.
122 "Positively Hateful," *Grace Under Fire*, ABC-TV, February 7, 1996, written by Tim Doyle.
123 "72 Hours," *The Golden Girls*, NBC-TV, February 17, 1990, written by Tracy Gamble and Richard Vaczy.
124 "Running With Scissors," *Sex and the City*, HBO, August 20, 2000, written by Michael Patrick King.
125 "If I Should Die Before I Wake," *A Different World*, NBC-TV, April 11, 1991, written by Susan Fales.
126 "The Test," *Titus*, Fox Network, October 10, 2000, written by Christopher Case.
127 "Killing All the Right People," *Designing Women*, CBS-TV, October 5, 1987, written by Linda Bloodworth-Thomson.
128 "For Peter's Sake," *Dream On*, HBO, June 20, 1992, writen by David Crane and Marta Kauffman.
129 "GAA slaps limp wrist," *The Advocate*, August 30, 1972.
130 "The New Gay Life," *Variety*, May 3, 1972.
131 *Corner Bar* review, *Variety*, June 28, 1972.
132 As quoted in "GAA slaps limp wrist."
133 "The Homecoming," *The Nancy Walker Show*, ABC-TV, September 30, 1976, written by Rod Parker. My discussion is based on a copy of the script in the Gay Media Task Force Records, 1972-1988, Collection #7315, Division of Rare and Manuscript Collections, Cornell University Library, Ithaca, NY.
134 "The Trouble With Trillions," *The Simpsons*, Fox Network, April 5, 1998, written by Ian Maxtone-Graham.
135 "Lisa the Skeptic," *The Simpsons*, Fox Network, November 23, 1997, written by David X. Cohen.
136 "Hank's New Assistant," *The Larry Sanders Show*, HBO, July 26, 1995, written by John Riggi.
137 "The Matchmaker," *The Larry Sanders Show*, HBO, January 8, 1997, written by John Riggi.
138 "Putting the Gay Back in Litigation," *The Larry Sanders Show*, HBO, May 17, 1998, written by Richard Day, Alex Gregory, and Peter Huyck.
139 "Veronica's Got a Secret," *Veronica's Closet*, NBC-TV, January 8, 1998, written by Eric Weinberg.
140 "Veronica's Great Model Search," *Veronica's Closet*, NBC-TV, October 8, 1998, written by Josh Bycel and Jon Fener.
141 "Veronica Helps Josh Out," *Veronica's Closet*, NBC-TV, June 20, 2000, written by Jeffrey Astroff & Mike Sikowitz.
142 Harry F. Waters, "99 and 44/100% Impure," *Newsweek*, June 13, 1977
143 For a detailed analysis of the *Soap* controversy, see Steven Capsuto, *Alternate Channels: The Uncensored Story of Gay and Lesbian* (New York: Ballantine Books, 2000), pp. 138-149; and Kathryn C. Montgomery, *Target: Prime Time* (New York: Oxford University Press, 1989), pp. 95-100.
144 For an excerpt from Deiter's letter to Kersey, see Capsuto, p. 140.
145 *Variety*, September 7, 1977.
146 Lisa de Moraes, "Ellen asked but won't tell on lesbianism," *The Hollywood Reporter*, September 13-15, 1996, p. 1, 40.
147 Brian Lowry, "*Ellen* gets ready to open the closet door," *Los Angeles Times*, March 1, 1997, pp. F1, F17.
148 Erika Milvy, "She's Gay and a Lot of Fans Are Happy," *The New York Times*, April 10, 1997, pp. B1, B6.
149 "America's Families Deserve Better!" (advertisement), *Variety*, April 17, 1997, p

322.

[150] Jess Cagle, "As Gay As It Gets?" *Entertainment Weekly*, May 8, 1998, p. 31.

[151] For a discussion of Bono's comment and DeGeneres's reaction, see Cagle, p. 30.

[152] A.J. Jacobs, "When Gay Men Happen to Straight Women," *Entertainment Weekly*, p. 24.

[153] Ibid.

[154] Richard Natale, "Will Power," *The Advocate*, September 15, 1998, p. 33.

[155] Ibid.

[156] Jacobs, p. 22.

[157] Ibid.

[158] "Will Works Out," *Will & Grace*, NBC-TV, April 22, 1999, written by Michael Patrick King, Tracy Poust, and Jon Kinnally.

[159] Steven Capsuto, *Alternate Channels: The Uncensored Story of Gay and Lesbian Images* (New York: Ballantine Books, 2000).

[160] Erik Meers, "The Triumph of Normal," *The Advocate*, December 19, 2000.

[161] For more about *Say Uncle* and the 2001-2002 TV season, see Steven M. Housman, "Drama Queens," *Genre*, September 2001, pp. 38-42.

[162] Frank Swerlow, "In Living Color Cast Makes Some See Red," *Daily News*, January 28, 1992.

[163] "GLAAD Seeks Fox's apology for off-*Color* Skit," *Variety*, December 22, 1992, p. 8.

[164] Ibid.

AFTERWORD

[1] Bill Carter, "MTV and Showtime Plan Cable Channel for Gay Viewers," *The New York Times*, January 10, 2002.

[2] Ibid.

[3] "ALTV1-TV Network to Launch in 2003," U.S. Newswire, January 14, 2002.